Security Monitoring with Wazuh

A hands-on guide to effective enterprise security using real-life use cases in Wazuh

Rajneesh Gupta

Security Monitoring with Wazuh

Group Product Manager: Pavan Ramchandani
Publishing Product Manager: Khushboo Samkaria
Book Project Manager: Ashwin Kharwa
Senior Editor: Roshan Ravi Kumar
Technical Editor: Nithik Cheruvakodan
Copy Editor: Safis Editing
Indexer: Pratik Shirodkar
Production Designer: Shankar Kalbhor
Senior DevRel Marketing Coordinator: Marylou De Mello

First published: April 2024
Production reference: 1150324

Published by
Packt Publishing Ltd.
Grosvenor House
11 St Paul's Square
Birmingham
B3 1RB, UK.

ISBN 978-1-83763-215-2

`www.packtpub.com`

To my beloved wife, Ankita, who has been my unwavering support and the beacon of love in my life.
To our wonderful son, Taneesh, whose innocence and curiosity remind me of the beauty of the world.

– Rajneesh Gupta

Foreword

The cybersecurity landscape is constantly evolving, and the need for effective and accessible security solutions has never been more critical. As the founder of Wazuh, I have been committed to developing an open-source security platform that meets the diverse needs of organizations worldwide. Our platform, Wazuh, has been designed to provide comprehensive security monitoring and has become a key tool for many in the industry.

In *Security Monitoring with Wazuh*, Rajneesh Gupta offers an in-depth look at how to leverage the full potential of Wazuh for enterprise security. The book is a valuable resource for anyone looking to understand and implement effective security monitoring practices. It offers practical insights and guidance on using Wazuh to protect against threats and ensure compliance with various security frameworks.

Wazuh's open-source nature offers significant advantages in terms of quality and security. The platform benefits from continuous testing and enhancements by a broad community of users and developers, ensuring a high standard of quality. Additionally, the transparency of the source code fosters a security model based on openness. Unlike traditional closed-source approaches, this openness allows for more extensive code review and validation, resulting in a more robust and trustworthy solution.

Flexibility is another key benefit of Wazuh. Open-source software such as Wazuh offers the potential for companies to adapt the source code, create new features or integrate a solution into their security stack. In addition, Wazuh provides configuration flexibility, allowing users to tune the platform to meet their specific security requirements. This versatility enables organizations to effectively address their unique security challenges.

Additionally, cost-effectiveness enhances Wazuh's appeal. The absence of software license fees and vendor lock-in democratizes access to advanced cybersecurity capabilities, making it accessible to a broader range of users. This accessibility not only supports the open-source community but also serves as a valuable educational resource.

I would like to express my appreciation to the Wazuh community for their ongoing contributions and support. Your dedication plays a crucial role in the continuous improvement of the platform.

I also commend Rajneesh for his efforts in creating this comprehensive guide. His work provides valuable insights and practical guidance for effectively using Wazuh to enhance security monitoring and response.

In conclusion, this book is a must-read for those seeking to fortify their security defenses. This book equips you with the knowledge needed to effectively deploy and utilize Wazuh, ensuring your organization remains resilient in the face of evolving cybersecurity threats.

Santiago Bassett

Founder and CEO of Wazuh

Contributors

About the author

With 11 years of experience, **Rajneesh Gupta**, a seasoned cybersecurity expert, specializes in open-source security, security monitoring, cloud security, security audit, and red-teaming exercises. Prior to this, he worked with Hewlett-Packard as security lead. A CISA-certified professional, he has played a pivotal role in building and automating **Security Operation Centers** (**SOCs**) for hundreds of businesses globally, conducting security audits, and guiding on frameworks and compliances.

Rajneesh is also passionate about mentoring, having helped numerous individuals kickstart their careers in cybersecurity. He is also the author of *Hands-On with Cybersecurity and Blockchain*, which is popular across both security and blockchain communities. Outside of work, Rajneesh enjoys spending time in hill stations and playing volleyball.

To my amazing wife – your unwavering support made writing this book possible. Your love, patience, and belief in me kept me going. Thank you for being my rock.

About the reviewers

Hasitha Upekshitha Karunarathna is a cybersecurity professional specializing in SOC services. With a focus on protecting digital environments, he has completed multiple successful projects in cybersecurity and SOC services. Known for his attention to detail and strategic approach, Hasitha is committed to enhancing cybersecurity resilience for a safer digital future.

I extend my gratitude to the global community of Wazuh SIEM professionals and novices for investing their precious time in delving into this book and acquiring these valuable skills. Thank you to all who have dedicated their time to read and engage with this content.

Jayaraman Manimaran is a seasoned security tester with over eight plus years of expertise in DevSecOps, penetration testing, red teaming, and purple teaming. Having navigated the complexities of testing as a service for diverse sectors, including banking, finance, and telecommunications, he brings a wealth of practical knowledge to the evaluation process. His commitment to knowledge dissemination is evident through his tech blogs, security research, and the publication of scripts aimed at simplifying the challenges faced by penetration testers. He holds certifications such as CARTP, CRTP, CRTA, eCPPT, CRT-ID, eWPT, CRT-COI, eJPT, and C|EH.

I extend my heartfelt gratitude to my family, particularly my supportive wife, for standing by me and understanding my demanding schedule. Special thanks to the author and Packt for the invaluable opportunity to contribute to this publication. Your support and understanding have made my role as a technical reviewer possible.

Table of Contents

Part 2: Threat Intelligence, Automation, Incident Response, and Threat Hunting

4

Security Automation Using Shuffle 123

5

Incident Response with Wazuh 151

8

Appendix 257

9

Preface

Hi there! Welcome to *Security Monitoring Using Wazuh*. In this book, we will explore the realm of security operations and management using Wazuh – an open source security platform that unifies **Security Incident and Event Management** (**SIEM**) and **Extended Detection and Response** (**XDR**) capabilities – to enhance threat detection, incident response, threat hunting, and compliance management within your organizations.

Wazuh combines powerful features such as intrusion detection, log analysis, file integrity monitoring, vulnerability detection, and security configuration assessment into a unified solution.

I will provide relevant information and guide you through the deployment of the Wazuh system, its integration with several third-party security tools, and practical use cases. My expertise in open source derives from two primary sources:

- A decade of experience in consulting and constructing open-source security solutions within enterprise networks
- Insights gleaned from podcasts, interviews, and discussions with industry experts

The demand for open-source security tools such as Wazuh is fueled by their affordability, community support, and flexibility, helping organizations to enhance threat detection, incident response, security monitoring, threat intelligence, and compliance management. Learning and gaining hands-on experience with tools such as Wazuh can significantly help aspirant security analysts or professionals in enhancing their skills in intrusion detection, log analysis, incident response, vulnerability management, and custom scripts, directly from a single platform. Engaging with open source communities helps you develop network opportunities and continuous learning, positioning you to become a valuable individual in the cybersecurity industry.

Who this book is for

Security analysts, SOC analysts, and security architects can gain practical insights into how to set up a Wazuh platform and leverage it to improve an organization's security posture.

The three main target audiences for this book are as follows:

- **Security engineers**: For security engineers, this book offers comprehensive guidance on deploying and configuring Wazuh for intrusion detection, malware detection, security monitoring, and so on.

- **Security architects**: They will gain information on designing security infrastructure with Wazuh as a core component, enabling them to build a scalable and compliant security solution that effectively mitigates risk and delivers real-time alerts.
- **SOC analyst**: They will benefit from practical insights and real-world use cases on the Wazuh platform. They will learn to analyze security alerts, create custom Wazuh rules and decoders, and respond promptly to threats.

What this book covers

Chapter 1, Intrusion Detection System (IDS) Using Wazuh, provides fundamentals on IDSs and Suricata and its capabilities and features, installing Wazuh and setting up Suricata, utilizing Suricata in threat detection, handling network scanning probes, identifying Metasploit exploits, simulating web-based attacks with DVWA, and measuring NIDS effectiveness with tmNIDS.

Chapter 2, Malware Detection Using Wazuh, introduces you to malware, using FIM for detection, integrating VirusTotal for enhanced analysis, and integrating Windows Defender and Sysmon.

Chapter 3, Threat Intelligence and Analysis, discusses enhancing Wazuh capabilities by integrating threat intelligence and analysis tools such as MISP, TheHive, and Cortex. This chapter includes real-world examples of threat intelligence in a variety of contexts, as well as instructions on configuring and utilizing TheHive, Cortex, and MISP for cooperative threat analysis and response.

Chapter 4, Security Automation and Orchestration Using Shuffle, covers the integration of **Security orchestration, Automation, and Response** (**SOAR**) with the Wazuh platform that can be utilized to streamline and enhance incident response processes. The chapter focuses on the implementation of automated workflows, playbooks, and response actions using Wazuh and Shuffle.

Chapter 5, Incident Response with Wazuh, focuses on Wazuh's Active response capability to remediate threats in real time, covering several practical use cases such as blocking brute-force attempts and automatically isolating Windows machines.

Chapter 6, Threat Hunting with Wazuh, delves into the methodology of proactive threat hunting using Wazuh, focusing on log analysis, attack mapping, Osquery utilization, and command monitoring.

Chapter 7, Vulnerability and Configuration Assessment, explores vulnerability and policy assessment using Wazuh. It will cover the important parts of finding vulnerabilities, monitoring configurations, and following standard compliance frameworks in a business. This chapter also covers the basics of vulnerability assessment and compliance standards such as PCI DSS, NIST 800-53, and HIPAA. It also provides ideas on how to use Wazuh's features to make sure your organization follows all of its security rules and policies.

Chapter 8, Appendix delves into a list of custom Wazuh rules to enhance security monitoring. It explores the creation of custom PowerShell rules to detect suspicious activities within Windows environments. Additionally, the chapter discusses the implementation of custom Auditd rules for auditing Linux systems, bolstering defense against potential threats. Moreover, it provides insights into crafting custom Kaspersky endpoint security rules, enabling comprehensive threat detection and response. Finally, it covers custom Sysmon rules mapped to certain MITRE ATT&CK® techniques.

Chapter 9, *Glossary*, provides a comprehensive glossary covering key terms and concepts essential for understanding security monitoring and Wazuh functionality. From *active response*, which automates response actions, to *Amazon EC2 instances* and beyond, each entry offers concise explanations. Terms such as *compliance*, *IDS*, and *vulnerability detection module* are elucidated, aiding you in grasping crucial security concepts. Additionally, tools such as *PowerShell*, *Docker*, and *YARA* are defined, highlighting their significance in modern cybersecurity practices. This glossary serves as a valuable reference for both novice and experienced security professionals who are navigating the complex landscape of security monitoring and threat detection.

To get the most out of this book

You need to have a basic understanding of cybersecurity concepts such as malware, network scanning, web application attacks, and security compliance.

Software/hardware covered in the book	Operating system requirements
Wazuh OVA	Windows and Ubuntu Linux
Suricata IDS and Osquery	
VirusTotal	

Download the example code files

You can download the code mentioned in the book from the GitHub repository here: `https://github.com/PacktPublishing/Security-Monitoring-using-Wazuh`

We also have other code bundles from our rich catalog of books and videos available at `https://github.com/PacktPublishing/`. Check them out!

Disclaimer on images

This book contains many horizontally long screenshots. These screenshots provide readers with an overview of Wazuh's execution plans for various operations. As a result, the text in these images may appear small at 100% zoom. Additionally, you will be able to examine these plans more thoroughly in the output of Wazuh as you work through the examples.

Conventions used

There are a number of text conventions used throughout this book.

`Code in text`: Indicates code words in text, database table names, folder names, filenames, file extensions, pathnames, dummy URLs, user input, and Twitter handles. Here is an example: "Copy the `curl` command to download the Wazuh module and start the Wazuh agent service as mentioned in the following diagram."

A block of code is set as follows:

```
<rule id="200101" level="1">
<if_sid>60009</if_sid>
<field name="win.system.providerName">^PowerShell$</field>
<mitre>
```

When we wish to draw your attention to a particular part of a code block, the relevant lines or items are set in bold:

```
policy:
   id: "rdp_audit"
   file: "sca_rdp_audit.yml"
   name: "System audit for Windows based      system"
   description: "Guidance for establishing a secure configuration for
Unix based systems."
```

Any command-line input or output is written as follows:

```
$ sudo systemctl restart wazuh-agent
```

Bold: Indicates a new term, an important word, or words that you see on screen. For instance, words in menus or dialog boxes appear in **bold**. Here is an example: "**Suricata** is an open-source network **intrusion detection and prevention system (IDS/IPS)**."

> **Tips or important notes**
> Appear like this.

Get in touch

Feedback from our readers is always welcome.

General feedback: If you have questions about any aspect of this book, email us at `customercare@packtpub.com` and mention the book title in the subject of your message.

Errata: Although we have taken every care to ensure the accuracy of our content, mistakes do happen. If you have found a mistake in this book, we would be grateful if you would report this to us. Please visit `www.packtpub.com/support/errata` and fill in the form.

Piracy: If you come across any illegal copies of our works in any form on the internet, we would be grateful if you would provide us with the location address or website name. Please contact us at `copyright@packt.com` with a link to the material.

If you are interested in becoming an author: If there is a topic that you have expertise in and you are interested in either writing or contributing to a book, please visit `authors.packtpub.com`.

Share Your Thoughts

Once you've read *Security Monitoring with Wazuh*, we'd love to hear your thoughts! Scan the QR code below to go straight to the Amazon review page for this book and share your feedback.

`https://packt.link/r/1-837-63215-4`

Your review is important to us and the tech community and will help us make sure we're delivering excellent quality content.

Download a free PDF copy of this book

Thanks for purchasing this book!

Do you like to read on the go but are unable to carry your print books everywhere?

Is your eBook purchase not compatible with the device of your choice?

Don't worry, now with every Packt book you get a DRM-free PDF version of that book at no cost.

Read anywhere, any place, on any device. Search, copy, and paste code from your favorite technical books directly into your application.

The perks don't stop there, you can get exclusive access to discounts, newsletters, and great free content in your inbox daily

Follow these simple steps to get the benefits:

1. Scan the QR code or visit the link below

`https://packt.link/free-ebook/9781837632152`

2. Submit your proof of purchase
3. That's it! We'll send your free PDF and other benefits to your email directly

Part 1: Threat Detection

In this part, we will focus on utilizing Wazuh for effective threat detection. You will learn to set up an **intrusion detection system** (**IDS**) to discover suspicious traffic. In addition to that, you will also learn the architecture, components, and core capabilities of the Wazuh platform. You will learn about several capabilities of Wazuh to detect malware with some practical use cases.

This part includes the following chapters:

- *Chapter 1, Intrusion Detection System (IDS) Using Wazuh*
- *Chapter 2, Malware Detection Using Wazuh*

1

Intrusion Detection System (IDS) Using Wazuh

Organizations of all sizes are increasingly concerned about protecting their digital landscape. With technology growing and digital systems becoming more important, cyber threats are escalating rapidly. Organizations must take a proactive approach toward cybersecurity and deploy mechanisms and appropriate visibility controls that not only prevent but also detect threats or intrusions. The main goal of prevention techniques is to keep threats from getting into a network or system. Like deploying perimeter security solutions such as firewalls, **intrusion prevention system** (**IPS**) infrastructure, visibility and control, and, most importantly, endpoint protection and insider threats. They intend to put up barriers that make it impossible for bad people to get in or execute any cyber-attacks.

Detection techniques, along with preventive measures, involve keeping an eye on systems all the time for any signs of compromise or strange behavior and taking the required steps to mitigate the execution of reported malicious activity/behavior. One of the popular tools for this purpose is an **intrusion detection system** (**IDS**). Wazuh can help organizations detect potential threats or ongoing attacks, and an IDS also allows a security team to enable the early detection of possible breaches or suspicious activity, and, as a result, the security team can quickly respond to mitigate potential damage. Wazuh is a popular IDS result, which works on various levels including host-level visibility along with the capability to collect, aggregate, index, and analyze logs from various sources at a perimeter and infrastructure level; it also offers end-user activity monitoring solutions and protection. It provides a ton of features, including log collection. In addition to log collection, it has various inbuilt modules including vulnerability management, file integrity, malware detection, automated incident response, and various external integrations. Another open source popular IDS/IPS solution is **Suricata**, which works on a network level that helps the security team detect anomalous network behavior. In this book, we get hands-on with Wazuh capabilities and features, however, in this chapter, our focus will be on integrating Suricata IDS/IPS with Wazuh. This will help us detect any network anomalous behavior.

In this chapter, we will learn the following:

- What is an IDS?
- Configuring an IDS on Ubuntu and Windows Server

- Getting started with Wazuh and Suricata
- Detecting network scanning probes
- Testing web-based attacks with **Damn Vulnerable Web Application** (**DVWA**).
- Testing a **network-based IDS** (**NIDS**) using **tmNIDS**

What is an IDS?

An IDS works by monitoring network traffic, system logs, and other relevant information to identify and analyze patterns and signatures associated with known threats or abnormal behavior. The primary goal of an IDS is to detect and alert security administrators about potential threats or breaches. When an IDS identifies suspicious behavior or patterns, it generates an alert, notifying the security team to take appropriate action.

Types of IDS

There are two main types of IDS: NIDS and **host-based IDS** (**HIDS**). The main difference between a NIDS and a HIDS is the monitoring scope and types of activities they detect. Have a look at the following table to look at the differences:

	NIDS	**HIDS**
Scope	It works at the network level, monitoring the data going to and from different devices to look for abnormal behaviors or events that might indicate an intrusion.	It is installed directly on the host's and monitor's log files, system calls, file integrity, and other host-specific files for any unusual activities.
Location	Functions at one or more central places in a network's infrastructure to monitor and analyze traffic going through those points.	Operates locally on individual hosts or devices, keeping an eye on actions that are unique to that machine.
Detection focus	A NIDS detects network attacks and anomalies. It can detect port scans, DoS attacks, intrusion attempts, and other network infrastructure threats.	A HIDS monitors host activity. It detects unauthorized access, file system changes, critical system file modifications, and suspicious processes or behaviors that may indicate a compromised host.
Popular tools	Suricata, Snort	Wazuh, OSSEC

Table 1.1 – NIDS versus HIDS

In the following diagram, you can see that a NIDS is installed to monitor network traffic while an HIDS monitors individual devices.

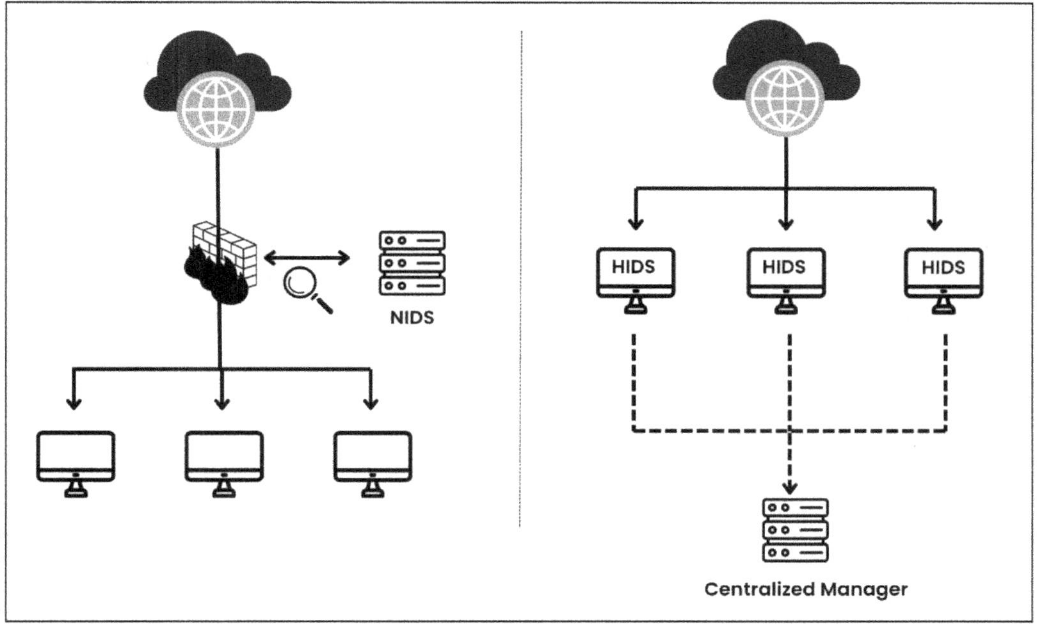

Figure 1.1 – NIDS versus HIDS

What is Suricata?

Suricata is an open-source network **intrusion detection and prevention system** (**IDS/IPS**). It is intended to monitor network traffic and detect a variety of threats, including malware, intrusion attempts, and network anomalies. Using a rule-based language, Suricata analyzes network packets in real time, allowing it to identify and respond to suspicious or malicious activities. The non-profit organization **OISF** (**Open Information Security Foundation**) owns and develops Suricata.

Suricata can also be deployed as an IPS in order to detect and block malicious traffic to the organization. Although IPS deployment might sound like the obvious option, unfortunately, it isn't that friendly; it often blocks legitimate traffic as well if they aren't configured properly. And yes, this is why the detection approach is sometimes better than the prevention approach.

You can download Suricata from the following link: `https://suricata.io/download/`.

There are multiple use cases of Suricata IDS; some of the important use cases are as follows:

- **Network traffic monitoring**: Suricata analyzes real-time network traffic for threats and anomalies. Organizations need to smartly deploy Suricata at various points in the network to analyze both incoming and outgoing traffic. This use case can help us detect malware, **Distributed Denial of Service** (**DDoS**) attacks, port scans, reconnaissance data exfiltration, and so on.
- **Signature and anomaly detection**: Suricata detects known attack patterns or signatures by checking network traffic against a library of rules and patterns that have already been set up. In this chapter, we will use the Suricata ruleset created by the **Emerging Threats** (**ET**) community. This ruleset can help us detect known malware, viruses, web-based attacks (SQL Injection, cross-site scripting attacks, etc.), known network attack signatures, and so on.
- **Protocol analysis**: Suricata can deeply examine many different network technologies, such as HTTP, DNS, and TLS. This helps us to discover anomalous behaviors of protocols, such as unusual HTTP requests, DNS tunneling, and unexpected SSL/TLS handshakes.
- **Logging and alerting**: Suricata keeps logs and sends out alerts when it detects possible threats. These alerts can be used to get security teams to act right away, or they can be added to **security information and event management** (**SIEM**) systems so that they can be analyzed further and linked to other security events. Wazuh, Splunk, Elastic, and all the popular SIEM solutions support integration with the Suricata IDS.

Let's learn about the deployment methods of the Suricata IDS.

How organizations use Suricata as an IDS

There are several ways to deploy the Suricata IDS and some of the important and popular deployment methods are explained in the following:

- **Inline deployment at network perimeter**: Suricata sits between the external internet connection and the internal network, actively monitoring and scrutinizing network traffic in real time. It can be deployed as a physical appliance or as a **virtual machine** (**VM**). The network traffic passes through Suricata, which analyzes the packets and acts based on the criteria that have been defined.

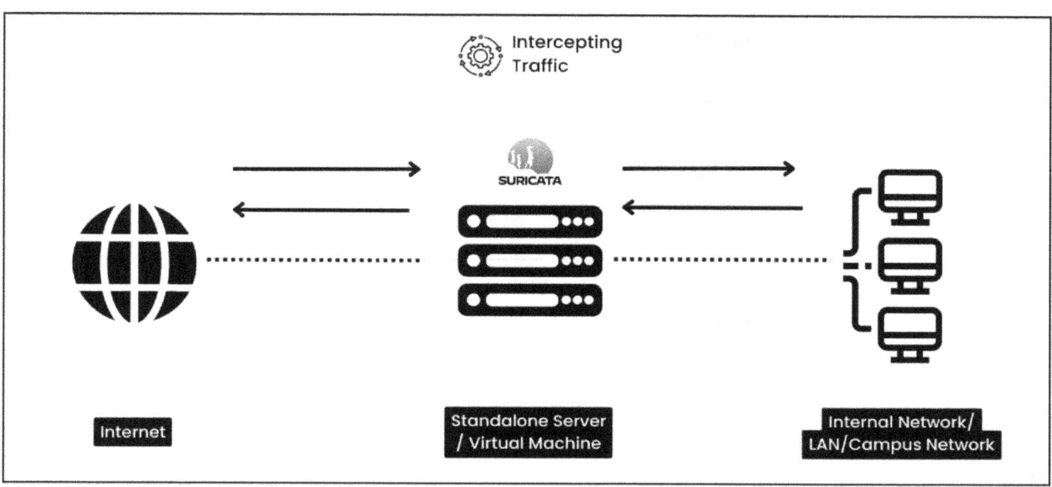

Figure 1.2 – Inline deployment at network perimeter

- **Internal network monitoring**: Suricata sensors are strategically located within the internal network in order to capture network traffic between segments or departments. These sensors could be physical or virtual devices. They analyze the captured traffic and transmit alerts or records to a centralized management system for additional analysis and response. As you can see in the following diagram, the sensors will export the data to a centralized server.

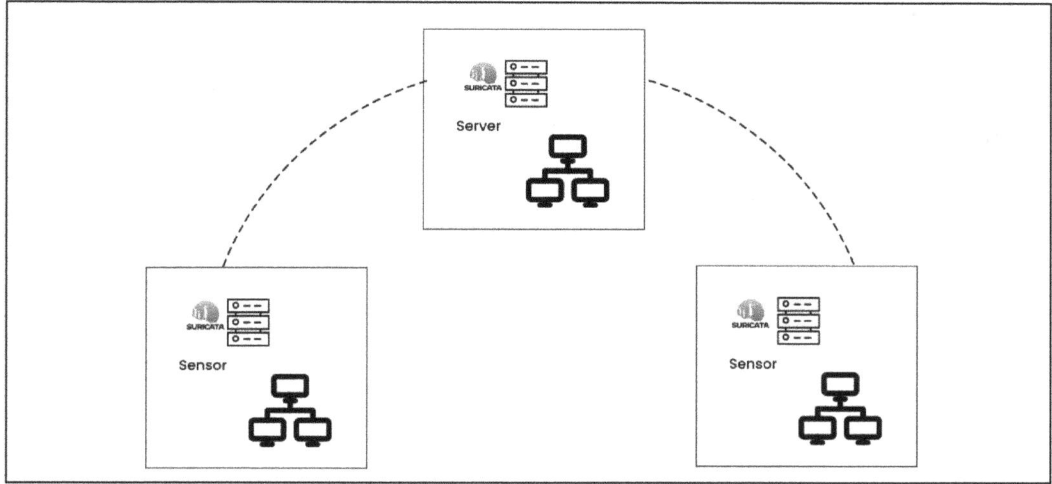

Figure 1.3 – Internal network monitoring

- **Cloud environment monitoring**: Suricata can be deployed as virtual appliances or containers in AWS and Azure cloud environments. It is installed within the cloud infrastructure and monitors network traffic within virtual networks and between cloud resources. The captured traffic is transmitted to a central analysis system for response detection.

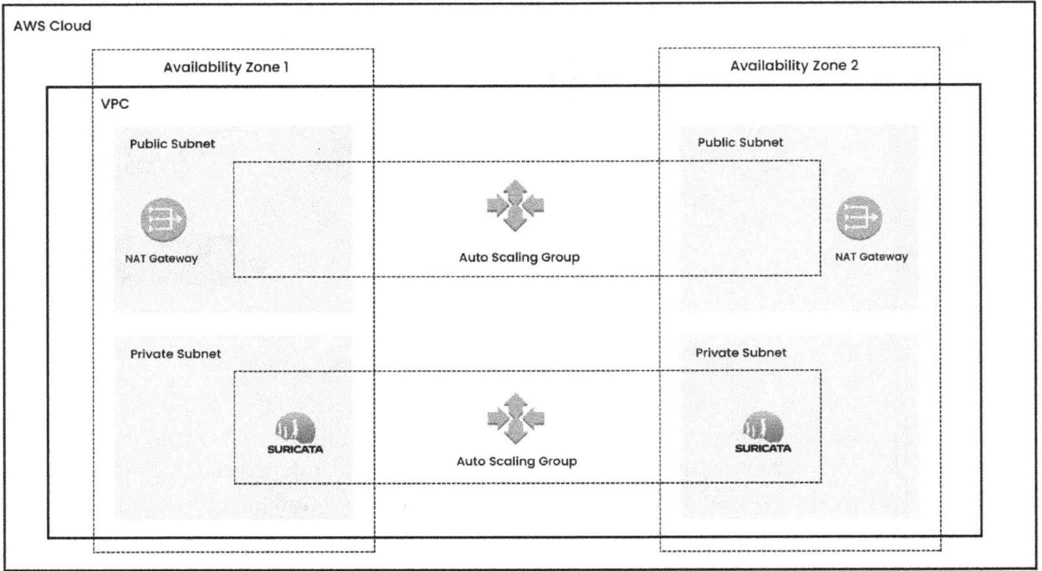

Figure 1.4 – Cloud security monitoring (AWS)

- **Network tap deployment**: Suricata is used in conjunction with **network taps** or **port mirroring**. Taps are strategically located at key network nodes to capture a copy of network traffic, which is then sent to Suricata for analysis. This deployment ensures accurate and comprehensive network activity visibility.

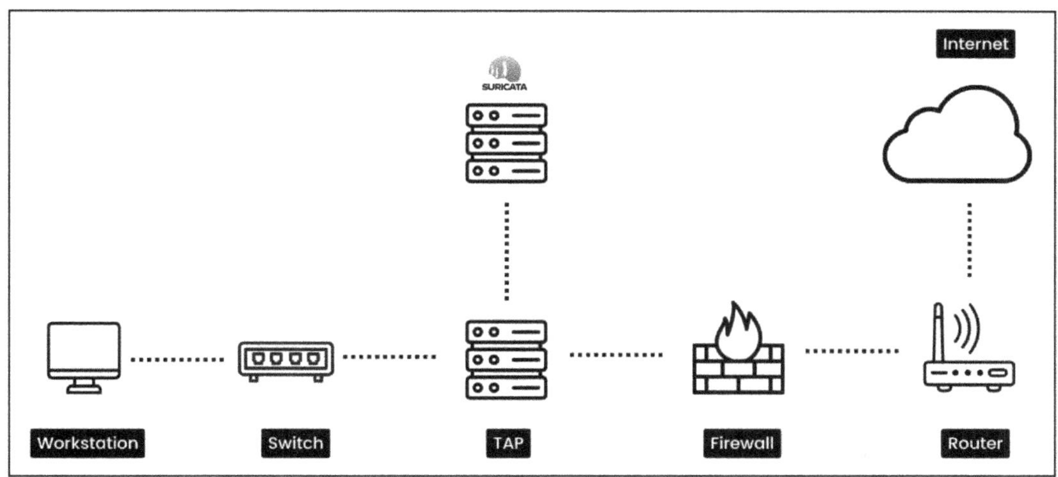

Figure 1.5 – Network tap deployment

We have learned about the different Suricata deployment methods. In the next section, we will learn about Wazuh, its core components and deployment methods, and then we will learn how to install Suricata IDS on Ubuntu Server.

Getting started with Wazuh and Suricata

Wazuh is an open-source security monitoring platform that provides **extended detection and response** (**XDR**) and SIEM functionality. Wazuh's capabilities include log analysis, intrusion detection, vulnerability detection, and real-time alerting, helping organizations enhance their security posture and respond to threats effectively. In this section, we will first get a basic understanding of the Wazuh platform and its core components and deployment methods, and then we will set up the Wazuh agent and connect with the Wazuh platform. Next, we will set up a Suricata IDS and integrate it with the Wazuh agent. Some of the main points we will explore are as follows:

- Core components of Wazuh
- Wazuh deployment options
- Wazuh core features
- Wazuh modules
- Wazuh administration
- Installing the Wazuh server
- Installing the Wazuh agent

- Installing Suricata on Ubuntu Server
- Setting up Windows Server with Suricata

The core components of Wazuh

Wazuh provides a centralized platform for monitoring and managing security events across the organization's IT infrastructure. Wazuh collects, analyzes, and connects log data from different sources, such as endpoints, network devices, firewalls, proxy servers, and cloud instances. Once the logs are collected, Wazuh provides several capabilities to the security team such as file integrity monitoring, malware detection, vulnerability detection, command monitoring, system inventory, threat hunting, security configuration assessment, and incident response. The Wazuh solution is made up of three main parts: the Wazuh server, the Wazuh indexer, and the Wazuh dashboard. The Wazuh agent is installed on the endpoints that need to be monitored.

The Wazuh server

This central component is also used to manage the agents and analyze the data received from them:

- It collects logs from several sources such as hosts, network devices, firewalls, proxy servers, and syslog servers.
- Normalizes and standardizes collected logs and events into a uniform format for analysis and correlation. It utilizes the Wazuh decoder to parse logs to display the logs in a uniform format.
- The Wazuh server is capable of integrating logs from several data sources such as syslog, Windows event logs, Windows Sysmon, Docker logs, Palo Alto firewall logs, and Check Point firewall logs.
- The Wazuh server also provides an API for interaction, allowing remote servers or systems to interact and query, for example, the number of active Wazuh agents, vulnerability information, Wazuh rule verification, and so on.

The Wazuh indexer

It is responsible for indexing and storing alerts generated by the Wazuh server:

- The Wazuh indexer stores alerts sent by the Wazuh server and acts as a primary repository
- It's made to handle a lot of security alerts, making sure that storage and indexing work well as the system grows

> **Note**
>
> Indexing is the process of arranging and arranging data to enable effective and quick retrieval. It involves creating a data structure called an **index**.

- The Wazuh indexer provides robust search features that make it possible to quickly and thoroughly search through saved alerts using particular criteria or patterns
- The Wazuh indexer uses four index patterns to store the data:
  - `wazuh-alerts-*`: This is the index pattern for alerts generated by the Wazuh server
  - `wazuharchives-*`: This is the index pattern for all events sent to the Wazuh server
  - `wazuh-monitoring-*`: This pattern is for monitoring the status of Wazuh agents
  - `wazuh-statistics-*`: This is used for statistical information about the Wazuh server

The Wazuh dashboard

The Wazuh dashboard is a web interface that allows you to perform visualization and analysis. It also allows you to create rules, monitor events, monitor regulatory compliances (such as PCI DSS, GDPR, CIS, HIPPA, and NIST 800-53), detect vulnerable applications, and much more.

Wazuh agents

Wazuh agents are installed on endpoints such as servers, desktops, laptops, cloud compute instances, or VMs. Wazuh utilizes the OSSEC HIDS module to collect all the endpoint events.

> Note
>
> OSSEC is a popular and open-source **host-based IDS** (**HIDS**). It is a powerful correlation and analysis module that integrates log analysis, file integrity monitoring, Windows registry monitoring, centralized policy enforcement, rootkit detection, real-time alerting, and active response. It can be installed on most **operating systems** (**OSs**) such as Linux, OpenBSD, FreeBSD, MacOS and Windows.Wazuh deployment options

Wazuh is known for its ability to fully monitor security and detect threats. It also has several flexible deployment options. Depending on your requirement, you can deploy Wazuh in an on-premises server, cloud, Docker container, Kubernetes, or another environment. For a production environment, Wazuh core components (i.e., the Wazuh server, the Wazuh indexer, and the Wazuh dashboard) should be installed in cluster mode. Cluster mode deployment involves setting up more than one Wazuh server node to work collectively. By spreading the work and duties among several nodes in the cluster, this configuration aims to improve speed, scalability, and resilience. Let's cover some important deployment options:

- **Servers**: Putting Wazuh on dedicated servers gives you more power and lets you make changes that work with your system. You can utilize on-premises servers or cloud instances. Remember, you need multiple server instances to deploy Wazuh in cluster mode.

- **VM image**: Wazuh gives you an **Open Virtual Appliance** (**OVA**) formatted VM image that is already set up. This can be imported straight into VirtualBox or any other virtualization software that works with OVA files. This is good for a lab purpose only. You can use this deployment option to test all the scenarios mentioned in this book. Download the OVA file from here: `https://documentation.wazuh.com/current/deployment-options/virtual-machine/virtual-machine.html`.
- **Docker container**: Docker is an open platform for building and running applications inside an isolated software container. Docker containers are the best way to quickly and easily set up Wazuh components in independent environments. This option is commonly used for testing, development, or situations where setup and takedown need to be done quickly. You can download the Docker image from the link here: `https://hub.docker.com/u/wazuh`.
- **Deployment on Kubernetes**: Kubernetes is an open-source container orchestration platform. You can opt for this method when managing large-scale deployment with multiple containers. This method gives you higher scalability, automated deployment, and resource optimization. You can check out the Wazuh Kubernetes repository at the following link: `https://github.com/wazuh/wazuh-kubernetes`.

If you want to test all the use cases throughout the book, I suggest you use the Wazuh VM deployment option by downloading the OVA file; however, for the production-level deployment, you can choose any of the remaining options. The Wazuh community has done a brilliant job in documenting the installation guide. You can refer to this link for step-by-step assistance: `https://documentation.wazuh.com/current/installation-guide/index.html`.

Wazuh modules

Wazuh has a set of modules that work together to help organizations handle security events, find threats, make sure they are following the rules, and keep their systems and data safe. Once you access the Wazuh manager, the topmost option is **Modules**. By default, you can find multiple modules categorized under four sections as mentioned in the following diagram:

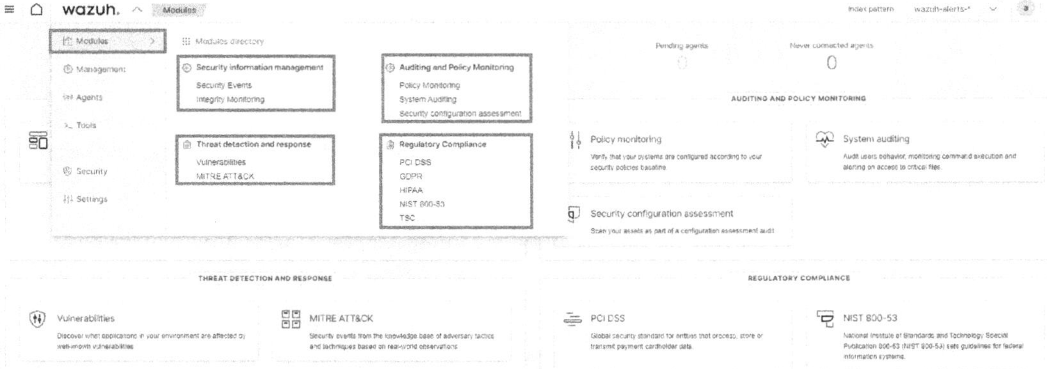

Figure 1.6 – Default Wazuh modules

Let us look into each of those four sections in detail:

- **Security information management**: This consists of the **Security Events** and **Integrity Monitoring** module. Security alerts will be triggered and displayed based on predefined Wazuh rules for identified security events. The Integrity Monitoring module monitors any unauthorized changes to critical system files and directories.
- **Threat detection and response**: By default, this section has two modules: **Vulnerabilities** and **MITRE ATT&CK®**. However, you can also add Osquery, VirusTotal, and more. The **Vulnerabilities** module identifies, and tracks known vulnerabilities in the systems or software. The **MITRE ATT&CK** module maps detected threats or incidents to the **MITRE ATT&CK** framework.

> Note
>
> **ATT&CK** stands for **adversarial tactics, techniques, and common knowledge**. **MITRE** is a government-funded research organization based in Bedford, MA, and McLean, VA. MITRE ATT&CK is a framework that helps organizations with attacker's tactics, techniques, and procedures to test their security controls.

- **Auditing and Policy Monitoring**: This section consists of three modules: the **Policy Monitoring** module, the **System Auditing** module, and the **Security configuration assessment** module.
  - The **Policy Monitoring** module monitors the systems to make sure security policies are properly established.
  - The **System Auditing** module tracks and audits use activities including use login attempts, file access, and privilege changes in the endpoint.
  - The **Security configuration assessment** module is a very popular feature that checks system configurations against best practices or predefined security standards. Wazuh utilizes the CIS benchmark for most of the security configuration checks.

> Note
>
> The **Center for Internet Security (CIS)** benchmarks are a set of best practices that are known around the world and are based on consensus. They are meant to help security professionals set up and manage their cybersecurity defenses.

- **Regulatory Compliance**: This section consists of multiple modules including PCI DSS compliance, GDPR, HIPPA, NIST 800-53, and TSC modules. Wazuh rules are created and tagged with some of these compliances. When any of those rules get triggered, we see the alerts. This is how we can align security compliances with Wazuh.

Next, let's talk about the Wazuh Administration, where we will discuss some core features of the Wazuh manager.

Wazuh Administration

Under the **Management** section of the Wazuh dashboard, we have the **Administration** section. As you can see in the following diagram, the **Administration** section includes capabilities such as **Rules**, **Decoders**, **CDB lists**, **Groups**, and **Configuration**.

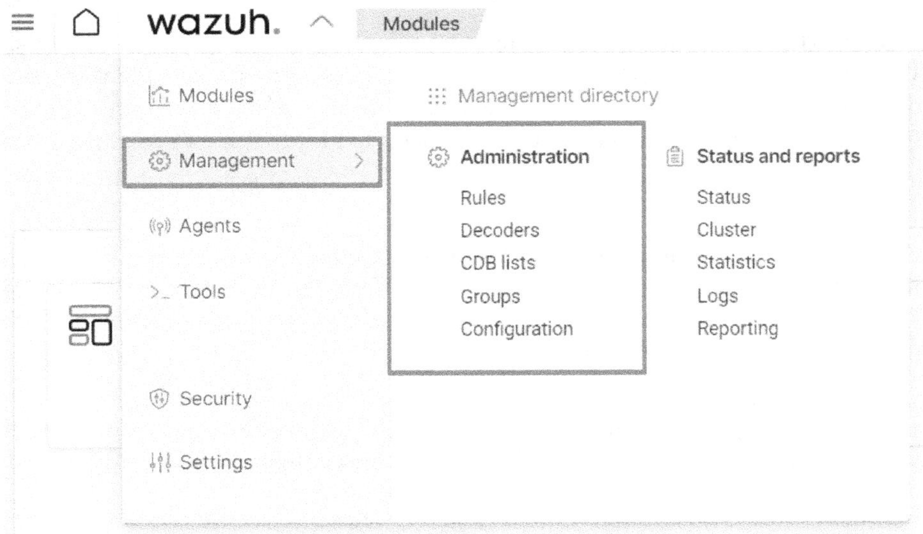

Figure 1.7 – Wazuh administration

All the features mentioned under the **Administration** tab play a pivotal role in ensuring the effectiveness of the Wazuh platform for real-time monitoring and threat detection. We will understand each of these features as explained in the following sections.

Decoders

Decoders are responsible for reading incoming log entries, pulling out the important information, and putting them into a standard format that the Wazuh system can easily understand and analyze. Raw log entries can be in different formats, such as syslog, JSON, XML, or custom text formats. The job of the decoder is to figure out how these logs are put together and pull out meaningful fields and values. There are many pre-built decoders in Wazuh such as the syslog decoder, OpenSSH decoder, Suricata decoder, and the Cisco ASA decoder. To understand what decoders are and how they work, let us look at how logs from the Barracuda **Web Application Firewall** (**WAF**) are processed:

```
<decoder name="barracuda-svf1">
    <parent>barracuda-svf-email</parent>
    <prematch>^\S+[\S+]|</prematch>
    <prematch>^\S+</prematch>
```

```
    <regex>^\S+[(\S+)] (\d+-\w+-\w+) \d+ \d+ |</regex>
    <regex>^(\S+) (\d+-\w+-\w+) \d+ \d+ </regex>
    <order>srcip, id</order>
</decoder>
```

Let's break down the parts of this Wazuh decoder:

- `decoder name`: This indicates the name of the decoder.
- `parent`: This gives us the name of the parent decoder. The parent decoder will be processed before the child decoders.
- `prematch`: This is like a condition that must match to apply the decoder. It uses regular expressions to look for a match.
- `regex`: This represents the regular expression to extract data. In the preceding decoder, we have two `regex` instances.
- `order`: This indicates the list of fields in which the extracted information or value will be stored.

Decoders have many more configuration options available to them. Visit the *Decoders Syntax* page (`https://documentation.wazuh.com/current/user-manual/ruleset/ruleset-xml-syntax/decoders.html`) in the Wazuh documentation to see all of the available options.

Rules

Wazuh rules help the system detect attacks in the early stages, such as intrusions, software misuse, configuration issues, application errors, malware, rootkits, system anomalies, and security policy violations. Wazuh comes with several pre-built rules and decoders but also allows you to add custom rules. Let's take a sample Wazuh rule:

```
<rule id="200101" level="1">
    <if_sid>60009</if_sid>
    <field name="win.system.providerName">^PowerShell$</field>
    <mitre>
      <id>T1086</id>
    </mitre>
    <options>no_full_log</options>
    <group>windows_powershell,</group>
    <description>Powershell Information EventLog</description>
  </rule>
```

Let's break this code down:

- `rule id`: This represents the unique identifier for the Wazuh rule.
- `level`: The rule's classification level ranges between 0 and 15. According to the rule categories page (`https://documentation.wazuh.com/current/user-manual/ruleset/rules-classification.html`) in the Wazuh documentation, each number indicates a distinct value and severity.
- `if_sid`: This specifies the ID of another rule (in our case, it's `60009`), which triggers the current rule. The "if" condition is considered as the "parent" rule that must be checked first.
- `field name`: This specifies the name of the field extracted from the decoder. The value is matched by a regular expression. In this case, we are looking for the field name `win.system.providerName` with a value of `PowerShell`.
- `group`: This is used to organize the Wazuh rules. It contains the list of categories that the rules belong to. We have organized our rule in the `windows_powershell` group.

There are tons of other options available for Wazuh rules. I would suggest you check out the *Rules Syntax* page at the following link: `https://documentation.wazuh.com/current/user-manual/ruleset/ruleset-xml-syntax/rules.html`) in the Wazuh documentation.

CDB lists

The **Constant Database** (**CDB**) list enables the categorization and management of IP addresses and domains based on their characteristics. These lists can include known malicious IP addresses, suspicious domains, trusted IP addresses, whitelisted domains, and more. Admins maintain these lists by adding or removing entries based on reputation or risk levels. To learn more about CDB lists, you can visit the official Wazuh documentation for CDB lists: `https://documentation.wazuh.com/current/user-manual/ruleset/cdb-list.html`.

Groups

Agents can be grouped based on their OS or functionalities using groups; for example, all Windows agents can be grouped under a single group named Windows Agents. This is helpful when you want to push configuration changes from the Wazuh manager to all Windows agents at once. This becomes a simple and single-step solution. To learn more about grouping agents, you can visit the official Wazuh documentation here: `https://documentation.wazuh.com/current/user-manual/agents/grouping-agents.html`.

Configuration

This helps security teams to fine-tune Wazuh's main configurations such as cluster configuration, alert and output management, log data analysis, cloud security, vulnerabilities, inventory data, active response, commands, Docker listeners, and monitoring (Amazon S3, Azure logs, Google Cloud,

GitHub, Office 365, etc.). All these features can even be customized from the command-line option as well. You need to locate the `ossec.conf` file in your Wazuh manager or Wazuh agent at the `/var/ossec/etc` directory.

Now, let's start deploying our Wazuh agent on the Ubuntu machine and then we will install Suricata on the same machine.

Installing the Wazuh server

The Wazuh server is the central component of the Wazuh security platform. It consists of two important elements: the Wazuh manager and Filebeat. The Wazuh manager collects and analyzes data from the Wazuh agents and triggers alerts when it detects any threats. Filebeat forwards alerts and events to the Wazuh indexer. The Wazuh server can be installed in multiple ways, however, I'd recommend the multi-node cluster method for a production environment and the VM method for a lab environment. You can follow the guidelines for both methods in the following sections.

For a production environment

To set up Wazuh in the production environment, it is recommended to deploy the Wazuh server and Wazuh indexer on different hosts. This helps you handle traffic from a large number of endpoints and also to achieve high availability. The step-by-step guide to install the Wazuh server along with the indexer and dashboard is mentioned here: `https://documentation.wazuh.com/current/installation-guide/index.html`.

For a lab environment

You can use the Wazuh VM OVA file for a lab environment as it is easy to deploy. All the Wazuh components including the Wazuh server, indexer, and dashboard are unified. To install Wazuh using an OVA file, follow these steps:

1. **Download the OVA file**: Start by downloading the Wazuh OVA file from the official Wazuh website: `https://documentation.wazuh.com/current/deployment-options/virtual-machine/virtual-machine.html`.
2. **Import the OVA file**: Use your favorite virtualization platform (e.g., VMware Workstation, VirtualBox, etc.) and import the downloaded OVA file.
3. **Configure VM settings**: Before powering on the VM, adjust the VM settings as needed:
    - **CPU cores**: 4
    - **RAM**: 8 GB
    - **Storage**: 50 GB

4. **Access the Wazuh web interface**: You can start the VM. Next, open the Web browser using the VM IP address and enter the default username and password as shown in the diagram.

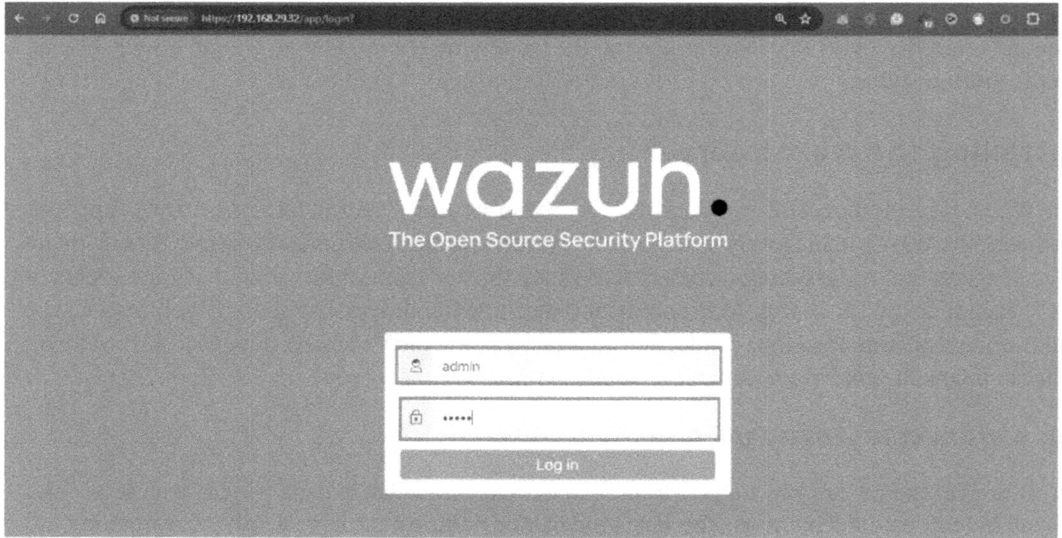

Figure 1.8 – Accessing the Wazuh web interface

You need to enter the following:

- Username: `admin`
- Password: `admin`

Installing Wazuh agent

A Wazuh agent is compatible with multiple OSs. Once a Wazuh agent is installed, it will communicate with the Wazuh server, pushing information and system logs in real-time using an encrypted channel.

Installing a Wazuh agent on Ubuntu Server

To deploy a Wazuh agent on the Ubuntu Server, you need to install the agent and configure the deployment variables. To get started with installation, you need to log in to your Wazuh dashboard, navigate to **Agents**, click on **Deploy an agent** and then follow these steps:

1. **Select an OS, version, and architecture**: As mentioned in the following diagram, navigate to the **LINUX** box and choose **DEB amd64** for AMD architecture or **DEB aarch64** for ARM architecture.

Figure 1.9 – Deploying a new agent

2. **Enter the server address and other optional settings**: Enter the Wazuh server address and agent name and select the group. Please make sure your desired agent group is created before you add any new agent.

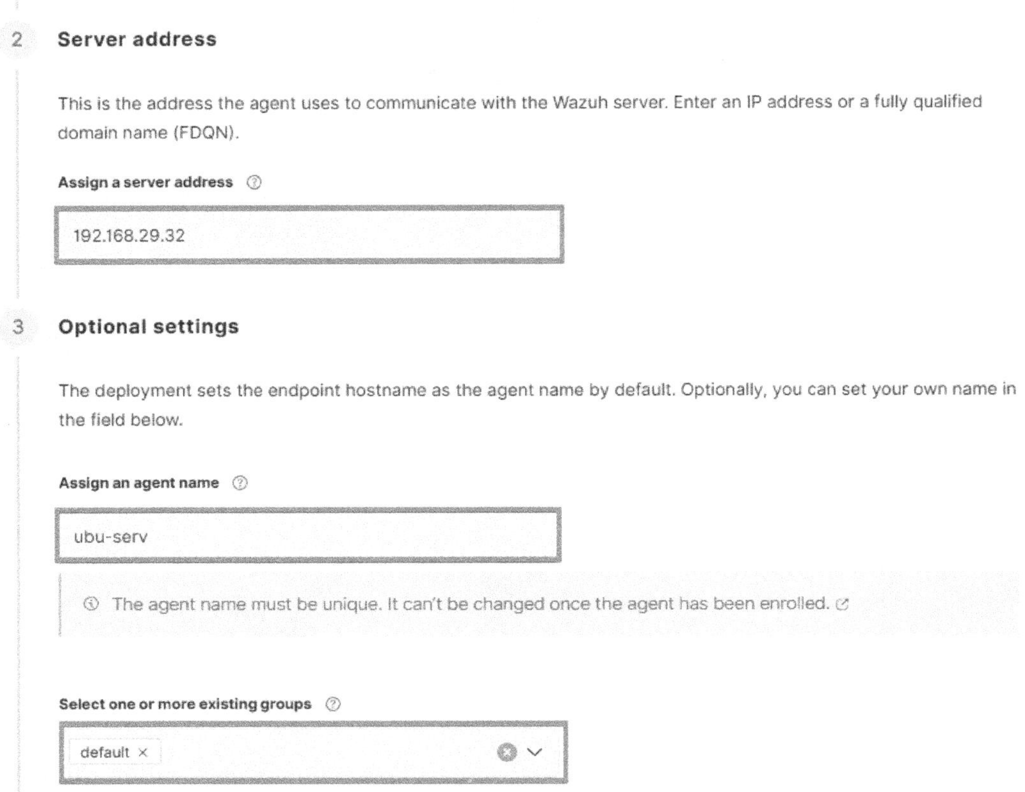

Figure 1.10 – Choosing a server address and optional settings

Let's break down what we've inputted:

- `192.168.29.32`: This is the IP address of the Wazuh server
- `ubu-serv`: This indicates the name of the Wazuh agent
- `default`: It represents the Wazuh agent group

3. **Download the package and enable the service**: Copy the `curl` command to download the Wazuh module and start the Wazuh agent service as mentioned in the following diagram.

4 **Run the following commands to download and install the Wazuh agent:**

```
wget https://packages.wazuh.com/4.x/apt/pool/main/w/wazuh-agent/wazuh-agent_4.6.0-1_amd64.deb &&
sudo WAZUH_MANAGER='192.168.29.32' WAZUH_AGENT_GROUP='Ubuntu' WAZUH_AGENT_NAME='ubu-serv' dpkg -i
./wazuh-agent_4.6.0-1_amd64.deb
```

5 **Start the Wazuh agent:**

```
sudo systemctl daemon-reload
sudo systemctl enable wazuh-agent
sudo systemctl start wazuh-agent
```

Figure 1.11 – Retrieving the commands to download and install a Wazuh agent

> **Note**
>
> Make sure that there are no firewall rules blocking communication between the agent and the Wazuh manager. The agent should be able to communicate with the manager over the configured port (the default is `1514/514` for syslog).

Finally, you can verify whether the agent is connected and activated by logging in to the Wazuh manager and navigating to **Agents**.

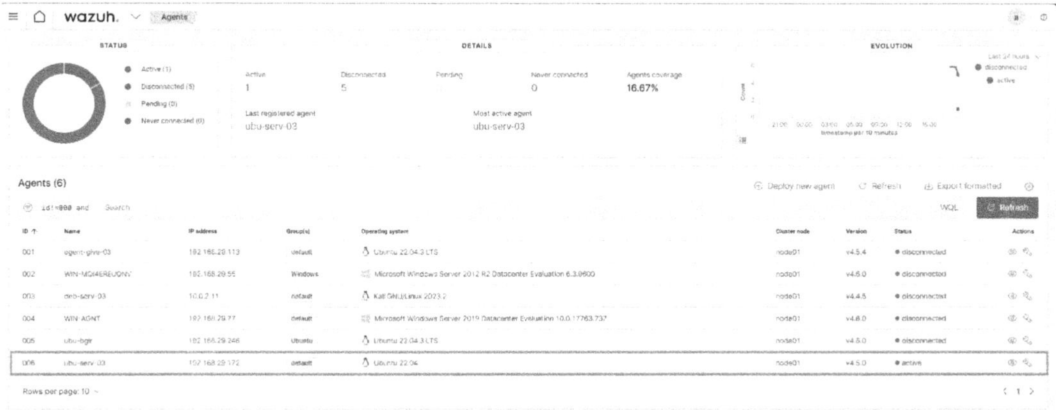

Figure 1.12 – Visualizing Wazuh agents

As you can see in the preceding diagram, the `ubu-serv-03` agent is connected with the following:

- **ID**: `006`
- **IP address**: `192.168.29.172`
- **Group(s)**: **default**
- **Operating system**: **Ubuntu 22.04**
- **Status**: **active**

Now, let's install the Wazuh agent on Windows Server. The process will be the same for the Windows desktop, too.

Installing a Wazuh agent on Windows Server

You can monitor real-time events from Windows Server or a desktop on the Wazuh server by using the **command line interface** (CLI) or **graphical user interface** (GUI). To get started with installation, you need to log in to your Wazuh dashboard, navigate to **Agents**, click on **Deploy an agent** and then follow these steps:

1. **Select an OS, version, and architecture**: As shown in the following diagram, navigate to the **WINDOWS** box, choose the **MSI 32/64 bits** package, and then enter the Wazuh server IP address.

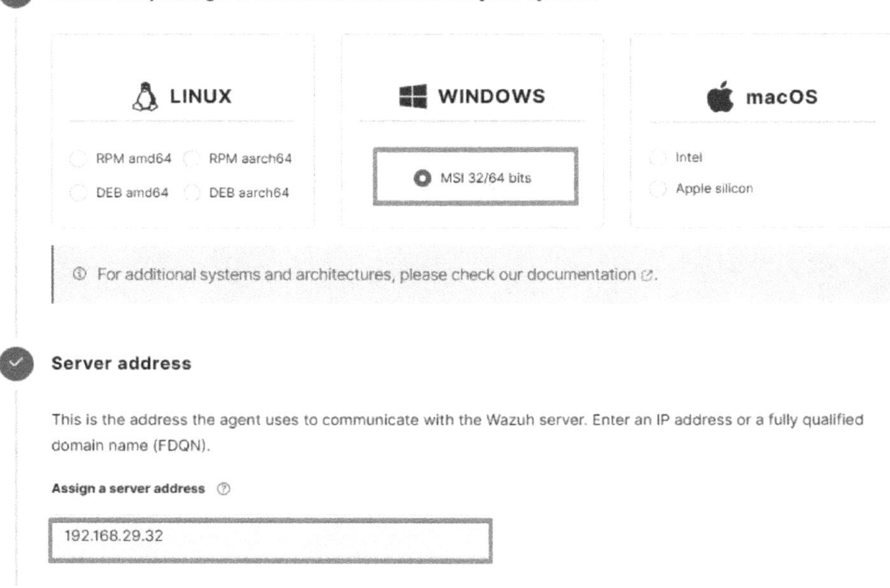

Figure 1.13 – Selecting the Windows package for the Wazuh agent

2. **Enter the server address and other optional settings**: Enter the Wazuh server address and agent name and select the group. Please make sure your desired agent group is created before you add any new agent.

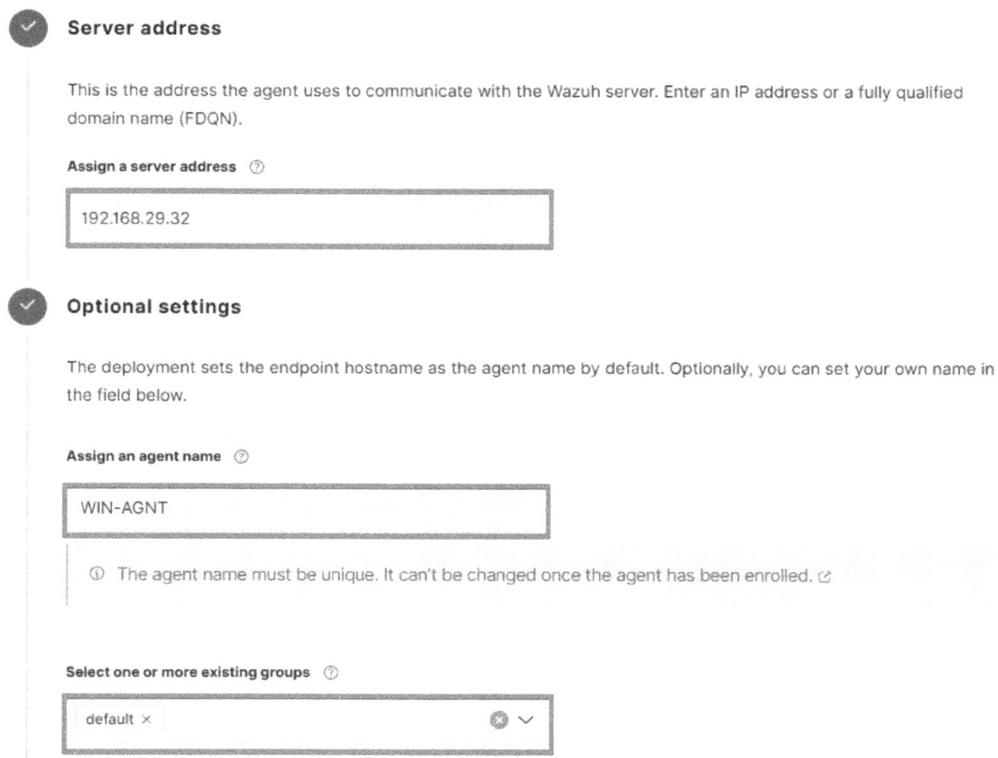

Figure 1.14 – Entering the server address and optional settings

3. **Download the package and enable the service**: Copy the PowerShell command to download the Wazuh module and start the Wazuh agent service as shown in the following diagram. The following command needs to be entered on a Windows PowerShell terminal.

4 **Run the following commands to download and install the Wazuh agent:**

```
Invoke-WebRequest -Uri https://packages.wazuh.com/4.x/windows/wazuh-agent-4.6.0-1.msi -OutFile
${env.tmp}\wazuh-agent; msiexec.exe /i ${env.tmp}\wazuh-agent /q WAZUH_MANAGER='192.168.29.32'
WAZUH_AGENT_GROUP='default' WAZUH_AGENT_NAME='WIN-AGNT' WAZUH_REGISTRATION_SERVER='192.168.29.32'
```

5 **Start the Wazuh agent:**

```
NET START WazuhSvc
```

Figure 1.15 – Retrieving the commands to download and install the Wazuh agent on a Windows machine

Finally, you can verify whether the agent is connected and activated by logging in to the Wazuh manager and navigating to **Agents**.

Figure 1.16 – Visualizing Wazuh agents installed on a Windows machine

As you can see in the preceding diagram, the `WIN-AGNT` agent is connected with the following:

- **ID:** `004`
- **IP address:** `192.168.29.77`
- **Group(s): default**

- **Operating system: Microsoft Windows Server 2019 Datacenter Evaluation 10.0.17763.737**
- **Status: active**

We have successfully learned how to deploy Wazuh agents on both the Ubuntu Server and Windows Server. In the next section, we will learn how to set up a Suricata IDS on Ubuntu Server.

Installing Suricata on Ubuntu Server

With the ability to detect malicious or suspicious activities in real time, Suricata is an NSM tool, which has the potential to work as an IPS/IDS. Its goal is to stop intrusion, malware, and other types of malicious attempts from taking advantage of a network. In this section, we will learn how to install Suricata on Ubuntu server. Let's first learn about the prerequisites.

Prerequisites

To install Suricata IDS on Ubuntu Server, the prerequisites are as follows:

- You will need to have Ubuntu Server installed (version 20.04 or higher)
- Sudo Privileges

Installation

This process involves the installation of Suricata packages using the `apt-get` command line tool and then we need to install the free and open source Suricata rules created by the ET community. The rules within the ET ruleset cover a broad spectrum of threat categories, including malware, exploits, policy violations, anomalies, botnets, and so on. To complete the installation, follow these steps:

1. **Install Suricata**: Log in to the terminal on Ubuntu Server and install the Suricata IDS package with the following commands:

   ```
   sudo add-apt-repository ppa:oisf/suricata-stable
   sudo apt-get update
   sudo apt-get install suricata -y
   ```

2. **Install the ET ruleset**: Install the ET ruleset. The ET Suricata ruleset comprises a compilation of rules created for the Suricata IDS. We are required to store all the rules in the `/etc/suricata/rules` directory:

   ```
   cd /tmp/ && curl -LO https://rules.emergingthreats.net/open/
   suricata-6.0.8/emerging.rules.tar.gz
   sudo tar -xvzf emerging.rules.tar.gz && sudo mv rules/*.rules /
   etc/suricata/rules/
   sudo chmod 640 /etc/suricata/rules/*.rules
   ```

> **Note**
>
> If the rule directory is not present, you can create one by using the `mkdir /etc/suricata/rules` and then you can enter the previously mentioned commands.

3. **Modify the Suricata configuration**: In order to fine-tune Suricata configuration, it is required to change the default setting under the Suricata configuration file located at `/etc/suricata/suricata.yaml`:

```
HOME_NET: "<AGENT_IP>"
EXTERNAL_NET: "any"

default-rule-path: /etc/suricata/rules
rule-files:
- "*.rules"
# Linux high speed capture support
af-packet:
  - interface: eth01
```

   Let's break down this code further:

   - `HOME_NET`: This is a variable that needs to be set with the agent IP address.
   - `EXTERNAL_NET`: This variable needs to be set with `"any"` to ensure Suricata will monitor the traffic from any external IP address.
   - `default-rule-path`: This is set to our Suricata rule path.
   - `af-packet`: This is a packet capture method used to capture network traffic directory from a **network interface card** (**NIC**). You can check your current NIC by using the `ifconfig` command and updating the `af-packet` settings.

4. **Restart the Suricata service**: In order for configuration changes to take effect, we are required to restart the Suricata service using the following command:

```
$ sudo systemctl restart suricata
```

5. **Integrate with Wazuh**: In order for the Wazuh agent to monitor and collect Suricata traffic, we need to specify the Suricata log file location under the Wazuh agent `ossec` config file located at `/var/ossec/etc/ossec.conf`. Suricata stores all the logs at `/var/log/suricata/eve.json`. You are required to mention this file under the `<location>` tag in the `ossec.conf` file:

```
<ossec_config>
  <localfile>
    <log_format>json</log_format>
    <location>/var/log/suricata/eve.json</location>
  </localfile>
</ossec_config>
```

6. **Restart the Wazuh agent service**: For the current changes to take effect, you need to restart the Wazuh agent services using the following command:

```
$ sudo systemctl restart wazuh-agent
```

This completes Suricata's integration with Wazuh. The Suricata IDS has been installed on Ubuntu Server along with the ET ruleset. Your endpoints are ready to trigger alerts if any malicious traffic is matched against any of the ET rulesets. Before getting into some practical use cases, let's first get a basic understanding of Suricata rules and how to create one.

Understanding Suricata rules

Suricata is powerful when you have a set of powerful rules. Although there are thousands of Suricata rule templates available online, it is still important to learn how to create a custom Suricata rule from scratch. In this section, we'll learn basic Suricata rule syntax and some common use cases with attack and defense.

Suricata rule syntax

Suricata uses rules to detect different network events, and when certain conditions are met, it can be set up to do things such as alert or block.

Here's an overview of the Suricata rule syntax:

```
action proto src_ip src_port -> dest_ip dest_port (msg:"Alert
message"; content:"string"; sid:12345;)
```

Let's break this code down:

- `action`: This says what should be done when the rule is true. It can be `alert` to send an alert, `drop` to stop the traffic, or any of the other actions that are supported.
- `proto`: This shows what kind of traffic is being matched, such as `tcp`, `udp`, and `icmp`.
- `src_ip`: This is the source IP address or range of source IP addresses. This is where the traffic comes from.
- `src_port`: This is the port or range of ports where the traffic is coming from.
- `dest_ip`: This is the IP address or range of IP addresses where the traffic is going.
- `dest_port`: This is the port or range of ports where the traffic is going.
- `msg`: The message that will be shown as an alert when the rule is true.
- `content`: This is an optional field that checks the packet payload for a certain string or content.

Now, based on our current Suricata configuration, we have the `$HOME_NET` and `$EXTERNAL_NET` network variables. Let's get an understanding of an example rule to detect an SSH connection:

```
alert tcp $EXTERNAL_NET any -> $HOME_NET 22 (msg:"SSH connection
detected"; flow:to_server,established; content:"SSH-2.0-OpenSSH";
sid:100001;)
```

Let's break this down:

- `alert`: The rule specifies that an alert should be generated if the specified conditions are met.
- `tcp`: This refers to **Transmission Communication Protocol** (**TCP**) based traffic.
- `$EXTERNAL_NET any -> $HOME_NET 22`: The traffic flow is defined by directing traffic from any external network IP address (`$EXTERNAL_NET`) to any home or local network IP (`$HOME_NET`) on port `22` (SSH).
- `(msg:"SSH connection detected";)`: This specifies a detailed message to be added to the alert. It indicates that the rule has identified an SSH connection in this instance.
- `flow:to_server,established`: This defines the direction of the traffic that initiates the rule. It is looking for established connections between the server (home network) and the server (external network). This portion of the rule prevents initial connection attempts from generating alerts.
- `content:"SSH-2.0-OpenSSH`: This part looks at the payload of the packet for a particular string (`"SSH-2.0-OpenSSH"`). It searches the traffic payload for this specific string, which signifies the utilization of the OpenSSH protocol and the SSH protocol in general.
- `sid:100001`: It is a unique identifier for a particular rule.

Now that we've learned how to create some basic Suricata rules, let's go through some Suricata IDS use cases with the Wazuh platform.

Network scanning probe attack and detection

Network scanning is the initial stage of most hacking exercises, and the most powerful tool used for this purpose is none other than the **Nmap** scanner. Nmap is a free and open source Linux command-line tool. Nmap helps us to scan any host to discover opened ports, software versions, OSs, and so on. It is used by security professionals for security testing, network exploration, and vulnerability detection. Threat actors also perform network scanning to discover any open ports, software versions, or vulnerability packages. In this section, we will initiate network scanning probes using the Nmap tool against our Wazuh agent (running Suricata services). The ET ruleset already consists of rules to detect Nmap-based scanning probes. We will verify it using this attack scenario.

We will be following the points in these sections:

- Lab setup
- Attack simulation
- Visualize on the Wazuh manager

Lab setup

In this mini lab setup, we need three parts: an attacker machine (Kali Linux or Ubuntu), an Ubuntu machine or Windows machine with the Wazuh agent installed on it, and finally, our Wazuh server. If you use a Kali Linux machine, Nmap is preinstalled; however, if you use an Ubuntu machine, you can install the Nmap package using the `sudo apt-get install nmap` command.

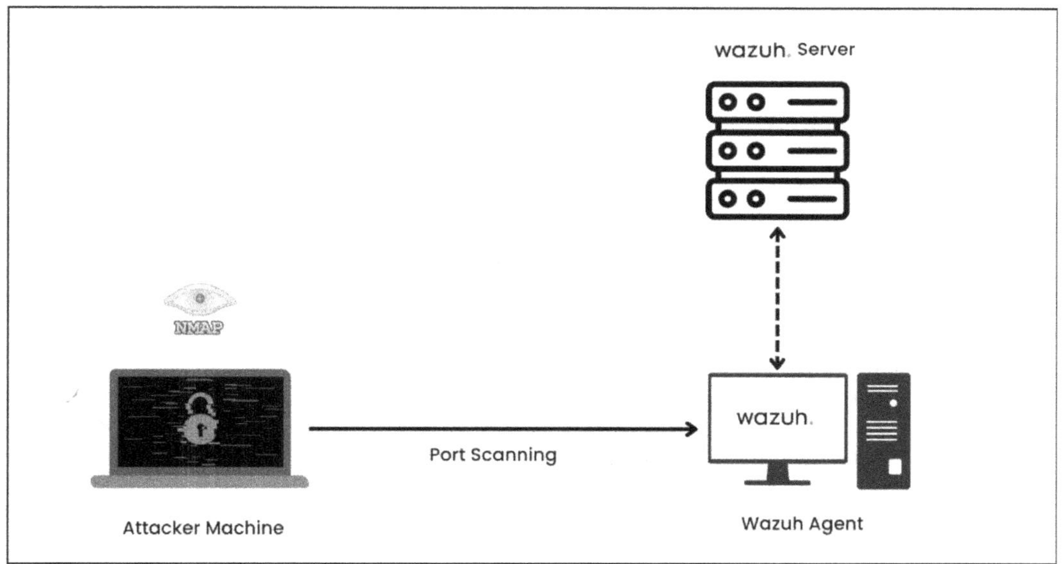

Figure 1.17 – Lab setup of network scanning probe detection using Nmap

Attack simulation

If you are using Kali Linux or Ubuntu as an attacker machine, you can open the terminal and enter the `nmap` command using the `-sS` keyword for an SYN scan and `-Pn` to skip host discovery. The Nmap SYN scan is a half-open scan that works by sending a TCP SYN packet to the target machine (the Wazuh agent). If the port is open, the target device responds with a **SYN-ACK** (**synchronize-acknowledgment**) packet. However, if the port is closed, the device may respond with an **RST** (**reset**) packet, which means the port is not open. In this testing, we will run two types of scan: first to check for open ports using `-sS` and second, to check for software version using `-sV` (version scan):

```
# nmap -sS -Pn 10.0.2.5. // Port Scanning
# nmap -sS -sV -Pn 10.0.2.5 // Version Scanning
```

Once you run the preceding command, you will learn what all the ports are open and second, what version of the package is installed on the target machine. Let's look at the output of the Nmap port scan command:

```
nmap -sS -Pn 10.0.2.5
Starting Nmap 7.94 ( https://nmap.org ) at 2023-12-10 02:53 IST
Nmap scan report for 10.0.2.5
Host is up (0.0037s latency).
Not shown: 998 closed tcp ports (reset)
PORT   STATE SERVICE
22/tcp open  ssh
80/tcp open  http

Nmap done: 1 IP address (1 host up) scanned in 1.45 seconds
```

As you can see, STATE of port `22/tcp` and `80/tcp` are open. Now, let's look at the output of the Nmap version check command:

```
nmap -sV -Pn 10.0.2.5
Starting Nmap 7.94 ( https://nmap.org ) at 2023-12-10 02:59 IST
Nmap scan report for 10.0.2.5
Host is up (0.0024s latency).
Not shown: 998 closed tcp ports (reset)
PORT   STATE SERVICE VERSION
22/tcp open  ssh     OpenSSH 8.9p1 Ubuntu 3ubuntu0.3 (Ubuntu Linux;
protocol 2.0)
80/tcp open  http    Apache httpd 2.4.52 ((Ubuntu))
Service Info: OS: Linux; CPE: cpe:/o:linux:linux_kernel

Service detection performed. Please report any incorrect results at
https://nmap.org/submit/ .
Nmap done: 1 IP address (1 host up) scanned in 7.59 seconds
```

From the output, you can see from the `VERSION` column that the target is running two software packages: `OpenSSH 8.9` and Apache with version `2.4.52`.

Visualize on the Wazuh dashboard

To visualize the Suricata alerts, log in to the Wazuh manager and navigate to **Security events**. Next, select the agent. You will find the security alert shown in the following diagram.

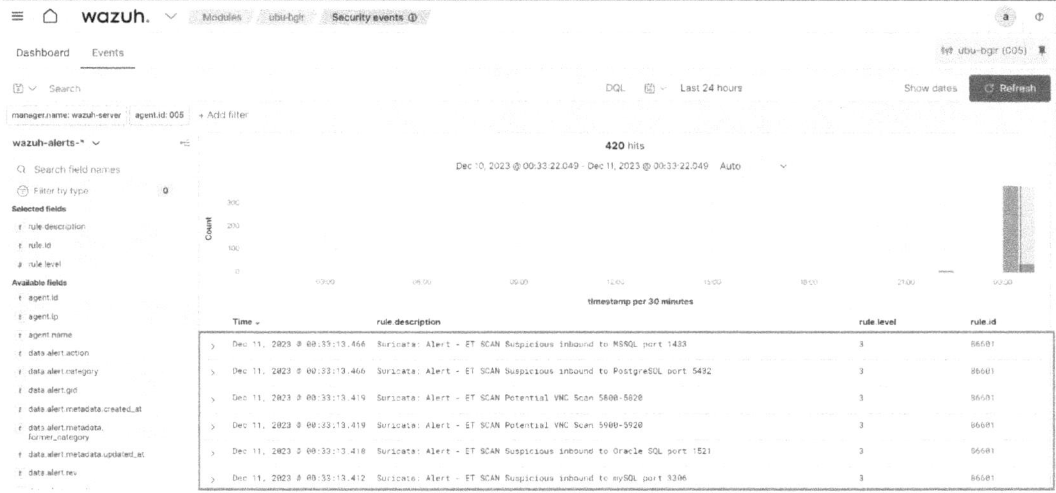

Figure 1.18 – Visualizing network scanning probes on the Wazuh dashboard

You can also apply a filter with `rule.group: suricata`.

Figure 1.19 – Visualizing network scanning probes using a Suricata filter

Let's expand one of the alerts, as shown in the following.

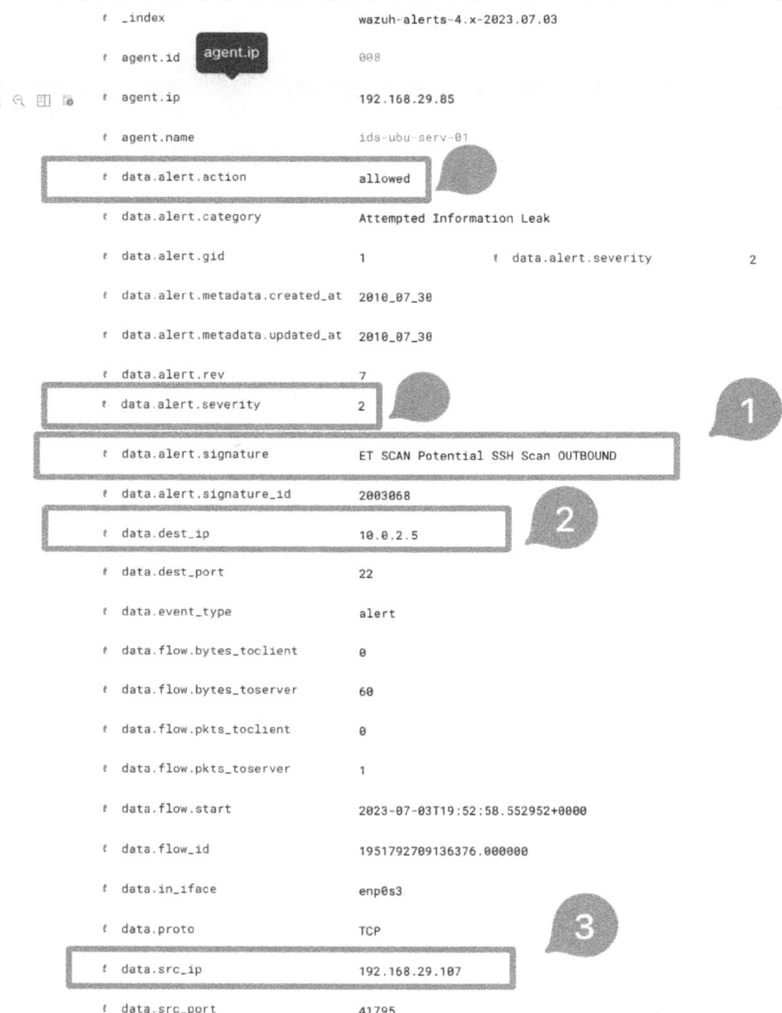

Figure 1.20 – The ET SCAN Potential SSH Scan OUTBOUND alert

Let's break some of the following down:

- `data.alert.signature`: This field talks about the `ET SCAN Potential SSH Scan OUTBOUND` Suricata rule that detected this abnormal traffic. `ET` represents the ET ruleset.
- `data.dest_ip`: This gives us the victim IP address.
- `data.src_ip`: This gives us the attacker IP address.
- `data.alert.action`: This field indicates the action taken by Wazuh in response to a detected security event.
- `alerts.severity`: This field represents the severity level assigned to the security event by Wazuh.

So, this was the simple use case of how Suricata can detect the network scanning probes and how Wazuh visualizes it on the dashboard. In the next section, we will learn how to detect web-based attacks on our intentionally vulnerable application DVWA.

Testing web-based attacks using DVWA

As per a CDNetworks report, around 45.127 billion web applications were detected and blocked throughout 2022, which is an increase of 96.35% compared to 2021 (`https://www.cdnetworks.com/news/state-of-waap-2022/`). Attacks on web applications have become so common that they are now the main cause of data breaches. Some of the most common types of web application attacks include **cross-site scripting** (**XSS**), DDoS, **cross-site request forgery** (**CSRF**), **XML External Entity** (**XXE**), and SQL Injection. Suricata with the ET ruleset can detect such attacks by dissecting packet payloads and scrutinizing HTTP/HTTPS protocol headers for anomalies or abnormal traffic patterns. In this section, we will utilize an intentionally infected web application, DVWA. DVWA is a PHP-based application and is popular among penetration testers and ethical hackers as it helps them get hands-on with security vulnerability and exploitation. We will cover these points in the following subsections:

- Lab setup
- Setting up the victim server with DVWA
- Test an SQL Injection attack
- Test a reflected XSS attack

Lab setup

In this lab setup, we need four parts: an attacker machine (Kali Linux or Ubuntu), a victim server (DVWA running on a Debian server), a TAP server (Wazuh and Suricata agents on Ubuntu), and a Wazuh server. The lab design is in the following figure:

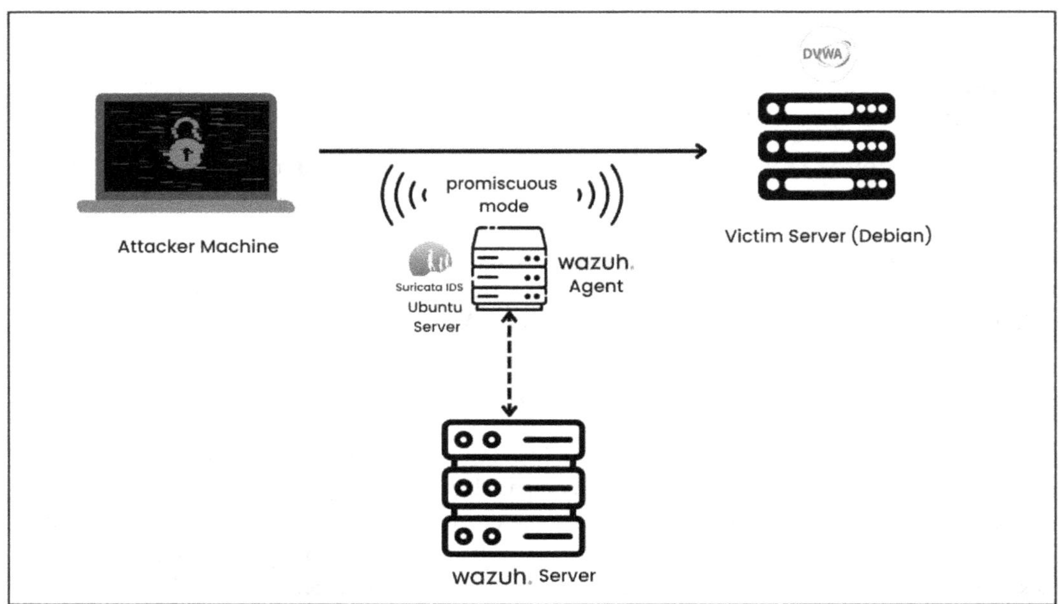

Figure 1.21 – The lab setup for detecting web-based attacks using Suricata

Let's break this down further:

- The attacker machine is Kali Linux, but you can use any other machine.
- The DVWA application has been installed on a Debian-based server.
- Ubuntu Server deployed in promiscuous mode (a network setting) and running a Suricata IDS and Wazuh agent. Promiscuous mode allows the network adapter to intercept and read all the network traffic that it receives.
- The Wazuh server is deployed as a VM.

Setting up the victim server with DVWA

We will be installing a DVWA application on a Debian-based Linux distribution. You can download it from the following link: `https://www.debian.org/distrib/`. Our DVWA application has some dependencies such as `php`, an `apache2` web server, and a MySQL database:

1. Let's first install all of them with the following command:

```
sudo apt -y install apache2 mariadb-server php php-mysqli php-gd
libapache2-mod-php
```

2. Next, prepare the database:

   I. We need to run the initial database setup:

   ```
   sudo mysql_secure_installation
   ```

   II. Type `yes` and then create a user and set its privileges:

   ```
   CREATE USER 'dvwa'@'localhost' IDENTIFIED BY 'password';
   GRANT ALL PRIVILEGES ON dvwa.* TO 'dvwa'@'localhost'
   IDENTIFIED BY 'password';
   ```

3. Next, install the DVWA application. The DVWA source code is available on GitHub. You can enter the following command under `/var/www/html`:

```
cd /var/www/html
sudo git clone <https://github.com/digininja/DVWA.git>
sudo chown -R www-data:www-data /var/www/html/*
```

4. Let's configure the PHP file. For this, go to the `/var/www/html/config` directory. You will find the `config.inc.php.dist` file. Just make a copy of this file:

```
cp /var/www/html/config/config.inc.php.dist /var/www/html/
config/config.inc.php
```

5. Update the database information under the `config.inc.php` file. Change the `db_user` to `dvwa` and `db_password` to `password`.
6. Start the `mysql` service:

```
systemctl start mysql or service mysql start
```

7. Update the `php` file and go to `/etc/php/x.x/apache2/` to open the `php.ini` file.
8. Search for `allow_url_include` and set to **On**.

9. Launch DVWA.
10. Open DVWA with `http://localhost/DVWA/setup.php` and then reset the database.
11. Now, log in to DVWA with the default credentials:

```
username: admin
password: password
```

This completes our DVWA application installation. Next, we can start testing the DVWA application from Kali Linux against SQL Injection and XSS as explained in the next section.

Test an SQL Injection attack

SQL Injection, or **SQLi**, is a type of cyberattack in which malicious SQL code is injected into an application. This lets the attacker extract or modify the contents of the database. This attack modifies the database by tricking the program into running SQL commands that weren't intended to be run. In order to test the DVWA application against SQL Injection vulnerability, we need to insert our malicious payload into the HTTP request itself:

```
http://<DVWA_IP_ADDRESS>/DVWA/vulnerabilities/sqli/?id=a' UNION SELECT
"Hello","Hello Again";-- -&Submit=Submit
```

Let's break this down:

- `UNION SELECT "Hello","Hello Again"`: The `UNION SELECT` statement is used to combine the results of two or more `SELECT` queries into a single result set. In this case, the attacker wants to add their own information to the query result. `"Hello"` and `"Hello Again"` are the text information that the attacker wants to inject into the query result.
- `-- -`: This is a comment in SQL. Everything following this on the same line is considered a comment and ignored by the SQL processor.
- `&Submit=Submit`: This part suggests that the query could be part of a form submission where the `Submit` parameter is sent with the `Submit` value.

Now, let's check on our Wazuh dashboard for the relevant security alerts.

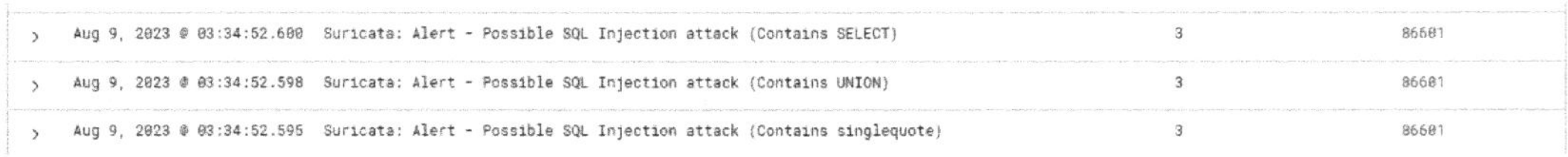

>	Aug 9, 2023 @ 03:34:52.600	Suricata: Alert - Possible SQL Injection attack (Contains SELECT)	3	86601
>	Aug 9, 2023 @ 03:34:52.598	Suricata: Alert - Possible SQL Injection attack (Contains UNION)	3	86601
>	Aug 9, 2023 @ 03:34:52.595	Suricata: Alert - Possible SQL Injection attack (Contains singlequote)	3	86601

Figure 1.22 – Visualizing SQL Injection alerts

As you expand the individual security alert, you will see detailed information about the alert, the Suricata ET rule, and the category as shown in the following figure:

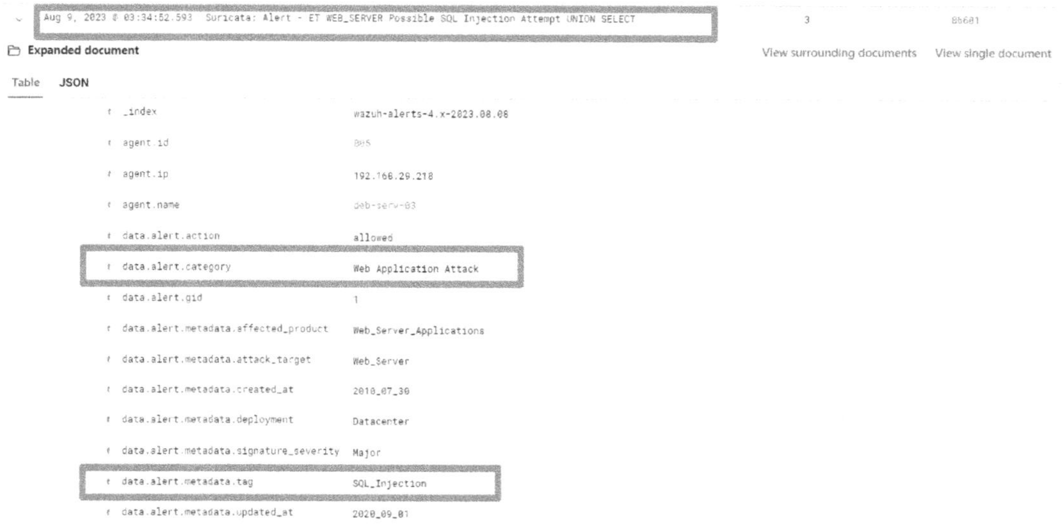

Figure 1.23 – Suricata alert for SQL Injection on the Wazuh dashboard

Let's break this down:

- `Suricata: Alert - ET WEB_SERVER Possible SQL Injection Attempt UNION SELECT`: This represents the security alert name
- `data.alert.category` `Web Application Attack`: This shows the category of the rule as specified in the Suricata ET ruleset
- `Data.alert.metadata.tag: SQL_Injection`: This shows the metadata of the Suricata ET ruleset for web application attacks

As we scroll down the alert information even further, we will see more information, as shown in the following figure.

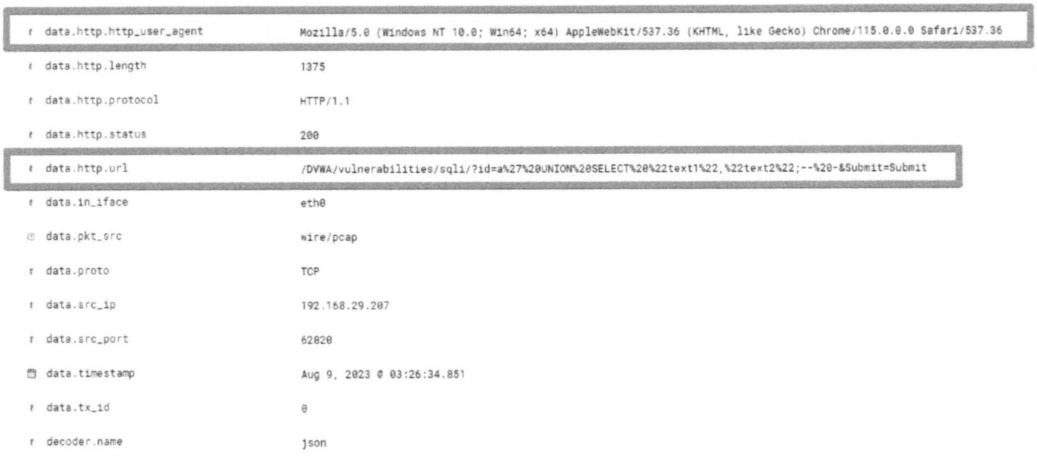

t data.http.http_user_agent	Mozilla/5.0 (Windows NT 10.0; Win64; x64) AppleWebKit/537.36 (KHTML, like Gecko) Chrome/115.0.0.0 Safari/537.36
t data.http.length	1375
t data.http.protocol	HTTP/1.1
t data.http.status	200
t data.http.url	/DVWA/vulnerabilities/sqli/?id=a%27%20UNION%20SELECT%20%22text1%22,%22text2%22;--%20-&Submit=Submit
t data.in_iface	eth0
data.pkt_src	wire/pcap
t data.proto	TCP
t data.src_ip	192.168.29.207
t data.src_port	62820
data.timestamp	Aug 9, 2023 @ 03:26:34.851
t data.tx_id	0
t decoder.name	json

Figure 1.24 – Detailed information of a Suricata alert for SQL Injection

Let's break this down:

- `data.http.http.user_agent`: This represents the browser information from where the attack has been attempted
- `data.http.url: /DVWA/vulnerabilities/sqli/?id=a%27%20UNION%20SELECT%20%22text1%22,%22text2%22;--%20-&Submit=Submit`: This represents a URL query string for the DVWA, specifically targeting a SQL Injection vulnerability.

Now, we have learned about how to detect SQL Injection attacks using a Suricata IDS and visualize them on a Wazuh dashboard. In the next section, we will test our DVWA application for XSS vulnerabilities. We will later detect and visualize them on a Wazuh dashboard.

Test a reflected XSS attack

XSS is a type of code injection attack that targets websites and sends malicious scripts to a user's web browser to execute. In a **reflected XSS** attack, the attacker inserts malicious script into a website or app, which is subsequently reflected onto the user's browser from the web server. This kind of attack is possible when a user inputs information into the application, and the application reflects it back to the user without enough sanitization or validation. To test if our intentionally vulnerable application, DVWA, for a reflected XSS attack, we can submit a piece of JavaScript code and verify whether it is reflecting the data back to our browser.

You can open the DVWA application and navigate to the **XSS (Reflected)** tab. Next, enter a sample JavaScript code as written here:

```
<script>alert("Hello");</script>
```

Let's break this down:

- `<script>` tag: This indicates a piece of JavaScript code that should be executed by the browser
- `Alert("Hello")`: This is a function that tells the browser to display a pop-up box with the **Hello** text when the script is executed

You can enter the JavaScript code and click on the **Submit** button as shown in the following diagram.

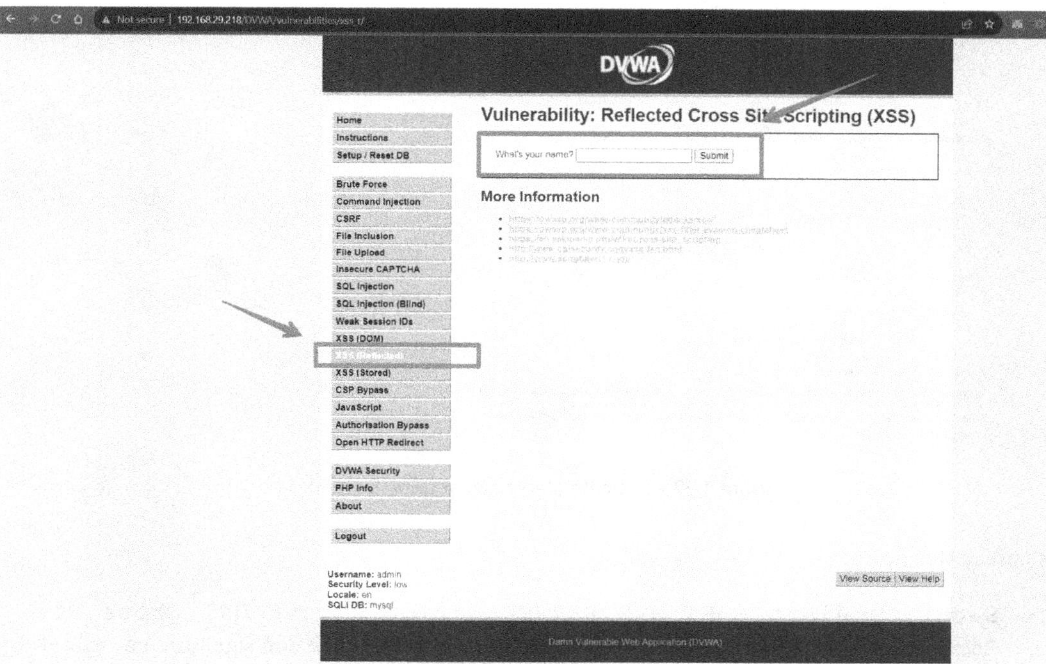

Figure 1.25 – Initiating a reflected XSS attack on DVWA

The DVWA application doesn't have a sanitization check for user inputs, making it vulnerable to reflected XSS attacks. As a result, we will see the **Hello** text reflected back to our browser as shown in the following diagram.

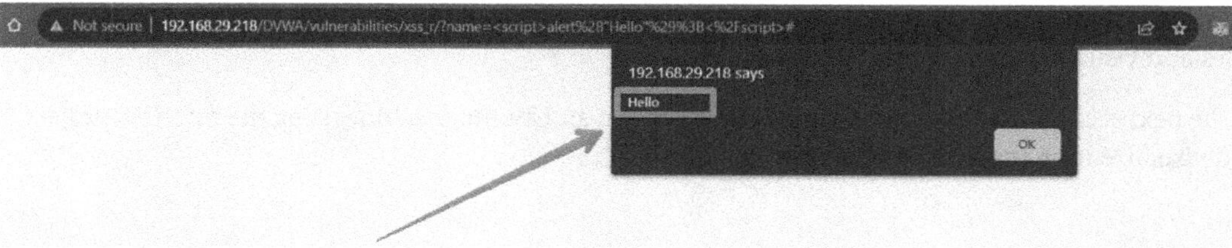

Figure 1.26 – Visualizing reflected XSS on DVWA

So, the attack was successful. Let's visualize the alert on the Wazuh dashboard. Navigate to **Security Alerts** and select the agent.

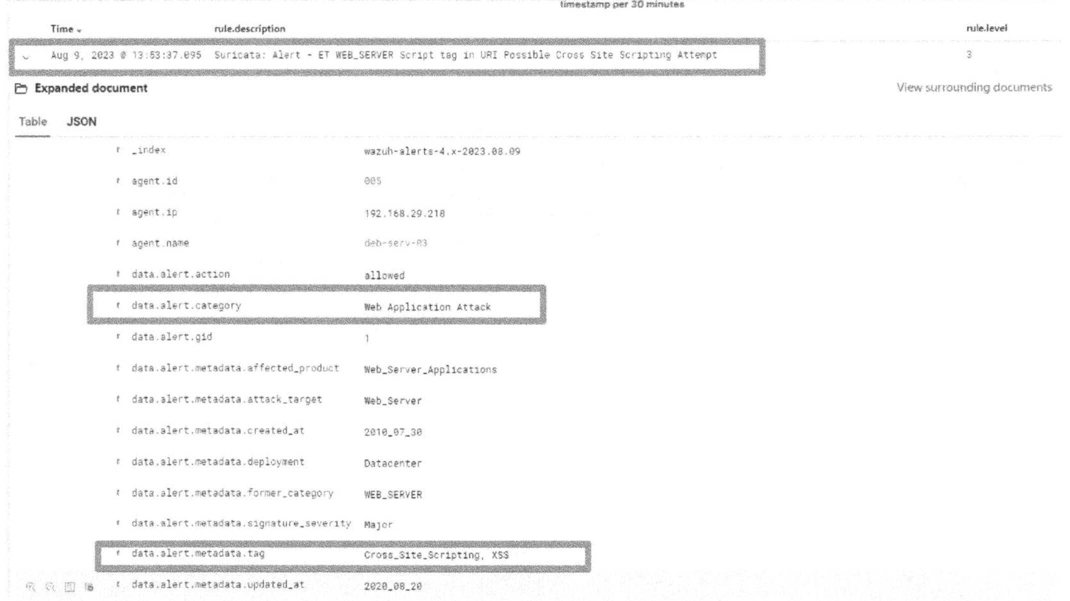

Figure 1.27 – Suricata alert against an XSS attack

Let's break this down:

- `Security Alert - ET WEB_SERVER Script tag in URI Cross Site Scripting Attempt`: This represents the security alert name and signature name.
- `data.alert.category Web Application Attack`: This represents the category of the alert based on the Suricata ET ruleset.
- `data.alert.metadata.tag Cross_Site_Scripting, XSS`: This represents the metadata of the security alerts. In our case, it's `Cross_Site_Scripting` and `XSS`.

In this section, we have successfully launched the SQL Injection and reflected XSS on the intentionally vulnerable application called DVWA. Finally, we were able to detect the attacks using Suricata ET rules and visualize them on the Wazuh dashboard.

In the next section, we will emulate multiple attacks on an Ubuntu machine using the tmNIDS project and visualize it on the Wazuh manager.

Testing NIDS with tmNIDS

tmNIDS is a GitHub project maintained by *3CoreSec*. tmNIDS is a simple framework designed for testing the detection capabilities of NIDS such as Suricata and Snort. The tests inside tmNIDS are designed to align with rulesets compatible with the ET community. The ET community builds and shares Suricata rules to detect a wide range of attacks such as web-based attacks, network attacks, and DDoS attacks. In this section, we will learn to simulate attacks using tmNIDS and we will visualize them on the Wazuh dashboard. We will cover these points in the following subsections:

- Lab setup
- Installing tmNIDS on Ubuntu Server
- Testing for a malicious User-Agent
- Testing for a Tor connection
- Test everything at once

Lab setup

In this lab setup, we have two devices: Ubuntu Server running the Wazuh agent, Suricata IDS, and tmNIDS, and second, the Wazuh server installed using a VM OVA file. The lab design is in the following figure.

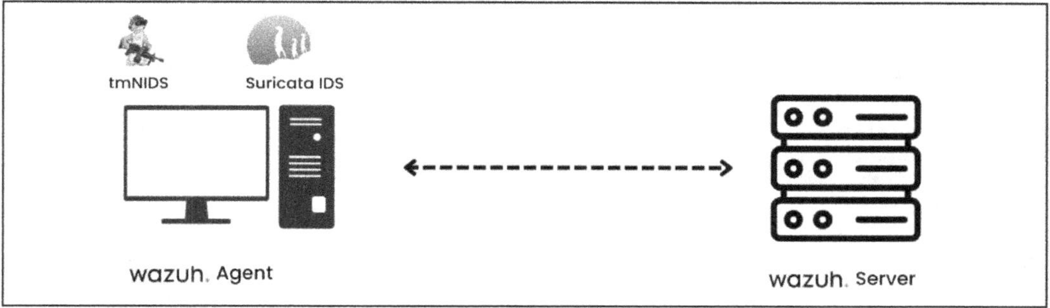

Figure 1.28 – Lab set for testing Suricata IDS rules using tmNIDS

Installing tmNIDS on Ubuntu Server

The source code of the tmNIDS project is published on GitHub (`https://github.com/3CORESec/testmynids.org`). To install tmNIDS, we can run a `curl` command to download the packages:

```
curl -sSL https://raw.githubusercontent.com/3CORESec/testmynids.org/
master/tmNIDS> -o /tmp/tmNIDS && chmod +x /tmp/tmNIDS && /tmp/tmNIDS
```

Let's break this down:

- `curl`: This is a utility tool that initiates a request to download data from the specific URL.
- `-sSL`: Here, `-s` stands for showing progress without any output. The `S` flag will show errors if `curl` encounters any problem during the request and the `L` flag represents redirection.
- `-o /tmp/tmNIDS`: This informs `curl` to save downloaded files as **tmNIDS** in the `/tmp` directory.
- `chmod +x /tmp/tmNIDS`: It changes the file permissions of the downloaded file to executable.

Once the package has been executed, you will see a list of 12 tests for Suricata IDS as in the following diagram.

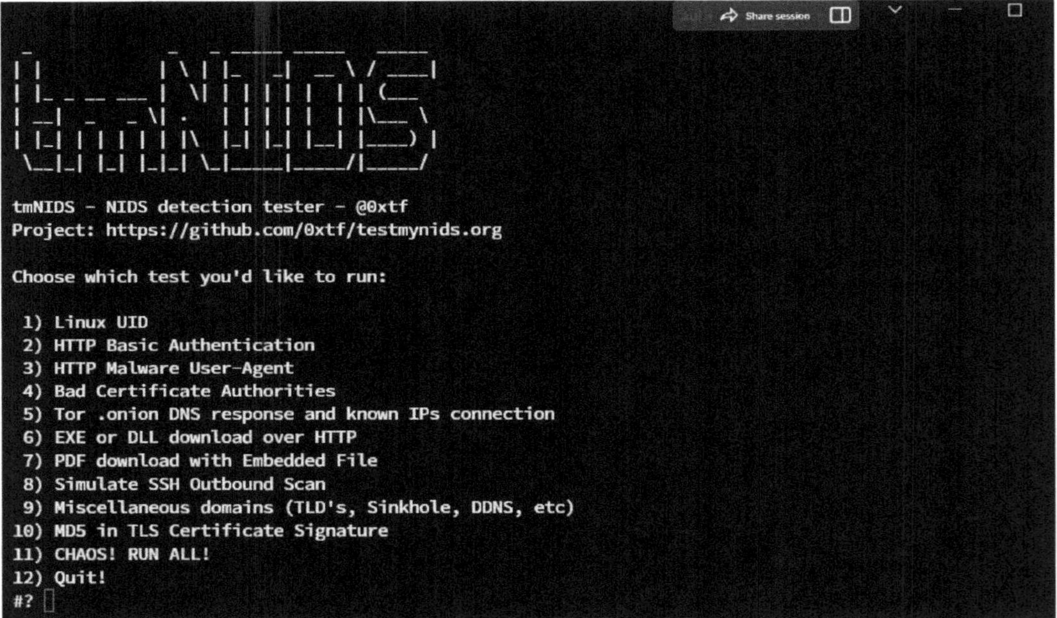

Figure 1.29 – Visualizing tmNIDS detection tester

So, now that our tmNIDS is ready, we can start testing our Ubuntu Server (running Suricata IDS) against multiple attacks as explained in the next sections.

Testing for a malicious User-Agent

In this scenario, we will execute test 3 from the tmNIDS tests, which is `HTTP Malware User-Agent`. For every HTTP request, there is a `User-Agent` header that describes the user's browser, device, and OS. When an HTTP web browser sends a request to a web server, it inserts this header to identify itself to the server. The `User-Agent` string usually contains information such as the browser's name and version, OS, device type, and sometimes extra data such as rendering engine details. If you take a closer look at the HTTP header using Google developer mode, you will find the `User-Agent` information:

```
User-Agent: Mozilla/5.0 (Windows NT 10.0; Win64; x64)
AppleWebKit/537.36 (KHTML, like Gecko) Chrome/96.0.4664.45
Safari/537.36
```

This `User-Agent` string says that the browser is running on a Windows 10 64-bit system, using the Chrome browser (version `96.0.4664.45`) with rendering engines associated with both WebKit (Safari) and Gecko (Firefox).

To test the Ubuntu Server (running Suricata IDS) against `HTTP Malware User-Agent test`, enter 3 on the `tmNIDS` prompt.

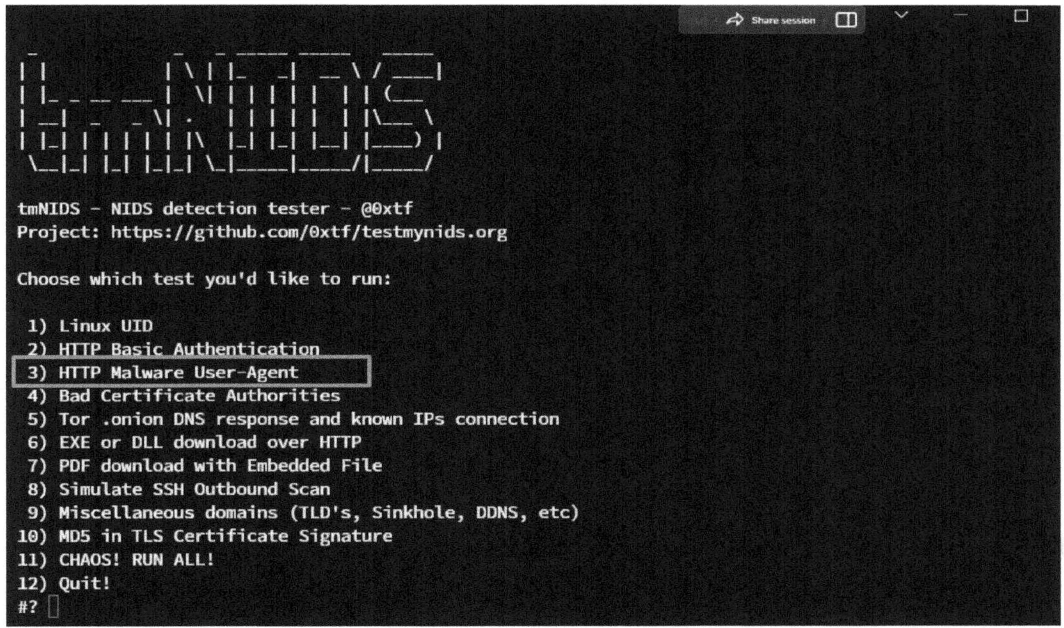

Figure 1.30 – Choosing option 3 from the tmNIDS detection tester

Now, let's visualize the alerts on the Wazuh dashboard. You can navigate to the **Security Alerts** module and select the endpoint. You can find the alerts as shown in the following diagram.

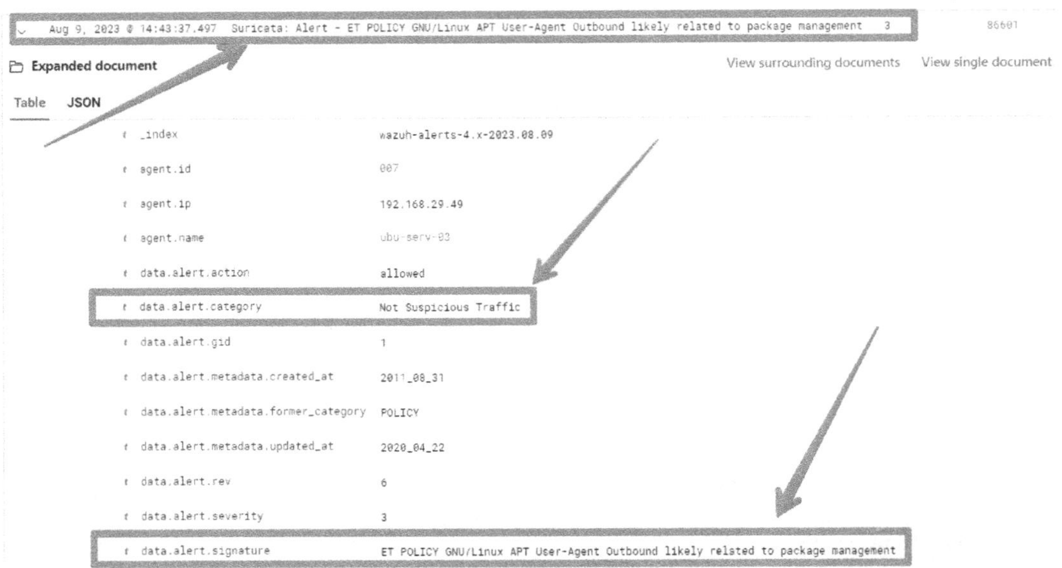

Figure 1.31 – Suricata alert against a suspicious User-Agent

Let's break some of the following down:

- `Suricata: Alert - ET POLICY GNU/LINUX APT User-Agent Outbound likely to package management`: This represents the **Security alerts** name and signature
- `data.alert.category : Not Suspicious Traffic`: This represents the category of the ET ruleset category
- `data.alert.signature : ET POLICY GNU/Linux APT User-Agent Outbound likely related to package management`: This suggests potential APT-related outbound network activity, possibly tied to package management.

After successfully testing `HTTP Malicious User-Agent` and visualizing alerts on the Wazuh dashboard, we will test the Tor connection in the next section.

Testing for Tor connection

In this scenario, we will execute test 5, which is `Tor`. **Tor** is a decentralized, anonymous network that users can use to browse the internet privately and safely. However, it is often used by hackers, malicious actors, and cybercriminals who access the dark web and sell stolen data and illegal goods online. Its anonymity features can keep attackers' identities secret, making it hard for the government to track their actions and hence, it is important for every organization to block any traffic from Tor services. The most popular Tor application is **Tor Browser**. When anyone accesses any website through the Tor Browser, it goes through proxy nodes, making it difficult for anyone to intercept. From a cybersecurity point of view, we can build a list of IP addresses of such nodes and eventually block them, or block Tor-based applications based on their signatures.

To test this scenario, go back to the tmNIDS prompt and enter `5`. The Tor attack will be executed on our Ubuntu Server running Suricata IDS.

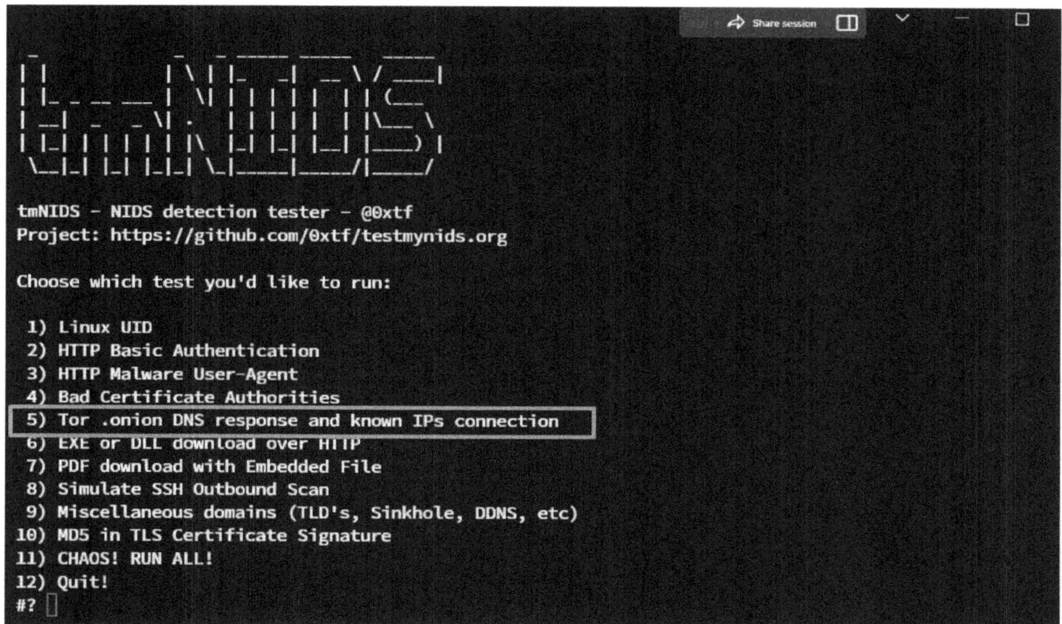

Figure 1.32 – Choosing option 5 from the tmNIDS detection tester

To visualize the alert, navigate to the **Security Alerts** module of Wazuh and check for the relevant alerts shown in the following diagram.

	Time	rule.description	rule.level	rule.id
›	Aug 9, 2023 @ 15:15:19.215	Suricata: Alert - ET POLICY DNS Query for TOR Hidden Domain .onion Accessible Via TOR	3	86601
›	Aug 9, 2023 @ 15:15:19.215	Suricata: Alert - ET MALWARE Cryptowall .onion Proxy Domain	3	86601

Figure 1.33 – Suricata alert against Tor hidden traffic

Both have been detected by the Suricata ET ruleset. There are two rule descriptions:

- `Suricata: Alert - ET POLICY DNS Query for TOR Hidden Domain .onion Accessible Via TOR`
- `Suricata: Alert - ET MALWARE Cryptowall .onion Proxy Domain`

We have successfully tested the Tor .onion DNS response test and visualized the alerts on the Wazuh manager. In the next section, we will run all the tests at once and visualize the alerts.

Testing everything at once

Now, this is like a non-stop rifle. You basically launch all the tests at once. To start, type `11` under the tmNIDS tests prompt and monitor the events on the Wazuh manager.

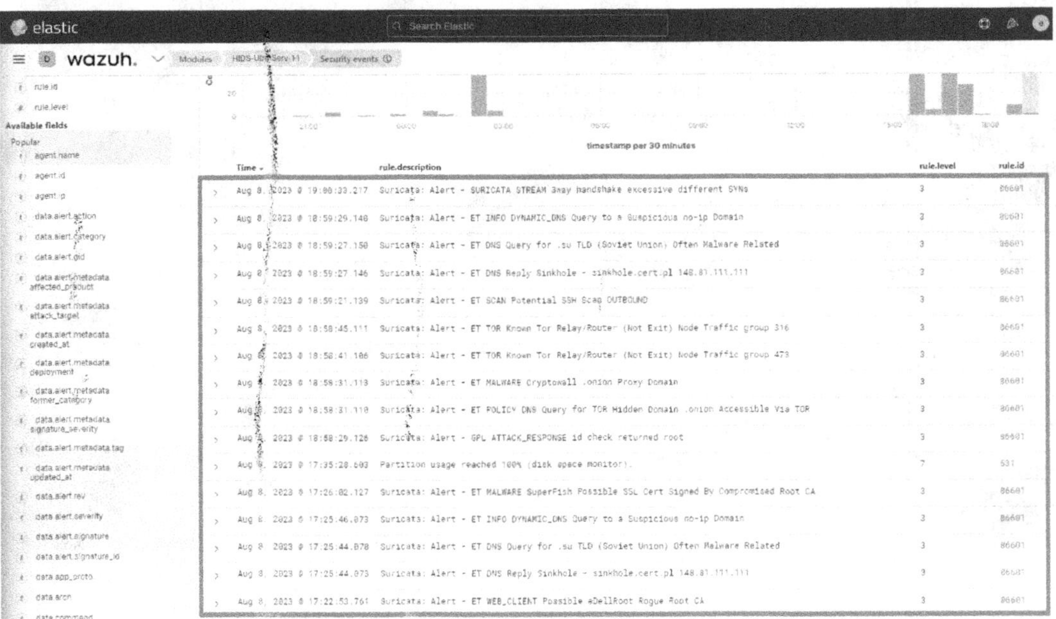

Figure 1.34 – Suricata alerts against all the tmNIDS tests

As you can see, we have received alerts against all the tests listed in the tmNIDS detection tester. This shows that our Suricata IDS along with the ET ruleset are effective against attacks launched by the tmNIDS project.

Summary

In this chapter, we learned about Wazuh and its integration with the Suricata IDS to effectively detect anomalous traffic behavior. We started by exploring the Suricata IDS and its deployment method. We then covered the setup of Wazuh, the configuration of Suricata rules, and practical threat detection using DVWA. We then learned about testing Suricata rulesets using a tmNIDS tester.

In the next chapter, we will learn about the different malware detection capabilities of the Wazuh platform. We will also explore third-party integration for the purpose of detecting advanced malware files and signatures.

2
Malware Detection Using Wazuh

Malware is short for **malicious software**, and it is installed on a computer without the user's permission. Attackers can use malware to encrypt, steal computer data, or spy on system activity. **Malware detection** is a process of monitoring and analyzing computer systems and networks for the presence of malicious software and files. Security products detect malware by matching the signature of known malware samples and also by monitoring anomalous behavior. However, some malware can evade detection using multiple techniques once it enters the system. Wazuh utilizes a wide range of approaches to address and counter those techniques to detect malicious files and suspicious activities. In this chapter, we will learn about different Wazuh modules to detect malicious files and integrate some third-party tools to enhance its detection capabilities.

In this chapter, we'll cover the following topics:

- Types of malware
- Wazuh's capabilities for malware detection
- Malware detection using **file integrity monitoring** (**FIM**)
- **VirusTotal** Integration
- The CDB list
- Integrating Windows Defender logs
- Integrating **System Monitor** (**Sysmon**) to detect fileless malware

> **Note**
> In this chapter, we will utilize a real malware sample for testing; please make sure your system is running in isolation or in a controlled environment.

Types of malware

Malware can take many forms, each with its own distinct capabilities and objectives. Some common types of malware include the following:

- **Viruses**: Malware that attaches itself to legitimate files and programs and spreads by infecting other files. Viruses can cause damage by corrupting or destroying data. Examples include ILOVEYOU, Mydoom, and Anna Kournikova.
- **Worms**: Malware that copies itself and spreads through networks by taking advantage of security holes to infect other connected systems. Examples include Blaster, Mydoom, and Slammer.
- **Trojans**: Malicious software that looks like legitimate files or programs. Once installed, Trojans can let cybercriminals in without permission, which can lead to data theft, espionage, or more damage. Examples are Zeus (designed to steal financial information such as credit or debit cards), SpyEye (targets online banking information), and Poison Ivy (controls the victim machine remotely).
- **Ransomware**: Malware that encrypts the data of a victim, making it impossible to access until a ransom is paid to the attackers. Businesses and people can suffer a lot from ransomware attacks. Examples include Locky, WannaCry, and Ryuk.
- **Spyware**: Malware that is designed to covertly monitor and collect information from an infected system, including sensitive data, passwords, and browsing habits. Examples include CoolWebSearch (delivered through pop-up ads) and FinSpy (used by law enforcement agencies to capture screenshots and intercept communications).
- **Rootkits**: Malware that gets privileged access to a system without being noticed. This lets attackers hide their presence and keep control of the system that has been compromised. Examples include Sony BMG Rootkit, Alureon, and ZeroAccess.

Malware is usually spread through different ways, such as phishing emails, malicious downloads, infected websites, and external devices such as USB drives that have been hacked. Cybercriminals are always changing their methods to avoid being caught and take advantage of new weaknesses. Now, let's learn about some of the important Wazuh capabilities for malware detection.

Wazuh capabilities for malware detection

Wazuh offers several capabilities that contribute to its effectiveness in detecting malware. This is accomplished through the use of a combination of log analysis, intrusion detection, and threat intelligence. It also provides real-time alerting, event correlation, and the ability to execute custom scripts for automated reaction activities, making it a powerful tool for effectively identifying and responding to malware attacks. The following are some of Wazuh's methods for malware detection:

- **Threat detection rules and FIM**: In this method, Wazuh utilizes its built-in capability to detect any critical file modification. Some of the capabilities are:
  - Wazuh employs a set of predefined, continuously monitored threat detection principles. The purpose of these principles is to identify suspicious activities, events, and patterns that may indicate malware infections or security breaches.
  - Wazuh's malware detection relies heavily on FIM. It monitors modifications to files and directories, such as additions and deletions. Wazuh generates an alert when an unauthorized or unanticipated change occurs, which may indicate malware activity.
- **Rootkit behavior detection**: Wazuh uses the rootcheck function to detect anomalies that might indicate the presence of malware in an endpoint:
  - Rootkits are a form of malware that can conceal their presence and other malicious actions on a compromised system. Wazuh identifies rootkit-like activities using behavior-based detection techniques.
  - Wazuh searches for suspicious system behavior, such as unauthorized privilege escalation, attempts to conceal files or processes, and other activities that are typically associated with rootkits. When such conduct is identified, an alert is triggered.
- **VirusTotal integration**: Wazuh detects malicious files through integration with VirusTotal:
  - VirusTotal is a web-based service that scans files and URLs for potential hazards using multiple antivirus engines and threat intelligence sources. Wazuh incorporates VirusTotal to improve its malware detection capabilities.
  - When Wazuh encounters a file or URL that it suspects to be malicious, it can automatically submit the sample for analysis by VirusTotal. The result includes findings from multiple antivirus engines, which are then integrated into Wazuh's alerting mechanism. If the file is identified as malicious by multiple engines, the confidence in the alert is increased.
- **YARA integration**: Wazuh detects malware samples using YARA, which is an open-source tool that identifies and classifies malware artifacts based on their binary patterns:
  - YARA is a powerful tool that lets you write your own rules to find malware and certain patterns in files and processes. Wazuh works with YARA, so users can make their own rules for YARA to use to find malware that fits their needs.
  - Security professionals can use YARA integration to create custom signatures that detect specific malware strains or behaviors that are not covered by the normal Wazuh rules. These custom rules can be added to the Wazuh ruleset and used to monitor the environment.

Now that we understand some important malware detection capabilities of the Wazuh platform, we can start to learn about different use cases with Wazuh. In the next section, we will learn how to detect malware using the FIM module of Wazuh.

Malware detection using FIM

When a system gets compromised by malware, it may create new files or modify existing files, such as the following file types:

- Executable files (`.exe`, `.dll`, `.bat`, and `.vbs`)
- Configuration files (`.cfg` and `.ini`)
- Temporary files (`.tmp`)
- Registry entries
- Log files (`.log`)
- Payload files
- Hidden files and directories
- Batch scripts (`.bat`)
- PowerShell (`.ps1`)
- Specially crafted documents with a malicious payload (`.doc`, `.xls`, and `.pdf`)

Using this information, we can create an FIM rule in Wazuh to detect any file changes. However, we will get a high number of false positive alerts, too. To solve this problem, we can focus on a specific directory or folder. We will learn more in this section.

In this section, we'll learn how to create Wazuh rules to detect some of the common malware patterns.

We'll cover the following use cases:

- Configuring and testing FIM on an Ubuntu machine
- Detecting suspicious files on a **PHP** server using the FIM module

Configuring and testing FIM on an Ubuntu machine

FIM is a technology that monitors the integrity of system and application files. It safeguards sensitive data, application, and device files by routinely monitoring, scanning, and confirming their integrity. It works by detecting changes to mission-critical files in the network and as a result, it brings down the risk associated with data breaches.

The good news is that Wazuh has a built-in capability for FIM. This is possible because Wazuh uses an **Open Source HIDS Security (OSSEC)** agent. OSSEC is a free, open-source host-based intrusion detection system. When a user or process creates, modifies, or deletes a monitored file, the Wazuh FIM module initiates an alert. Let's understand a file integrity check by setting up a FIM module on an Ubuntu machine. In order to test this use case, you need to follow these steps.

Requirements

To test the FIM use case, we would require the following:

- The Wazuh manager
- An Ubuntu machine (with the Wazuh agent installed)

Step 1 – Setting up the Wazuh agent on an Ubuntu machine

By default, the FIM module is enabled on the Wazuh agent. The configuration of the FIM module is present in the `<syscheck>` tag under the `ossec.conf` file located at `/var/ossec/etc`. We only need to add directories (to be monitored) under the `<syscheck>` block. The following configuration will monitor specified files and directories for any types of changes or modifications:

```
<syscheck>
  <disabled>no</disabled>
  <frequency>720</frequency>
  <scan_on_start>yes</scan_on_start>
  <directories check_all="yes" report_changes="yes" real_time="yes">/
etc,/bin,/sbin</directories>
  <directories check_all="yes" report_changes="yes" real_time="yes">/
lib,/lib64,/usr/lib,/usr/lib64</directories>
  <directories check_all="yes" report_changes="yes" real_time="yes">/
var/www,/var/log,/var/named</directories>
  <ignore>/etc/mtab</ignore>
  <ignore>/etc/hosts.deny</ignore>
  <ignore>/etc/mail/statistics</ignore>
  <ignore>/etc/random-seed</ignore>
  <ignore>/etc/adjtime</ignore>
  <ignore>/etc/httpd/logs</ignore>
  <ignore>/etc/utmpx</ignore>
  <ignore>/etc/wtmpx</ignore>
  <ignore>/etc/cups/certs</ignore>
  <ignore>/etc/dumpdates</ignore>
  <ignore>/etc/svc/volatile</ignore>
  <ignore>/sys/kernel/security</ignore>
  <ignore>/sys/kernel/debug</ignore>
  <ignore>/sys</ignore>
  <ignore>/dev</ignore>
```

```
    <ignore>/tmp</ignore>
    <ignore>/proc</ignore>
    <ignore>/var/run</ignore>
    <ignore>/var/lock</ignore>
    <ignore>/var/run/utmp</ignore>
  </syscheck>
```

Let's break down the preceding configuration:

- The `<disabled>` tag is set to `no` to enable the syscheck module on Wazuh.
- The `<scan_on_start>` tag is set to `yes` to conduct the initial scan when the Wazuh agent shows up.
- The `<frequency>` tag is set to `720` to conduct a file monitoring scan every 720 minutes.
- The `<directories>` tags talk about all the directories to monitor. In this example, we're monitoring important system directories such as `/etc`, `/bin`, `/sbin`, `/lib`, `/lib64`, `/usr/lib`, `/usr/lib64`, `/var/www`, `/var/log`, and `/var/named`.
- The `<ignore>` tags indicate files or directories to ignore during the monitoring process. These are common system files that are not generally important for FIM analysis.

Step 2 – Restart the Wazuh agent

For the configuration changes to take effect, we need to restart the `wazuh-agent` service as shown in the following:

```
sudo systemctl restart wazuh-agent
```

Step 3 – Visualizing the alerts

To visualize the alerts, you can navigate to **Security Alerts** or the **Integrity Monitoring** module in the Wazuh dashboard and check for the file-added alerts as shown in the following figure:

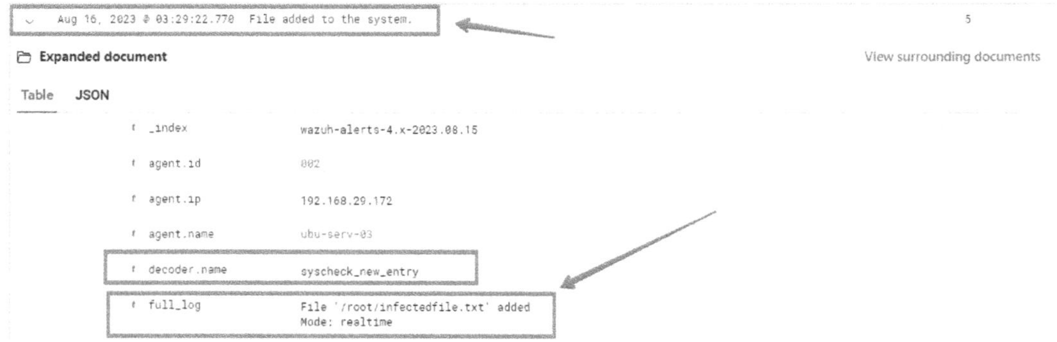

Figure 2.1 – Visualizing the file-added alert on the Wazuh manager

Let's break this down:

- `decoder.name: syscheck_new_entry`: This field represents a new entry related to system checks or FIM that have been detected by the Wazuh agent. In this case, a file has been added.
- `full.log: File '/root/infectedfile.txt'added`: This represents that a new file called `infectedfile.txt` has been added.

In this use case, we have learned to detect file changes in `/root` using the FIM module of Wazuh. In the next section, we will learn to detect possible malware in the PHP server.

Detecting suspicious files in the PHP server using the FIM module

PHP is known for its simplicity, speed, and flexibility. Currently, there are more than 33 million websites that use PHP. The most common PHP file extensions are `.php`, `.phtml`, `.php3`, `.php4`, `.php5`, `.php7`, and `.phps`.

These files are commonly found in the `/var/www/html/`, `/var/www/public_html/`, and root directory. In order to test possible malware using the FIM module in the PHP server, you need to follow these steps.

Requirements

To detect possible malicious files in the PHP server using Wazuh's FIM module, you need the following system requirements:

- The Wazuh manager
- An Ubuntu server, which should have the PHP server package and Wazuh agent installed

Creating a Wazuh rule

We will create a Wazuh rule to detect file creation and modification on the PHP server. We will add different types of PHP file extensions under the `<field>` tag of the Wazuh rule. We will cover this use case along with testing and finally, we will visualize the alerts on the Wazuh manager:

Create a Wazuh rule to detect PHP file creation/modification

To create a Wazuh rule, go to **Management | Rules** and click on **Create a new rule**. Next, we'll name it `custom_fim.xml` and add the following rule:

```
<group name="linux, webshell, windows,">
  <!-- This rule detects file creation. -->
  <rule id="100500" level="12">
    <if_sid>554,550</if_sid>
```

```
    <field name="file" type="pcre2">(?i).php$|.phtml$|.php3$|.php4$|.
php5$|.phps$|.phar$|.asp$|.aspx$|.jsp$|.cshtml$|.vbhtml$</field>
    <description>[File creation]: Possible web shell scripting file
($(file)) created</description>

  </rule>
</group>
```

Let's break this code down:

- `<if_sid>554</if_sid>`: This tag represents a list of rule IDs. This rule will match when a rule ID on the list has previously been matched. In this case, rule ID `100500` will match when rule ID `554` gets triggered. Rule ID `554` is fired when a file is added, and rule ID `550` represents the change in the integrity checksum.
- `<field name="file" type="pcre2">(?i).php$|.phtml$|.php3$|.php4$|.php5$|.phps$|.phar$|.asp$|.aspx$|.jsp$|.cshtml$|.vbhtml$</field>`: This is used as a requisite to trigger the rule. It will check for a match in the content of a file extracted by the decoder. In this case, the content is the list of all possible PHP file extensions.

Testing

To test our FIM rule, we will add a new file called `antivirusupdate.php` in the root directory using the `touch` command as shown in the following figure.

```
root@haxcamp:~# touch antivirusupdate.php
root@haxcamp:~# ls
antivirusupdate.php  attack1.txt  infectedfile.txt  snap  wazuh-agent.deb
root@haxcamp:~#
```

Figure 2.2 – Creating a blank file in the root directory

Visualizing the alerts

To visualize the FIM alerts, navigate to the **Security Alerts** module of the Wazuh dashboard and you will find the alert as shown in the following figure.

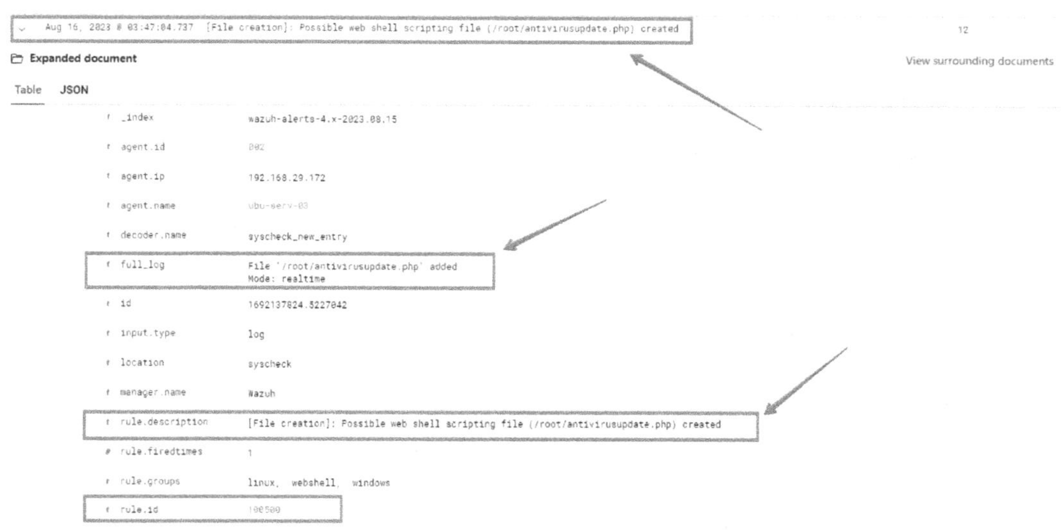

Figure 2.3 – Visualizing possible web shell alerts on the Wazuh manager

Let's break this down:

- `full.log`: `File '/root/antivirusupdate.php' added Mode`: This represents the full logs on the Wazuh manager
- `rule.description`: This represents the triggered rule ID. In this case, the rule ID is 100500

> **Note**
>
> This FIM rule may lead to a lot of false positive alerts on the Wazuh dashboard. To overcome this situation, you can fine-tune your `<syscheck>` block by adding more `<ignore>` tags.

In the next section, we will detect malicious files using the CDB list in the Wazuh manager.

The CDB list

The CDB list in Wazuh serves as a repository for distinct hashes or checksums of malicious and benign files. The Wazuh security platform can precisely compare the files' cryptographic representations on a system and those kept in the CDB. The CDB list consists of lists of users, file hashes, IP addresses, domain names, and so on. In this section, we will cover the following topics:

- The workings of the CDB list
- Setting up the Wazuh server
- Configuring Windows endpoints

- Testing
- Visualizing the alerts

The workings of the CDB list

You can save a list of users, file hashes, IP addresses, and domain names in a text file called a CDB list. A CDB list can have entries added in a `key:value` pair or a `key:only` format. Lists on CDBs can function as allow or deny lists. Wazuh processes the CDB list in the process mentioned here:

1. **Hash generation**: CDB lists consist of hashes of both good and bad content such as IP addresses, malware hashes, and domain names. A hash is a unique fixed-length value generated based on the CDB list content.
2. **File comparison**: Wazuh computes file hashes during a system scan and compares them to the CDB entries.
3. **Identification**: Wazuh marks a file as possibly malicious if its hash matches a known malicious hash in the CDB.
4. **Alerts and reactions**: Based on the set policies, Wazuh has the ability to trigger alerts or responses upon detection.

We've learned about how Wazuh processes the CDB list. Now, let's go through the first practical use case of the CDB list wherein we will detect malicious IP addresses using the CDB list.

Setting up the Wazuh server

We need to set up our Wazuh server with the CDB list of malware hashes and create the required rules to trigger alerts when a file with a hash matches CDB malware hashes. We need to follow these steps to accomplish that:

1. **Create a file in the CDB list**: CDB lists are stored in the `/ossec/etc/lists` directory on the Wazuh server. To add a new CDB list for malware hashes, create a new file with the name `malware-hashes` using the following command:

   ```
   nano /var/ossec/etc/lists/malware-hashes
   ```

2. **Add malware hashes**: We need to enter the known malware hashes in the `key:value` pair where `key` will be the actual malware hash and `value` will be the name or keyword. Now, there are several sources from where we can download and use the malware hashes for the CDB list. One of the popular sources is a list published by Nextron Systems. You can view and download the list from the official GitHub page (`https://github.com/Neo23x0/signature-base/blob/master/iocs/hash-iocs.txt`). For testing purposes, we will use a few popular malware hashes such as Mirai and Fanny.

Open the file using the `Nano` editor:

```
nano /var/ossec/etc/lists/malware-hashes
```

Then enter the malware hash in the format shown in the following:

```
GNU nano 2.9.8                /var/ossec/etc/lists/malware-hashes

e0ec2cd43f71c80d42cd7b0f17802c73:mirai
55142f1d393c5ba7405239f232a6c059:Xbash
F71539FDCA0C3D54D29DC3B6F8C30E0D:fanny
```

Figure 2.4 – The CDB list of malware hashes

In the preceding image, we have the hash of three types of malware: `mirai`, `Xbash`, and `fanny`.

3. **Add the CDB list under the default ruleset**: By providing the location of the CDB list in the `<ruleset>` block, you may add a reference to the CDB list in the `/var/ossec/etc/ossec.conf` Wazuh manager configuration file:

```
<ruleset>
 <!-- Default ruleset -->
<list>etc/lists/malware-hashes</list>
 <ruleset>
```

4. **Write a rule to compare hashes**: Create a custom rule in the Wazuh server's `/var/ossec/etc/rules/local_rules.xml` file. When Wazuh finds a match between the MD5 hash of a recently created or updated file and a malware hash in the CDB list, this rule triggers. When an event occurs that indicates a newly created or modified file exists, rules `554` and `550` will be triggered:

```
<group name="malware,">
  <rule id="110002" level="13">
    <if_sid>554, 550</if_sid>
    <list field="md5" lookup="match_key">etc/lists/malware-
hashes</list>
    <description>Known Malware File Hash is detected: $(file)</
description>
    <mitre>
      <id>T1204.002</id>
    </mitre>
  </rule>
</group>
```

5. **Restart the manager**: We have to restart the Wazuh manager to apply the changes:

```
systemctl restart wazuh-manager
```

We have successfully created a CDB list of malware hashes and security rules to compare it with the hash of each file in the Wazuh agent. In the next step, we will set up a Windows endpoint to detect any file changes so that it can trigger the CDB list to perform a comparison of file hashes.

Configuring the Windows endpoint

We need to set up our Windows endpoint to detect file changes. We will configure `<syscheck>` to track file changes in the `Downloads` folder. You can choose any folder:

```
<ossec_config>
 <syscheck>
<disabled>no</disabled>
<syscheck> <disabled>no</disabled>
<directories check_all="yes" realtime="yes">/PATH/TO/MONITORED/
DIRECTORY</directories>
 </syscheck>
</ossec_config>
```

Let's break this code down:

- `check_all="yes"`: This ensures that Wazuh verifies every aspect of the file, such as its size, permissions, owner, last modification date, inode, and hash sums
- `realtime="yes"`: Wazuh will perform real-time monitoring and trigger alerts

Next, restart the Wazuh agent using the following command:

```
systemctl restart wazuh-agent
```

Testing

Download the Mirai malware sample and put it in the area that the FIM module is monitoring to make sure everything is working right. In our case, it is a `Downloads` folder.

> **Note**
> Be careful as these malicious files are harmful, so only use them for tests. Do not put them in places where they will be used.

Use the following PowerShell command to download the Mirai malware sample and store it in the `Downloads` folder:

```
Invoke-WebRequest -Uri https://wazuh-demo.s3-us-west-1.amazonaws.com/
mirai -OutFile C:/Users/Administrator/Downloads/mirai
```

Visualizing the alerts

Wazuh immediately detects the malware sample. As you can see in the following figure, we have an alert with the `Known Malware File Hash is detected` description:

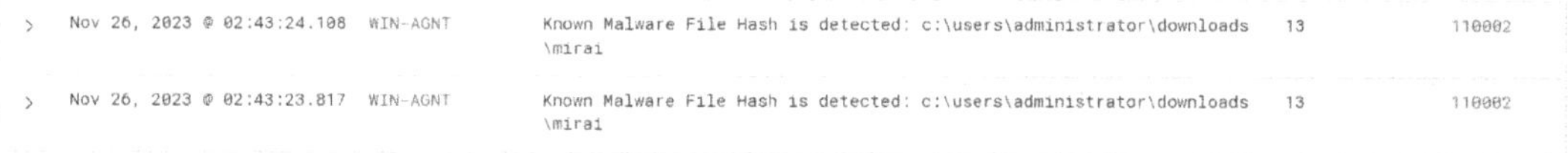

Figure 2.5 – Know Malware File Hash is detected

If you expand the alert, you can see the full log, rule ID, and other information as shown in the following figure:

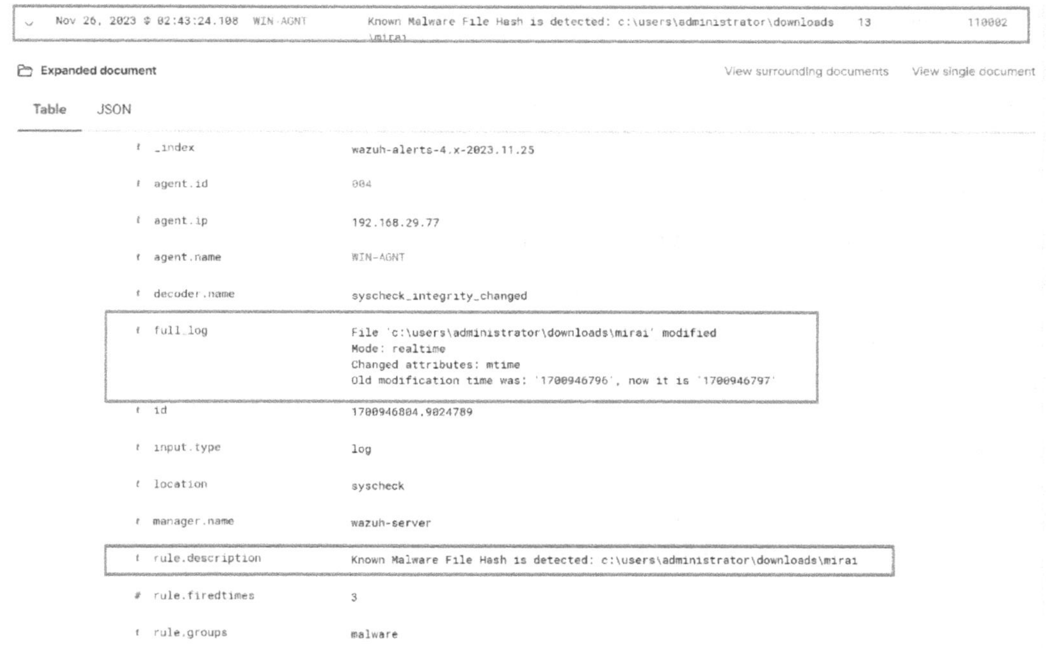

Figure 2.6 – Visualizing the Mirai malware alerts

Let's break this down:

- `rule.description: Know Malware File Hash is detected`: This represents the description of rule ID 11002
- `full.log: File 'c:\users\administrator\downloads\mirai' modified`: This shows the full log information with the location, mode, attributes, and old/new modifications

We have successfully tested the CDB list to detect known malware using file hashes stored in the form of `key:value` pairs within the CDB list. Moreover, there are some more use cases of the CDB list such as detecting unknown users and detecting blacklisted IP addresses. In the next section, we will learn to detect malware using the VirusTotal API.

VirusTotal integration

VirusTotal is a free online service that analyzes files and URLs to detect malware and other malicious content. It uses over 70 types of antivirus software and URL blocklisting engineers to provide detailed information about the submitted file, URL, or IP address. VirusTotal allows users to contribute their own findings and submit comments on files and URLs. These contributions can help improve the service's accuracy and provide valuable insights to other users. VirusTotal provides an API with multiple paid plans. However, it also has a free plan where you can request four lookups per minute with a daily quote of 500 lookups.

In this use case of malware detection, we will use a FIM module to monitor the changes and then trigger VirusTotal to scan the files in that directory. We will cover the following points:

- Set up a VirusTotal account
- Integrate VirusTotal with the Wazuh manager
- Create a Wazuh rule on the Wazuh manager
- Set up a FIM check on Ubuntu Server
- Testing malware detection

Set up VirusTotal account

In order to set up the VirusTotal account, simply visit `VirusTotal.com` and sign up. After signing up, go to your profile and click **API key**. Copy the API key safely as shown in the following figure:

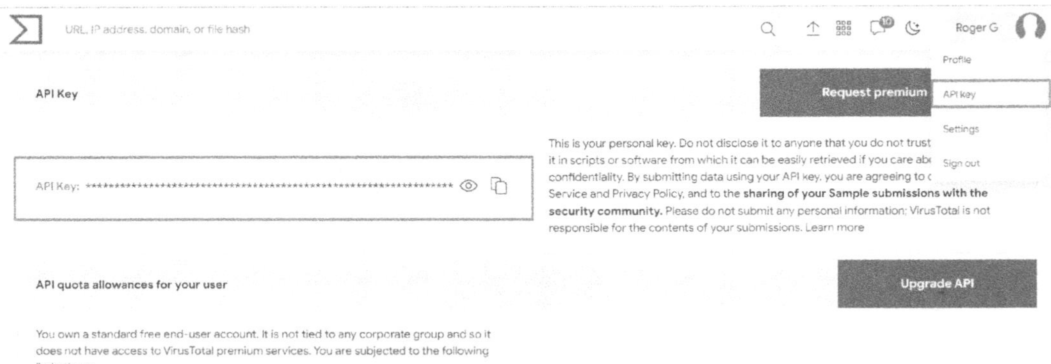

Figure 2.7 – Retrieving the VirusTotal API key

Integrate VirusTotal with the Wazuh manager

Wazuh has prebuilt VirusTotal integration scripts located in `/var/ossec/integrations`. Now, all you have to do is to call this VirusTotal script in `/var/ossec/etc/ossec.conf` file, and to do that, add a `<integration>` tag as shown in the following:

```
<ossec_config>
  <integration>
    <name>virustotal</name>
    <api_key><YOUR_VIRUS_TOTAL_API_KEY></api_key> <!-- Replace with
your VirusTotal API key -->
    <rule_id>100200,100201</rule_id>
    <alert_format>json</alert_format>
  </integration>
</ossec_config>
```

Let's break this code down:

- `<api_key>`: This represents the VirusTotal API key. You need to replace the `YOUR_VIRUS_TOTAL_API_KEY` text with your API key.
- `<rule_id>100200,100201</rule_id>`: This represents the rule that triggers the VirusTotal inspection. In this case, we have rule ID 100200 and `100201`. We haven't created these rules yet; we will write these rules to detect file changes in a specific folder of the endpoint. This will be covered in the next step.

Create a Wazuh rule on the Wazuh manager

Now, we want to trigger VirusTotal scanning only when any file is changed, added, or deleted to avoid tons of false positive alerts. We will create an FIM rule with an ID of `100200` and `100201` in the `local_rule.xml` file located at `/var/ossec/etc/rules` in the Wazuh manager. The Wazuh rules can be written as shown in the following:

```
<group name="syscheck,pci_dss_11.5,nist_800_53_SI.7,">
    <!-- Rules for Linux systems -->
    <rule id="100200" level="7">
        <if_sid>550</if_sid>
        <field name="file">/root</field>
        <description>File modified in /root directory.</description>
    </rule>
    <rule id="100201" level="7">
        <if_sid>554</if_sid>
        <field name="file">/root</field>
        <description>File added to /root directory.</description>
    </rule>
</group>
```

Let's break this down:

- `<if_sid>550</if_sid>`: This specifies a condition that triggers this rule. It's triggered when the event ID (SID) `550` occurs. The Wazuh rule `550` indicates that the integrity checksum changed.
- `<if_sid>554</if_sid>`: This rule triggers when the event ID `554` occurs. The Wazuh rule indicates that a file has been added to the system.

Set up an FIM check on Ubuntu Server

We want the Wazuh agent to first detect any file changes in the `/root` directory and this will trigger the Wazuh rule ID `100200` and `100201`. To enable syscheck to detect any file changes in the `/root` directory, we need to make the following changes:

1. **Ensure <syscheck> is enabled**: Search for the `<syscheck>` block in the `/var/ossec/etc/ossec.conf` Wazuh agent configuration file. Make sure that `<disabled>` is set to `no`. This enables the Wazuh FIM to monitor directory changes.
2. **Track the root directory for any file changes**: In the Wazuh Ubuntu agent, you need to add a `/root` directory to enable an FIM check of `<directories check_all="yes" report_changes="yes" realtime="yes">/root</directories>`.
3. **Restart the Wazuh agent**: Now, for the FIM changes to take effect in the `ossec.conf` file, we need to restart the Wazuh agent with the following command:

```
sudo systemctl restart wazuh-agent
```

This completes the Wazuh agent restart process. In the next step, we will test VirusTotal using a sample malware file.

Testing malware detection

To test malware detection using VirusTotal, we will use the **European Institute for Computer Antivirus Research** (**EICAR**) test file. An EICAR test file is used to test the response of antivirus software and it is built by the European Institute for Computer Antivirus Research (hence, EICAR) and the **Computer Antivirus Research Organization** (**CARO**). You can download the test file from their official website: `https://www.eicar.org/download-anti-malware-testfile/`.

> **Note**
>
> If you are testing this for a Windows machine, you need to disable the **Enhanced security** option on Google Chrome and **Real-time protection** on Windows Defender to allow the download.

Once the EICAR file is downloaded, move it to the root directory.

Visualizing the alerts

To view the alerts, navigate to the **Security Alerts** module of the Wazuh dashboard and you should find the alerts as shown in the following figure.

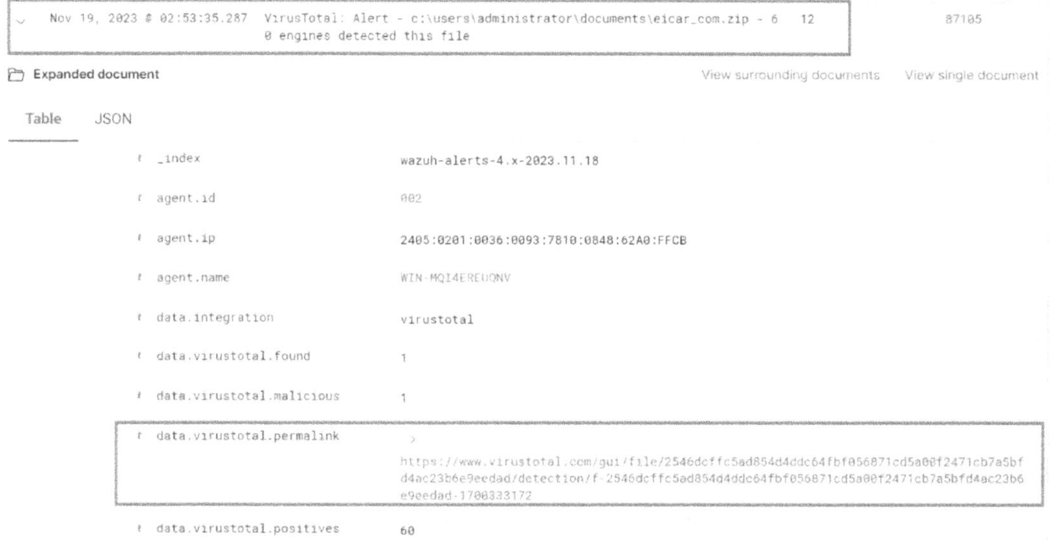

Figure 2.8 – Visualizing the VirusTotal alert on the Wazuh dashboard

Let's break this down:

- `data.integration: virustotal`: This represents the third-party integration used in Wazuh. In this case, it is VirusTotal.
- `data.virustotal.permalink`: This represents the URL of the VirusTotal detection page.

We have successfully detected an EICAR file using VirusTotal and Wazuh. In the next section, we will learn how to integrate Windows Defender (an antivirus solution) with the Wazuh platform.

Integrating Windows Defender logs

Windows Defender is an antivirus software module of Microsoft Windows. As per the *2023 Antivirus Market Report*, Windows Defender is the most common free antivirus product for PC users, with around 40% of the market share of free antivirus software. For more information on this, you can check the following link: `https://www.security.org/antivirus/antivirus-consumer-report-annual/`. Additionally, Microsoft also offers endpoint security solutions for enterprises called Windows Defender for Endpoint. This makes us put more attention on integrating Windows Defender with Wazuh. By default, Wazuh cannot read the Windows Defender logs. Hence, it is important for us to put extra effort into making it possible.

In this section, we'll learn to push Windows Defender logs to the Wazuh manager. You will learn about the following:

- How to get started with Windows Defender logs
- Setting up the Wazuh agent to collect Windows Defender logs
- Testing for malware detection
- Visualizing the alerts

Getting started with Windows Defender logs

Windows Defender logs help SOC analysts understand the security status of endpoints, identify potential cyber threats, and also help them investigate any security incidents. Windows Defender logs encompass several pieces of information such as scan activities, threat detection, updates, quarantine, remediation, firewall and network activities, and real-time protection.

Let's first understand where the Defender logs are stored. Well, You can view the logs in **Event Viewer**.

Go to **Event Viewer** | **Applications and Services Logs** | **Microsoft** | **Windows** | **Windows Defender** | **Operational**.

The general tab will give you information about the scan type and user information. However, the **Details** tab will give you complete information on that threat detection.

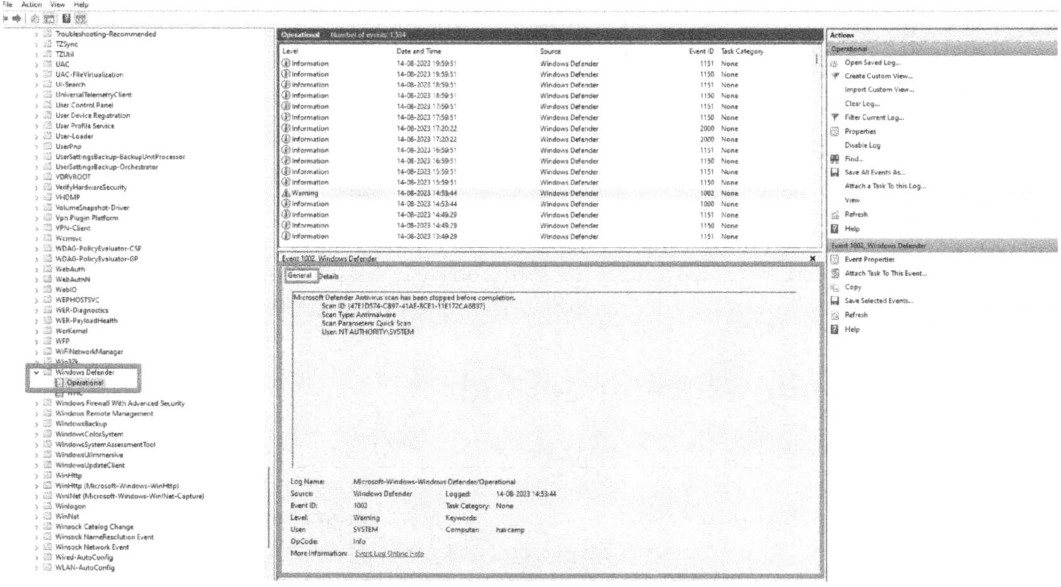

Figure 2.9 – Visualizing Windows Event Viewer

To get more detailed information about this event, you can navigate to the **Details** tab shown in the following figure:

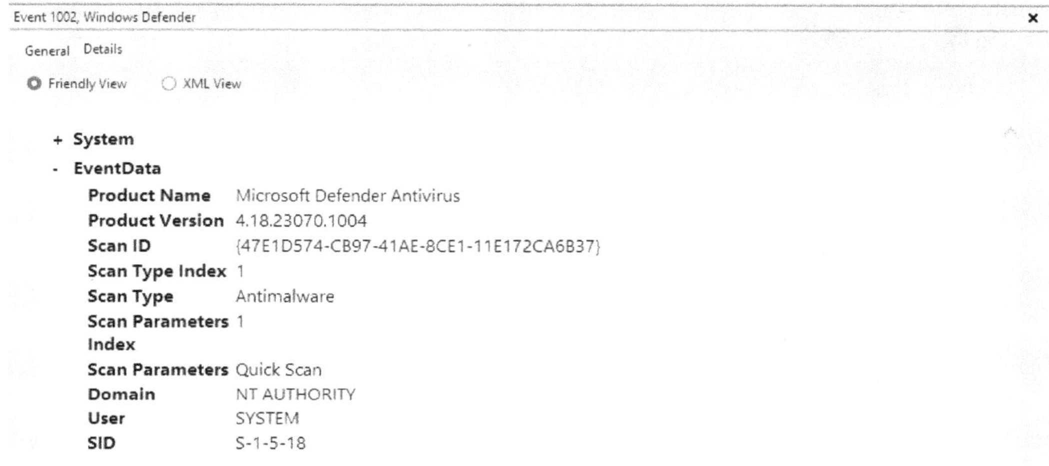

Figure 2.10 – Details of the Windows Defender event

Setting up the Wazuh agent to collect Windows Defender logs

We need to push the Defender logs in the `ossec.conf` file of the Wazuh agent. To collect Windows Defender logs, you must configure the Wazuh agent using the Wazuh manager or locally using the `ossec.conf` agent file located at `C:\Program Files (x86)\ossec-agent`.

In a large network, manually going to each Wazuh agent and making the changes in each agent is a cumbersome task. Wazuh helps us with the `agent.conf` file, which pushes the configuration to specific agent groups.

Login to the Wazuh dashboard, go to **Management** | **Groups**, and select the **Windows** group. You can also create a new group if you haven't created one. In order to push the Microsoft Defender logs to the Wazuh agent, you need to add `<localfile>` tag in the `agent.conf` file as shown in the following:

```
<localfile>
<location> Microsoft-Windows-Windows Defender/Operational</location>
<log_format>eventchannel</log_format>
</localfile>
```

Let's break this down:

- `<localfile>`: This tag is used to define the local log file or file path that the Wazuh agent should monitor.

- `<location> Microsoft-Windows-Windows Defender/Operational</location>`: This represents the location or path of the log file that Wazuh should monitor. In this case, it is monitoring the `Microsoft-Windows-Windows Defender/Operational` log location.
- `<log_format>`: This tag specifies the format.

Now, for these changes to take effect, you need to restart the Wazuh agent using the following command:

```
sudo systemctl restart wazuh-agent
```

> **Note:**
> To verify the location of Windows Defender events, you can also navigate to the `Microsoft-Windows-Windows Defender/Operational` location under **Event Viewer** and check for the log name as shown in the following figure.

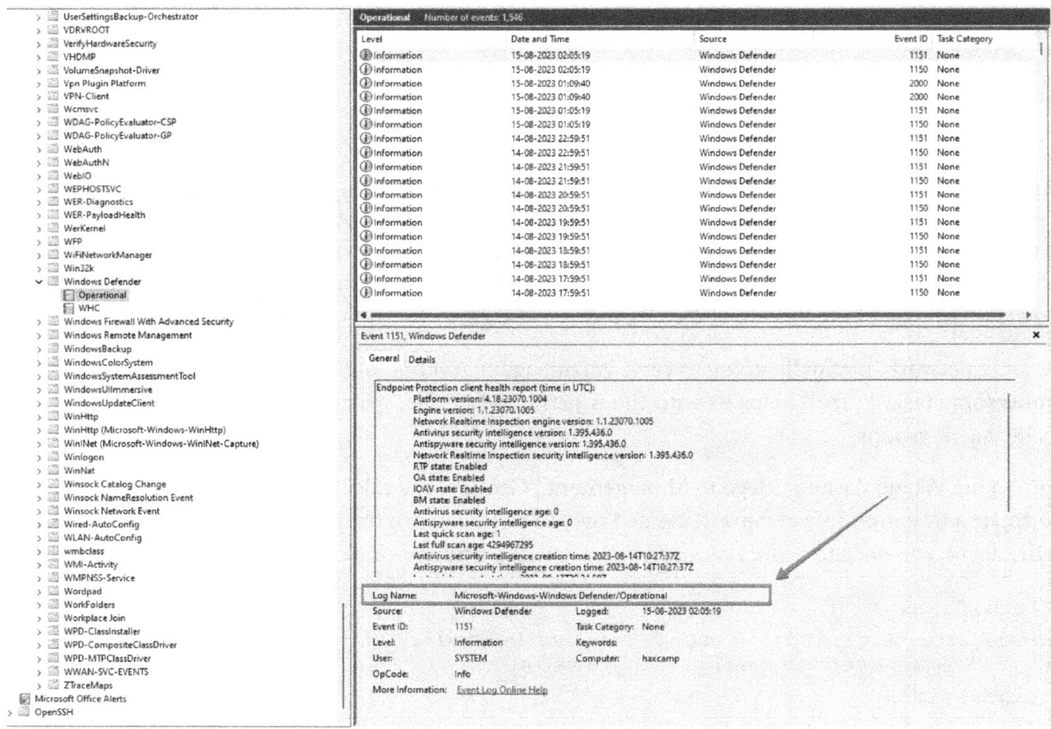

Figure 2.11 – Checking Log Name for Windows Defender events

Testing for malware detection

To test the malware detection using VirusTotal, we will use an EICAR test file. You can download the EICAR test file from their official website: `https://www.eicar.org/download-anti-malware-testfile/`.

> **Note**
>
> You need to disable the **Enhanced security** option on Google Chrome and **Real-time protection** on Windows Defender to allow the download.

Visualizing the alerts

To visualize the alerts related to the EICAR test file, you can navigate to **Security Alerts** in the Wazuh manager and check for the Windows Defender alerts as shown in the following figure:

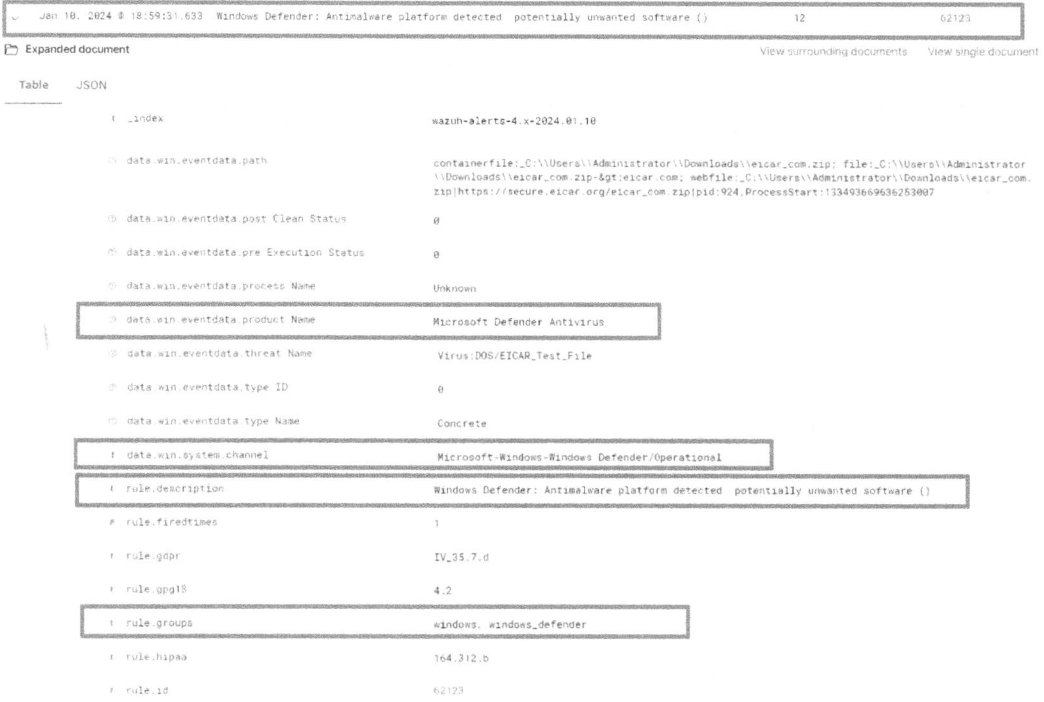

Figure 2.12 – Visualizing Windows Defender alerts in the Wazuh manager

Let's break this down:

- `data.win.eventdata.product Name: Microsoft Defender Antivirus`: This represents the name of the product that generated the alert. In this case, it is Microsoft Defender Antivirus.
- `data.win.system.channel: Microsoft-Windows-Windows Defender/Operational`: This indicates the channel or source from where the alert originated. In this case, it is the `Microsoft-Windows-Windows Defender/Operational` channel.
- `rule.description: Windows Defender: Antimalware platform detected potentially unwanted software ()`: This provides the description of the triggered rule.
- `rule.groups: windows, windows_defender`: This field specifies the groups or categories to which the rule or alert belongs. In this case, we have `Windows` and `Windows_defender` indicating that it's a Windows-specific alert related to Windows Defender.

We have successfully collected and visualized the alerts from the Windows Defender solution. In the next section, we will learn to install and integrate Sysmon modules on a Windows machine to enhance the detection capabilities of the Wazuh platform.

Integrating Sysmon to detect fileless malware

Malicious code that operates directly within a computer's memory rather than the hard drive is known as fileless malware. It is "fileless" in the sense that no files are downloaded to your hard drive when your machine is infected. This makes it more difficult to detect using traditional antivirus or anti-malware tools, which primarily scan disk files.

Sysmon is a device driver and Windows system service that provides advanced monitoring and logging capabilities. It was created by Microsoft's Sysinternals team to monitor various aspects of system activity, such as processes, network connections, and file changes. While Sysmon does not specifically focus on detecting fileless malware, its comprehensive monitoring capabilities can undoubtedly assist in identifying and mitigating the impact of fileless malware attacks. We can enhance Wazuh's malware detection capabilities by installing Sysmon on each Windows machine. To test the fileless attack detection, we will use the APTSimulator tool to simulate the attack and visualize them on the Wazuh manager.

In this section, we will learn how to detect fileless malware using Sysmon and finally, we will visualize them on the Wazuh dashboard. We will cover the following items in this section:

- How do fileless attacks work?
- Requirements for lab setup
- Setting up Sysmon on a Windows machine
- Configure the Wazuh agent to monitor Sysmon events

- Creating Sysmon rules on the Wazuh manager
- Testing malware detection
- Visualizing the alerts

How do fileless malware attacks work?

In its operation, a fileless malware attack is fairly unique. Understanding how it works can help an organization protect against future fileless malware attacks. Let's learn about the different stages involved in the fileless malware attack. Each attack stage will be explained, and the techniques and tools used by the attackers will be explained in the following subsections.

Stage 1 – Gain access

Threat actors must first gain access to the target machine in order to carry out an attack. Some of the common techniques and tools involved in this stage are mentioned here:

- **Techniques**: Remotely exploit a vulnerability and gain remote access via web scripting or a social engineering scheme such as phishing emails
- **Tools**: ProLock and Bumblebee

Stage 2 – Steal credentials

Using the access gained in the previous step, the attacker now attempts to obtain credentials for the environment he has compromised, which will allow him to easily move to other systems in that environment. Some of the techniques and tools that he could have used are as follows:

- **Techniques**: Remotely exploit a vulnerability and gain remote access via web scripting (e.g., Mimikatz)
- **Tools**: Mimikatz and Kessel

Stage 3 – Maintain persistence

Now, the attacker creates a backdoor that will allow him to return to this environment at any time without having to repeat the initial steps of the attack. Some of the techniques and tools are as follows:

- **Techniques**: Modify the registry to create a backdoor
- **Tools**: Sticky Keys Bypass, Chinoxy, HALFBAKED, HiKit, and ShimRat

Stage 4 – Exfiltrate data

In the final step, the attacker collects the data he desires and prepares it for exfiltration by copying it to a single location and then compressing it with commonly available system tools such as Compact.

The attacker then uploads the data via FTP to remove it from the victim's environment. Some of the techniques and tools are as follows:

- **Techniques**: Using DNS tunneling, traffic normalization, use of an encrypted channel, and so on
- **Tools**: FTP, SoreFang, and SPACESHIP

Requirement for the lab

To test the fileless malware detection, we need the following system:

- The Wazuh server
- Windows 10 or 11 or Windows Server 2016 or 2019, which should have the Wazuh agent installed

Setting up Sysmon on a Windows machine

In this step, we'll set up our Windows 11 endpoint with the Sysmon package.

Sysmon offers comprehensive data about process creation, network connections, and file creation time changes. Sysmon generates events and stores them in `Applications and Services Logs/Microsoft/Windows/Sysmon/Operational`. To install Sysmon on a Windows machine, you need to follow the steps as explained in the following sections.

Step 1 – Download and extract Sysmon

To download Sysmon on your Windows machine, visit its official website: `https://learn.microsoft.com/en-us/sysinternals/downloads/sysmon`. Once downloaded, extract the Sysmon archive to a folder of your choice on your Windows machine.

Step 2 – Download the SwiftOnSecurity Sysmon configuration

SwiftOnSecurity's Sysmon configuration is a well-known and simple configuration file created by popular security professionals. Using this configuration can enhance our Windows monitoring capabilities. To download the SwiftOnSecurity Sysmon configuration file, visit their official GitHub repository (`https://github.com/SwiftOnSecurity/sysmon-config`) and download the latest version of the configuration file called `SysmonConfig.xml`.

> **Note**
>
> Make sure you place the `SysmonConfig.xml` file in the same folder where you extracted Sysmon.

Step 3 – Install Sysmon with the SwiftOnSecurity configuration

To install Sysmon using the SwiftOnSecurity configuration file called `SysmonConfig.xml`, you need to follow some steps as explained here:

1. Open a command prompt or PowerShell with administrative privileges.
2. Navigate to the folder where Sysmon is extracted.
3. Now, run the following command to install Sysmon with the SwiftOnSecurity configuration:

   ```
   sysmon.exe -accepteula -i SysmonConfig.xml
   ```

   Let's break this down:

   - `-accepteula`: It represents the **end user license agreement** (**EULA**) for Sysmon. By including this flag, you are acknowledging and agreeing to the terms of use.

Verify installation

After the installation, you can verify that Sysmon is running properly by checking **Event Viewer**. To do so, open **Event Viewer**, navigate to `Applications and Services Logs/Microsoft/Windows/Sysmon/Operational`, and you should start getting Sysmon-related events as shown in the following figure:

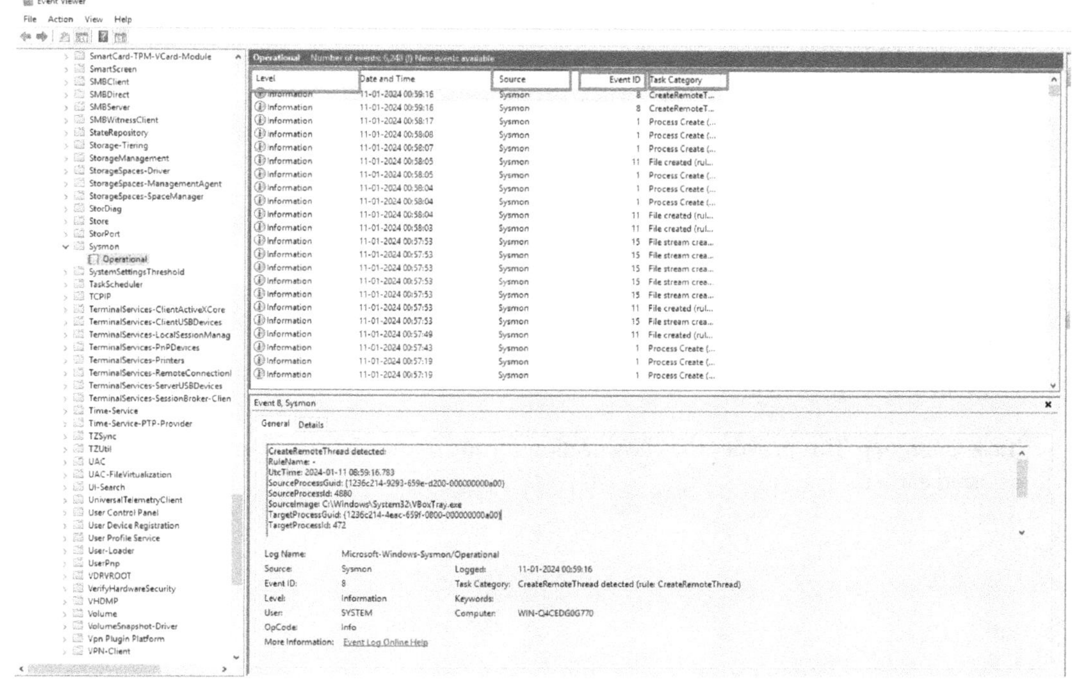

Figure 2.13 – Visualizing Sysmon events in Event Viewer

Let's break this down:

- **Level**: This refers to the severity of an event. The levels are usually categorized as follows:
    - **0**: Information
    - **1**: Warning
    - **2**: Error
    - **3**: Critical
- **Source**: This field indicates the software or component that generated the event. In this case, it is Sysmon.
- **Event ID**: It is a unique value assigned to each type of event. Sysmon uses different event IDs for various purposes:
    - **Event ID 1**: Process creation
    - **Event ID 2**: File creation
    - **Event ID 3**: Network connection
    - **Event ID 7**: Image loaded
    - **Event ID 10**: Process access
    - **Event ID 11**: File creation
    - **Event ID 12**: Registry event (object create and delete)
    - **Event ID 13**: Registry event (value set)
    - **Event ID 14**: Registry event (key and value rename)
    - **Event ID 15**: File creation stream hash
    - **Event ID 17**: Pipe event (pipe created)
    - **Event ID 18**: Pipe event (pipe connected)
    - **Event ID 22**: DNS request
- **Task Category**: This provdes the classification for the events. It is the name of the event IDs as listed earlier.

Configure the Wazuh agent to monitor Sysmon events

Assuming the Wazuh agent is already installed and running, you need to inform the agent to monitor Sysmon events. To do that, we need to include the following block in the `ossec.conf` file:

```
<localfile>
<location>Microsoft-Windows-Sysmon/Operational</location>
<log_format>eventchannel</log_format>
</localfile>
```

To ensure our changes take effect, we need to restart the agent.

Configure the Wazuh manager

We are required to create a custom rule in the Wazuh manager to match the Sysmon events generated by the Windows machine. This rule will ensure that the Wazuh manager triggers an alert every time it gets a Sysmon-related event.

To create a rule, go to the Wazuh dashboard and navigate to **Management** | **Rules**, select **Manage rules** | **Add new rule** | **Enter a name** (`custom_sysmon.xml`), and paste the following rules:

```
<!-- Log Sysmon Alerts -->
<group name="sysmon">
<rule id="101100" level="5">
<if_sid>61650</if_sid>
<description>Sysmon - Event 22: DNS Query.</description>
<options>no_full_log</options>
</rule>
<rule id="101101" level="5">
<if_sid>61603</if_sid>
      <options>no_full_log</options>
<description>Sysmon - Event 1: Process creation.</description>
</rule>
<rule id="101102" level="5">
<if_sid>61604</if_sid>
      <options>no_full_log</options>
<description>Sysmon - Event 2: A process changed a file creation
time.</description>
</rule>
<rule id="101103" level="5">
<if_sid>61605</if_sid>
      <options>no_full_log</options>
<description>Sysmon - Event 3: Network connection.</description>
</rule>
<rule id="101104" level="5">
```

```
<if_sid>61606</if_sid>
      <options>no_full_log</options>
<description>Sysmon - Event 4: Sysmon service state changed.</
description>
</rule>
<rule id="101105" level="5">
<if_sid>61607</if_sid>
      <options>no_full_log</options>
<description>Sysmon - Event 5: Process terminated.</description>
</rule>
<rule id="101106" level="5">
<if_sid>61608</if_sid>
      <options>no_full_log</options>
<description>Sysmon - Event 6: Driver loaded.</description>
</rule>
<rule id="101107" level="5">
<if_sid>61609</if_sid>
      <options>no_full_log</options>
<description>Sysmon - Event 7: Image loaded.</description>
</rule>
<rule id="101108" level="5">
<if_sid>61610</if_sid>
      <options>no_full_log</options>
<description>Sysmon - Event 8: CreateRemoteThread.</description>
</rule>
<rule id="101109" level="5">
<if_sid>61611</if_sid>
      <options>no_full_log</options>
<description>Sysmon - Event 9: RawAccessRead.</description>
</rule>
<rule id="101110" level="5">
<if_sid>61612</if_sid>
      <options>no_full_log</options>
<description>Sysmon - Event 10: ProcessAccess.</description>
</rule>
<rule id="101111" level="5">
<if_sid>61613</if_sid>
      <options>no_full_log</options>
<description>Sysmon - Event 11: FileCreate.</description>
</rule>
<rule id="101112" level="5">
<if_sid>61614</if_sid>
      <options>no_full_log</options>
<description>Sysmon - Event 12: RegistryEvent (Object create and
```

```
delete).</description>
</rule>
<rule id="101113" level="5">
<if_sid>61615</if_sid>
      <options>no_full_log</options>
<description>Sysmon - Event 13: RegistryEvent (Value Set).</
description>
</rule>
<rule id="101114" level="5">
<if_sid>61616</if_sid>
      <options>no_full_log</options>
<description>Sysmon - Event 14: RegistryEvent (Key and Value
Rename).</description>
</rule>
<rule id="101115" level="5">
<if_sid>61617</if_sid>
      <options>no_full_log</options>
<description>Sysmon - Event 15: FileCreateStreamHash.</description>
</rule>
</group>
```

Let's break this down:

- `<group>`: This tag is used to organize rules and helps in managing and categorizing rules based on their functionality.
- `<rule>`: This defines the individual rule with the `id` and `level` attributes. In the preceding ruleset, the rule ID ranges from 101100 to 101107 with `level=5`.
- `<if_sid>`: This tag is used as a requisite to trigger any rule when a rule ID has previously matched. Let's look at a couple of the following rules:
    - `Rule ID "101100"` with `if_sid "61650"` will be checked when the requisites of rule ID 61650 are satisfied
    - `Rule ID "101101"` with `if_sid "61603"` will be checked when the requisites of rule ID 61603 are satisfied
    - `Rule ID "101102"` with `if_sid "61604"` will be checked when the requisites of rule ID 61604 are satisfied
    - `Rule ID "101103"` with `if_sid "61605"` will be checked when the requisites of rule ID 61605 are satisfied
    - `Rule ID "101104"` with `IF_SID "61606"` will be checked when the requisites of rule ID 61606 are satisfied

- `Rule ID "101105"` with `IF_SID "61607"` will be checked when the requisites of rule ID 61607 are satisfied
- `Rule ID "101106"` with `IF_SID "61608"` will be checked when the requisites of rule ID 61608 are satisfied
- `Rule ID "101107"` with `IF_SID "61609"` will be checked when the requisites of rule ID 61609 are satisfied

> **Note**
> You can review the details of each of the mentioned `IF_SID` under the Wazuh rule file called `0595-win-sysmon_rules.xml`. You can find this file under the **Rules** section of the Wazuh dashboard or in the Wazuh's official GitHub repository located at `https://github.com/wazuh/wazuh-ruleset/tree/master/rules`.

For changes to take effect, you have to restart the Wazuh manager on the dashboard as shown in the following figure:

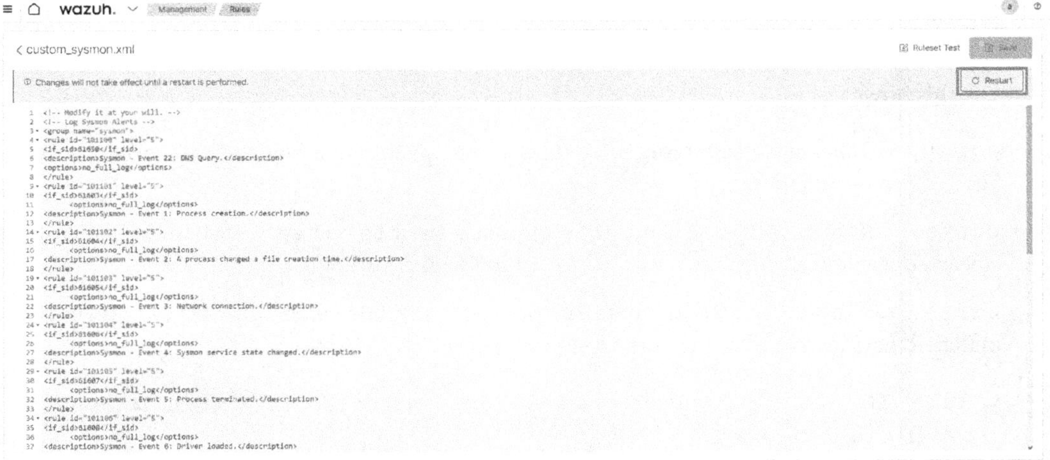

Figure 2.14 – Restarting the Wazuh manager

To restart the Wazuh manager using the command line, you can enter the following command:

```
systemctl restart wazuh-manager
```

In the next step, we will test our Wazuh rules by initiating attacks simulated by the APTSimulator tool and will visualize the alerts on the Wazuh dashboard.

Testing

To test a fileless malware scenario, we will use the APTSimulator tool developed by Florian Roth. It is a Windows batch script that employs several tools and output files to make a system appear to be compromised. To execute this APTSimulator script, download the file on a Windows machine and execute the `.bat` file.

Here is the link to download: `https://github.com/NextronSystems/APTSimulator`.

Once you download this script on your Windows Server, open the command prompt, go to the `APTSimulator-0.9.4` folder, and execute the bat file `APTSimulator.bat`, as shown in the following figure.

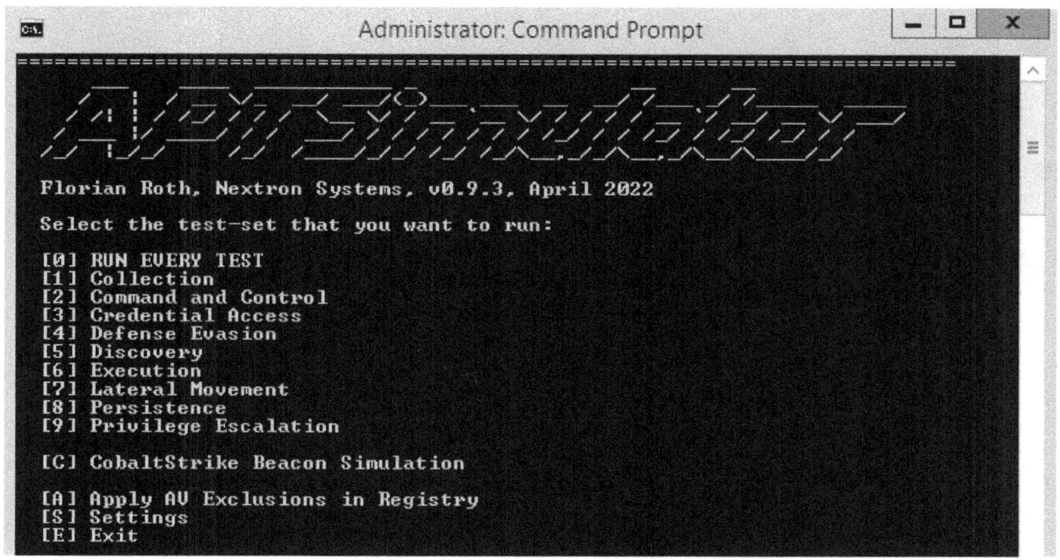

Figure 2.15 – Executing APTSimulator for testing Sysmon alerts

Type `0`. This will run every test including Collection, Command and Control, **Credential Access**, **Defense Evasion**, **Discovery**, **Execution**, **Lateral Movement**, **Persistence**, and **Privilege Escalation**.

> **Note**
>
> Some of the attacks might not work so you can skip them.

Visualizing the alerts

To visualize the Sysmon alerts from the Windows machine, navigate to the **Security Alerts** module in the Wazuh dashboard and you should see multiple alerts as shown in the following figure:

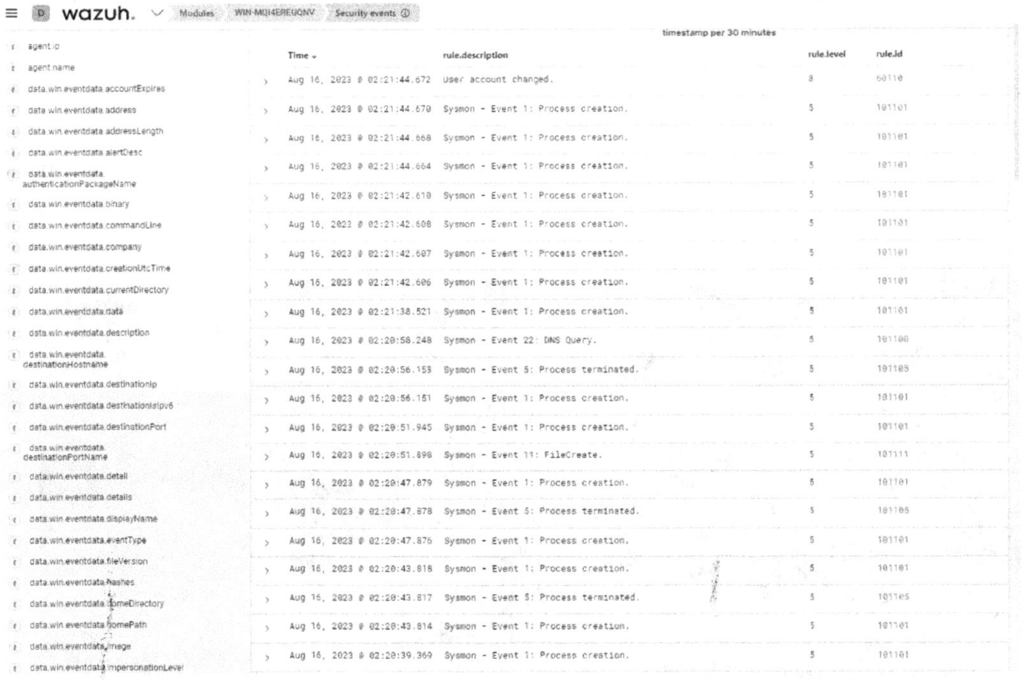

Figure 2.16 – Visualizing the Sysmon alerts in the Wazuh dashboard

Here, you can see that we got a wide range of Sysmon events such as **Process Creation (Event 1)**, **DNS Query (Event 22)**, **Network Connection (Event 3)**, and **RegistryEvent (Event 13)**. All these Sysmon events can be used to conduct further analysis.

Summary

This chapter introduced us to the synergy between Wazuh and malware detection, covering its capabilities in FIM and using VirusTotal for enhanced threat intelligence and the CDB list to build a list of known malware hashes. The integration of Windows Defender logs with Wazuh provided us with a unified look at security events on a Windows machine. In the end, we talked about the integration of Sysmon with a Windows machine to detect fileless malware on the Windows machine.

In the next chapter, we will learn how to enhance Wazuh's threat intelligence capabilities by integrating the **Malware Information Sharing Platform** (**MISP**). To build a scalable system, we will also integrate TheHive and Cortex with the MISP platform.

Part 2: Threat Intelligence, Automation, Incident Response, and Threat Hunting

In this part, you will learn how to extend the Wazuh threat intelligence capability by integrating the MISP platform. You will learn to integrate TheHive with Wazuh and MISP to perform threat analysis. In addition to that, you will learn how to automate security operations and management of the Wazuh platform using the **security orchestration, automation, and response** (**SOAR**) tool, **Shuffle**. You will also learn to perform automated incident responses using a Wazuh-native feature called Active Response such as blocking brute force attempts and automatically isolating infected machines. Lastly, we will learn how to leverage the Wazuh platform to conduct proactive threat hunting.

This part includes the following chapters:

3
Threat Intelligence and Analysis

According to a Ponemon Institute study (`https://webroot-cms-cdn.s3.amazonaws.com/9114/5445/5911/ponemon-importance-of-cyber-threat-intelligence.pdf`), organizations with robust threat intelligence respond to cyberattacks 53% faster, highlighting its importance in threat analysis, incident response, and mitigation. Simply put, threat intelligence is data that is gathered, processed, and studied to figure out why a threat actor does what they do, who they attack, and how they do it. Threat intelligence data empowers security operations teams to proactively defend against potential security incidents, improving their ability to detect, analyze, and eradicate the threat effectively. When you integrate threat intelligence capabilities into the Wazuh platform, **security operations center** (**SOC**) analysts can get more context for each security alert. In this chapter, we aim to enhance Wazuh's threat intelligence capabilities. To achieve this, we will leverage the **Malware Information Sharing Platform** (**MISP**), an open-source project designed for the collection and sharing of threat intelligence. Additionally, we will incorporate TheHive/Cortex, a comprehensive suite tailored for scalable threat analysis and incident response. By integrating these tools with Wazuh, we enable security teams to conduct thorough threat analyses and streamline incident response processes. This integration facilitates the automation of threat intelligence tasks, resulting in reduced response times and enhanced security for organizations.

In this chapter, we will cover the following topics:

- What is threat intelligence?
- Automated threat intelligence
- Setting up TheHive and Cortex
- Setting up an MISP project
- Integrating Wazuh and TheHive
- Integrating TheHive and Cortex with MISP
- Use cases

What is threat intelligence?

Threat intelligence, or **cyber threat Intelligence**, is basically knowledge about threat actors (an individual or group of attackers that carry out hacking campaigns against companies or government bodies), their motives, and their capabilities. Threat intelligence is all about staying on top of the latest threats and risks lurking on the internet. Threat intelligence enables us to make faster, more informed, data-backed security decisions and change our behavior from reactive to proactive in the fight against attackers. Threat intelligence helps every domain of cybersecurity, including SOC analysts, intel analysts, **chief information security officers** (**CISOs**), etc. By collecting and analyzing threat intelligence information, organizations can be empowered through early detection and prevention, informed decision-making using context, improved incident response, a better understanding of attackers' tactics, **techniques, and procedures** (**TTPs**), better security defense against growing threats, and more.

In this section, we will talk about:

- Types of threat intelligence
- How SOC analysts use threat intelligence

Types of threat intelligence

In the constantly changing world of cybersecurity, companies that want to strengthen their defenses must stay ahead of new risks and utilize threat intelligence. Threat intelligence is mainly offered in three types: *tactical intelligence*, *operational intelligence*, and *strategic intelligence*. By using these types of threat intelligence, businesses can not only learn about how threat actors' strategies change over time but also plan their defenses to successfully deal with cyber threats that are always changing. Let's understand all three types of threat intelligence in detail:

- **Tactical intelligence**: Tactical intelligence is concerned with the immediate future, is technical in nature, and identifies simple **indicators of compromise** (**IOC**). IOCs are technical information collected during investigations, threat-hunting activities, or malware analyses. IOCs are actual pieces of data, such as IP addresses, domains, file hashes, etc. They can even be collected via open source and free data feeds such as:
    - AlienVault OTX (`https://otx.alienvault.com/`
    - Abuse.ch (`https://abuse.ch/`)
    - Blocklist.de (`https://www.blocklist.de`), and
    - Proofpoint Emerging Threats (`https://rules.emergingthreats.net`).
- This tactical intelligence data is consumed by IT analysts and SOC analysts. It typically has a very short lifespan because IOCs such as malicious IP addresses or domain names can become obsolete in a matter of days or even hours.

- **Operational intelligence**: Every attack has a "*who*," a "*why*," and a "*how*." The "*who*" is referred to as identification. The "*why*" is referred to as motivation or intent. The "*how*" is made up of the threat actor's TTPs. This gives the blue team or security operations team insight into how adversaries plan, conduct, and sustain campaigns and major operations. This is called operational intelligence. Tactical intelligence plus human analysis gives this intelligence a longer useful lifespan.
- **Strategic intelligence**: Strategic intelligence assists decision-makers in understanding the threats that cyber threats pose to their organizations. With this knowledge, they can make cybersecurity investments that protect their organizations while also aligning with their strategic priorities. CISOs and management teams are the real consumers of this intelligence. Strategic intelligence requires human data collection and analysis, which requires a deep understanding of cybersecurity and geopolitics. Strategic intelligence is usually prepared in the form of reports.

Combining these different types of threat data can help businesses create complete and flexible cyber defenses against a wide range of cyber threats.

Next, we will focus on how SOC analysts can consume threat intelligence data (especially tactical and operational intelligence) for better detection and analysis of threats.

How SOC analysts use threat intelligence

In the previous section, we learned how SOC teams utilize both tactical and operational intelligence information. Threat intelligence provides valuable information about the latest threats, attack methods, malicious actors, and vulnerabilities. Let's talk about the practical steps SOC analysts take when using threat intelligence:

1. **Gather observables**: Observables are pieces of possible threat information. Examples include IP addresses, domain names, URLs, file hashes, email addresses, and more. Observables can be collected via SIEM tools, EDR, email security tools, open source and free threat intelligence feeds, etc.
2. **Enrichment and context**: After identifying suspicious observables, gather context and enrich the information to better understand the threat. For example, you discovered an IP address (123.45.67.89) connecting to a newly registered domain (`malicious-website.com`). You begin by enriching this data by searching threat intelligence databases and historical data. This IP address has previously been linked to several phishing campaigns, and the domain is hosted in a high-risk region known for cybercriminal activity.
3. **IOC creation**: On the basis of the enriched information, you generate IOCs that can be used in the future to detect similar malicious activities. For example, from the information gathered, you create the following IOCs:
   - IP address IOC: `123.45.67.89`
   - Domain IOC: `malicious-website.com`
   - URL path IOC: `malicious-website.com/login`

These IOCs are now added to the security tools in your organization, such as firewalls, intrusion detection systems, and SIEM solutions. If any of these IOCs are matched, it indicates malicious activity that warrants investigation.

4. **Detection and response**: With the enhanced IOCs in place, the security systems of your organization, such as SIEM, IDS, or XDR, actively monitor network traffic and logs for matches against these indicators. When a match is discovered, an alert is generated, and the SOC team is prompted to initiate incident response procedures. For example, an employee clicks a link that leads to the IOC-mentioned URL path (`malicious-website.com/login`). This triggers an alert in the intrusion detection system of your organization (e.g. Suricata). The SOC team investigates the incident after receiving the alert. They verify that the user's computer has visited a malicious URL and may have been exposed to malware. The SOC team isolates the compromised system, initiates malware analysis, and initiates the containment and eradication processes to prevent further spread.
5. **Continuous improvement**: After the incident has been resolved, the SOC team conducts a post-incident analysis. This involves evaluating the efficacy of the threat detection process, refining the IOCs, and learning from past responses to improve future response strategies. During analysis, the SOC team determines that the phishing attempt originated from an email with a subject line referencing a fake job offer. They decide to add email subject patterns to their IOCs to detect similar phishing campaigns more effectively in the future.

> **Note**
>
> IOCs are not just limited to domains, IP addresses, or URLs; they can also be file hashes, email addresses, email subjects and patterns, registry keys, network signatures (data payloads or packet headers), behavioral indicators (unusual file modification, new user accounts), custom YARA rules, user agents, HTTP headers, DNS records, SSL certificates, hosting information, etc.

We learned about how SOC analysts utilize threat intelligence information; however, in order to make it more efficient, we need to automate the threat intelligence process, including collection, observable analysis, and updates.

Automated threat intelligence

As of now, you might have realized the importance of threat intelligence for SOC analysts or blue team. But imagine, if there are thousands of observables generated every day, it will be very difficult to manually copy/paste each observable and search them in the threat intelligence database or feeds. This brings a lot of challenges to SOC, such as delayed threat detection, missed alerts, a lack of consistency, and slow response times. In this section, we will design an automated threat intelligence system and integrate it with Wazuh. We will cover the following:

- Designing automated threat intelligence
- Introduction to MISP

- TheHive and Cortex
- The workings of threat intelligence and analysis

Designing automated threat intelligence

Wazuh is a security platform that collects security events from all endpoints. To integrate threat intelligence capabilities, we will use an MISP project—an open-source threat intelligence sharing platform. The integration between Wazuh and MISP can be accomplished by using MISP API, as shown in the following figure:

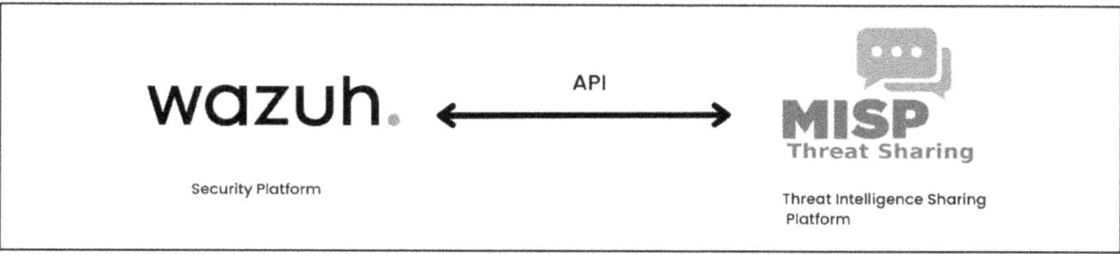

Figure 3.1 – Proposed integration of Wazuh with MISP

However, the design will not allow the security team to track every observable and security incident. We need to build a system wherein we can take the security events from Wazuh and analyze the observables of each event separately against threat intelligence feeds. In short, we have three tools in this design:

- Wazuh (security events collection)
- A security incident management tool (for receiving alerts from Wazuh and performing a lookup with threat intelligence data)
- A threat intelligence tool (this tool is created to provide threat intelligence data to the security incident management tool)
- Top of Form

We will use the TheHive tool for security incident management and an MISP project for threat intelligence management. The following figure gives you an idea of the proposed integration of Wazuh with TheHive/Cortex and MISP:

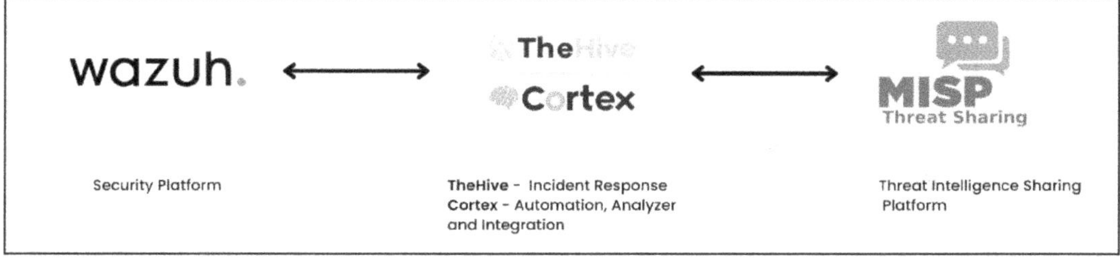

Figure 3.2 – Proposed integration of Wazuh with TheHive/Cortex and MISP

This integration of Wazuh, TheHive, and MISP has some major advantages:

- **Centralized threat intelligence**: The integration lets threat intelligence from MISP be put together in TheHive, creating a central location for Wazuh to store and analyze security events and decide what to do about them. This integration lets security teams correlate events with known risks and IOCs, which makes responding to incidents more accurate and quicker.
- **Scalable security operations**: The integration streamlines the handling of security events, enabling scalable security operations. Through the utilization of Wazuh's detection capabilities, TheHive's case management skills, and MISP's threat intelligence capabilities, organizations can effectively handle and address an increasing volume of security incidents without requiring significantly more manual effort.
- **Automated incident response**: Although this chapter is about threat intelligence integration, by integrating TheHive, we can also accomplish automated incident response capabilities. By utilizing information from MISP, security analysts can generate response playbooks in TheHive, which enables them to provide more consistent and prompt responses to security incidents identified by Wazuh.

Let's first quickly understand the capabilities of each of these tools. Then, we will set them up and integrate them with each other.

Introduction to MISP

MISP is an open-source threat intelligence platform that enables organizations and security professionals to collect, share, and collaborate on structured threat information. MISP has seven core layers:

- **Data layer**: This layer focuses on gathering detailed information about security incidents and threats from the actual threat intelligence data. The primary components of the data layer are as follows:
  - **Events**: Security events or threat information.
  - **Attributes**: Describes aspects of threats such as IP addresses, domains, hashes, email addresses, etc.
  - **Objects**: A template that specifies contextualized and organized information about threats.
- **Context layer**: This layer is concerned with creating links and correlations between various pieces of threat intelligence data.
- **Correlation layer**: This layer is responsible for identifying patterns and correlations between various events and properties.
- **Warning list layer**: Warning lists are collections of indicators that are considered to be malicious or suspicious.
- **Taxonomies layer**: Taxonomies standardize threat intelligence data categorization and classification. They aid in the consistent and orderly organization and description of threats.

- **Galaxies layer**: Galaxies are groups of connected information regarding various threats, such as threat actors, methods, malware families, and so on. They provide contextual information to help you understand dangers better.
- **Feed layer**: Feeds entail incorporating external threat intelligence sources into MISP. This layer enables MISP to automatically retrieve and incorporate data from a variety of reliable sources, thereby enhancing the threat intelligence database.

As we discussed earlier, we need TheHive as a broker that accepts the security alerts from Wazuh and allows us to analyze each observable against MISP threat intelligence data.

TheHive consists of two tools: TheHive for incident management and Cortex for integration with tons of threat intelligence platforms. TheHive and Cortex constitute a potent integration designed for SOC analysts. This integration bridges the gap between effective collaboration and advanced threat analysis, thereby enhancing the SOC's ability to identify, mitigate, and respond to cybersecurity threats.

TheHive

TheHive is an incident response platform designed to help SOC analysts analyze security alerts and incidents. It facilitates collaboration and information sharing among different team members during security investigations and incident responses. Some of the important capabilities of TheHive are as follows:

- **Observable analysis**: TheHive can analyze the alerts received from Wazuh, and this enables SOC analysts to pre-qualify alerts before deciding whether to ignore them or convert them into cases.

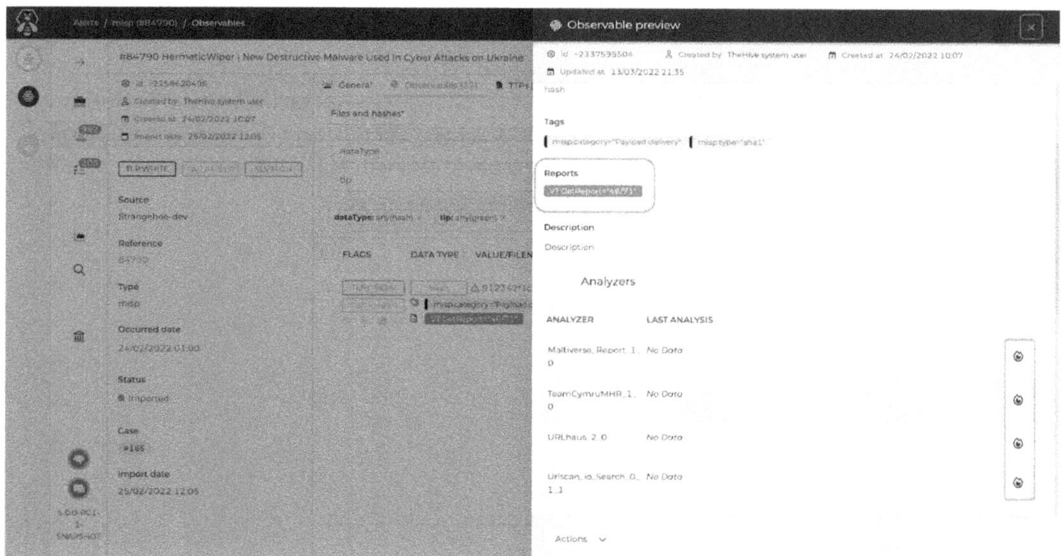

Figure 3.3 – Observable preview

- **Case timeline**: A case timeline illustrates the entirety of the case's lifecycle, including initial alerts, ongoing and completed tasks, identified IOCs, and much more.

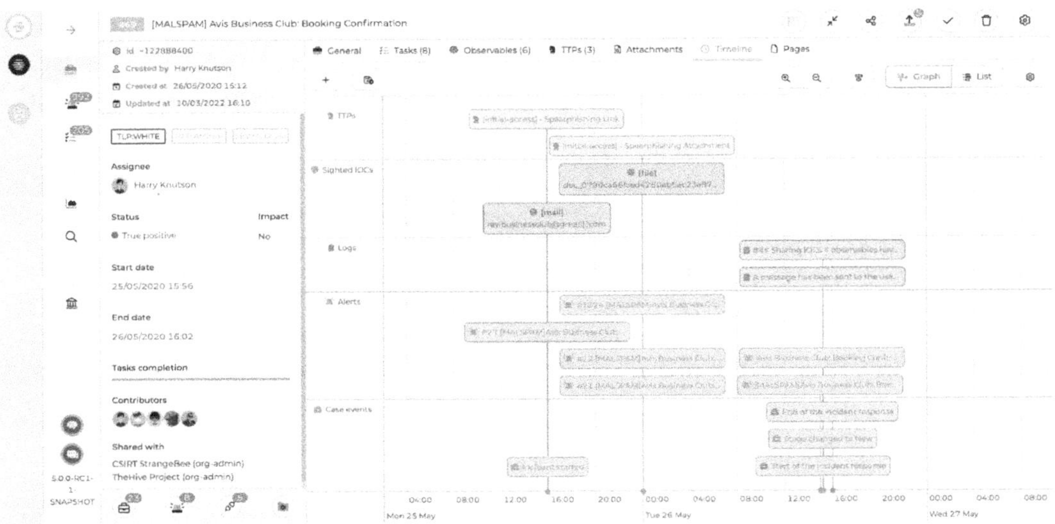

Figure 3.4 – Case timeline in TheHive

- **Integration**: TheHive version 5 has strong and default integration capabilities with Cortex, Wazuh, and MISP. However, it can also be integrated with IBM QRadar, Splunk SIEM, Elasticsearch, VirusTotal, and many more.
- **Alert TTPs**: TheHive can contain a set of MITRE ATT&CK TTPs with ATT&CK mapping post-integration with MISP. MITRE ATT&CK (standing for **Adversarial Tactics, Techniques, and Common Knowledge**) is a framework that classifies cyber threat behaviors and techniques employed by attackers at various stages of an attack. We will learn more about the MITRE ATT&CK framework in *Chapter 6, Threat Hunting with Wazuh*.

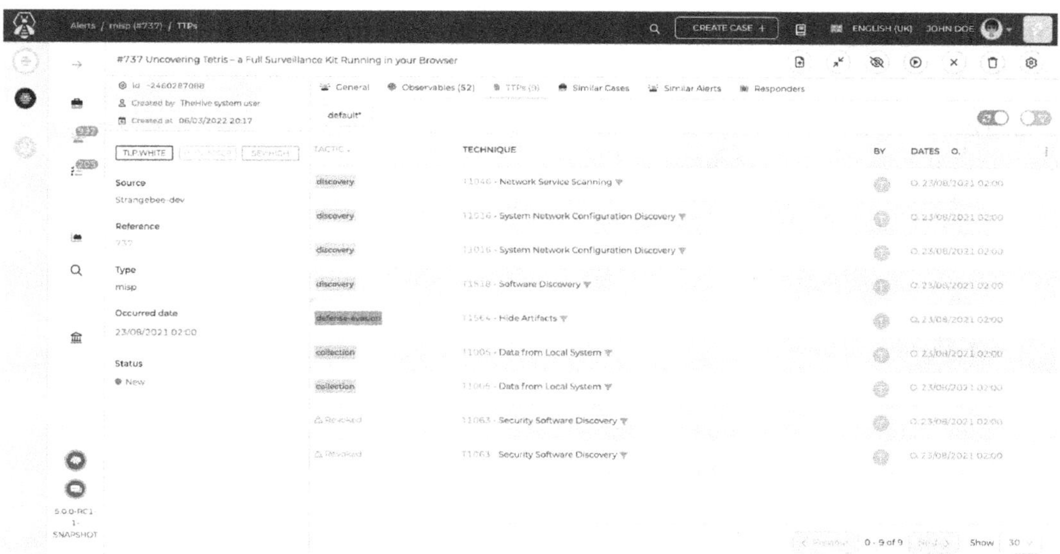

Figure 3.5 – Visualizing TTPs in the TheHive platform

TheHive and Cortex are made to work together without any problems. TheHive can send observables from incidents to Cortex so that the preset analyzers can look at them. Some jobs can be automated with this integration, which cuts down on the amount of work that needs to be done by hand in the incident response process. Let's explore the capabilities of Cortex.

Cortex

Cortex is a part of the TheHive project. It automates threat intelligence and response, providing SOC analysts with the ability to detect and respond to threats quickly and effectively. One of the core features of Cortex is its ability to integrate several security tools, threat intelligence feeds, security services, and more. Cortex serves as a central repository for this intelligence, allowing analysts to manage and access the information they require with ease.

Cortex has two major components:

- **Analyzers**: Analyzers gather and enrich data from various sources to help SOC analyst teams. There are many types of analyzers that connect to online security services, threat feeds, and databases. After transforming the data, the analyzer can enrich it by checking it against a list of known malicious indicators, querying online services for more information, or running custom scripts for more advanced analysis.
- **Responders**: Responders are used for acting in accordance with the enriched data supplied by the analyzers. Responders come in a variety of forms, each intended to carry out a particular task, such as blocking an IP address, isolating an infected device, or alerting a security analyst.

Understanding the workings of automated threat intelligence and analysis

The final design workflow involves all three components: Wazuh, TheHive/Cortex, and MISP. This recommended design helps enterprises build an effective and scalable incident response system. Some of the important steps involved in this automated threat intelligence and analysis design with Wazuh, TheHive/Cortex, and MISP are as follows:

- **Event transfer**: Post-integration, TheHive can receive the security events from Wazuh. We can also configure Wazuh to send only specific types of alerts, such as security alerts matching rule level three or higher.
- **Alert triage**: Once the alert is received from Wazuh by TheHive, it can invoke Cortex to immediately look at the observables that are linked to it. This can include things such as running security scans, comparing observables to MISP threat intelligence feeds, or getting more information from the internet.
- **Response action**: TheHive can initiate response actions based on Cortex analysis results, such as altering the status of an event, providing tasks for analysts, or generating reports. It helps in the automation of portions of the incident response workflow.

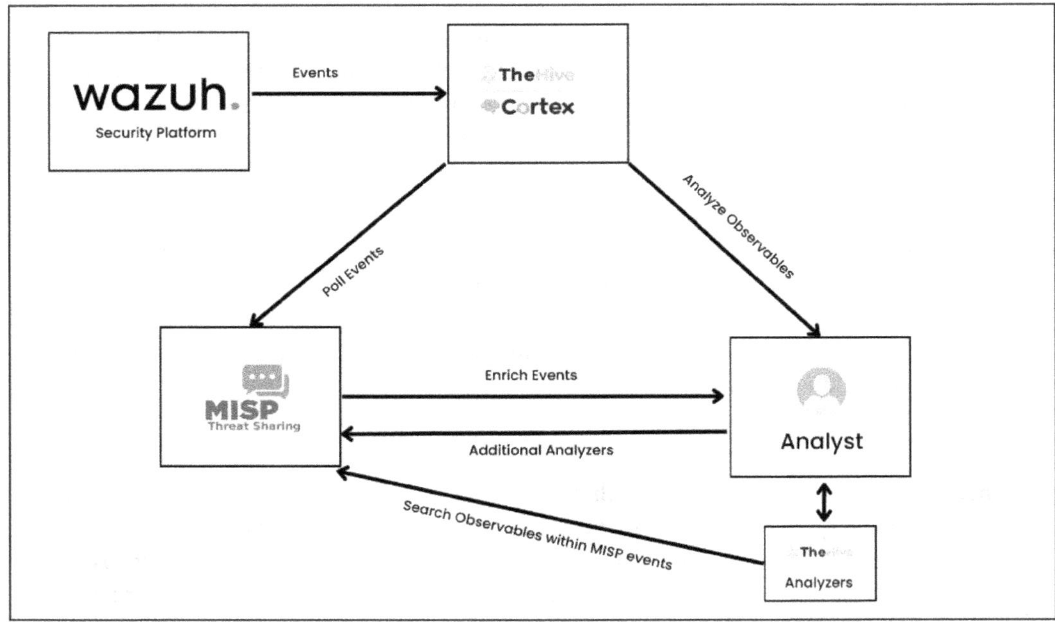

Figure 3.6 – Workflow of threat intelligence and analysis with Wazuh, TheHive, and MISP

Now that we have learned the entire flow of automated threat intelligence, incident management, and analysis, let's begin to set up Wazuh, TheHive/Cortex, and MISP tools and integrate them to work seamlessly.

Setting up TheHive and Cortex

The deployment design of TheHive provides companies with flexibility by allowing for both standalone server deployments (deployment on a single server) and clustered deployments (multiple servers work together to handle the TheHive application load). It is recommended to use cluster mode deployment for large production environments. Some of the software components of TheHive are as follows:

- **Apache Cassandra**: TheHive utilizes the Apache Cassandra database to store its data. Cassandra is a distributed NoSQL database known for its scalability and capability to manage massive amounts of data across a cluster of numerous nodes. Cassandra is utilized within the framework of TheHive to store data pertaining to cases, incidents, and other pertinent information.
- **Elasticsearch**: TheHive uses Elasticsearch for indexing. It is a powerful analytics and search engine that makes data indexing, querying, and searching more effective. It improves TheHive's search performance and speed, which makes it simpler for users to find and evaluate data.
- **S3 MINIO**: When a clustered deployment is necessary or when organizations need scalable and distributed file storage, TheHive provides support for S3-compatible storage solutions such as **MINIO**. AWS provides a scalable object storage, called **S3** (**Simple Storage Service**). An open-source substitute called MINIO is compatible with the S3 API.

The TheHive application, database, index engine, and file storage can be run separately so each layer can be a node or cluster. TheHive could be set up in a complex clustered architecture using virtual IP addresses and load balancers.

We can set up TheHive and Cortex in different environments, such as Ubuntu servers, Docker, Kubernetes, etc. To simplify the installation process, we are going to use Docker Compose. We need to take the following steps:

1. Install Docker Compose
2. Prepare the YML script for the TheHive module
3. Launch and test
4. Create an organization and user on TheHive
5. Create an organization and user on Cortex

Install Docker Compose

Let's start with the Ubuntu Server. I'll use Ubuntu 23.10 and take the following steps to install Docker Compose:

1. **Install pre-requisites packages for Docker**: Log in to Ubuntu 20.04 and run the following `apt` commands to install Docker dependencies:

   ```
   $ sudo apt update
   $ sudo apt install -y apt-transport-https ca-certificates curl gnupg-agent software-properties-common
   ```

2. **Set up the official Docker repository**: Although Docker packages are available in the default Ubuntu 20.04 repositories, it is recommended that you use the official Docker repository. Run the following commands to enable the Docker repository:

   ```
   $ curl -fsSL https://download.docker.com/linux/ubuntu/gpg | sudo apt-key add -
   $ sudo add-apt-repository \ "deb [arch=amd64] https://download.docker.com/linux/ubuntu \ $(lsb_release -cs) stable"
   ```

3. **Install Docker with apt command**: We are now ready to install the most recent and stable version of Docker from its official repository. Run the following to install it:

   ```
   $ sudo apt-get update
   $ sudo apt install docker-ce -y
   ```

   After installing the Docker package, run the following command to add your local user to the Docker group:

   ```
   $ sudo usermod -aG docker rajneesh
   $ sudo usermod -aG docker root
   ```

   Verify the Docker version by executing the following:

   ```
   $ docker version
   ```

   Verify whether the Docker daemon service is running:

   ```
   $ sudo systemctl status docker
   ```

4. Install Docker Compose on Ubuntu 23.10. To install Docker Compose on Ubuntu Linux, run the following commands sequentially:

   ```
   $ sudo curl -L "https://github.com/docker/compose/releases/download/1.29.0/docker-compose-$(uname -s)-$(uname -m)" -o /usr/local/bin/docker-compose
   $ sudo chmod +x /usr/local/bin/docker-compose
   ```

   Check the Docker Compose version by running the following command:

   ```
   $ docker-compose --version
   ```

If the Docker installation is good, you should see the output with the Docker compose version, OpenSSL version, CPython version, etc.

Prepare the YML script for the TheHive module

The primary distinction between `docker run` and `docker-compose` is that `docker run` is entirely command line-based, whereas `docker-compose` reads configuration data from a YAML file. So, the beauty of Docker Compose is that we can install all the modules of TheHive with a single YML script, and once this YML script is executed by Docker, all the modules will be turned up. Now, let's prepare our TheHive YML script:

1. **Create a new directory**: To keep our project organized, let's create a new directory named `theHive` and change the directory:

   ```
   $ mkdir theHive
   $ cd theHive
   ```

2. **Create a docker-compose file**: The `docker-compose.yml` is a configuration file that allows us to configure and launch multiple Docker containers within a single file. Let's create a `docker-compose.yml` file with the code shared in the GitHub repository at `https://github.com/PacktPublishing/Security-Monitoring-using-Wazuh/blob/main/Chapter%203/theHive_Docker_Compose.yml`.

   You can also find the YML code from the link here: `https://docs.strangebee.com/thehive/setup/installation/docker/`

Launch and test

To deploy the TheHive, run the following command from the TheHive directory:

```
$ docker-compose up -d
```

Next, wait for two or three minutes. Open your browser and access TheHive at `http:://<Server_IP>:9000` and Cortex at `http:://<Server_IP>:9001`.

The default credentials of TheHive application are as follows:

- **Login**: `admin@thehive.local`
- **Password**: `secret`

Next, Cortex doesn't provide default credentials; you have to reset the database and set a new username and password. These will be our default admin credentials.

Once you have admin credentials for both theHive and Cortex, we will create an organization and a user under it and generate an API key.

Create an organization and user on TheHive

Once you're logged in, we need to do a few things. We need to first create an organization and then a user:

1. To create an organization, go to **Organization** and click **Add**. Enter a **Name** and **Description** and set the tasks sharing rule to **Manual**.
2. Next, create two users for the haxcamp organization—a user and an API user. Go to **Users** and click **Add** to create a normal user account. Enter the following:
   - **Name**: This represents the field to enter the name.
   - **Login**: This indicates your login name. You can use a username or an email address.
   - **Type**: This represents the type of user. You can select Normal or Administrator. Here, we will be selecting **Normal**.
   - **Password**: You can set or reset the password for the user.
   - **Organization**: This represents the organizations the user belongs to. In this case, we have `admin` and `haxcamp` organizations. Let us assign the user to the `haxamp` organizations.
3. Now, let's create API users. This user account will be used to integrate TheHive with the Wazuh manager. To create an API user, go to **Users** and click **Add**. Enter `API User` for the **Name**, enter `api@haxcamp.local` for the login ID, set the account type to **Service**, and set haxcamp organization as `org-admin user`. Once the API user is created, click on **Reveal**:

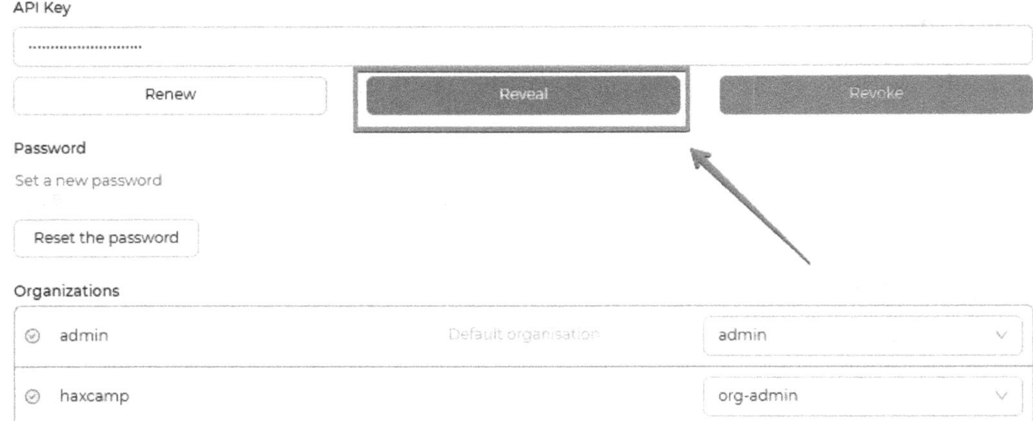

Figure 3.7 – Retrieve TheHive API

Copy the API key and save it somewhere. We will require this API key when integrating TheHive with the Wazuh manager.

Create an organization and user on Cortex

Once you've set your admin credentials on Cortex, you need to create an organization. Fill in **Name** and **Description**:

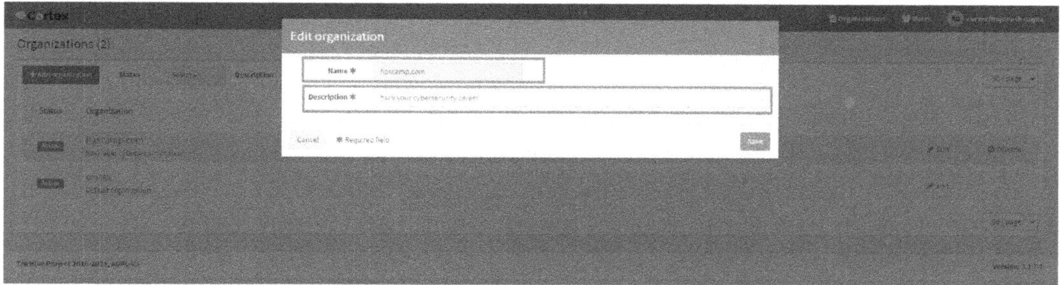

Figure 3.8 – Setting up organization details in Cortex

Next, we need to create a user. To do that, go to **Users**, click on **Add user**, and fill in **Login**, **Full name**, **Organizations & Roles**:

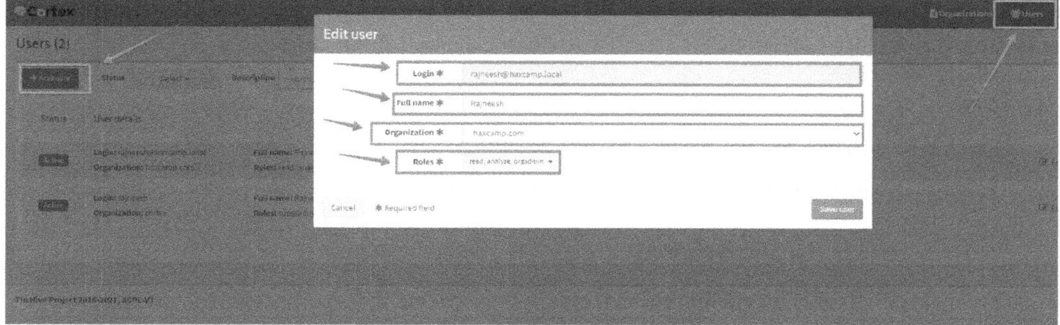

Figure 3.9 – Creating and adding a user in Cortex

You will notice the following in the preceding screenshot:

- **Login**: This represents the login username or email address of the user.
- **Organization**: This represents the organization the user belongs to.
- **Roles**: This shows the role of the user.

After creating the user, you can click on **Reveal** to reveal the API key and save that for future use when we integrate Cortex with MISP:

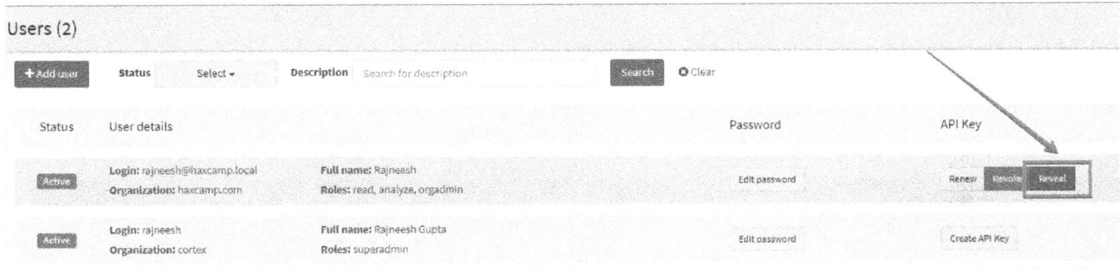

Figure 3.10 – Retrieving the Cortex API

Alright, now one of the three tools is deployed and ready to use. Let's work on deploying our MISP project before we finally get to Wazuh.

Setting up MISP

MISP is an open source software and there are different ways we can install it to build our own threat intelligence and share it with the community. MISP can be installed on most Linux distributions, and the MISP community has created simple install scripts. MISP has many dependencies and combines various software to function properly. This is also known as the **LAMP** stack:

- Linux operating system
- Apache for web server
- MySQL relational database
- Miscellaneous—PHP, Perl, Python

We can deploy MISP in different environments (`https://www.misp-project.org/download/`), such as Docker, VirtualBox VM, and VMware VM. Deploying MISP and its dependencies via Docker is by far the simplest installation process I've found. VirtualBox VM and VMware VM are good for lab and testing environments. Take the following steps to set up MISP:

1. Fulfill the requirements.
2. Install Docker and Docker Compose.
3. Set up and launch MISP.
4. Add an organization and users.
5. Add feeds.

Fulfill the requirements

To set up MISP in the Docker environment, we require Ubuntu Server 22.04.

Install Docker and Docker Compose

To set up Docker and Docker Compose, refer the *step 1* of *Setting up TheHive/Cortex*.

Set up and Launch MISP

Now that we've installed Docker, we need to install the MISP Docker image and configure the environmental variable. This will have four sub-steps:

1. Clone the Git repository.
2. Modify the environmental variable file.
3. Start Docker Compose.
4. Launch MISP.

We will initiate the installation of MISP using their official GitHub repository, as explained:

1. **Clone the Git repository**: Let's clone the get repository with the following command:

   ```
   $ git clone https://github.com/MISP/misp-docker
   ```

   This will clone the Git repository under a directory `misp-docker`. Now, change the directory as follows:

   ```
   $ cd misp-docker
   ```

2. **Modify the environmental variable file**: Let's configure the environment variable file to update the server URL.

   Copy `template.env` to `.env` (on the root directory) and edit the environment variables in the `.env` file:

   ```
   $ cp template.env .env
   ```

   Next, open the file and edit it using the GNU nano editor:

   ```
   $ nano .env
   and set the MISP_BASEURL to https://<Server_IP>
   ```

The final file should look like this:

```
MYSQL_HOST=misp_db
MYSQL_DATABASE=misp
MYSQL_USER=misp
MYSQL_PASSWORD=misp
MYSQL_ROOT_PASSWORD=misp
MISP_ADMIN_EMAIL=admin@admin.test
MISP_ADMIN_PASSPHRASE=admin
MISP_BASEURL=https://<Server_IP>
POSTFIX_RELAY_HOST=relay.fqdn
TIMEZONE=Europe/Brussels

DATA_DIR=./data
```

3. **Start Docker Compose**: To start the MISP Docker container, we need to build it using this command:

```
$ docker-compose build
```

   Next, run the containers in detach mode using this command:

```
$ docker-compose up -d
```

4. **Launch MISP**: Now it's the moment of truth. Open your browser and enter `https://<MISP_Server_IP>`.

   The default credentials are as follows:

   - Username: `admin@admin.test`
   - Password: `admin`

Add an organization and users

We need to create a local organization and add a user to it. Go to **Administration** and enter the **Organization** identifier, Generate **UUID**, Upload the company logo (optional), and click on **Submit**.

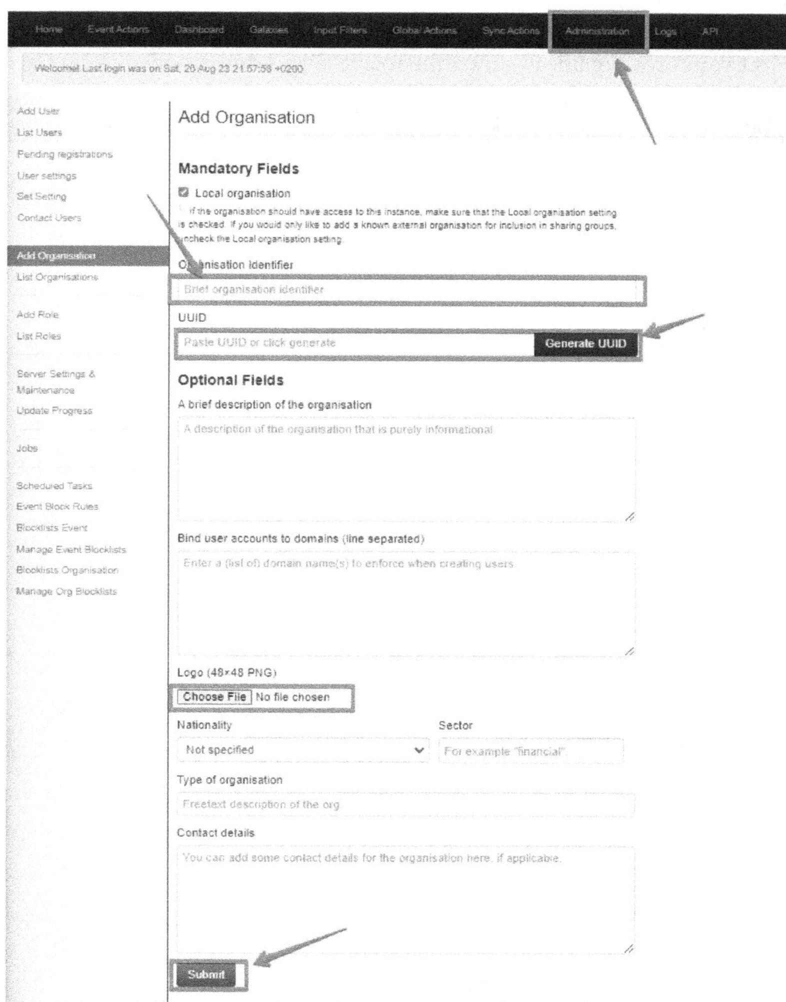

Figure 3.11 – Setting up organization details in the MISP platform

You will notice the following in the preceding screenshot:

- **Organization Identifier**: This represents a unique name for each organization.
- **UUID**: This is a unique identifier that ensures that each piece of information has a global unique identifier. You can even generate UUID online from a website such as `www.uuidgenerator.net`.

Now, to add a user to your organization, go to **Administration** > **Add User** and enter your email, set the password, select your own organization, set the role to **Org Admin**, and click on **Create User**.

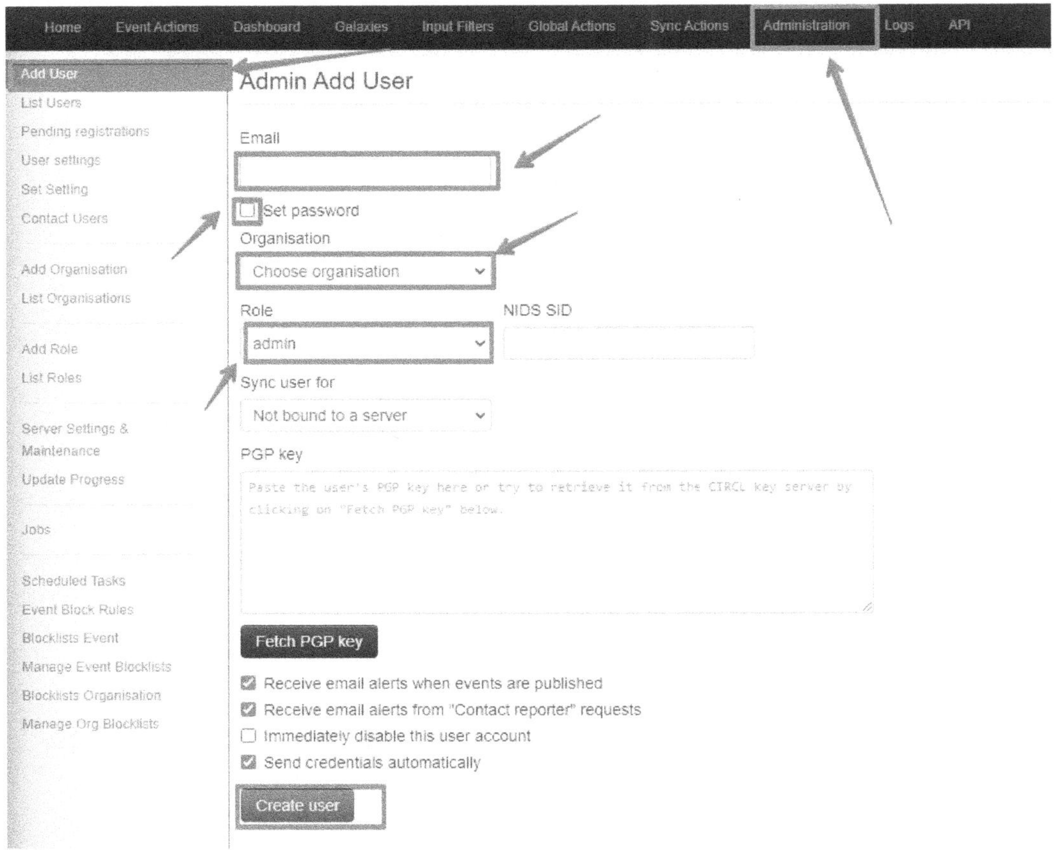

Figure 3.12 – Adding an admin user on MISP

You will notice the following in the preceding screenshot:

- **Email**: This represents the email address of the admin user.
- **Organization**: This represents the organization's name.
- **Role**: This represents the role of the user. In this case, you should set it to **admin**.

Add feeds

MISP uses feeds to download threat reports, IOCs, and other information. These feeds contain all of the data stored by MISP. Feeds are not enabled by default when configuring MISP. To use our feeds, we must import and enable them. Fortunately, MISP helps us with some good threat intelligence feeds. This feed information is fetched in JSON format and can be downloaded from their official GitHub repository at `https://github.com/MISP/MISP/blob/2.4/app/files/feed-metadata/defaults.json`.

Copy the raw data. Next, visit the MISP application, go to **Sync Actions**, click on **Import Feeds from JSON**, and paste the metadata there:

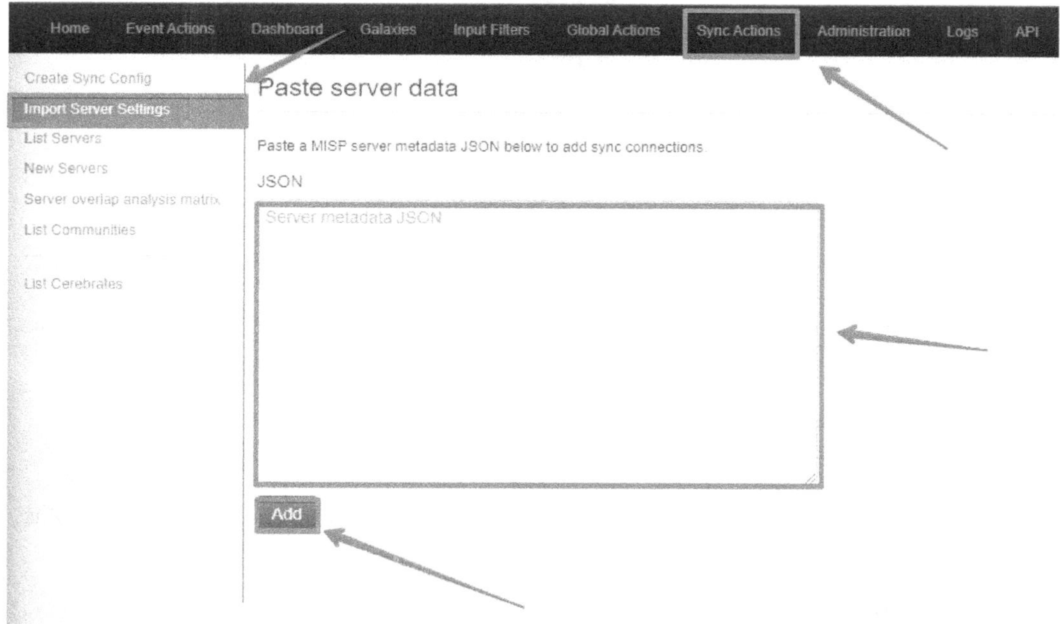

Figure 3.13 – Adding feeds to MISP

Here, **Server metadata** represents the JSON value of the threat intelligence feeds.

Next, enable the feeds. To do that, go to **Sync Actions** and click on **List Feeds**. Select all the feeds and click on **Enable Selected**:

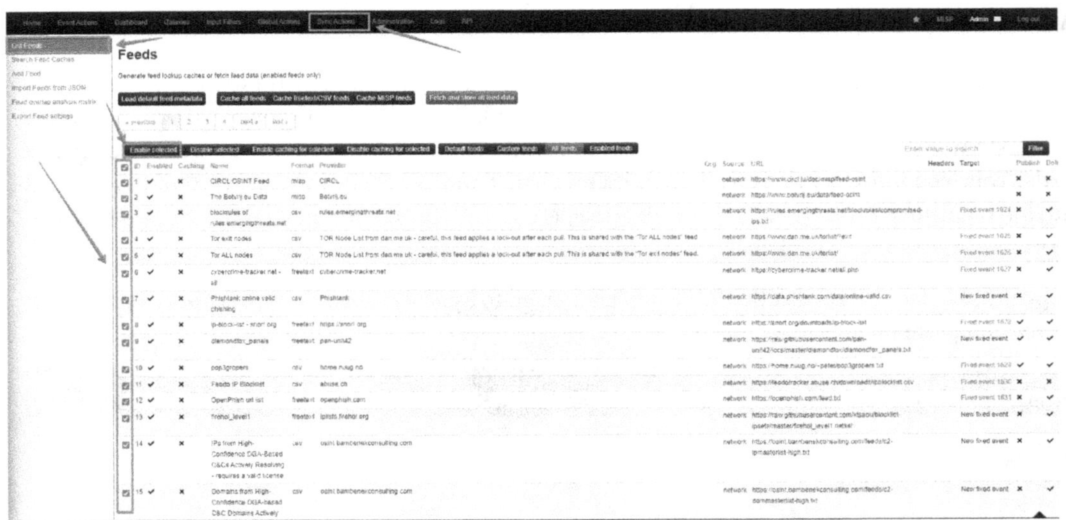

Figure 3.14 – Visualizing feeds in MISP

Here **List Feeds** represents a list of all the threat intelligence feeds with their providers' details.

This completes our task of setting up MISP applications. Next, we will work on integrating Wazuh and MISP with TheHive.

Integrating Wazuh with TheHive

We will integrate Wazuh with TheHive to automatically send Wazuh alerts to TheHive. SOC analysts will then be able to investigate and respond to these alerts, as well as create cases if necessary. In this section, we will take the following steps:

1. Install the TheHive Python script on the Wazuh manager.
2. Create an integration Python script on the Wazuh manager.
3. Create a Bash script on the Wazuh manager.
4. Integrate TheHive server in Wazuh server configurations.
5. Restart the manager.
6. Visualize the alerts on TheHive.

Install TheHive Python script on the Wazuh manager

We will use a Python script that will enable custom integration of TheHive with the Wazuh manager. We'll write in the following step which we will use as a reference. This module is operational as of the time of this writing after being tested with TheHive version 5.2.1.

Let's first install the thehive4py module using the following command:

```
sudo /var/ossec/framework/python/bin/pip3 install thehive4py
```

Create an integration Python script on the Wazuh manager

It is necessary to build the script custom-w2thive.py in the /var/ossec/integrations/ directory to allow for the integration of TheHive with Wazuh. You can find the full code from the GitHub repository at https://github.com/PacktPublishing/Security-Monitoring-using-Wazuh/blob/main/Chapter%203/custom_thehive_integration_Wazuh.py. Let me explain the import statement of this code to clarify how it is being built. I have broken down the first part (the import statement).

Import statement

This part of the python code defines the imported module or packages.

```
#!/var/ossec/framework/python/bin/python3
import json
import sys
import os
import re
import logging
import uuid
from thehive4py.api import TheHiveApi
=
```

Here, the lines import various Python modules, including json, sys, os, re, logging, uuid, and specific modules from the thehive4py package.

User configuration

This section of the code defines the user-configurable parameters as global variables:

```
lvl_threshold=0
suricata_lvl_threshold=3
debug_enabled = False
info_enabled = True
```

Let us break down the code:

- lvl_threshold=0: This indicates that TheHive will receive all the alerts generated by Wazuh. If you have a large network with thousands of monitored agents, keep it higher so that you get more relevant alerts.

- `debug_enable = False`: This represents the debugging option. In this case, it is set to `False`.
- `info_enabled= True`: This is the information logging option. In this code, it is set to `True`.

Now, let's set proper permissions and ownership using the `chmod` and `chown` commands:

```
sudo chmod 755 /var/ossec/integrations/custom-w2thive.py
sudo chown root:wazuh /var/ossec/integrations/custom-w2thive.py
```

Create a Bash script on the Wazuh manager

To successfully execute the `.py` script developed, we must construct a bash script called `custom-w2thive` and place it in `/var/ossec/integrations/custom-w2thive`. You can copy the entire code from the GitHub repository at `https://github.com/PacktPublishing/Security-Monitoring-using-Wazuh/blob/main/Chapter%203/custom_thehive_bash_script_Wazuh..sh`. Let me break down this bash script to help you understand its functionality.

Setting variables

In this part of the bash script, some variables are defined as shown in the code:

```
WPYTHON_BIN="framework/python/bin/python3"
SCRIPT_PATH_NAME="$0"
DIR_NAME="$(cd $(dirname ${SCRIPT_PATH_NAME}); pwd -P)"
SCRIPT_NAME="$(basename ${SCRIPT_PATH_NAME})"
```

- `WPYTHON_BIN` is set to the path of the Python 3 interpreter
- `SCRIPT_PATH_NAME` is set to the full path of the script
- `DIR_NAME` is set to the absolute path of the directory containing the script
- `SCRIPT_NAME` is set to the base name of the script

Determining the Python script path

This part of the script is used to get the location of the `custom-w2thive.py` file:

```
case ${DIR_NAME} in
    */active-response/bin | */wodles*)
        if [ -z "${WAZUH_PATH}" ]; then
            WAZUH_PATH="$(cd ${DIR_NAME}/../..; pwd)"
        fi
    PYTHON_SCRIPT="${DIR_NAME}/${SCRIPT_NAME}.py"
    ;;
    */bin)
```

```
    if [ -z "${WAZUH_PATH}" ]; then
        WAZUH_PATH="$(cd ${DIR_NAME}/..; pwd)"
    fi
    PYTHON_SCRIPT="${WAZUH_PATH}/framework/scripts/${SCRIPT_NAME}.py"
    ;;
     */integrations)
        if [ -z "${WAZUH_PATH}" ]; then
            WAZUH_PATH="$(cd ${DIR_NAME}/..; pwd)"
        fi
    PYTHON_SCRIPT="${DIR_NAME}/${SCRIPT_NAME}.py"
    ;;
Esac
```

Let us break them down the preceding code:

- `*/active-response/bin | */wodles*)`: This is a pattern that if matched, sets `WAZUH_PATH` and `PYTHON_SCRIPT` to `${DIR_NAME}/${SCRIPT_NAME}.py`.
- `(*/bin)`: This is another pattern that, if matched, sets `WAZUH_PATH` and `PYTHON_SCRIPT` to `${WAZUH_PATH}/framework/scripts/${SCRIPT_NAME}.py`.
- `(*/integrations)`: This is the third pattern that, if matched, sets `WAZUH_PATH` and `PYTHON_SCRIPT` to `${DIR_NAME}/${SCRIPT_NAME}.py`.

Setting the Python script path

Once the Python script is set in `PYTHON_SCRIPT`, this script executes the Python script:

```
${WAZUH_PATH}/${WPYTHON_BIN} ${PYTHON_SCRIPT} $@
```

Here, `(${WAZUH_PATH}/${WPYTHON_BIN})` with any command-line arguments is passed to the Bash script (`$@`).

As we did earlier, let's again set the required permissions and ownership using `chmod` and `chown`, respectively:

```
sudo chmod 755 /var/ossec/integrations/custom-w2thive
sudo chown root:wazuh /var/ossec/integrations/custom-w2thive
```

Integrate the TheHive server in the Wazuh server configurations

Now, you need to modify /var/ossec/etc/ossec.conf using your favorite text editor and insert the following code:

```
<ossec_config>
...
  <integration>
    <name>custom-w2thive</name>
    <hook_url>http://TheHive_Server_IP:9000</hook_url>
    <api_key>RWw/Ii0yE6l+Nnd3nv3o3Uz+5UuHQYTM</api_key>
    <alert_format>json</alert_format>
  </integration>
...
</ossec_config>
```

Let us break down the code:

- <integration>: This specifies the integration with the external applications or platforms.
- <hootk_url>: This defines the URL endpoint. In this case, it is the URL of the TheHive platform.
- <api_key>: This represents the API key associated with the integration. In this case, it is the API key of the TheHive platform.

Restart and test

Once complete, you need to restart the Wazuh manager:

```
sudo systemctl restart wazuh-manager
```

Visualizing the alerts on TheHive

If everything went according to plan, you should soon start seeing notifications generated under the **Alerts** tab in TheHive. As you can see in the screenshot, it worked:

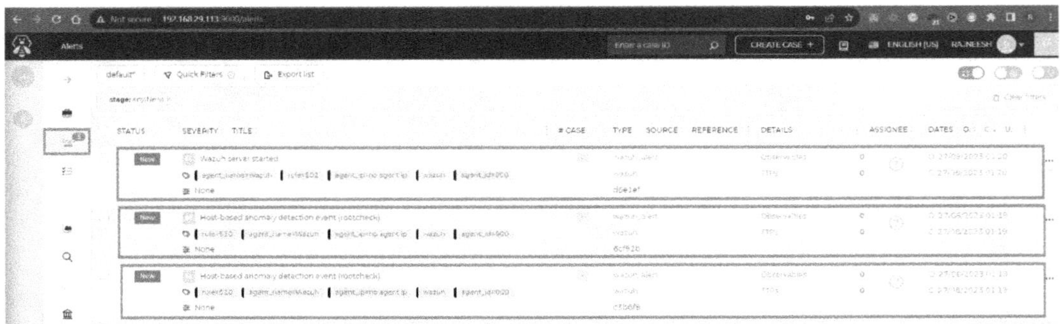

Figure 3.15 – Visualizing alerts on TheHive

Next, we need to integrate TheHive/Cortex with MISP threat intel to perform observable analysis.

Integrating TheHive and Cortex with MISP

TheHive and Cortex are powerful when they work together. TheHive is helpful in incident response, case management, collaboration, and threat analysis while Cortex is a powerful threat intel aggregator. Once we Integrate TheHive and Cortex with MISP, we can even run the observable analyzer directly from TheHive as a result; we don't have to manually perform analysis by going to Cortex. In order to achieve this automation, we need to do three things:

1. Integrate TheHive with Cortex
2. Integrate Cortex with MISP
3. Integrate TheHive with MISP

Integrate TheHive with Cortex

To integrate TheHive and Cortex, you need to enter the Cortex API key in the TheHive settings. I hope you've copied the Cortex API key, as explained in the earlier section *Setting up TheHive and Cortex | Create an organization and user on Cortex*. Now, in order to complete the integration, log in with the admin account or switch to the admin profile and click on the **Platform Management** tab. Test the server connection, as shown in the screenshot:

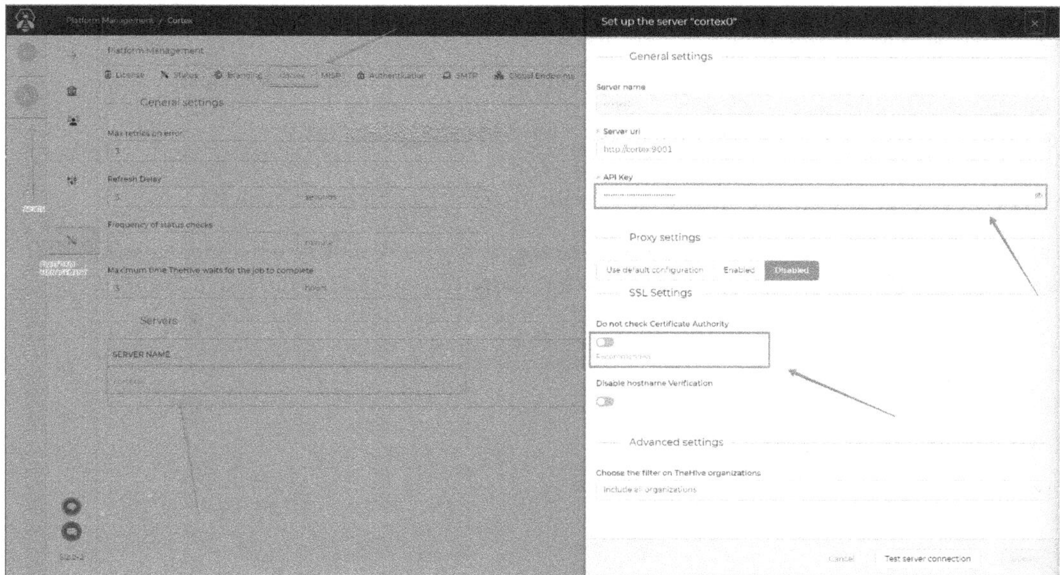

Figure 3.16 – Testing the server connection between TheHive and Cortex

You will notice the following in the preceding screenshot:

- **API Key**: This represents the API key of the Cortex server
- **Do not check Certificate Authority**: It is recommended to keep this disabled if you have not installed SSL on the server

Integrate Cortex with MISP

Log in to Cortex with your newly created account and then go to **Organizations**, click on the **Analyzer** tab, and search for `MISP_2_1 Analyzer`:

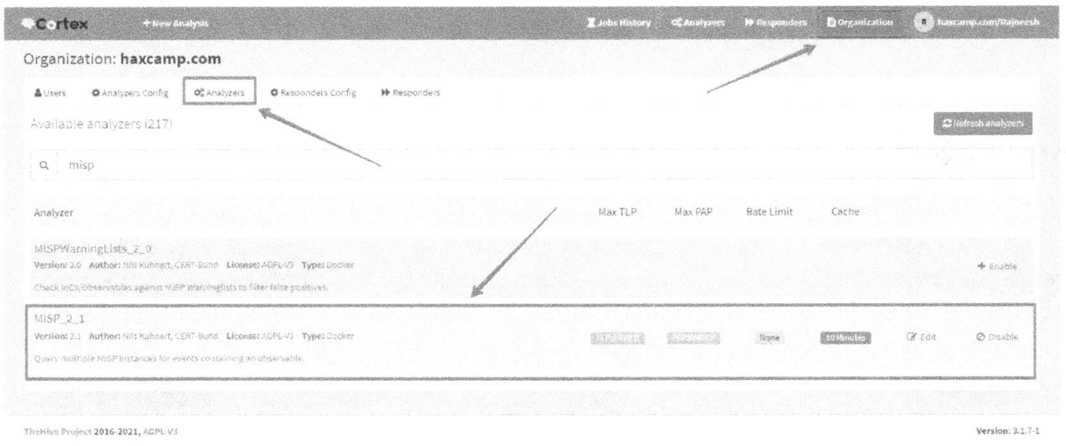

Figure 3.17 – Searching for MISP analyzer under Cortex

Here, **MISP_2_1** represents the MISP analyzers for performing observable analysis.

Next, click on **Edit** and a prompt will appear to configure the MISP integration. Enter a name, MISP base URL, and MISP API key, and set **cert_check** to **False** (if you haven't configured the SSL):

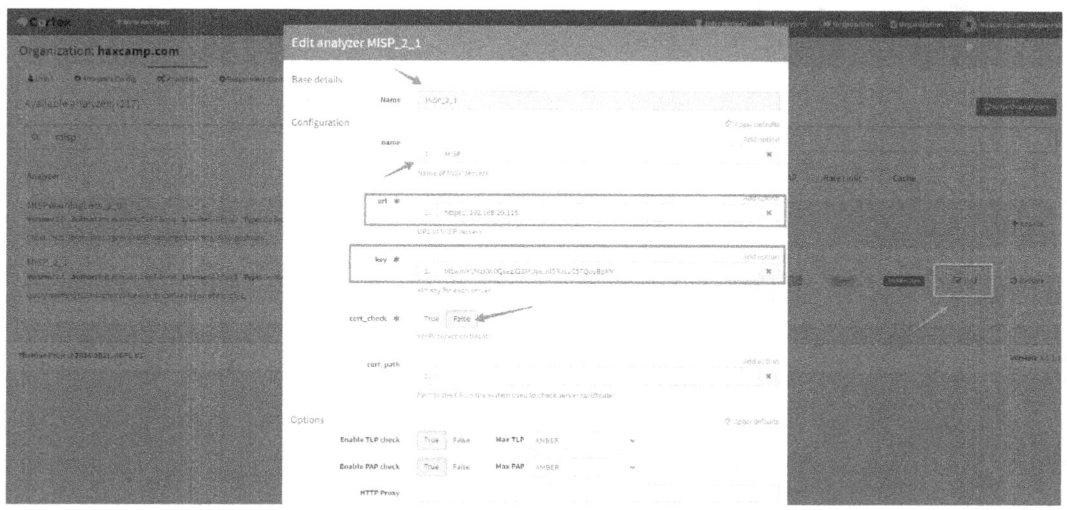

Figure 3.18 – Integrating MISP with Cortex

You will need to enter the following:

- **Name**: This indicates the name of the MISP analyzer.
- **URL**: This represents the URL of the MISP platform.
- **Key**: This indicates the API key of the MISP server.
- **cert_check**: This will dictate whether the Cortex will perform an SSL check or not. In this case, we will keep it **False**.

Now, it's time to verify the integration with a sample analyzer. In the top left, you have a **New Analysis** button. Now, set **TLP** to **AMBER**, **PAP** to **AMBER**, and **Data Type** to **domain**. Immediately, you get a new **Button MISP_2_1**, as shown:

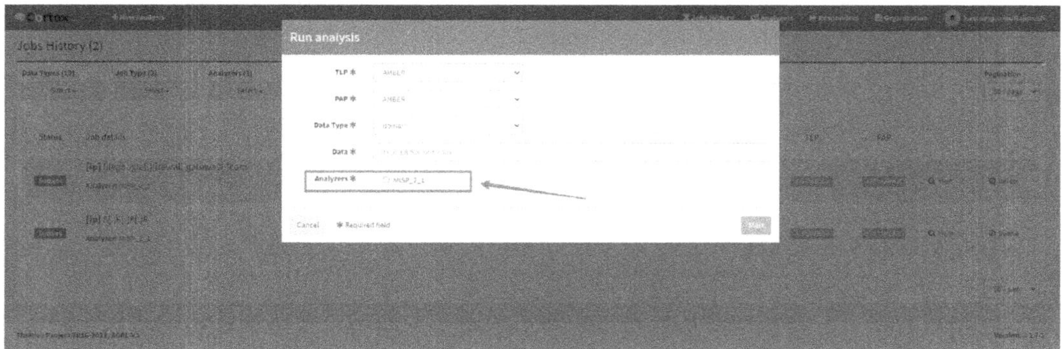

Figure 3.19 – Running MISP analyzer on Cortex

Integrate TheHive with MISP

The best part about TheHive suite is that MISP is already integrated with it. You only need to enter the API key of MISP in the TheHive platform. To complete the integration, log in with an admin account or switch to an admin profile and click on the **Platform Management** tab. You need to set up the MISP server name, server URL, and API key, and then you can test the connection, as shown in the screenshot:

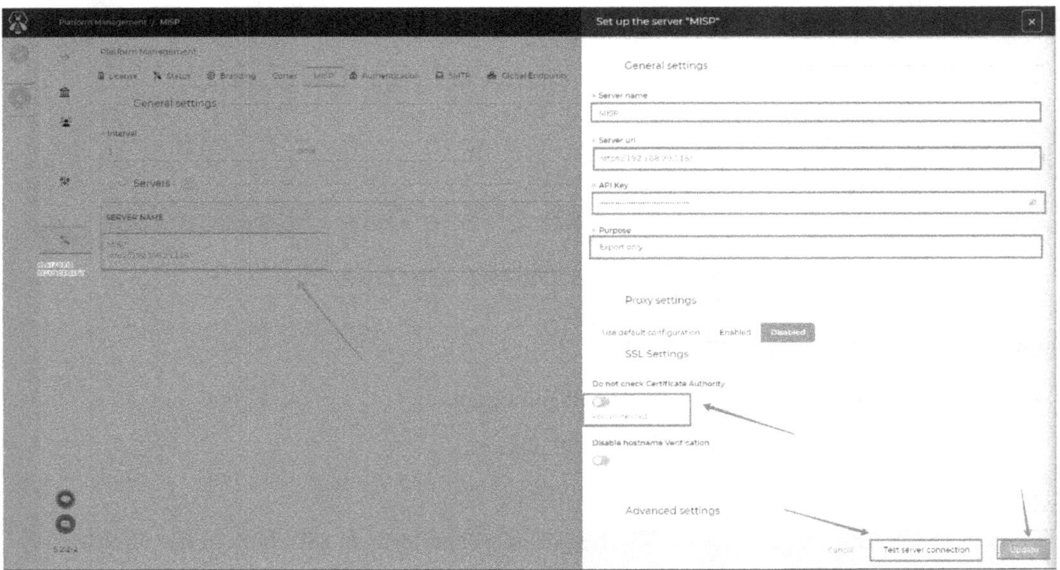

Figure 3.20 – Testing the connection between TheHive and MISP

You will notice the following in the preceding screenshot:

- **Server name**: This is the name of the MISP server.
- **Server url**: This represents the URL of the MISP server.
- **API Key**: This indicates the API key of the MISP server.
- **Purpose**: This shows how this API integration will be used. It can be **Export**, **Import**, or both. In this case, we will set it to **Export** to send queries.
- **Do not check Certificate Authority**: It is recommended to keep this disabled if you have not installed SSL on the server.
- **Test server connection**: This runs a connection check between TheHive and the MISP server.

Finally, the installation and integration of all three tools—Wazuh, TheHive/Cortex, and MISP—is complete. We will now focus on some important use cases of threat intelligence and analysis.

Use cases

Wazuh and TheHive integration offers a lot of benefits to SOC analysts and incident response teams. We will go through different use cases to explore several features of TheHive and MISP that work extremely well with Wazuh. We will go through some common use cases such as investigating suspicious file and network connections and tracking TTPs. In this section, we will cover the following topics:

- Pre-requisites
- Reviewing alerts
- Creating a case
- Analyzing file observable
- Analyzing network observable
- Managing TTPs

Pre-requisites

Before we get into some use cases of threat intelligence and analysis with Wazuh, TheHive, and MISP, we need to ensure these requirements are fulfilled:

- A Wazuh server
- An Ubuntu server running TheHive and Cortex using Docker
- An Ubuntu server running an MISP server
- Ubuntu Desktop or Ubuntu Server with the Wazuh agent installed

Reviewing alert

Once you integrate Wazuh with TheHive, you will start getting security alerts. Before you start investigating alerts or analyzing any observable against the MISP server, you need to get a good understanding of TheHive alert attributes. You can review all the important attributes of an alert in the following screenshot:

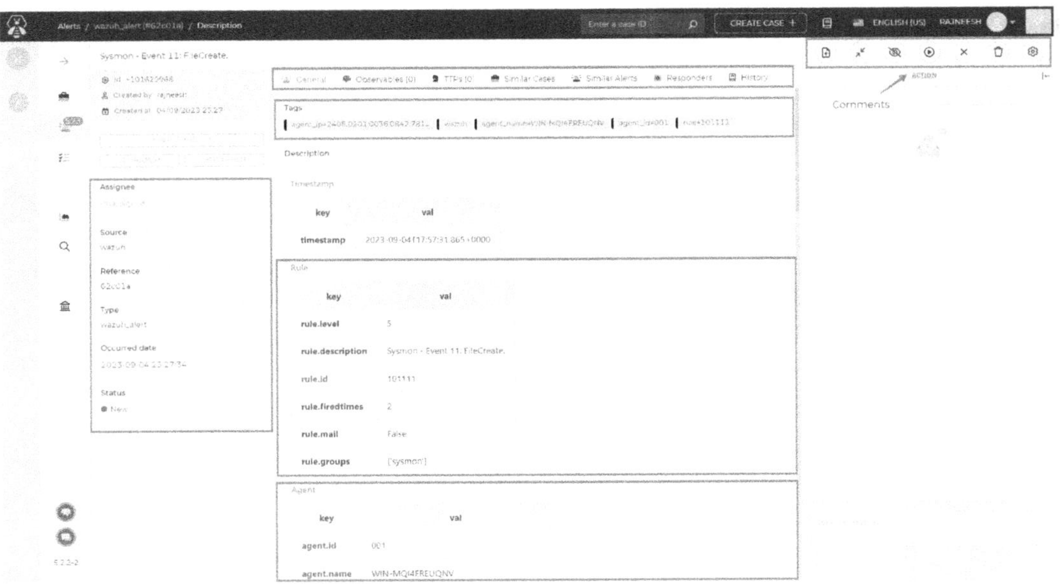

Figure 3.21 – Reviewing security alerts on TheHive

You will notice the following in the preceding screenshot:

- **General**: This is a tab that has **Tags**, **Description**, Wazuh **Rule**, and Wazuh **Agent** information
- **Observable**: This shows information such as IP addresses, domains, URLs, hashes, etc.
- **TTPs**: This shows MITRE attack tactics and techniques
- **Similar Cases**: This will show you existing related cases
- **Similar Alerts**: This will show you similar alerts
- **Responder**: This shows TheHive responder reports
- **History**: This shows the history of alerts

In the top left, you have action items, such as the following:

- **Create case from alert**: You can create a brand new case with this alert. I recommend you do this only when you're certain that it is not a false positive.
- **Merge selection into case**: You can merge alerts into a single case.
- **Ignore new update**: Once selected, you will not get any update on this alert.

- **Start**: Once you click on this play button, you can take it ahead without creating a case. You can change the status of the alert to **Pending**, add some summary notes, and assign it to another analyst or Tier 2 analyst.
- **Close**: If you are certain that it's a false positive or duplicate, you can close the alert.

Based on your investigation, you can also change the status of the alert, as shown in this screenshot:

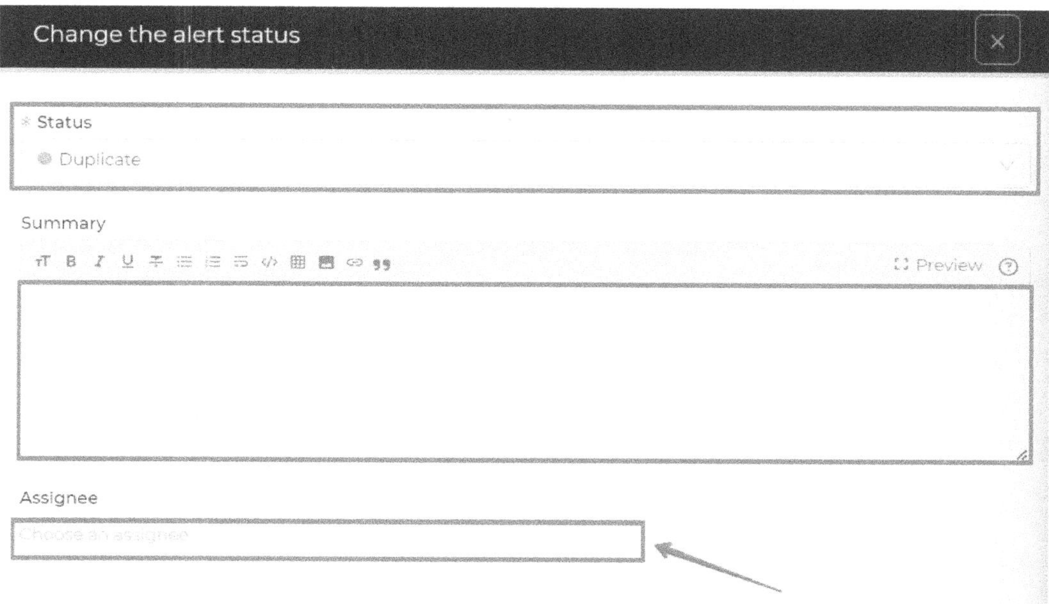

Figure 3.22 – Changing the alert status

You will notice the following in the preceding screenshot:

- **Status**: This is the alert status, and it can be **New**, **In Progress**, **Pending**, **Imported**, **Duplicate**, **False Positive**, or **Ignored**. In this case, it is set to **Duplicate**.
- **Assignee**: This states whom you want to assign this alert to. It can be your team member, SOC Level 2, the threat intelligence team, etc.

Creating a case

Once you are confident that you need to work on a certain alert, you can either create a fresh case or use a case template. Once you click on an empty case, you need to enter details such as the case title, severity, tasks, etc. You can create multiple tasks and assign them to different team members, as shown in screenshot:

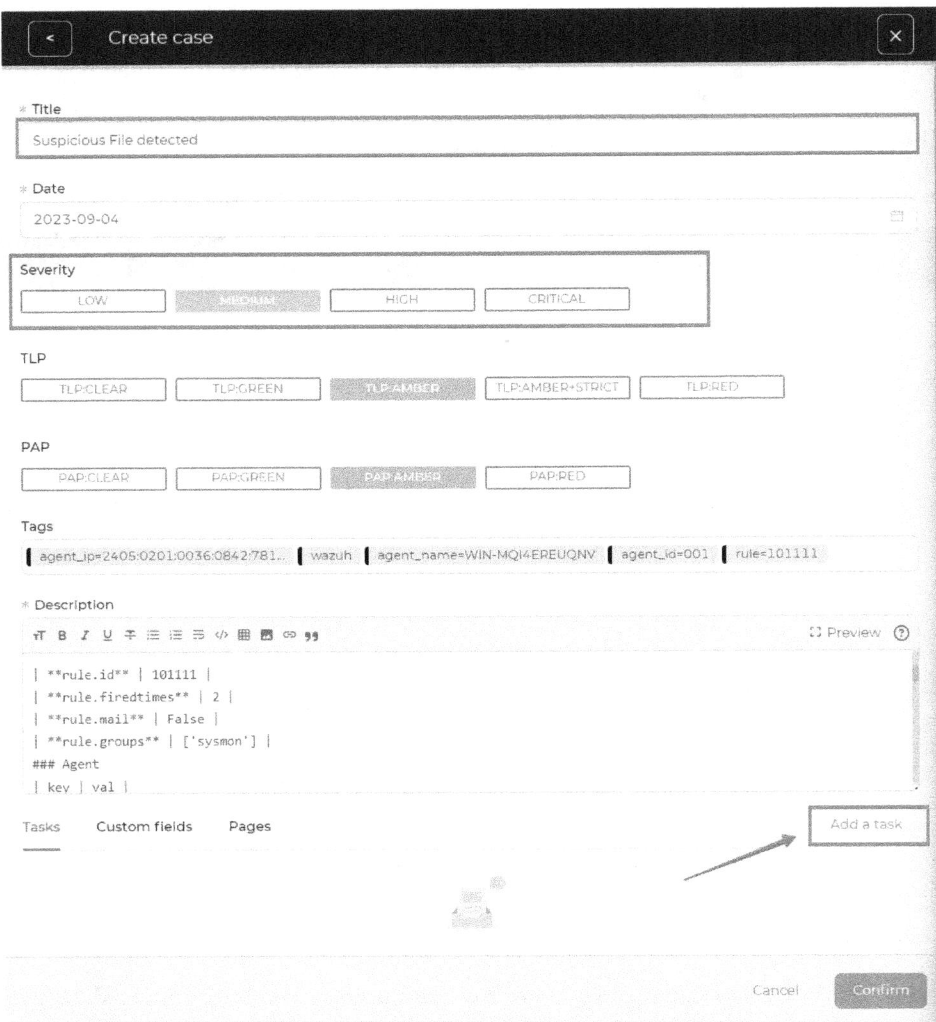

Figure 3.23 – Creating a new case in TheHive

You will notice the following in the preceding screenshot:

- **Title**: This represents the case name. In this case, it is `Suspicious File detected`.
- **Severity**: This represents how critical the case is.
- **Add a task**: This allows you to add multiple tasks.

Analyzing file observables

As we know, observables are initial information that needs to be analyzed before it is marked as an IOC. TheHive detects observables from Wazuh security events. Then, we can analyze the observables against multiple threat Intelligence feeds. The pre-defined observable types are IPs, email addresses, URLs, domain names, files, and hashes.

When you create a case from an alert, observables from alerts are also transferred to the theHive case. Even if you don't have any observables, you can create an observable and analyze it against MISP threat intelligence feeds. You can click on **Add an Observable** and enter the details, as shown in the following screenshot:

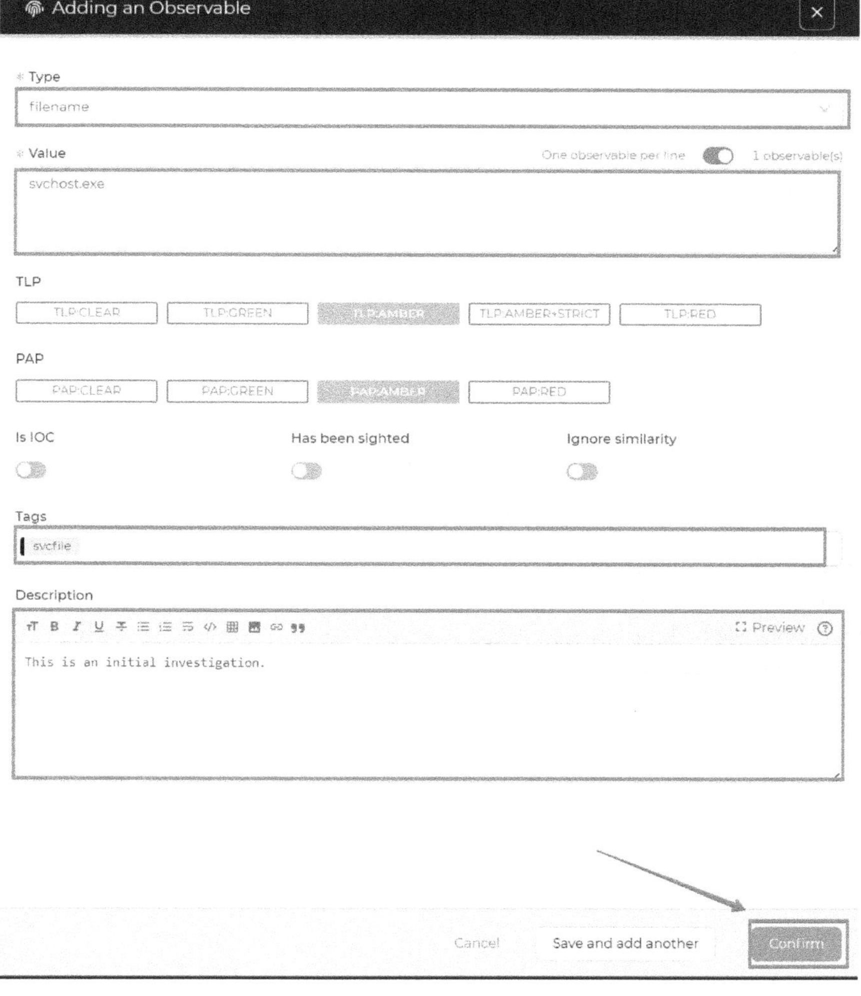

Figure 3.24 – Adding an observable in TheHive

You will notice the following in the preceding screenshot:

- **Type**: This represents the observable's type. In this case, it is `filename`.
- **Value**: I want to look for the `svchost.exe` file.
- **Tags**: Write any relevant tags.
- **Description**: Write a simple and relevant description.

Next, let's click on hamburger menu on the left of the `filename` observable and select **Run analyzers**, as shown in the following screenshot:

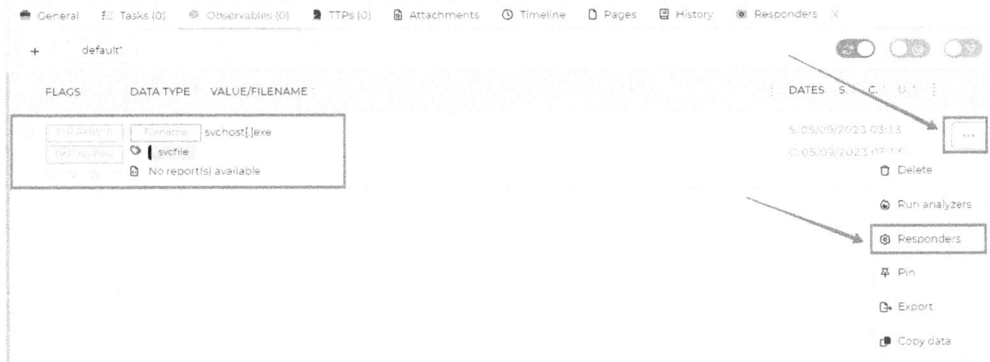

Figure 3.25 – Information about the observable

You will notice the following in the preceding screenshot:

- **Svchost[.]exe**: This is the sample file and is added as an observable.
- **Run analyzers**: This represents an action to execute the Cortex analyzer. In this case, we want to take the observable `Svshost[.]exe` and run the analyzer against the MISP server for threat intelligence lookup. Once we select **Run analyzers**, you should see **MISP_2_1**. Select it and click on **Run Selected Analyzer**, as shown in this screenshot:

Analyzer

Filename Analyzer Select all / Deselect all

MISP_2_1 [cortex0]

Cancel Run Selected Analyzers

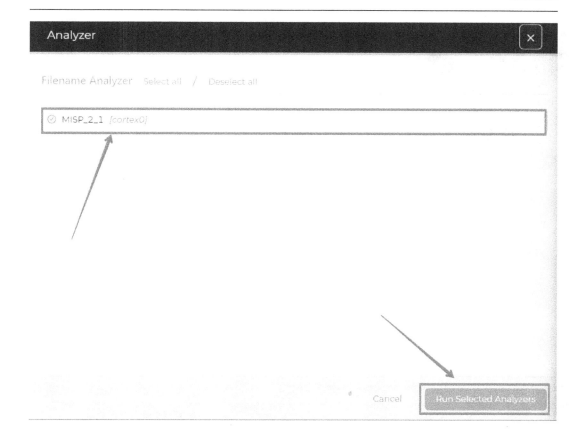

Figure 3.26 – Executing the MISP analyzer

Next, wait for 10 to 20 seconds and you should get a report under the same observable from the MISP Server. Bingo! As shown in the screenshot, you can find the result from the MISP server:

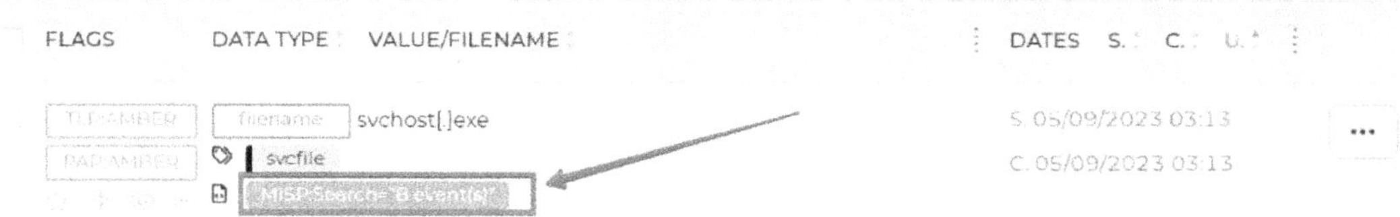

Figure 3.27 – Receiving the threat intelligence result from the MISP server

Once you click on it, you will see all eight matching events (threat intel feeds) in MISP, as shown:

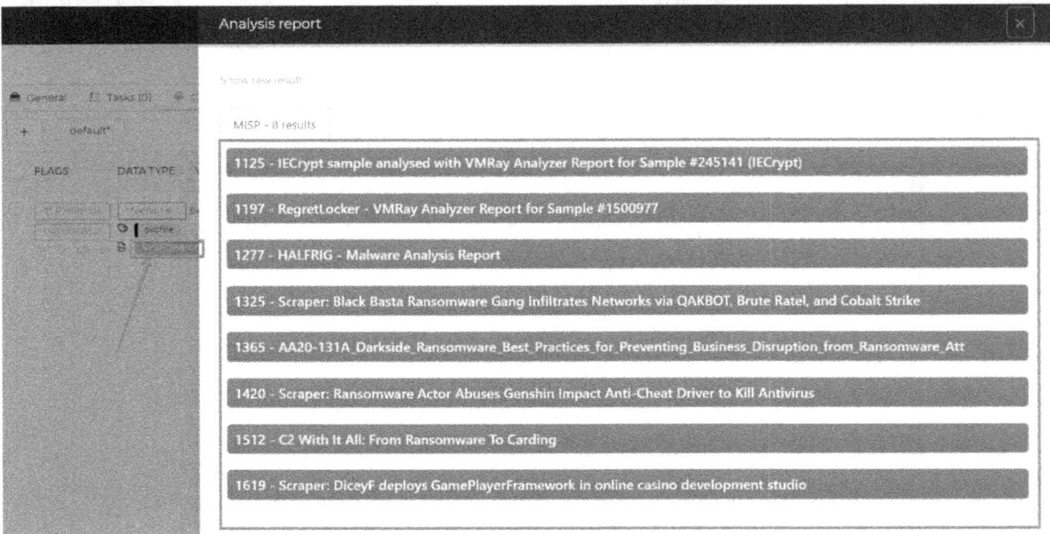

Figure 3.28 – Visualizing the observable analysis report from the MISP Server

You can go to any of the MISP events and click on **EventID**. You will be redirected to the MISP server for a specific event, as shown in this screenshot:

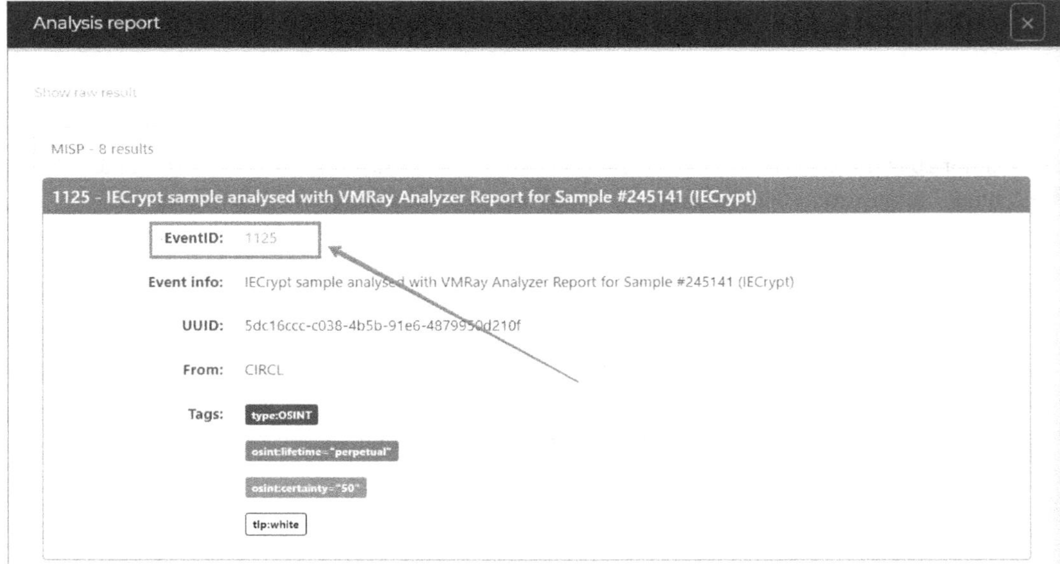

Figure 3.29 – Visualizing the threat intelligence event from the MISP server

You will notice the following in the preceding screenshot:

- **EventID**: This represents the event ID from the MISP server. In this case, the event ID is **1125**.
- **From**: This represents the threat intelligence feed provider. In this case, it is **CIRCL**.

To explore this specific event even further, we can log in to our MISP server and navigate to **View Event**. You can search for the event ID `1125` and find the result, as shown in this screenshot:

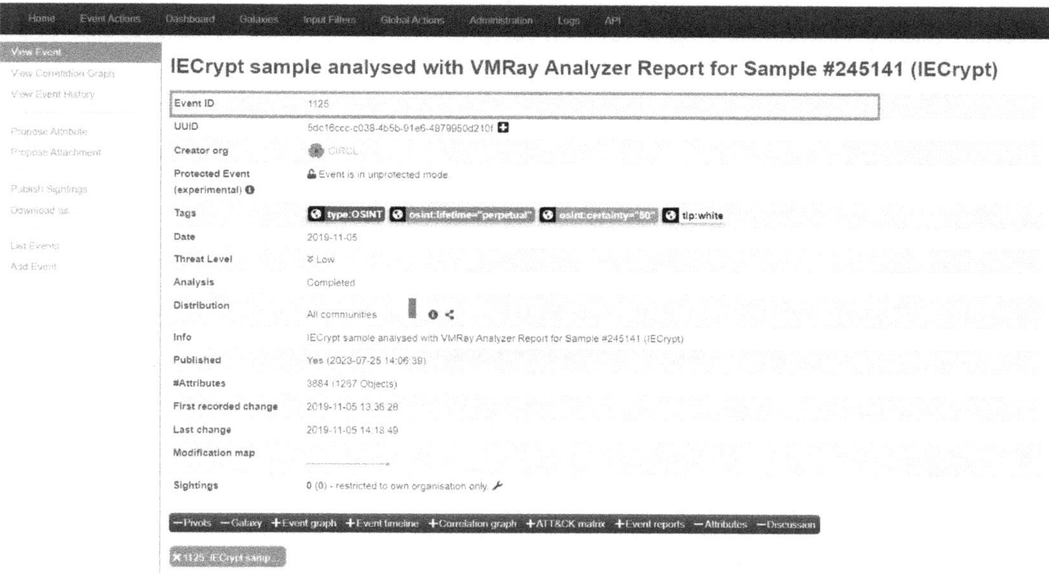

Figure 3.30 – Visualizing the event in the MISP server

Let us break down some of the entries:

- **Info**: This is a brief and descriptive summary of the event. In this case, it is **IECrypt sample analyzed with VMRay Analyzer Report for Sample #245141**.
- **Date**: This is the date and time when the event was created.
- **Threat Level**: This represents the severity or criticality of the threat. It can be low, medium, or high.
- **Analysis**: This indicates the current analysis state of the event, e.g., initial, ongoing, or completed.
- **Distribution**: This specifies the distribution level of the event, finding out who can access the information, such as only the organization, the sharing group, or the community. In this case, it is **All Communities**.
- **Tags**: This is a list of tags associated with the event, delivering additional categorization or metadata.

Analyzing network observables

Now, let's suppose you have some IP and domain observables. We can also test them in the same manner, or you can add related observables found during the investigation of other events. You can navigate to the **Observables** tab and, as you can see in the screenshot, we have some IP addresses as observables:

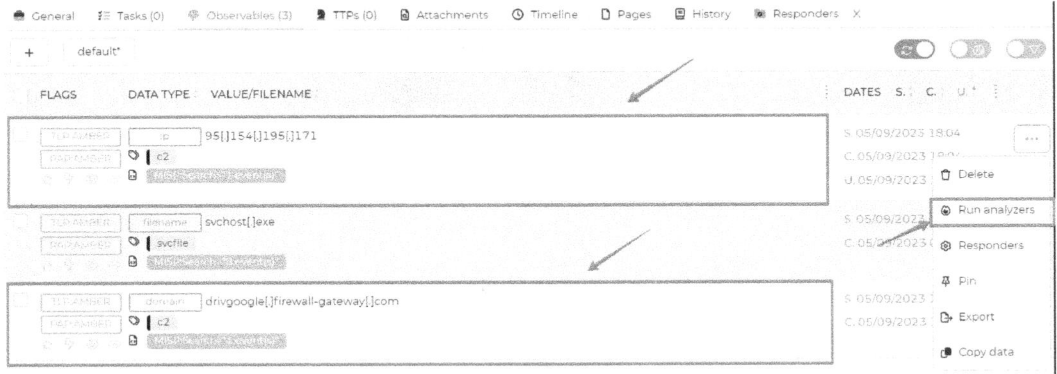

Figure 3.31 – Visualizing IP address observables in TheHIve

Let us break down the highlighted boxes in the screenshot:

- **95[.]154[.]195[.]171**: This is a sample IP address observable that needs to be analyzed by the MISP server
- **drivgoogle[.]firewall-gateway[.]com**: This is a sample domain name in the observable list that needs to be analyzed by the security team

Next, wait for 10 to 20 seconds and you should get a report under the same observable from the MISP Server. Awesome! As shown in the next screenshot, you can find the result from the MISP server:

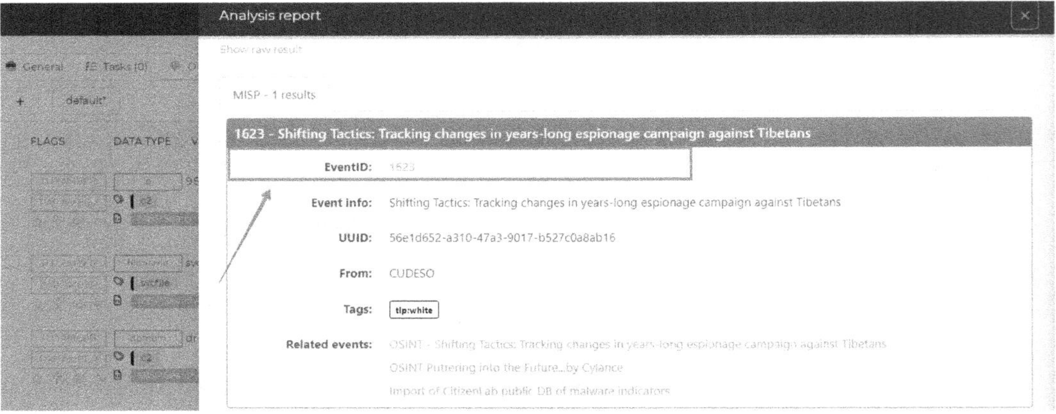

Figure 3.32 – Visualizing the observable analysis report from the MISP Server

Here, **EventID: 1623** represents the event ID from the MISP server. In this case, the event ID is `1125`.

Managing TTPs

TTP analysis can aid security teams in detecting and mitigating attacks by revealing how threat actors conduct their operations. TTPs are tactics, techniques, and procedures used by threat actors. The MITRE ATT&CK framework empowers SOC teams to identify and address TTPs they encounter. The MITRE ATT&CK framework consists of 14 tactics and hundreds of associated techniques and procedures. TheHive imports TTPs from Wazuh events and enhances our security investigation. You can also add a new TTP to any case by taking these steps:

1. Go to a specific case.
2. Click on TTPs at the top.
3. Click on Add.
4. Enter occur data.
5. Choose the tactic.
6. Choose a technique ID.

You can add a new TTP and enter the relevant information, as shown in the following screenshot:

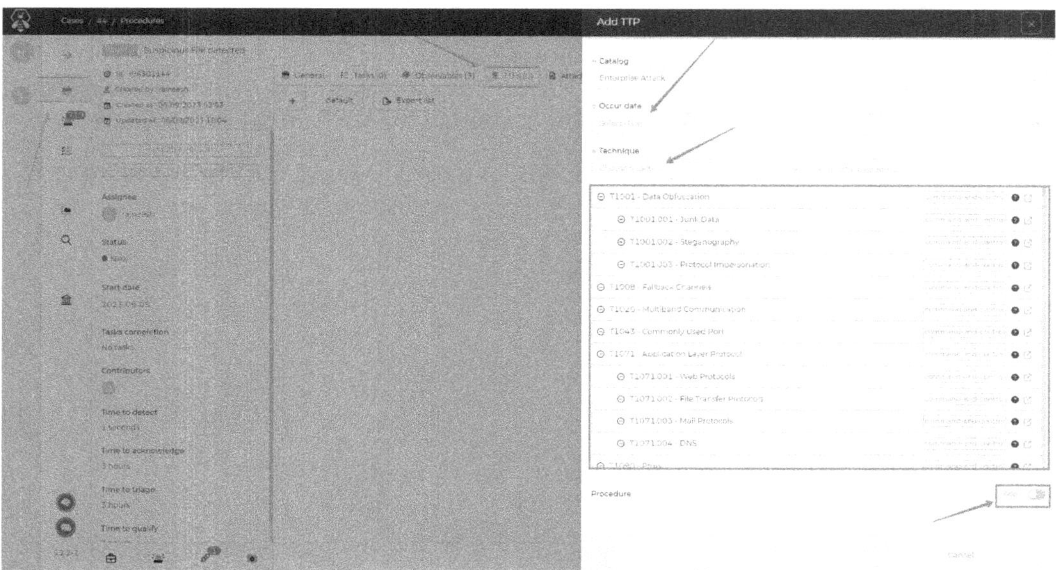

Figure 3.33 – Adding TTPs in TheHive

You will notice the following:

- **Catalogue**: This represents the category of attack. In this case, we selected **Enterprise Attack**.
- **Occur date**: This indicates the date on which the attack happened.
- **Technique**: This represents the technique and its ID from the MITRE ATT&CK matrix.
- **Procedure**: This requires you to manually enter the step-by-step instructions or sequences of actions that threat actors follow to execute a specific technique.

This completes our overview of the use cases of threat intelligence and analysis using Wazuh, TheHive, Cortex, and the MISP server. To learn more about the administration, features, and integration, you can visit their official websites:

- TheHive: `https://docs.strangebee.com/thehive/setup/`
- Cortex: `https://docs.strangebee.com/cortex/`
- MISP: `https://www.misp-project.org/documentation/`

Summary

This chapter on threat intelligence and analysis using MISP provided a comprehensive guide to understanding and implementing a practical threat intelligence and analysis system. We learned the critical role of MISP—when integrated with Wazuh and TheHive—in helping security analysts perform observable analyses and add TTPs. We also covered some important use cases of TheHive and Cortex for performing analyses of files, IP addresses, domains, etc. against the MISP threat intelligence database.

In the next chapter, we will learn how to enhance Wazuh's capabilities using security automation tools such as Shuffle. We will learn the importance of security automation and the integration of Shuffle with Wazuh, and we will also go through some use cases as well.

4
Security Automation Using Shuffle

Every day, the average security operations team receives over 11,000 security alerts (`https://start.paloaltonetworks.com/forrester-2020-state-of-secops.html`), including suspicious activity, intrusion attempts, privileged user and account monitoring, abnormal external communication, and unauthorized access attempts.

The majority of an analyst's time (almost 70%) is spent investigating, triaging, or responding to alerts, and the majority of these alerts must be processed manually, greatly slowing down a company's alert triage process. According to the same report, about 33% of these alerts turn out to be false positives. An SOC analyst can get frustrated with this overwhelming number of security alerts and repetitive false positives. This leads to the need for security automation, and this is where **SOAR** (**Security Orchestration and Automation Response**) plays a critical role. SOAR is a set of security features that enables businesses to collaborate on incident investigation and automate security operations tasks. The ultimate goal of this SOAR is to reduce the **MTTR** (**Mean Time to Respond**). This is achieved by automating every action or response taken by the SOC analyst. As a result, organizations stop alert fatigue for the SOC analyst and save them time. There are six core elements of SOAR: investigation, incident management, automation, reporting, vulnerability management, and threat intelligence. All of these elements are crucial for building powerful security automation in a network. Although Wazuh has some of these capabilities to build a strong security automation system, we need a third-party tool. In this chapter, we will use the Shuffle platform. Shuffle is an open-source security automation tool.

In this chapter, we will cover the following topics:

- What is SOAR?
- How a SOC analyst uses SOAR
- Setting up Shuffle SOAR
- Retrieving Wazuh Alerts
- Remotely managing Wazuh
- Important Shuffle apps

What is SOAR?

According to Gartner, "*Security orchestration, automation and response (SOAR) solutions combine incident response, orchestration and automation, and threat intelligence (TI) management capabilities in a single platform.*" SOAR tools are used to implement processes such as security playbooks, workflows, or processes to support a security operation analyst or incident analyst. The functionalities of SOAR are as follows:

- **Security orchestration**: Security orchestration involves the coordination of security tasks and workflows across several security tools and teams. It aims to streamline and optimize a response to security incidents and threats. We can create workflows that automate a sequence of security tasks, such as alert triage, investigation, containment, and remediation. This also involves the integration of a wide range of security tools, such as SIEM, firewalls, endpoint protection, and threat intelligence feeds. An example could be orchestrating the isolation of a compromised device from a network when a malware alert is detected.
- **Security automation**: Security automation focuses on the execution of predefined actions in response to security events or incidents. With event-driven workflows and the integration of various security tools, security automation enhances operation efficiency, reduces manual errors, and ensures that security responses align with organizational policies. An example of security automation in SOAR is automatically updating and patching software vulnerabilities as soon as they are discovered.
- **Incident response**: Incident response involves the processes and actions taken when a security incident or data breach occurs. In a SOAR system, incident response is made more efficient by orchestrating and automating security tools, tasks, executions, and so on. For example, when a data breach is detected, the SOAR platform can automatically generate an incident report, notify the relevant stakeholders, and initiate a predefined incident response plan.

SOAR integrates the concepts of security orchestration and security automation to provide an all-encompassing incident response strategy.

Next, let's discuss how an SOC analyst uses a SOAR platform throughout the alert and incident life cycle.

How a SOC analyst uses SOAR

A **Security Operation Center** (**SOC**) analyst is a cybersecurity professional responsible for monitoring, detecting, analyzing and mitigating security incidents in an organization. The SOC analyst leverages a SOAR platform to enhance the efficiency and effectiveness of security operations. By utilizing SOAR, SOC analysts can make jobs easier, cut down on reaction times, and make sure that security incidents are handled in a more coordinated and consistent way. There are several stages within the incident response process where the SOAR platform can be utilized, as shown in the following diagram.

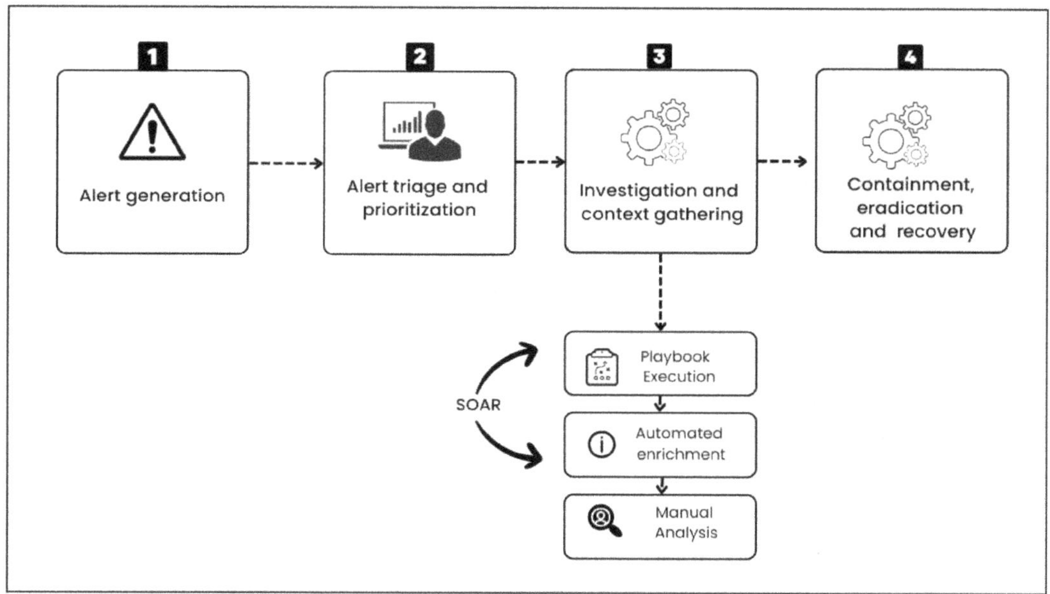

Figure 4.1 – The flow of the incident response and SOAR

Based on the diagram, each stage can be explained as follows:

1. **Alert generation**: SIEM (**Security Information and Event Management**) systems, an **IDS/IPS** (**Intrusion Detection System/Intrusion Prevention System**), and endpoint security solutions monitor network and system activity continuously for potential threats. Wazuh triggers an alert when there is an event matching Wazuh rules, and these alerts can be as follows:

    - **Log analysis alerts**: The Wazuh platform monitors endpoints, network, and application logs for any suspicious activities, and if there is a match based on the rule, it will trigger an alert – for example, detecting multiple failed login attempts within a short period

- **Intrusion detection system (IDS) alerts**: When integrated with Suricata Network-based IDS, Wazuh can analyze network traffic for signs of malicious activities – for example, an alert gets triggered when there is a known vulnerability, network scanning, or known exploits
- **File Integrity Monitoring (FIM) alerts**: Wazuh has an in-build FIM module to detect any unauthorized file changes – for example, unauthorized file modification alerts in the root directory of the Ubuntu server

2. **Alert triage and prioritization**: The SOAR platform uses predefined security rules and logic to prioritize incoming alerts according to their severity, origin, and potential impact, such as a brute-force attempt or potential ransomware attack.
3. **Investigation and context gathering**: This step involves three sub-steps – playbook execution, automated enrichment, and manual analysis:

   I. **Playbook execution**: For each alert, SOAR can use an incident response playbook. Playbooks are sets of automated and manual actions that guide an analyst through the investigation process.

   II. **Automated enrichment**: The SOAR platform can automatically add context to notifications, such as threat intelligence data, historical logs, and asset information. This contextual information assists the analyst in determining the alert's veracity and severity.

   III. **Manual analysis**: The analyst evaluates the enriched alert and may perform additional manual investigation. They may query systems, examine records, and utilize their knowledge to determine the nature and scope of the incident.

   Once the investigation and content gathering are completed, the SOAR playbook can be triggered for different actions, as mentioned in the next step.

4. **Containment, eradication and recovery**: During the containment phase of incident response, immediate actions are taken to limit the intensity of an incident, involving the isolation of affected endpoints to prevent further damage. This is followed by the eradication phase, where organizations focus on removing threats from the network. It also involves identifying and eliminating the root cause of the incident. Finally, the recovery phase takes care of restoring systems and services to their normal operational state.

We've learned about how an SOC analyst uses a SOAR platform, using an incident response example. In the next section, we will learn about the Shuffle platform.

Introduction to Shuffle

Shuffle is an open-source interpretation of SOAR. It was built by Fredrik Oedegaardstuen. It brings automation with Plug and Play enterprise apps. Shuffle relies heavily on Docker and microservices, making its design modular and powerful. Let's discuss some important components and features of Shuffle:

- **Apps and workflows**: Apps are building blocks in workflows. Workflows are the part of Shuffle where everything comes together. When you first configure Shuffle, it should provide you with more than 100 existing apps. Shuffle covers many of the popular apps, as shown in the following screenshot.

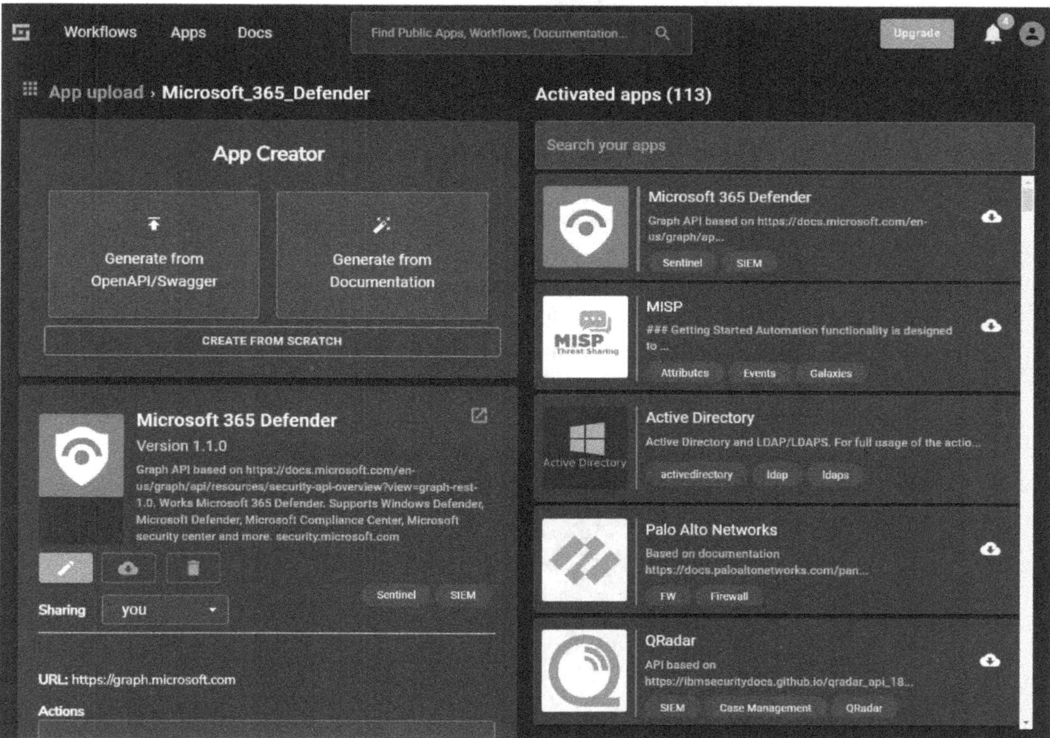

Figure 4.2 – App and workflows in Shuffle

- **File analysis**: Shuffle can help you upload and analyze an email attachment file with Yara. You can also manually upload a file by going to **Admin** | **Files**.

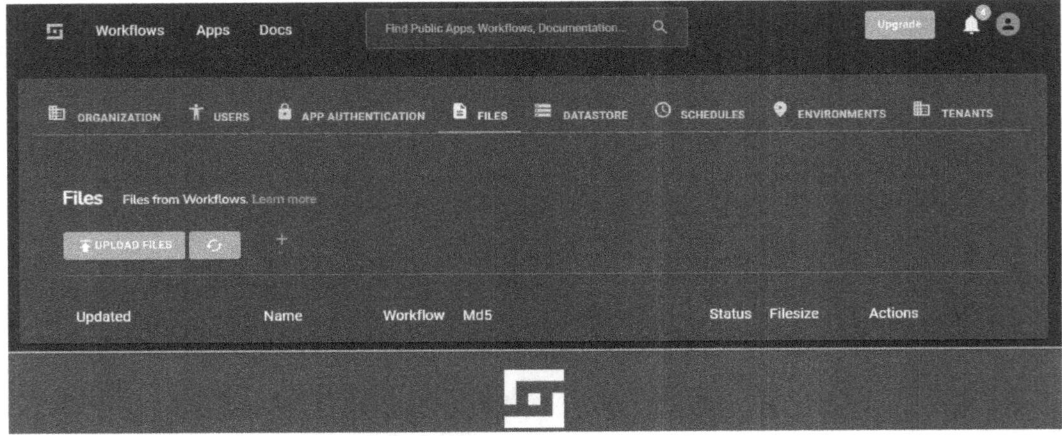

Figure 4.3 – Files for workflows in Shuffle

- **Shuffle cache**: Shuffle can help you store any information in the key-value pair format. The value will be sticky in nature, and hence, it can be used in a timestamp for security reports, maintaining **IOC** (**Indicators of Compromise**) lists, and so on. This is available in the form of Shuffle Tools. Whenever we use the Shuffle Tools app, we need to set the action type to **Set cache value** for caching to work.

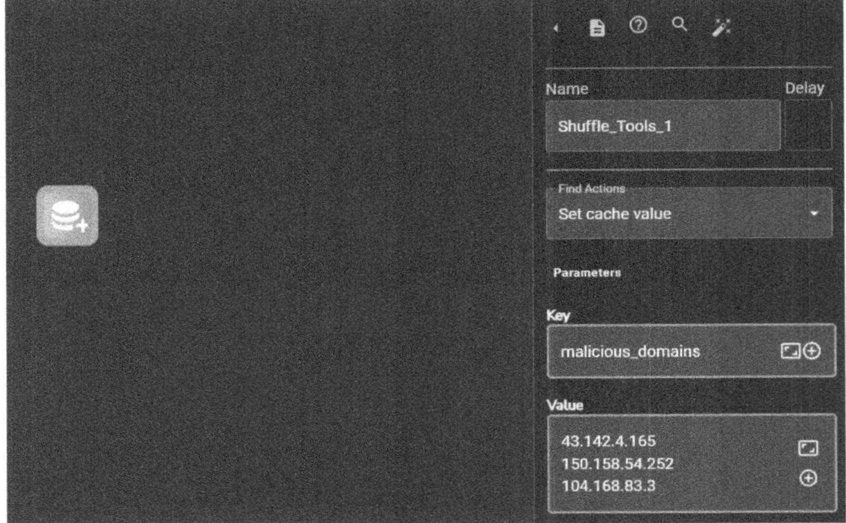

Figure 4.4 – The Shuffle cache

- **Trigger**: To achieve better security automation, Shuffle provides six types of Triggers:
    - **Webhooks**: These allow any outside source to send data in real time to Shuffle.
    - **Schedules**: These make it possible to start a workflow on a schedule
    - **Subflows**: Want to run another workflow from within your current one? This does that exactly.
    - **User input**: Starting or continuing an action based on what an analyst decides.
    - **Office365 Email Trigger**: This gets triggered when an email is received. It is useful for phishing analysis.
    - **Gmail email trigger**: Similar to Office365, Gmail gets a trigger when a Google user gets an email.
- **Use cases**: Users can create custom workflows to set up security use cases. The use cases in Shuffle are divided into five types – *Collect*, *Enrich*, *Detect*, *Respond*, and *Verify*. Each category can have multiple use cases. You can find the list all use cases here: `https://shuffler.io/usecases`.

Shuffle is a powerful security automation platform, offering full user management, multi-factor authentication, single sign-on, multi-tenancy, and a lot more. Now, let's learn to set up Shuffle using a Docker container.

Setting up Shuffle SOAR

Shuffle SOAR can be deployed in self-hosted or in the cloud. For cloud-based deployment, you simply have to visit their official website (`https://shuffler.io/register`) and create an account. In this section, we will learn how to deploy Shuffle SOAR using a self-host deployment method. We need to complete the following steps:

1. Requirements
2. Install Shuffle.
3. Fix the prerequisites for the Shuffle database.
4. Launch Shuffle.

Requirements

Shuffle can be installed using **Docker Compose**. Docker Compose helps us to define and run a multi-container docker application using `docker-compose.yml` script. As pre-requisites, we need to have the following:

- Ubuntu Server 22.0 (`https://ubuntu.com/download/server`)
- Docker and Docker Compose installed

Install Shuffle

When it comes to a Shuffle SOAR self-hosted deployment, currently it is only supported by Docker and Kubernetes. Here, we will utilize the Docker deployment method, and the package can be downloaded from Docker's official GitHub repository by following these steps:

1. **Clone the Shuffle module from GitHub**: Use the `git clone` command to download the Shuffle codebase from its GitHub repository:

   ```
   git clone <https://github.com/Shuffle/Shuffle>
   ```

2. **Change the directory to Shuffle**: Move into the directory where the Shuffle code has been cloned:

   ```
   cd shuffle
   ```

Once you have downloaded the packages, you need to fix some dependency issues with the database, as detailed in the next step.

Fixing the prerequisites for the Shuffle database

To avoid issues with the backend database, you are required to set the permissions and change the ownership, as follows:

1. **Create a directory for the OpenSearch database**: To store information in the OpenSearch database, create a directory called `shuffle-database`:

   ```
   mkdir shuffle-database.
   ```

2. **Set permissions and ownership for the directory**: Change the permissions with `chmod` to supposedly make the directory executable:

   ```
   sudo chmod +x shuffle-database
   ```

3. **Change the database ownership**: To change the ownership of the directory, use `chown`. You can also use it to assign the directory to a particular user or group (`1000:1000` in this example):

   ```
   sudo chown -R 1000:1000 shuffle-database
   ```

Launch Shuffle

To start Docker Compose, set up and execute Shuffle SOAR in detached mode (`-d flag`), which means it will run in the background, and you can continue to use your Terminal for other tasks. Use the following command to run Docker compose in detached mode:

```
sudo docker compose up -d
```

These instructions essentially walk you through the installation and configuration of Shuffle, ensuring that all necessary components (the OpenSearch database directory, Docker, and Compose) are installed, and then we use Docker Compose to launch the Shuffle SOAR platform.

In the next section, we will learn to integrate Wazuh with Shuffle SOAR and start receiving alerts from the Wazuh platform.

Retrieving Wazuh alerts

Wazuh and Shuffle SOAR's combination offers an excellent synergy for automating a variety of security activities. Renowned for its strong threat detection and response capabilities, Wazuh gathers data from multiple sources throughout the infrastructure to produce alerts and insights. When combined with Shuffle, a SOAR platform created to make incident response and automation easier, it makes it possible for these alerts to be coordinated easily. By using Shuffle's automation features, the integration lets security teams set up predefined responses to Wazuh alerts that are immediately carried out. Shuffle SOAR automates the initial analysis of alerts generated by Wazuh, filtering out false positives and prioritizing alerts based on severity. This helps security analysts focus on relevant security incidents.

This integration makes it possible to automate security tasks that used to be done manually, such as sorting alerts, investigating, and taking corrective actions. This frees up security teams to work on more important tasks while still protecting the network. To integrate Wazuh with Shuffle, we need to follow some steps:

1. Integrate Wazuh with Shuffle.
2. Retrieve Wazuh alerts for abnormal user login analysis.
3. Retrieve Wazuh alerts for successful login analysis.

Integrating Wazuh with Shuffle

The best part about Wazuh and Shuffle integration is that Shuffle integration scripts are already present in the current version of Wazuh, and hence, we don't have to manually create a new one. We only need to do the following:

1. **Create a new Shuffle workflow**: Go to the Shuffle self-hosted or cloud platform, and then create a new workflow. Next, from the **Trigger** section, add a Webhook node and copy the Webhook URI. Also, start the Webhook.

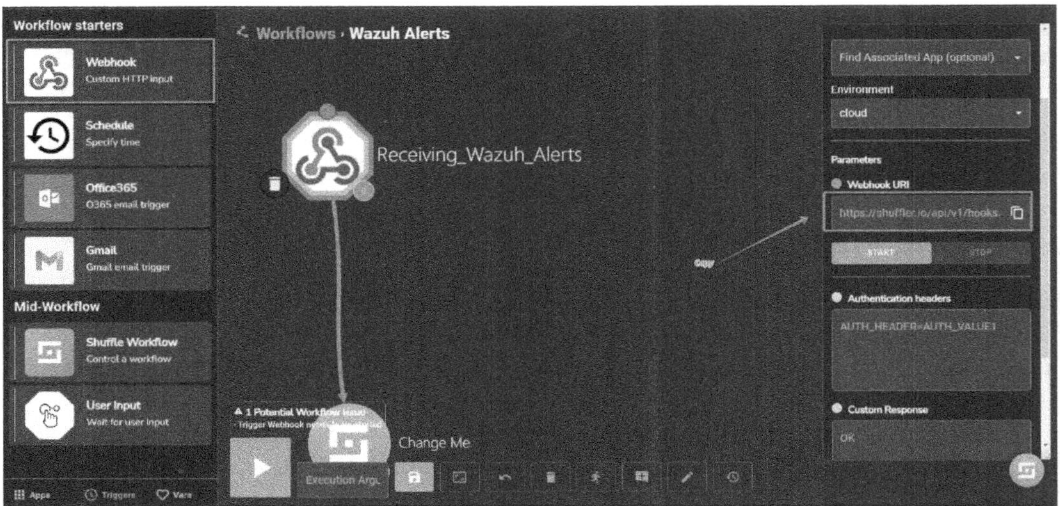

Figure 4.5 – Create a new Workflow in Shuffle

2. **Add a Hook URL to the Wazuh ossec.conf file**:

   Log in to the Wazuh manager and open the `ossec.conf` file located at the following path:

   ```
   /var/ossec/etc/ossec.conf
   ```

   Next, add the following script:

   ```
   <integration>
    <name>shuffle</name>
   <level>3</level>
   <hook_url>[https://<Shuffle_Server_IP>/api/v1/hooks/webhook_
   b68508da-0727-436c-8f33-412419222441](<https://shuffler.io/api/
   v1/hooks/webhook_b68508da-0727-436c-8f33-412419222441>)
   </hook_url>
   <alert_format>json</alert_format>
   </integration>
   ```

   Here, we request Wazuh to push all the level 3 alerts to Shuffle at the Hook URL: `https://<Shuffle_Server_IP>/api/v1/hooks/webhook_b68508da-0727-436c-8f33-412419222441`.

   In order for Wazuh to take effect, we need to restart the Wazuh dashboard:

   ```
   systemctl restart wazuh-manager
   ```

3. **Testing**: Once the integration is complete, we can come back to Shuffle. You need to save the workflow and run the test execution.

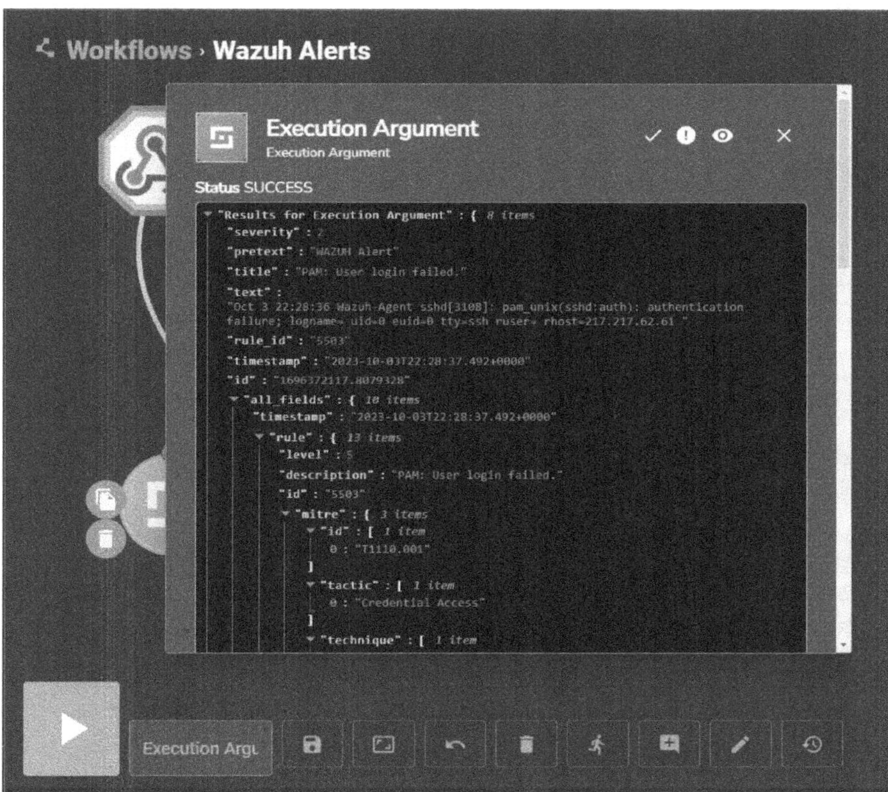

Figure 4.6 – Test execution

Retrieve Wazuh alerts for abnormal user login analysis

Abnormal user login attempts refer to any login activities that deviate from established patterns of normal behavior. It can be because of excessive failed login attempts, unusual login times, unfamiliar locations, multiple concurrent logins, and much more. Let's set up Shuffle SOAR to receive Wazuh alerts for abnormal user login attempts. The Wazuh alert name is `sshd: Attempt to login using a non-existent user`, and the alert is shown in the following screenshot.

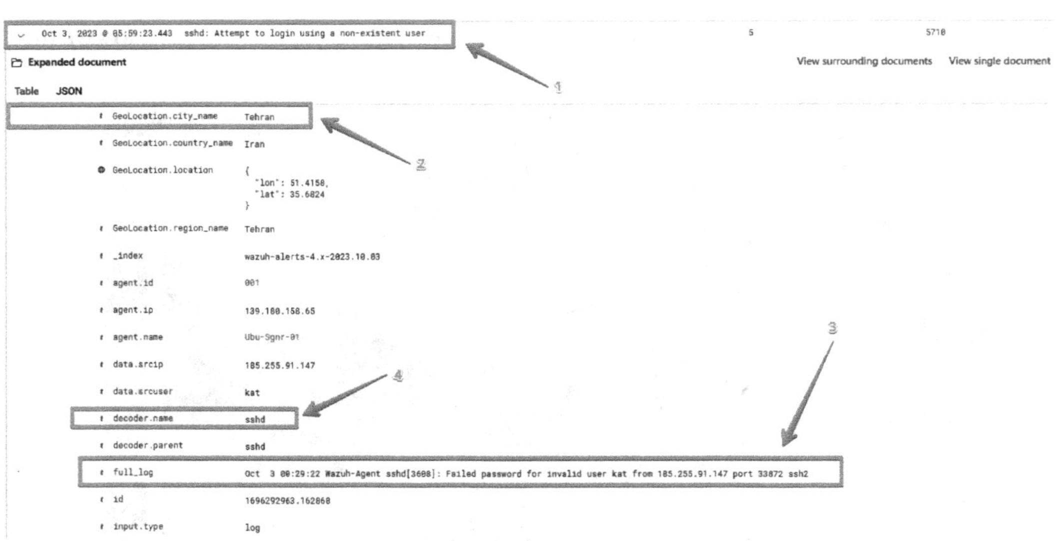

Figure 4.7 – A Wazuh alert – sshd: Attempt to login using a non-existent user

Let's break down the preceding screenshot:

1. **Oct 3, 2023 @ 05:59:23.443 sshd: Attempt to login using a non-existent user**: This represents the name of the alert.
2. **GeoLocation.city_name**: This represents the city name.
3. **Oct 3 00:29:22 Wazuh-Agent sshd[3608]: Failed password for invalid user kat from 185.255.91.147 port 33872 ssh2**: This represent the full log.
4. **decoder.name: sshd**: This represents the extracted Wazuh's decoder. In this case, it is **sshd**.

Retrieving alerts on Shuffle

In order to retrieve these alerts on Shuffle, we need to follow a three-step process:

1. **Create a Shuffle workflow**:

    I. Go to the Shuffle platform and click on **New workflows**. Then, select **Webhook** from the left-side **Workflow starters** menu under **Triggers**, and drag and drop it to the workflow editor.

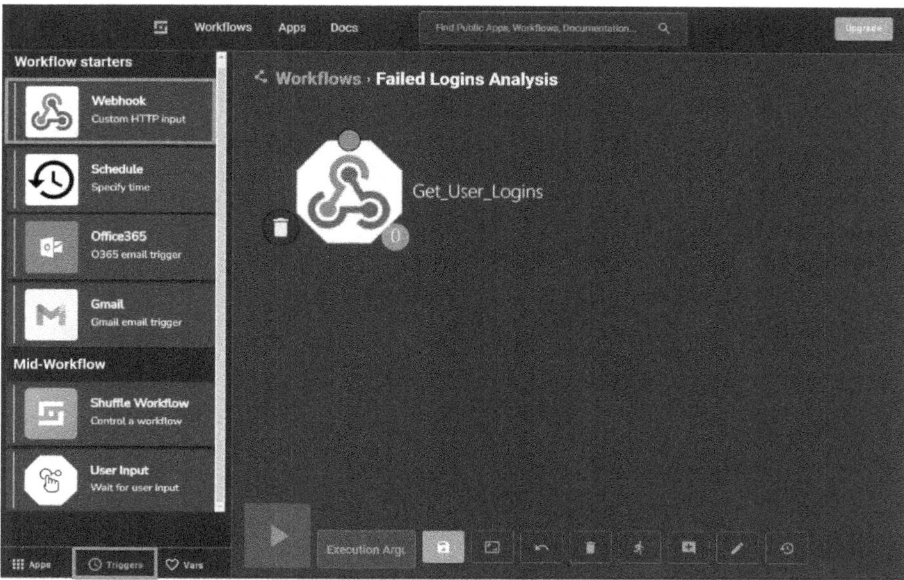

Figure 4.8 – A Shuffle workflow with a Webhook

II. Next, click on the Webhook node and copy the Webhook URI. This URI will be used as the hook URL in the Wazuh manager. If you chose a self-hosted version of Shuffle, you would see the IP address instead of shuffler.io (`http://shuffler.io`) in the URI.

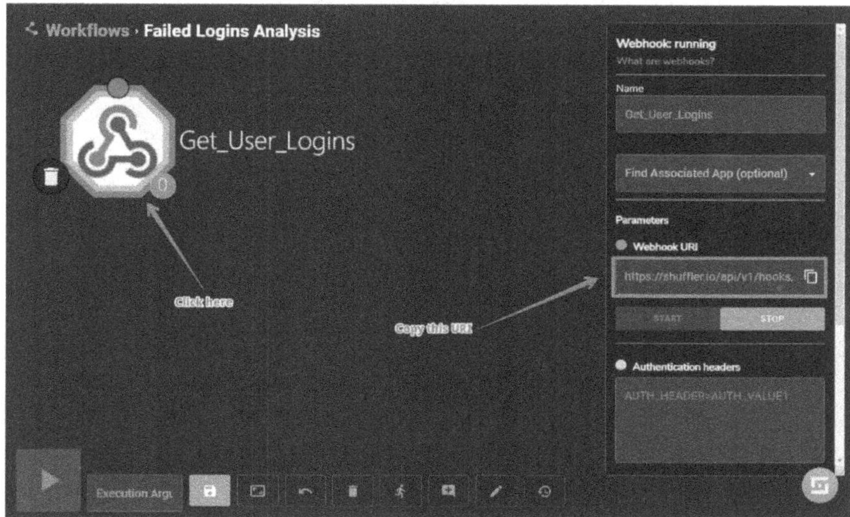

Figure 4.9 – Retrieving the Shuffle Webhook URI

2. **Add integration tags**: Log in to the Wazuh manager and open the `ossec.conf` file, located in the following path:

```
/var/ossec/etc/ossec.conf
```

Next, add the following script:

```
<integration>
<name>shuffle</name>
<rule_id>5710</rule_id>
<rule_id>5503</rule_id>
<rule_id>5760</rule_id>
<hook_url>[https://<Shuffle_Server_IP>/api/v1/hooks/webhook_
b68508da-0727-436c-8f33-412419222441] (<https://shuffler.io/api/
v1/hooks/webhook_b68508da-0727-436c-8f33-412419222441>)
</hook_url>
<alert_format>json</alert_format>
</integration>
```

Let's break down the preceding code:

- `Rule_id 5710` is the Wazuh in-built rule used to detect the `Attempt to login` using a non-existent user alert
- `Rule_id 5503` and `5760` are related to SSH login failure

3. **Run the execution**:

   I. First, give a name such as `Get_User_Logins` node and save the workflow. Next, start the node.

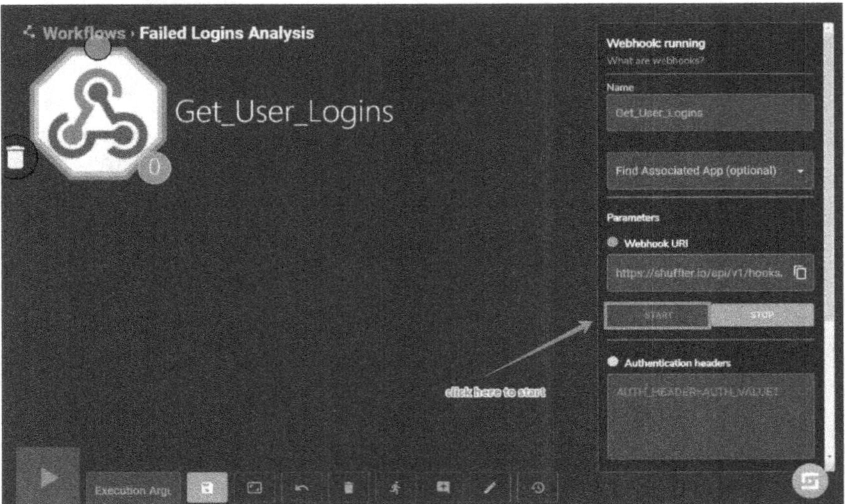

Figure 4.10 – Start the Webhook URI

II. Next, add Shuffle Tools from the **Apps** section. This will help us to view all the alerts and connect the Shuffle tools with `Get_User_Logins` node. Make sure you set the following:

```
Name: View_response
Find Actions: Repeat back to me
Call: $exec
```

Now, let's run the test execution and then click on the show execution button. If everything is good, you should see all the alerts, as shown in the following screenshot:

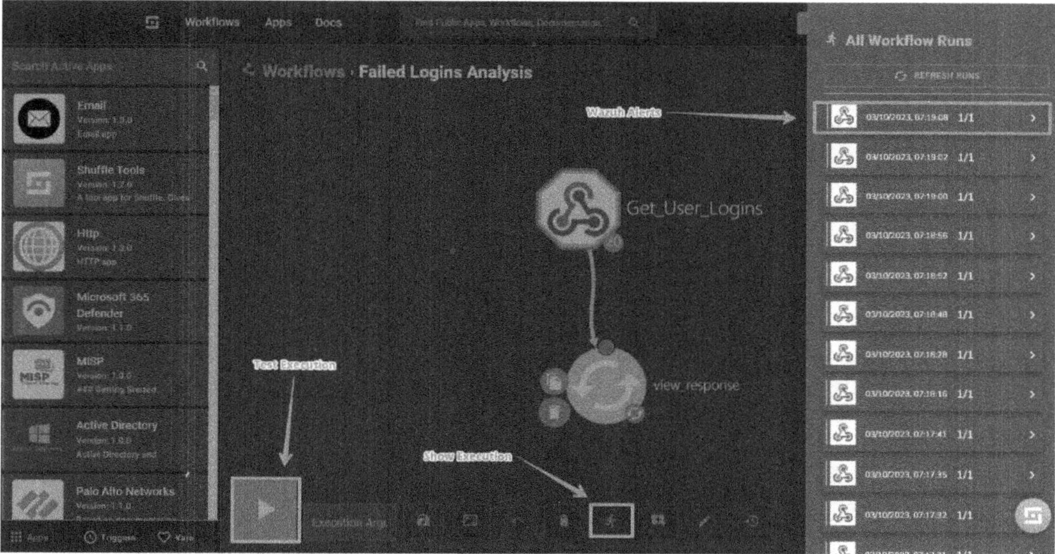

Figure 4.11 – Wazuh alerts received on Shuffle

Once you expand any part of the alert, you will see the entire alert in JSON format.

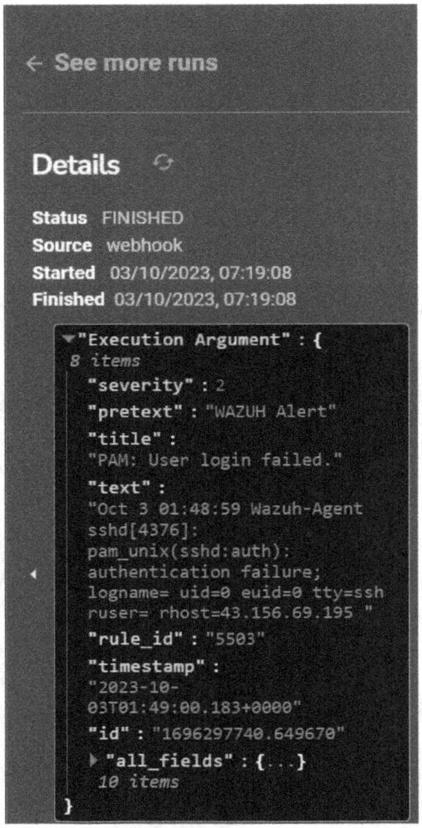

← See more runs

Details

Status FINISHED
Source webhook
Started 03/10/2023, 07:19:08
Finished 03/10/2023, 07:19:08

"Execution Argument" : {
8 items
"severity" : 2
"pretext" : "WAZUH Alert"
"title" : "PAM: User login failed."
"text" : "Oct 3 01:48:59 Wazuh-Agent sshd[4376]: pam_unix(sshd:auth): authentication failure; logname= uid=0 euid=0 tty=ssh ruser= rhost=43.156.69.195 "
"rule_id" : "5503"
"timestamp" : "2023-10-03T01:49:00.183+0000"
"id" : "1696297740.649670"
"all_fields" : {...}
10 items
}

Figure 4.12 – A Wazuh alert in the JSON format

Retrieving Wazuh alerts for successful login analysis

Analyzing successful logins is just as important as analyzing failed or abnormal login attempts, as it helps to detect unauthorized access, monitor privileged access, monitor for anomalies, and much more. To retrieve Wazuh alerts for successful logins, we only need to make the following changes to the previous steps:

1. Create a new workflow,
2. Add new integration tags, as follows:

```
<integration>
<name>shuffle</name>
<rule_id>5715</rule_id>
<hook_url>[https://<Shuffle_Server_IP>/api/v1/hooks/webhook_
```

```
b68508da-0727-436c-8f33-412419222441] (<https://shuffler.io/api/
v1/hooks/webhook_b68508da-0727-436c-8f33-412419222441>)
</hook_url>
<alert_format>json</alert_format>
</integration>
```

Here, `rule_id 5715` indicates a successful login to the device. Additionally, you need to replace `hook_url` with a newly generated URI.

Now that we understand how to retrieve Wazuh alerts, we should be made aware of some advanced nodes to conduct enrichment, security investigation, incident responses, and so on.

Remotely managing Wazuh

Shuffle SOAR is capable of automating multiple security operation activities. When it comes to managing the Wazuh manager and its agent, there is a manual element where a security analyst has to manually add/remove/modify different attributes. The good news is that Wazuh provides a Wazuh API to allow a trusted party to communicate and send required data. In this section, we will remotely manage multiple Wazuh-related tasks, such as managing agents, rules, CDB lists, agent groups, and decoders. We will cover the following topics in this section:

- Requirements
- Managing Wazuh agents

Requirement

To remotely manage Wazuh using Shuffle SOAR, we need to set up three things – authentication, JWT token generation, and subsequent API requests.

Authentication

In order to allow Shuffle to talk to the Wazuh manager, Shuffle initiates the authentication process by providing valid authentication. The default credential of the Wazuh API is the username `wazuh-wui` and the password `wazuh-wui`.

Go to Shuffle and create a new workflow, and then follow these steps:

1. From the **Search Active Apps** section, find the **Http** app and drag and drop it into the workflow editor.

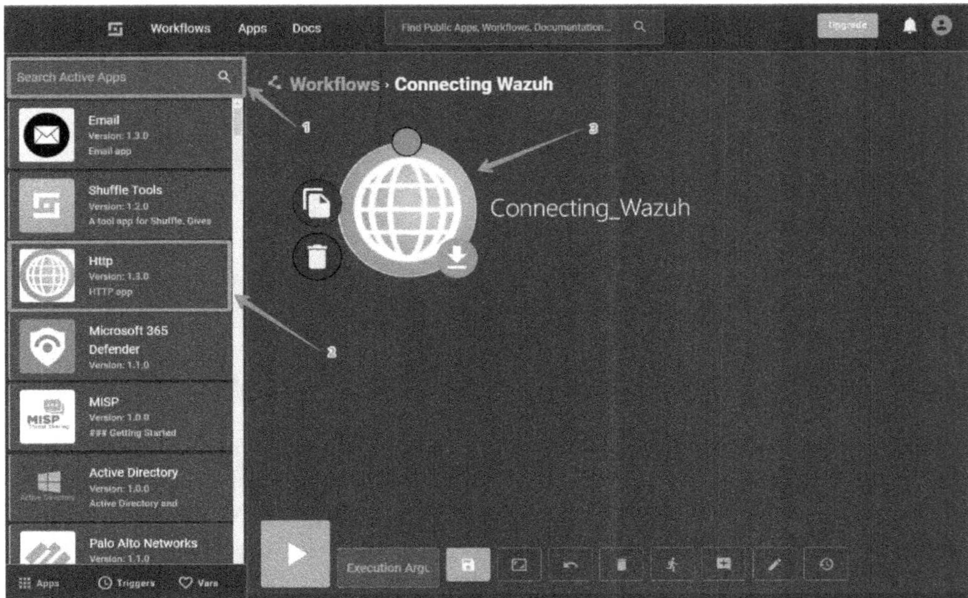

Figure 4.13 – Creating an Http app in a workflow

2. Next, we will create a `curl` query for authentication, as shown in the following diagram:

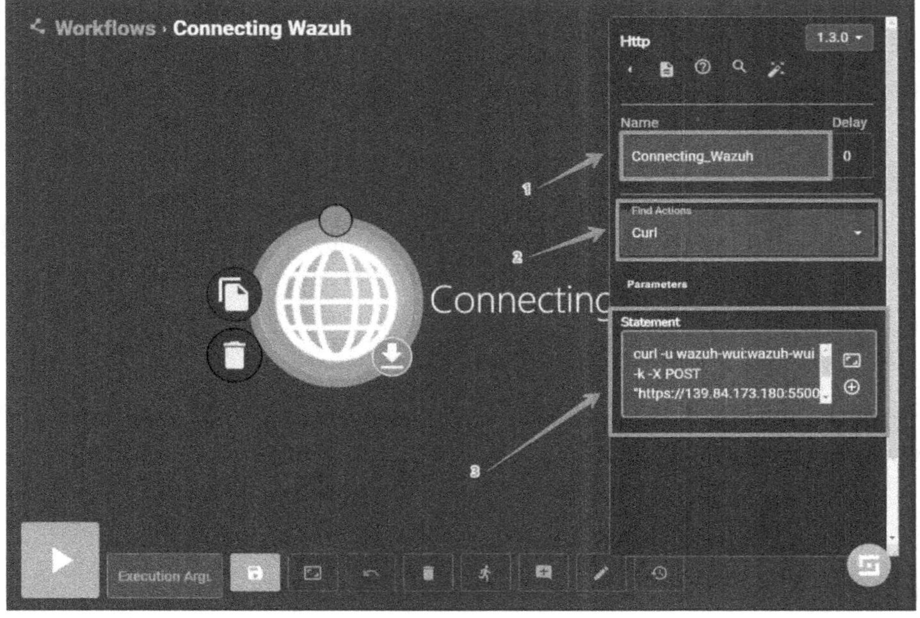

Figure 4.14 – Authentication using the curl command

3. Set a relevant name for the node.
4. Set **Action** to **Curl**.
5. Write a `curl` statement:

```
curl -u wazuh-wui:wazuh-wui -k -X POST
"<https://192.168.29.32:55000/security/user/
authenticate?raw=true>"
```

Finally, save and click the **Test Execute** button.

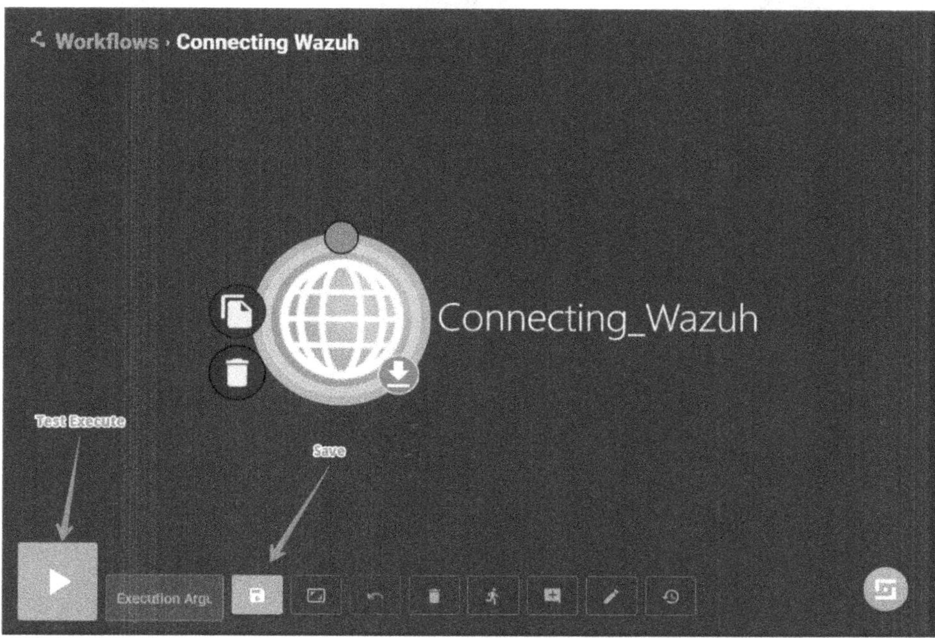

Figure 4.15 – Save and execute the curl Command on Shuffle

JWT token generation

Upon successful authentication, Wazuh generates a **JSON Web Token** (**JWT**). JWTs are often used for authentication and authorization in web applications and APIs.

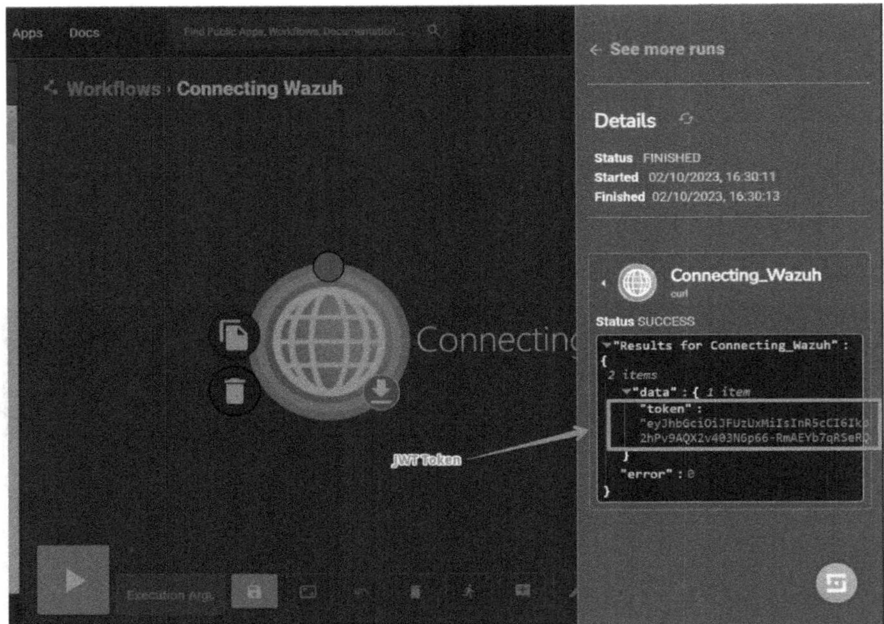

Figure 4.16 – JWT Token generation

The subsequent API request

Shuffle can now access all of Wazuh's protected resources by inserting a JWT token into the HTTP request:

```
curl -k -X <METHOD> "https://<HOST_IP>:55000/<ENDPOINT>" -H
"Authorization: Bearer <YOUR_JWT_TOKEN>"
```

Let's break down the preceding code:

- `-k`: This states that `curl` will allow connections to SSL/TLS-protected (HTTPS) sites without verifying the server's SSL certificate.
- `-X <Method>`: This `curl` option talks about HTTP request methods such as `GET`, `POST`, `PUT`, and `DELETE`.
- `<ENDPOINT>`: This represents the specific endpoint or resource on the Wazuh manager, such as agents, groups, lists, rules, and decoders.
- `-H`: This is another `curl` option that adds an HTTP header to the request. In the preceding example, we added an `Authorization` header with a `Bearer` value to the JWT token.

Managing Wazuh agents

We can use the Shuffle tool to manage Wazuh agents for information gathering and incident response. Wazuh API allows you to add a new agent, remove agents, restart agents, upgrade agents, and retrieve outdated agents using the Shuffle tool.

If you follow the previous steps, you must have retrieved the JWT token. Let's create a new Shuffle workflow with HTTP nodes, as shown in the following screenshot:

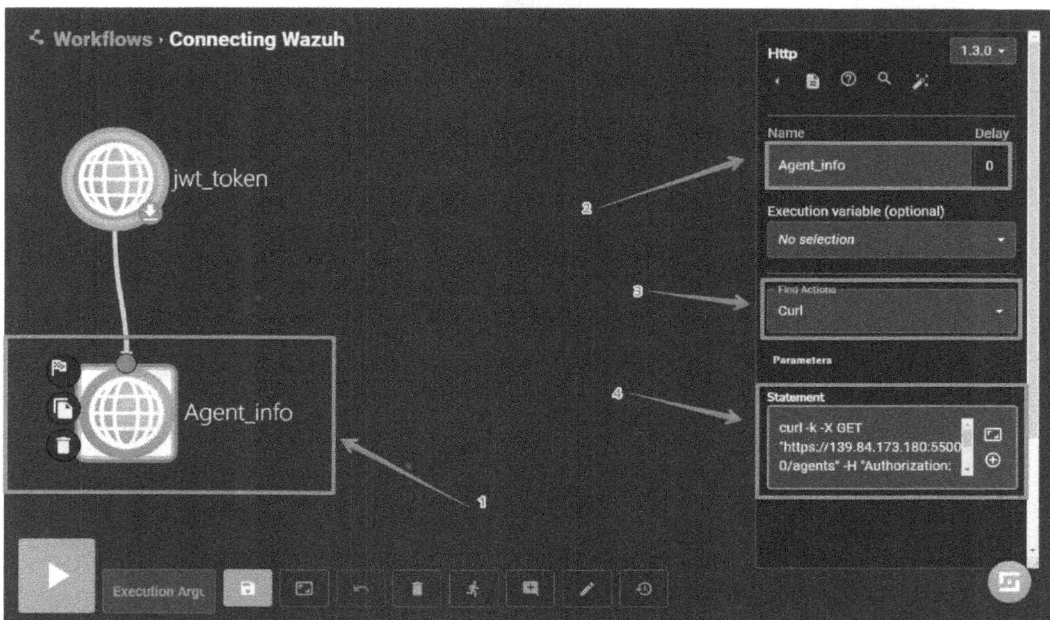

Figure 4.17 – Retrieving Wazuh agent information

To configure the new workflow, you need to follow the following steps:

1. Add a new **Http** node.
2. Enter a name – `Agent_info`.
3. Set **Find Actions** to **Curl**.
4. Write a `curl` command:

```
curl -k -X GET "<https://139.84.173.180:55000/agents>"
-H "Authorization: Bearer $jwt_token" -H "Content-Type:
application/json"
```

Let's break down the preceding code:

- `$jwt_token`: This is a variable that holds the JWT token. This variable name should be the same as the node name.

Next, save and test execute the workflow. You will get an output with all the agent information.

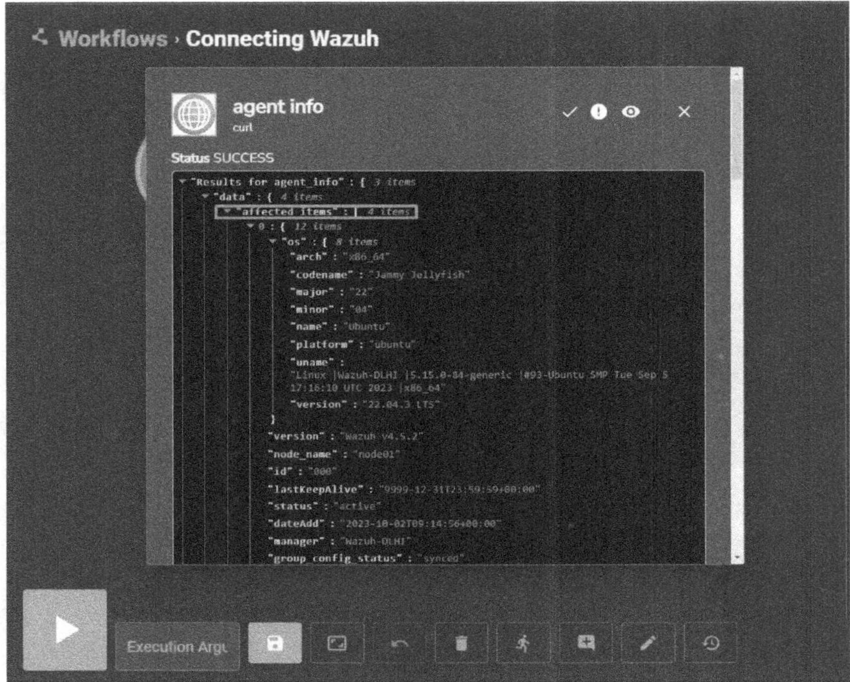

Figure 4.18 – Receiving the Wazuh agent information

Let's break down the preceding screenshot:

- **Status SUCCESS**: This shows that the API request was successful.
- **"affected items"**: This shows the content of the response message. In this case, we have four items about the agent information.

To learn more about managing Wazuh agents, refer to Wazuh's official documentation at `https://documentation.wazuh.com/current/user-manual/api/reference.html#tag/Agents`.

We have learned to manage Wazuh remotely using its API. In the following section, we will learn about some important apps and the integration of Shuffle.

Important Shuffle apps

The integration of Wazuh and Shuffle SOAR helps a security team to automate multiple recurring activities. It introduces a paradigm shift in approaching incidents, faster response time, phishing analysis, managing Wazuh, and much more. Shuffle SOAR support integration with hundreds of security tools. In this section, we will discuss some important apps and their integration with Wazuh.

Incident enrichment using TheHive

TheHive is a powerful and a scalable security incident response tool designed for SOCs , **CSIRTs** (**Computer Security Incident Response Teams**), and **CERTs** (**Computer Emergency Response Teams**). We can use TheHive app in a Shuffle workflow to add enrichment to every alert before conducting a manual security investigation. Once you integrate TheHive with a Shuffle workflow, you can execute multiple tasks on TheHive by using API endpoints, as shown here.

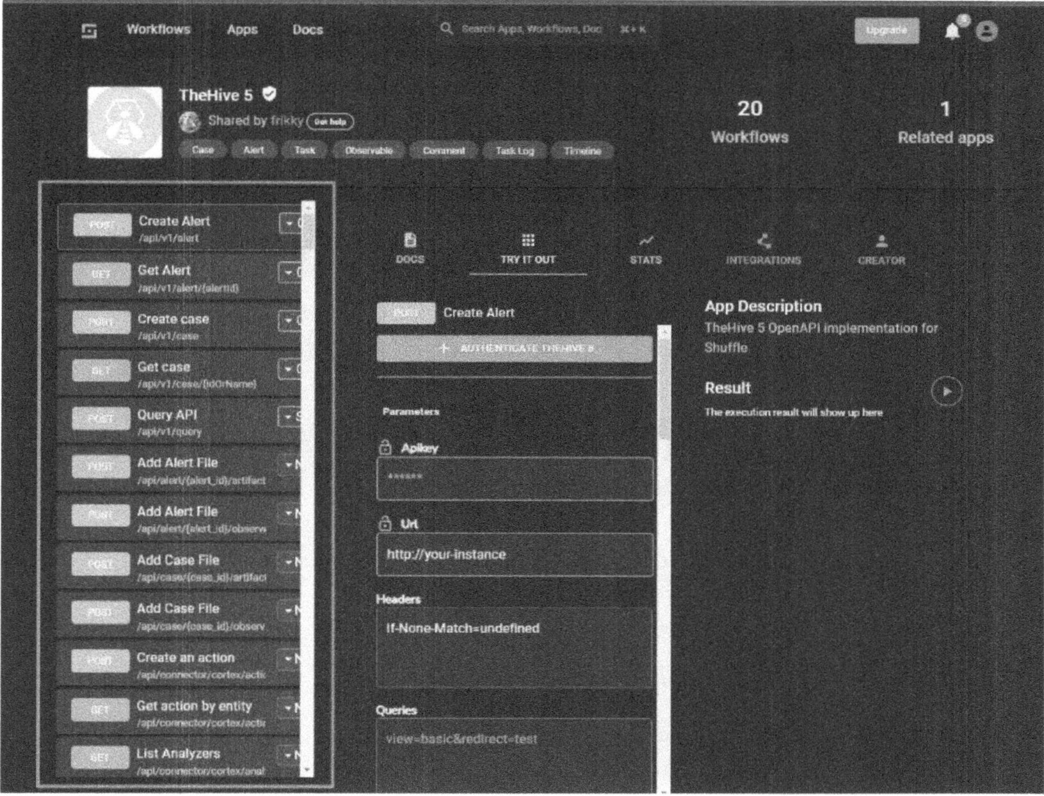

Figure 4.19 – TheHive API endpoints

An **API endpoint** is essentially a unique **Uniform Resource Identifier** (**URL**) or URI that provides access to an API. It facilitates communication between various software applications by serving as a point of interaction. In our case, TheHive allows Shuffle to access its capabilities using different API endpoints. For example, if you want to create a case in TheHive tool, you can use the **Create case** endpoint using the **POST** method, as shown here:

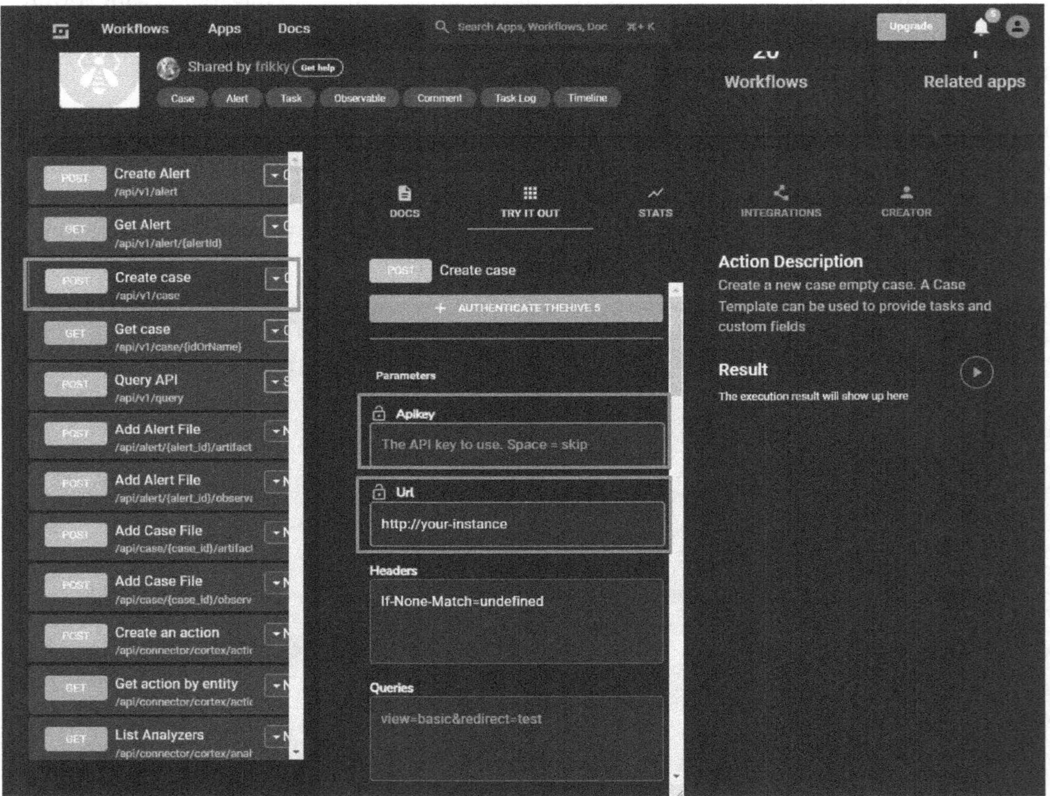

Figure 4.20 – The Create case endpoint on TheHive platform

Let's break down the preceding screenshot:

- **Apikey**: This is the API key for the TheHive platform
- **Url**: This is the complete URL for TheHive platform

Let's look at sample workflow published by the Shuffle community. The following workflow starts by receiving a Wazuh alert and then creating a case in TheHive, adding an observable to TheHive case, retrieving artifacts, and finally, running TheHive/Cortex analyzer against MISP and VirusTotal.

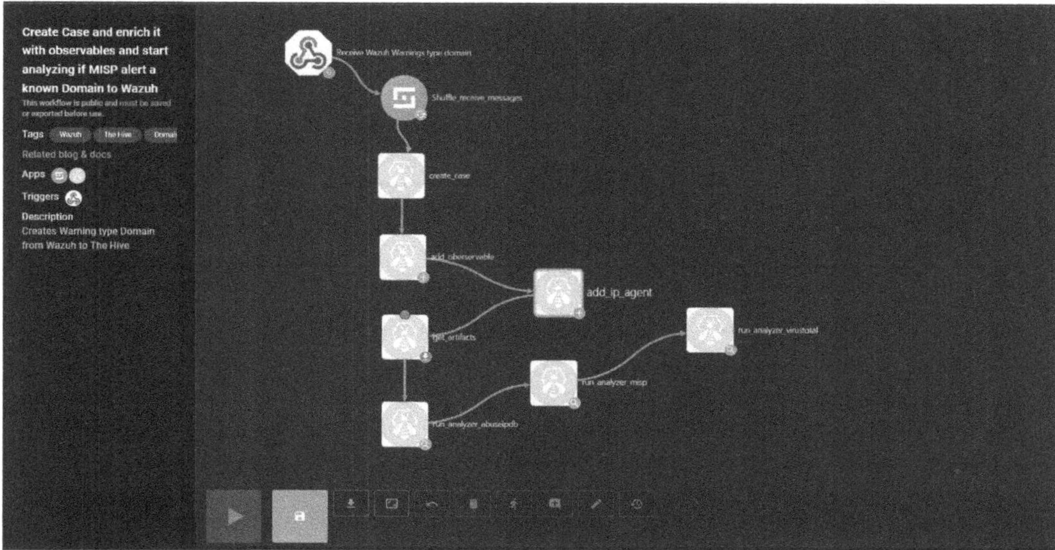

Figure 4.21 – Automating TheHive case enrichment using Shuffle

The link to access this sample workflow is available here: `https://shuffler.io/workflows/4e9f5826-a7fc-4cc1-b21d-0c7d231bcfa7?queryID=17e8f00cbed5d69823b1a0ad665d4b48`.

> **Note**
>
> The preceding sample workflow can be used once you submit all the required information, such as the Wazuh Webhook URI, TheHive API key and URL, and other essential information. Also, ensure that MISP and VirusTotal are already integrated with TheHive/Cortex to execute the analyzer, as mentioned in the preceding workflow.

Malware analysis using YARA

YARA is a tool that empowers malware researchers in identifying and categorizing malware samples. It's a free and open source program that works on Linux, Windows, and macOS. We can use the YARA tool in a Shuffle workflow to analyze an email attachment file or any other file, based on the custom rules defined by malware researchers. Let's take a look at the sample workflow here.

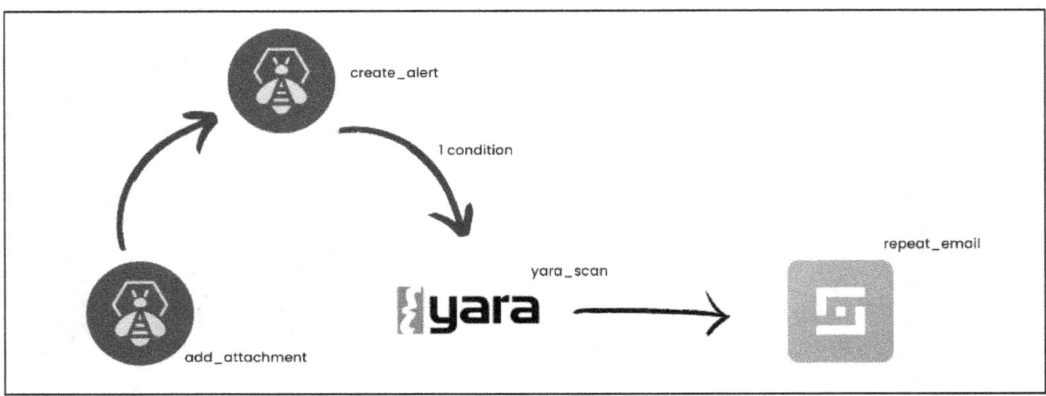

Figure 4.22 – Automated file analysis using YARA

The preceding workflow was created by Taylor Walton. This workflow starts by adding an email attachment to TheHive, then creating an alert on TheHive, and finally, running a YARA scan. To run the YARA scan against each email attachment, we can prepend this workflow as follows.

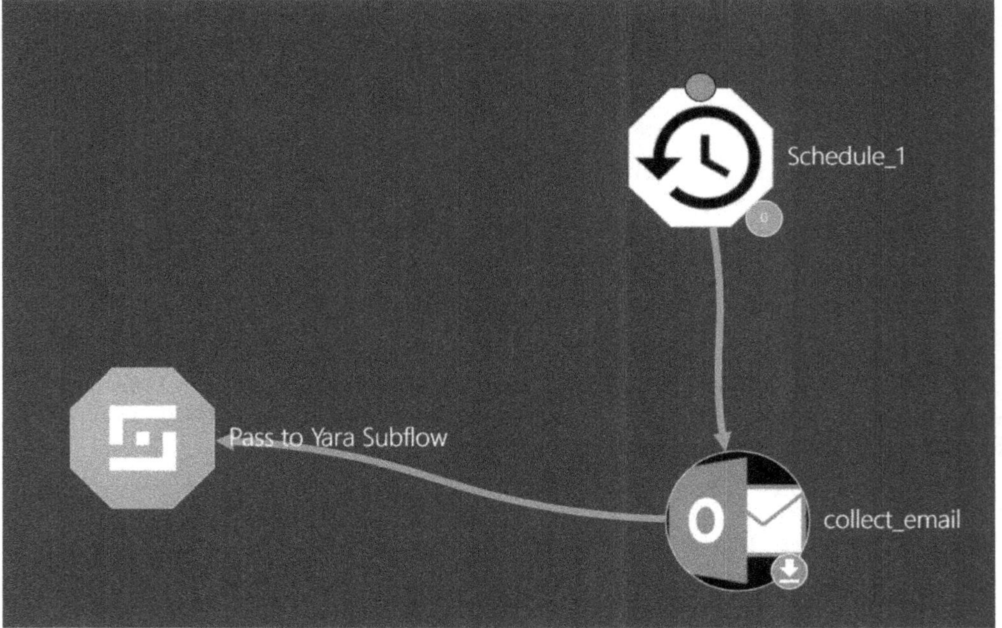

Figure 4.23 – An email collection workflow

Messaging and collaboration tools

Shuffle has a range of workplace collaboration application integration tools, such as Microsoft Teams, Slack, Discord, Outlook, and Gmail. Each application provides tons of API endpoints such as the following:

- Retrieving emails and creating a message on Outlook
- Creating a new chat on Slack
- Writing a message to a group on Microsoft Teams and so on

Threat intelligence platforms

Shuffle SOAR can be integrated with threat intelligence platforms such as MISP, AbuseIPDB, and AlienVault OTX, expanding its ability to collect and correlate different threat data:

- **MISP**: Shuffle SOAR connects to MISP to gain access to a collaborative threat intelligence-sharing platform, facilitating the exchange of structured threat information.
- **AbuseIPDB**: Integration with AbuseIPDB provides quick access to crowdsourced threat data relating to malicious IP addresses, improving the platform's ability to detect and block possible threats.
- **AlienVault OTX**: Integrating with AlienVault OTX improves threat visibility by leveraging its vast store of threat indicators and worldwide data. This thorough connection enables Shuffle SOAR users to investigate and respond to security issues in depth by accessing richer, real-time threat intelligence from a variety of trusted sources.

Endpoint protection/antivirus software

Shuffle provides a seamless integration with top-tier endpoint protection and antivirus solutions such as CrowdStrike Falcon, Windows Defender, Sophos, and BlackBerry Cylance, improving its efficacy in incident response and threat prevention. This integration enables direct communication and orchestration between the centralized platform of Shuffle SOAR and these security technologies, enabling automated response actions based on identified threats or incidents. Once integrated, we can create a Shuffle workflow to retrieve alerts from endpoint protection and send them to TheHive for further analysis, get detection rules from CrowdStrike, and so on.

Summary

In this chapter, we learned about the purpose of SOAR and how an SOC analyst uses SOAR in a real-world environment. We also learned how to set up a Shuffle SOAR platform using a Docker Compose environment and fixed some backend related issues. This chapter continued with the integration of Wazuh with Shuffle to receive alerts from Wazuh in real time. Finally, we learned how to remotely manage Wazuh using API integration and also covered some popular third-party integrations with Shuffle.

In the next chapter, we will learn about Wazuh's active response module to build a proactive incident response system. We will also cover some practical incident response use cases.

5

Incident Response with Wazuh

It is of utmost importance to have a rapid and efficient response plan in place to handle any security events that may arise in the ever-changing world of cybersecurity. For example, a sales employee opened up a malicious file with a name attached to an email pretending to be from an authorized business partner. This can result in a ransomware attack and bring down many mission-critical services. When such an incident happens, responding promptly can help to minimize the overall damage to the network. An efficient **incident response** (**IR**) can help businesses to promptly resume normal operations, thereby reducing the amount of downtime that occurs and the expenses connected with it.

In this chapter, we will learn how to leverage the Wazuh platform and other Wazuh-supported third-party tools to build an effective IR system. We will cover the following topics in this chapter:

- Introduction to incident response
- What is Wazuh active response?
- Blocking unauthorized SSH access
- Isolating an infected Windows machine
- Blocking RDP brute-force attack attempts

Introduction to incident response

IR is the process by which an organization handles situations such as data breaches, **distributed denial of service** (**DDoS**), and ransomware attacks. It is an effort to immediately identify an attack, mitigate the impacts of the attack, contain any damage caused by the attack, and fix the cause in order to reduce the risk of future attacks. In practice, IR refers to a collection of information security rules, processes, and tools that can be used to detect, contain, and remove intrusions. Let's discuss the two most popular IR frameworks, the **National Institute of Standards and Technology** (**NIST**) and SANS, as shown in the following diagram.

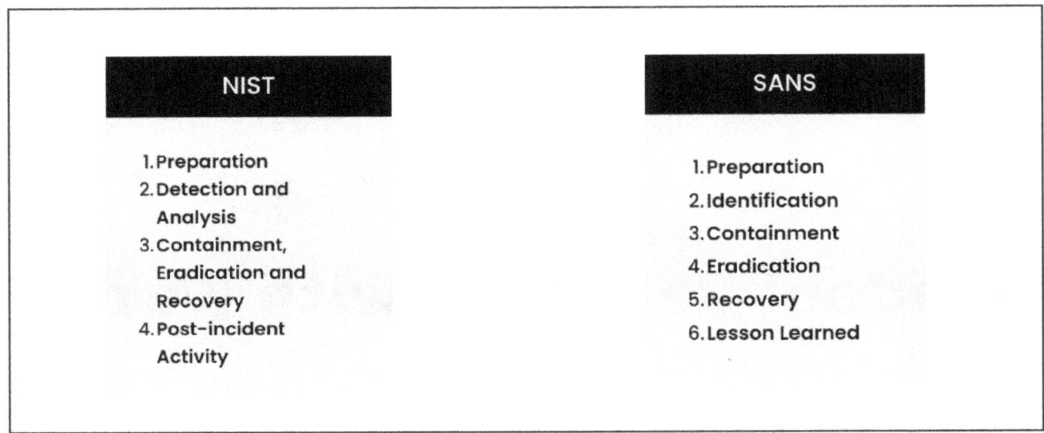

Figure 5.1 – NIST and SANS IR

Different methods of incident response process

There are various methods for developing a structured IR process. There are two IR frameworks and processes that are most popular: NIST and SANS. Let us see each of them in detail.

SANS six-step procedure

The SANS Institute recommends six processes for IR: *preparation*, *identification*, *containment*, *eradication*, *recovery*, and *lessons learned.*

Let's elaborate on the SANS six-step procedure. SANS defines IR as having six stages. When an incident occurs, these six processes are repeated in a cycle. The steps are as follows:

1. Preparation of systems and procedures
2. Identification of incidents
3. Containment of attack
4. Eradication of intrusion
5. Recovery from accidents, including system restoration
6. Lessons gained and feedback applied to the next stage of planning

Let us understand each of the processes step by step:

1. **Preparation**: During the first step of preparation, you evaluate the efficiency of existing security measures and regulations. This entails doing a risk assessment to identify current vulnerabilities and the priority of your assets. Some of the important action items are listed here:

   - Create a policy and plan for IR
   - Create an IR team
   - Determine and categorize important assets
   - Acquire the tools and technology required for incident detection and response

2. **Identification of incidents**: The emphasis is on the constant monitoring and identification of potential security issues using techniques such as **intrusion detection systems** (**IDSs**), **security incident and event management** (**SIEM**), **endpoint detection and response** (**EDR**), and log analysis. Some of the important steps are listed here:

   - Continuous surveillance for indications of security incidents
   - Use host-based and network-based IDSs
   - Gather and examine logs from various sources
   - Make use of threat intelligence streams

3. **Containment of attack**: When an incident occurs, this phase focuses on immediately isolating compromised systems, implementing temporary solutions or workarounds, and updating access restrictions and firewall rules to avoid additional compromise. This is where digital forensics plays a critical role.
4. **Eradication of intrusion**: The incident's root cause is recognized and treated here. Vulnerabilities that allowed the incident to occur are remedied, and policies and configurations are modified to prevent the same occurrence from occurring again.
5. **Recovery from accidents, including system restoration**: This phase focuses on resuming the normal operation of affected systems, certifying their integrity, and ensuring that the incident has been thoroughly resolved. It also entails analyzing and upgrading IR processes depending on the incident's lessons gained.
6. **Lessons learned phase**: During this phase, organizations undertake a post-event review, documenting the incident, the reaction, and the lessons learned. The purpose is to develop IR plans and policies, as well as to offer IR team members additional training.

NIST four-step procedure

NIST defines IR as having four steps: *preparation*, *detection and analysis*, *containment, eradication, and recovery*, and *post-incident activity*. Let us understand each of these processes in detail:

1. **Preparation**: The NIST framework for IR emphasizes preparation as a critical component, much like the SANS framework does. During this phase, systems, procedures, and plans must be put in place in order to get ready for incidents. Organizations should have the following in place to be ready for incidents:

    - A precise IR strategy
    - Clearly defined roles and duties
    - A successful communication strategy
    - Reporting plan
    - Determining the vital systems and resources
    - Testing and updating the IR plan on a regular basis

2. **Detection and analysis**: During this phase, companies identify and examine occurrences to comprehend their extent and consequences. Making decisions regarding how to respond to an incident at this time is crucial. The following should be in place inside businesses in order to recognize and analyze occurrences effectively:

    - Keeping an eye on escalation processes and mechanisms
    - Prompt incident detection and analysis

3. **Containment, eradication, and recovery**: The containment, eradication, and recovery stages in the NIST framework are similar to those in the SANS framework. The following should be in place inside organizations in order to contain, eliminate, and recover from incidents:

    - Isolating the impacted systems
    - Eliminating the incident's cause
    - Returning to regular operations

4. **Post-incident activity**: In the NIST system, post-incident activity is the last phase. Organizations evaluate their IR procedure and evaluate the effects of incidents at this point. The following should be in place for organizations to examine and enhance the IR process:

    - A procedure to evaluate the IR methodology
    - A process for recording the lessons discovered
    - A plan for bringing enhancements to the IR procedure into practice

Objectives of the NIST and SANS procedures

The objectives of the NIST and SANS IR frameworks are similar and offer an organized method for handling incidents. Nonetheless, the two frameworks differ in a few significant ways:

- Both frameworks emphasize the significance of having a precise IR plan, defined roles and duties, and efficient communication when it comes to the preparation stage. On the other hand, having a reporting plan in place and identifying key systems and assets are given more weight in the NIST framework.
- Both frameworks concentrate on the prompt detection and examination of occurrences in terms of detection and analysis. But whereas the NIST framework is more concerned with monitoring systems and escalation protocols, the SANS approach prioritizes triage and prioritizing.

In the next section, we will discuss the importance of automating IR activities.

Incident response automation

Effective IR is time-sensitive and requires teams to identify threats and initiate an **incident response plan (IRP)** as soon as possible. A security team receives thousands of security alerts from security tools every day and hence it is difficult to manually analyze events or assess every alarm that security tools generate. These constraints are addressed via automated IR. In *Chapter 4*, *Security Automation and Orchestration Using Shuffle*, we learned how shuffle SOAR makes this possible by creating workflows, helping the security team with automated incident enrichment, automated observable analysis with TheHive tool integration, automating Wazuh activities, and many more. In this chapter, our focus will be on using Wazuh's in-built capability called active response to perform IR. In general, IR automation can help the security team with the following:

- **Immediate containment**: Once compromised systems are identified, automated IR systems should isolate them to stop threats from spreading
- **Dynamic firewall rules**: In response to certain risks, the IR automation system can dynamically develop and deploy firewall rules that block malicious traffic or isolate vulnerable systems
- **Automated account disabling**: Automated reaction steps can quickly disable compromised user accounts in the case of a security incident, blocking future unauthorized access
- **User access restrictions**: To improve the security posture, the IR automation system can impose access controls, such as removing users who indicate suspicious behavior or restricting access privileges
- **GeoIP blocking**: To strengthen defense against targeted attacks, automated IR can use GeoIP blocking rules to limit access from particular geographic regions known for malicious activity

We can create tons of different use cases for automating IR. In the next section, we will practically deploy and test some of the automated IR using Wazuh's active response capability.

Wazuh active response

One of the main components of the Wazuh platform that enables automatic responses to security events and incidents is called active response. Security analysts can respond quickly to specific security threats or triggers identified by the Wazuh system by utilizing active response. By utilizing active response features, Wazuh enables organizations to respond to security incidents quickly and aggressively. With Wazuh active response, you may develop and execute automated responses against most security alerts. These responses may include executing custom scripts, banning IP addresses, or deactivating user accounts. Automating response actions makes sure that incidents with a high significance are dealt with and mitigated in a timely and consistent way. This is especially helpful when security teams don't have a lot of resources and have to decide how to respond first.

In this section, we will cover the following topics:

- Active response scripts
- Configuring active response
- The working of Wazuh active response

Active response scripts

Wazuh provides pre-built Active response scripts for Linux, Windows, and macOS systems. Additionally, it also helps security professionals to write custom active response scripts based on specific requirements. The default active response scripts are stored in the following folders/directories:

Endpoint	**Location (Directory/Folder)**
Windows	`C:\Program Files (x86)\ossec-agent\active-response\bin`
Linux	`/var/ossec/active-response/bin`
macOS	`/Library/ossec/active-response/bin`

Table 5.1 – Location of active response scripts

The Wazuh team and the entire community have done a brilliant job in building powerful active response scripts. Some of the popular scripts are mentioned in the following table:

Operating System	**Scripts**
Windows	• `Netsh.exe`: Blocks an IP address using `netsh` • `Restart-wazuh.exe`: Restarts the Wazuh agent • `Route-null.exe`: Adds an IP address to the null route

Operating System	Scripts
Ubuntu	• `firewall-drop`: Adds an IP address to the IP tables deny list • `start.sh`: Restarts the Wazuh agent or manager • `Route-null`: Adds an IP address to a null route

Table 5.2 – List of default active response scripts

Now, let's learn how to set up active response on the monitored endpoints.

Configuring active response

Active response configuration needs to be done only on the Wazuh server. However, both the server and agent must have an active response script. Wazuh requires three things to execute an active response, and these are as follows:

- Active response script
- The `<command>` tag
- The `<active-response>` tag

Active response script

The Wazuh manager and agents have out-of-the-box active response scripts, supporting Linux, macOS, and Windows endpoints. We can also create custom active response scripts that run when an alert of a specific rule ID, rule group, or alert level triggers. All the default active response scripts are stored in the /var/ossec/active-response/bin directory. If you create a custom script, make sure you save them in the same directory.

The <command> tag

The `<command>` tag specifies which script should be executed when a certain rule is triggered. The `<command>` elements for out-of-the-box active response scripts are automatically included in the Wazuh server `/var/ossec/etc/ossec.conf` instance type; therefore, it is not required to add them. Let me share an example of the `<command>` block:

```
<command>
  <name>firewall-drop</name>
  <executable>firewall-drop</executable>
  <timeout_allowed>yes</timeout_allowed>
</command>
```

Here, we have the following:

- `<name>`: Name of the command
- `<executable>`: Defines the script or executable that must be executed in response to a trigger
- `<timeout_allowed>`: Enables a timeout following a specified duration

The <active-response> tag

Insert an `<active-response>` tag within the `<ossec_config>` element in the `/var/ossec/etc/ossec.conf` file of the same Wazuh server. The `<active-response>` block specifies the location and condition of command execution, as shown:

```
<active-response>
    <command>firewall-drop</command>
    <location>local</location>
    <rules_id>5712</rules_id>
    <timeout>60</timeout>
  </active-response>
```

Here, we have the following:

- `<command>`: It provides the configuration command. In our case, we have used `firewall-drop`.
- `<location>`: It indicates the location where the command must be executed. We have three types of locations: `Local`, `Server`, or `Defined-agent`. The purpose of these options is as follows:
  - `Server`: It executes the script on the Wazuh server.
  - `Defined-agent`: It runs the script on a predefined agent. We require the `<agent-id>` tag to specify the ID of the Wazuh agent.

How Wazuh active response works

These active response scripts (hosted at `/var/ossec/active-response/bin`) are run on monitored endpoints by Wazuh in response to alerts triggered by a particular rule ID, level, or rule group. You can write a variety of scripts to start in response to a trigger, but you need to carefully plan these actions. Inadequate execution of rules and replies may make an endpoint more vulnerable.

Let's talk about how Wazuh active response works:

1. **Event generated**: The Wazuh agent pushes the events to the manager. The Wazuh manager analyzes and triggers alerts based on the matched rule.

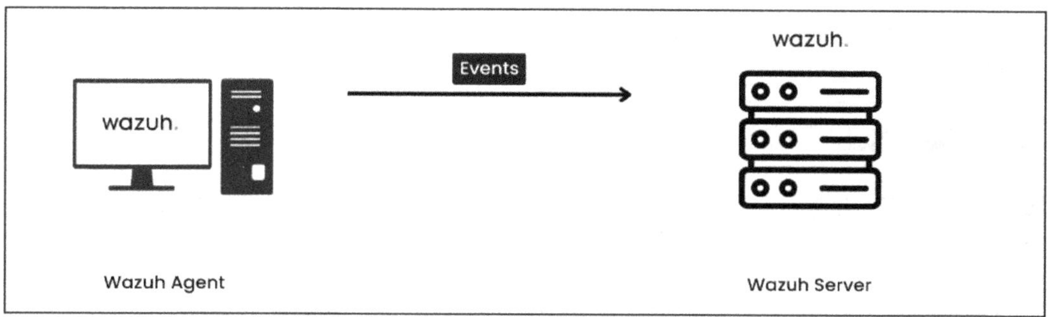

Figure 5.2 – Event generated

2. **Triggering active response**: Every security alert you see on the Wazuh dashboard is generated by the corresponding rule (pre-built by Wazuh or custom). If you add an `<active-response>` block within the `<ossec_config>` tag in the Wazuh server with the `<rule_id>` tag and there is a matching security alert, it will trigger our newly created `<active-response>`.
3. **Responding to the Wazuh agent**: Now, our Wazuh server will order the agent to perform an action defined by the `<command>` block. Wazuh agents will have the default active response scripts; however, if you want to implement any custom active response, you need to write and save the code in the Wazuh agent.
4. **Executing active response**: Active response scripts are stored within the Wazuh agent at the `/var/ossec/active-response/bin` location. You can troubleshoot or verify the Wazuh active response by checking the logs present at `/var/ossec/active-response/active-response.log`.

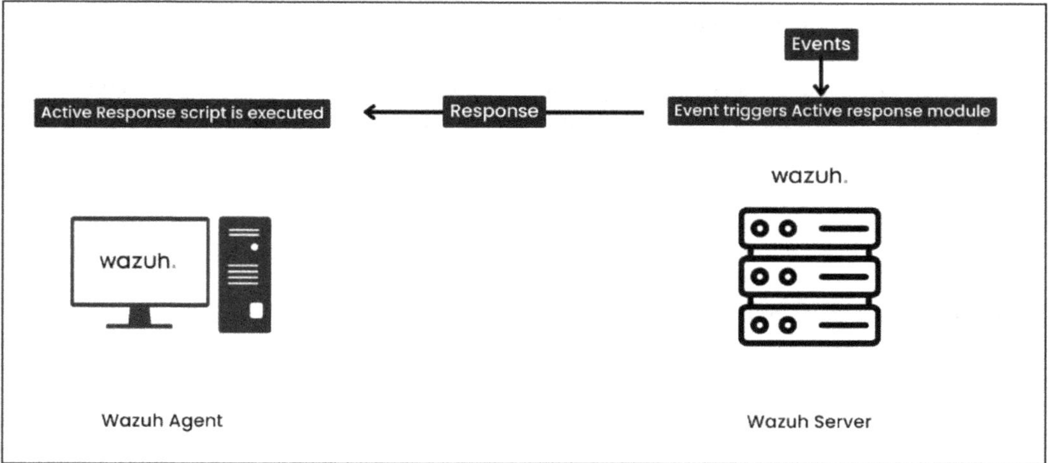

Figure 5.3 – Executing active response on Wazuh agent

5. **Active response alert**: Once the active response script is executed, our Wazuh manager will take that alert from the Wazuh agent and show it to us on the security alert dashboard.

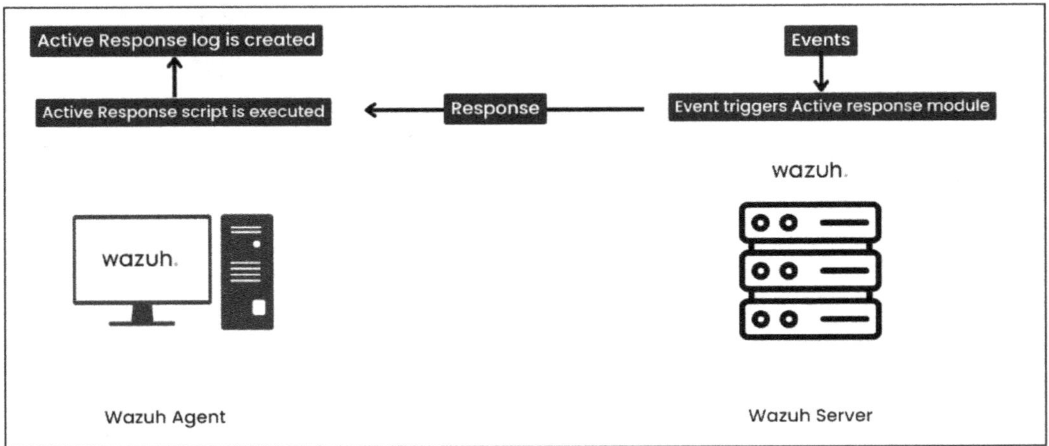

Figure 5.4 – Active response log

Now that we understand how Wazuh active response works and how to configure it, let's cover some practical use cases.

Blocking unauthorized SSH access

SSH attacks are among the most prevalent types of attacks against servers accessible via the internet. Automated bots that regularly monitor the internet for SSH servers with inadequate security setups carry out the major share of SSH attacks. Because attack sources are frequently scattered globally, with no single country dominating, it is a global cybersecurity threat. Organizational losses, data breaches, and compromised servers are all possible outcomes of successful SSH attacks. In this section, we will learn how to automatically block unauthorized SSH access to a victim's machine.

We will learn about the following:

- Lab setup
- Setting up active response
- Testing

Lab setup

In this lab setup, we require three things: an Ubuntu Server with a Wazuh agent installed, an attacker machine (Kali Linux), and, finally, our Wazuh server (we have used a Virtual Machine OVA file for Lab purposes only). The lab is designed as follows.

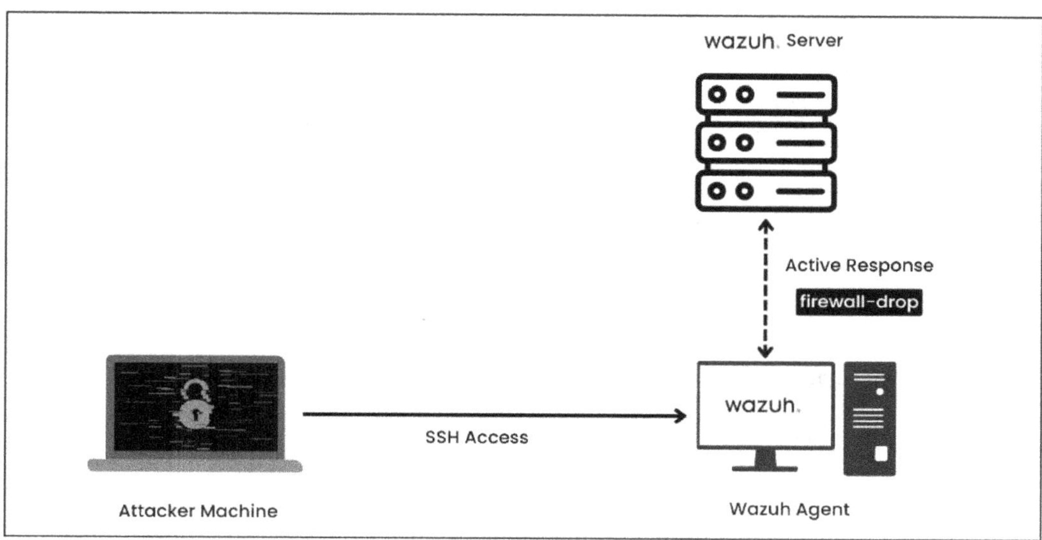

Figure 5.5 – Lab setup: Blocking unauthorized SSH access using Wazuh active response

In this lab, we are going to use the `firewall-drop` scripts as the default active response script for the monitored Ubuntu agent. Next, we need to modify the active response script to be triggered when an unauthorized SSH connection is detected.

Setting up Wazuh active response

In order to set up the Wazuh platform to block unauthorized SSH access attempts, we need to execute the firewall-drop active response script once Wazuh rule `5710` is triggered. We need to take the steps that follow to accomplish this task.

Modifying the active response on the Wazuh manager

As we have learned, `<active-response>` executes a specific `<command>` block. In our case, we are utilizing the firewall-drop active response, which executes the `firewall-drop` command. We can find both the `<command>` and `<active-response>` blocks in the `ossec.conf` file located at `/var/ossec/etc`. We want to make sure the `<active-response>` block for firewall-drop is executed once rule `5710` is triggered. Wazuh rule `5710` represents `sshd: Attempt to login using a non-existent user`. The final modified `<command>` and `<active-response>` blocks are shown here:

```
    <name>firewall-drop</name>
    <executable>firewall-drop</executable>
    <timeout_allowed>yes</timeout_allowed>
  </command>

  <active-response>
    <command>firewall-drop</command>
    <location>local</location>
    <rules_id>5710</rules_id>
    <timeout>60</timeout>
  </active-response>
```

Here, we have the following:

- `<executable>`: It is set to `firewall-drop`, which indicates the name of the script located at `/var/ossec/active-response/bin` of the Wazuh agent
- `<location>`: It is set to `local`, which indicates it only runs the script on the monitored endpoint that generated the alert
- `<timeout>`: It is set to 60 seconds and specifies that for 60 seconds the active response action will be effective

Restarting the Wazuh manager

In order for the Wazuh manager to implement the configuration change, we need to restart the manager, as shown:

```
systemctl restart wazuh-manager
```

Testing

To test the unauthorized SSH brute-force attack, you can log in to a Kali Linux machine and run the following-mentioned `hydra` tool command:

```
hydra -l  voldemort -P <PASSWORD_TEXT_FILE>  <WAZUH_AGENT_IP> ssh
```

Here, we have the following:

- `hydra`: This is the name of the tool used to perform the SSH brute-force attack.
- `-l voldemort`: The `-l` flag is used to indicate the username for the SSH login attempt. In this case, the username is `voldemort`.
- `-P <PASSWORD_TEXT_FILE>`: The `-P` flag is used to specify the path to the text file containing the list of passwords.
- `<WAZUH_AGENT_IP>`: This represents the IP address of the Wazuh agent.
- `SSH`: This specifies the service that `hydra` will attempt to attack.

Once you hit **Enter**, the SSH brute-force attack will be executed as shown in the following diagram:

```
┌──(root㉿haxcamp)-[~]
└─# hydra -l voldemort -P pass.txt 192.168.29.172 ssh
Hydra v9.5 (c) 2023 by van Hauser/THC & David Maciejak - Please do not use in military or s
ecret service organizations, or for illegal purposes (this is non-binding, these *** ignore
 laws and ethics anyway).

Hydra (https://github.com/vanhauser-thc/thc-hydra) starting at 2023-12-21 14:05:02
[WARNING] Many SSH configurations limit the number of parallel tasks, it is recommended to
reduce the tasks: use -t 4
[DATA] max 16 tasks per 1 server, overall 16 tasks, 72 login tries (l:1/p:72), ~5 tries per
 task
[DATA] attacking ssh://192.168.29.172:22/
[STATUS] 46.00 tries/min, 46 tries in 00:01h, 27 to do in 00:01h, 15 active
[STATUS] 36.50 tries/min, 73 tries in 00:02h, 1 to do in 00:01h, 12 active
1 of 1 target completed, 0 valid password found
Hydra (https://github.com/vanhauser-thc/thc-hydra) finished at 2023-12-21 14:07:35
```

Figure 5.6 – Launching an SSH brute-force attack

Visualizing alerts

Now, once the SSH brute-force attack is executed, we will see two alerts: first, an SSH unauthorized access attempt, and second, an active response blocking user access. To visualize the alerts, go to the Wazuh manager and navigate to **Security alerts**. You will see the following:

>	Dec 21, 2023 @ 14:06:50.826	ubu-serv-03	Host Blocked by firewall-drop Active Response	3	651
>	Dec 21, 2023 @ 14:06:48.838	ubu-serv-03	sshd: Attempt to login using a non-existent user	5	5710

Figure 5.7 – Wazuh alerts after the SSH brute-force attack

Let's look into the first alert, **ssh: Attempt to login using a non-existing user**, as shown in the following figure.

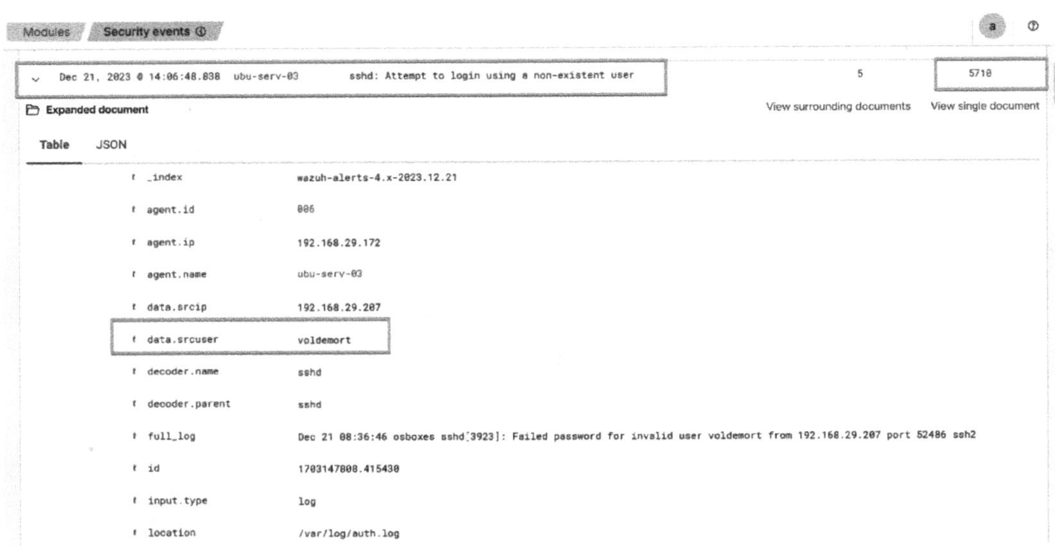

Figure 5.8 – Wazuh alert – ssh: Attempt to login using a non-existing user

Here, we have the following:

- `5710`: This represents the Wazuh rule ID `5710`, **sshd: Attempt to login using a non-existing user**.
- `data.srcuser: voldemort`: This represents the username of the unauthorized account. In this case, it is `voldemort`.

Next, we will look into an active response alert triggered by Wazuh rule ID `5710`, as shown in the following figure.

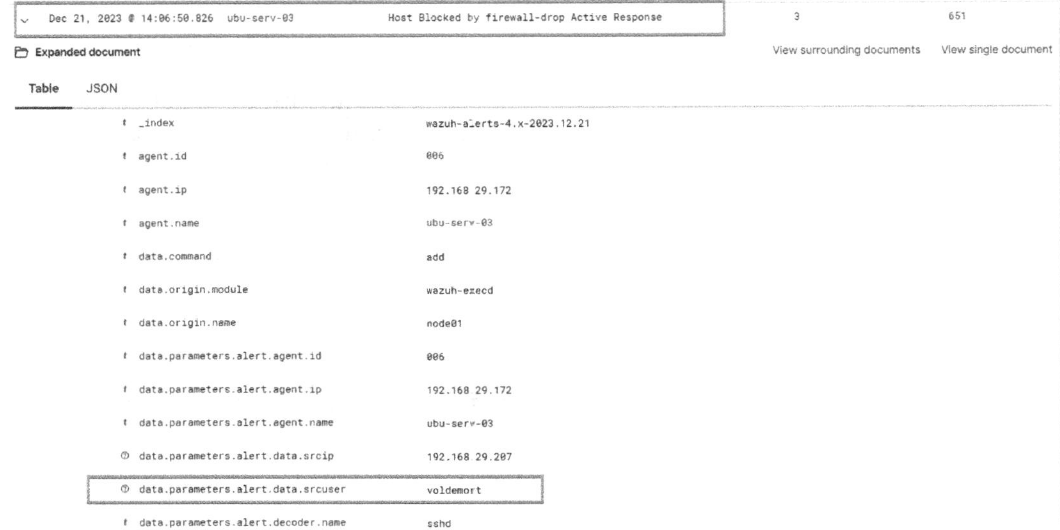

Figure 5.9 – Security alert – Host Blocked by firewall-drop Active Response

Here, we have the following:

- `data.parameters.alert.data.srcuser: voldemort`: This represents the username blocked by the firewall-drop active response script.

In this use case, we have automatically blocked any unauthorized SSH attempt to our Ubuntu server running the Wazuh agent. In the next section, we will learn how to automatically isolate a Windows machine after getting infected by malware.

Isolating a Windows machine post-infection

The process of isolating a compromised endpoint is an essential part of IR in a SOC. In order to stop the threat from spreading and inflicting further damage, you must isolate the infected device or system from the network immediately. Also remember that it is important to examine the severity of the compromise, the value of the asset, and the potential impact on the business before deciding on an isolation strategy; isolation is not a silver bullet. A ransomware attack is an essential attack scenario in which isolation is a crucial step. Ransomware is a type of malware that encrypts the data of a victim and demands payment for the decryption key. It frequently spreads quickly throughout a network, potentially affecting many endpoints. In this section, we will isolate a Windows machine post-infection by malware. We will utilize the Wazuh active response capability to create an automatic outbound rule to block all outgoing traffic. In this section, we will cover the following:

- Requirement
- Approach
- Setting up a Windows machine with a batch and PowerShell file
- Setting up Wazuh manager with VirusTotal and active response
- Testing

Requirement

In this use case, we are going to write a custom active response script to isolate a Windows machine. In order to demonstrate this detection, we need the following:

- A Windows 10 or 11 machine with the Wazuh agent installed
- PowerShell version 7
- VirusTotal integration
- A PowerShell script to block all outgoing traffic
- A Windows batch file (active response script) to trigger a PowerShell script

VirusTotal integration

In this step, we will integrate the VirusTotal platform with the Wazuh manager. VirusTotal is an online platform that aggregates several antivirus software and detects malicious content and false positives. We will cover three steps:

1. Set up a VirusTotal account.
2. Integrate VirusTotal with Wazuh.
3. Create a file integrity rule.

To complete all three steps, you can follow the steps described in the *VirusTotal integration* section of *Chapter 2, Malware Detection Using Wazuh.*

Setting up a Windows machine with a batch and PowerShell file

In this step, we will set up our Windows machine with an active response script. We will use a batch file to create an active response script. Next, to create a Windows Firewall rule to block all outgoing traffic, we need a PowerShell script. This PowerShell script will only be triggered when the batch file is executed. To complete the entire process, follow these steps.

Installing PowerShell version 7

Log in to your Windows 10 or 11 machine and install PowerShell version 7 from the official website:

`https://learn.microsoft.com/en-us/powershell/scripting/install/installing-powershell-on-windows?view=powershell-7.3`

Once downloaded and installed, you can find the executable at `C:\\Program Files\\PowerShell\\7\\"pwsh.ex`.

Writing a batch file as an active response script

Next, let's create our active response script first. This will be done by using a Windows batch script, which will then trigger a PowerShell script to block all outgoing traffic from a Windows machine.

Write an active response script in Notepad and save it with the name `fw.cmd` at the following location:

```
C:\\Program Files (x86)\\ossec-agent\\active-response\\bin
@ECHO OFF
ECHO.

"C:\\Program Files\\PowerShell\\7\\"pwsh.exe -executionpolicy ByPass
-File "C:\\Program Files (x86)\\ossec-agent\\active-response\\bin\\
wfblock.ps1"

:Exit
```

Writing a PowerShell script

Next, write a PowerShell script in Notepad and save it with name `wfblock.ps1` at the same location:

```
C:\\Program Files (x86)\\ossec-agent\\active-response\\bin\\wfblock.
ps1
#Author Rajneesh Gupta

# Set ConfirmPreference to None to automatically answer "No" to
confirmation prompts
$ConfirmPreference = "None"

# Define the rule name
$ruleName = "BlockOutgoingTraffic"

# Check if the rule already exists
$existingRule = Get-NetFirewallRule | Where-Object {$_.Name -eq
$ruleName}

if ($existingRule -eq $null) {
    # Create a new outbound block rule
    New-NetFirewallRule -DisplayName $ruleName -Direction Outbound
-Action Block -Enabled True
    Write-Host "Outgoing traffic is now blocked."
} else {
    Write-Host "Outgoing traffic is already blocked."
}
```

Here, we have the following:

- `$ruleName = "BlockOutgoingTraffic"`: It creates a `$ruleName` variable with the value `BlockOutgoingTraffic`. This will create a name for the Windows Firewall rule.
- `$existingRule`: This will check whether the rule already exists. If it doesn't exist, then create a new rule to block all outgoing traffic.

Once you set up the Windows machine configuration, you need to set up the Wazuh manager with an active response block and Wazuh rules.

Active response block in the Wazuh manager

In order to make sure, we need to modify or add the `<command>` and `<active-response>` blocks under the `/var/ossec/etc/conf` file:

```
<command>
    <name>windowsfirewall</name>
```

```
    <executable>fw.cmd</executable>
    <timeout_allowed>yes</timeout_allowed>
</command>
```

Here, make sure the `<executable>` tag has `fw.cmd`, which is the same as the Windows batch file we created earlier.

Second, we need to add an `<active-response>` block, as shown:

```
<active-response>
  <disabled>no</disabled>
  <command>windowsfirewall</command>
  <location>local</location>
  <rules_id>87105</rules_id>
  <timeout>60</timeout>
</active-response>
```

Here, we have the following:

- `<command>` is using the Windows firewall command.
- `<rules_id>` is selected as `87105` so that it will trigger when VirusTotal detects any malware sample. Wazuh rule `87105` defines the VirusTotal alert related to the sample file against the defined number of antivirus engines. To learn more, you can check the `0490-virustotal_rules.xml` Wazuh rule file under the **Management** tab of the Wazuh manager.

Testing

In order to test this use case, we will use a malware sample from `eicar.org`. You can download it using this URL: `https://www.eicar.org/download-anti-malware-testfile/`.

To make sure VirusTotal detects our testing malware sample, you need to save it in the document folder of a Windows 10/11 machine. Once you save the file, a file integrity check will be executed, and it will trigger VirusTotal to scan the sample. You can also find the corresponding alerts on the Wazuh dashboard.

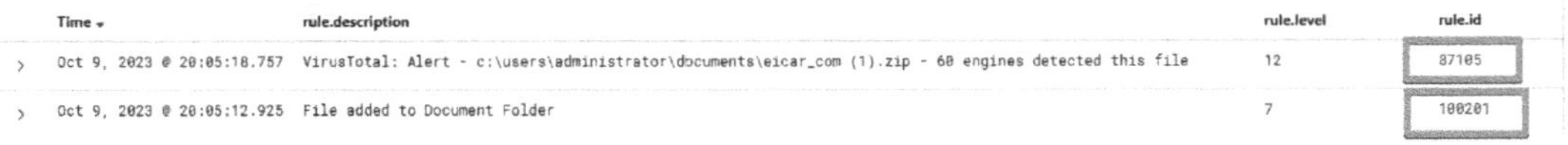

Time	rule.description	rule.level	rule.id
Oct 9, 2023 @ 20:05:18.757	VirusTotal: Alert - c:\users\administrator\documents\eicar_com (1).zip - 60 engines detected this file	12	87105
Oct 9, 2023 @ 20:05:12.925	File added to Document Folder	7	100201

Figure 5.10 – Visualizing VirusTotal alerts on the Wazuh manager

Let's take a closer look at the **File added to Document Folder** file integrity alert. You can see the `full.log` and rule description as follows.

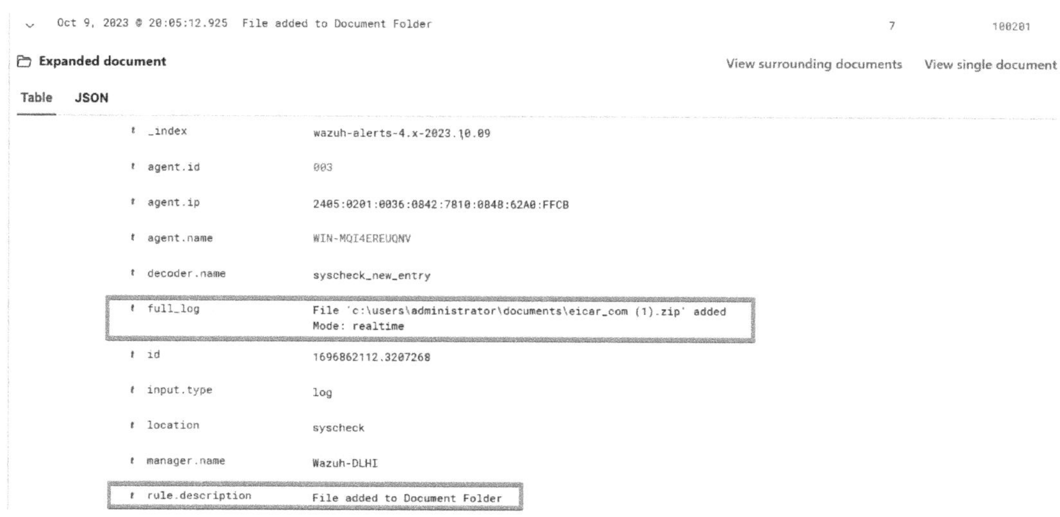

Figure 5.11 – Visualizing a Wazuh alert about the eicar.com(1) file

We can also check the second alert, **VirusTotal: Alert**. You can see the malware sample in the `data.virustotal.source.file` data field and rule ID `87105`.

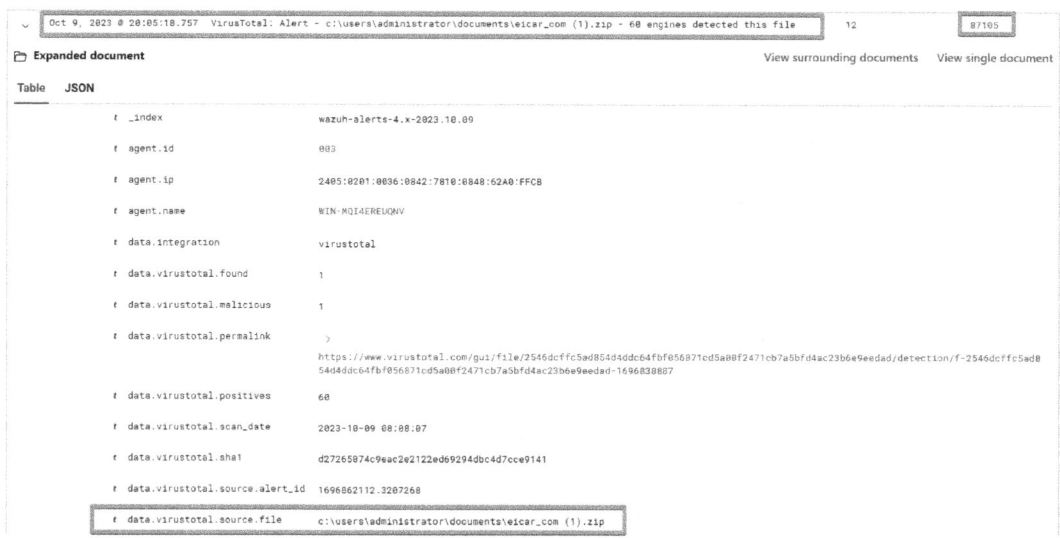

Figure 5.12 – Expanding a VirusTotal security alert on the Wazuh manager

Now, our <active-response> block will be executed as it is tied with rule ID 87105, which belongs to the VirusTotal alert, and our command, fw.cmd, will be executed on a Windows 10 machine. This fw.cmd active response script will trigger a PowerShell script and block all the outgoing traffic, as you can see in the following figure.

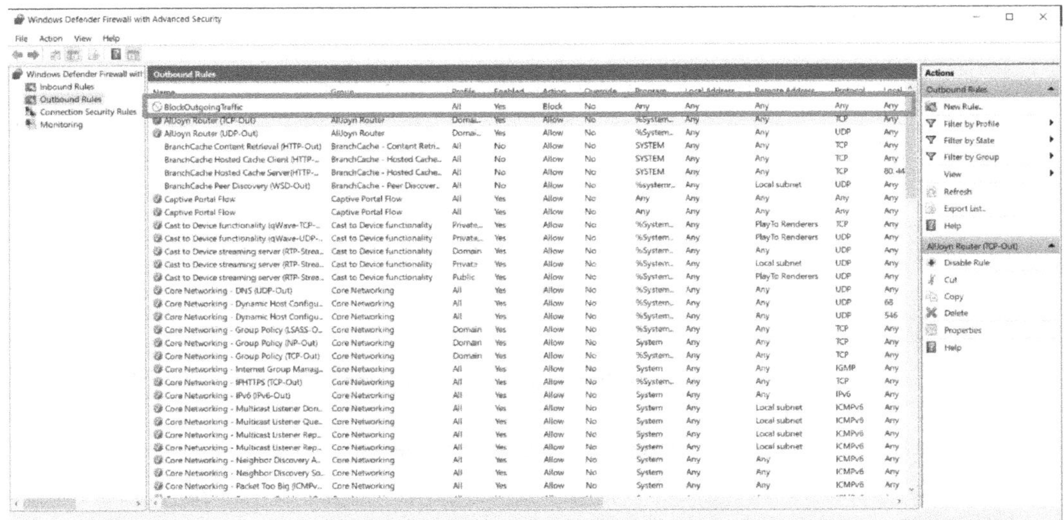

Figure 5.13 – Status of newly created BlockOutgoingTraffic rule on a Windows machine

So, we have successfully tested how Wazuh active response automatically blocks all outgoing traffic when our Windows machine is compromised by malware. This was possible by using our custom PowerShell script to create a security rule in the Windows Firewall service. In the next section, we will use active response to block RDP brute-force attack attempts.

Blocking RDP brute-force attacks

According to Sophos, in the first half of 2023, adversaries leveraged **Remote Desktop Protocol** (**RDP**) in 95% of attacks, increased by 88% from 2023. RDP is a Microsoft-developed proprietary protocol that allows users to connect to and remotely operate another computer or device via a network connection. Attackers employ automated software to try many login and password combinations in order to obtain unauthorized access to systems via RDP. Mitigating such risks involves proactive measures as well as quick action to block malicious IP addresses that try these assaults. In this section, we will utilize Wazuh active response to block the attacker's IP address against an RDP brute-force attack. We will cover the following points:

- Requirement
- Setting up a Windows agent with an active response script

- Setting up the Wazuh server with a rule and active response script
- Testing
- Visualization

Requirement

In this use case, we will use the default Wazuh active response script of a Windows machine called `netsh.exe`, located at `C:\Program Files (x86)\ossec-agent\active-response\bin`. We don't need to create any custom script for this. In order to make this entire use case work, we will use the following:

- Windows 10 or Windows Server
- Kali Linux for testing

Setting up a Windows agent with an active response script

In this step, we need to add the `netsh` command and the `netsh` active response block to the Wazuh agent's `C:\\Program Files (x86)\\ossec-agent\\ossec.conf` file:

```
<command>
    <name>netsh</name>
    <executable>netsh.exe</executable>
    <timeout_allowed>yes</timeout_allowed>
  </command>

<active-response>
    <disabled>no</disabled>
    <command>netsh</command>
    <location>local</location>
    <rules_id>100100</rules_id>
  </active-response>
```

Here, we have the following:

- `netsh.exe`: This is the network shell script located at `C:\Program Files (x86)\ossec-agent\active-response\bin`.
- `<rules_id>`: This indicates that the active response `netsh` script will be executed when rule `100100` is triggered. We will be creating rule `100100` to detect RDP brute-force attacks on the Wazuh server in the next step.

Save the `ossec.conf` file and restart the Wazuh agent.

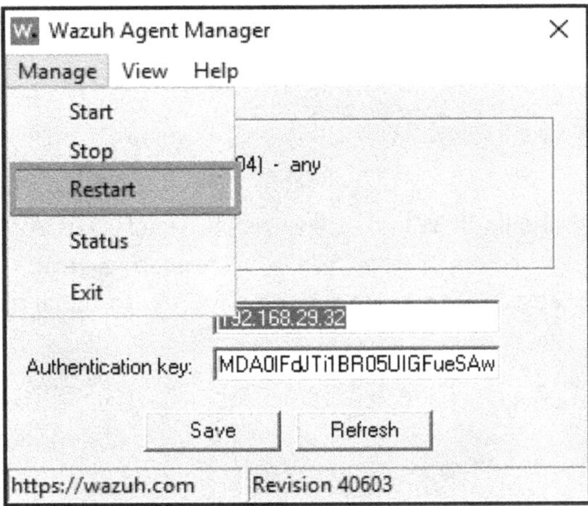

Figure 5.14 – Restart the Wazuh agent on the Windows Server

Setting up Wazuh Server with a brute-force attack rule and active response script

We want our Wazuh to execute the active response `netsh` script against a brute-force attack and hence, we will write a Wazuh rule to detect RDP login attempts with `level="10"`, `frequency="3"`, and `timeframe="120"`. This rule will be triggered when three failed login attempts are detected within 120 seconds of the timeframe. The following-mentioned rule block needs to be added to the `local_rules.xml` file located in the `/var/ossec/etc` directory:

```
<group name="rdp">
  <rule id="100100" level="10" frequency="3" timeframe="120">
    <if_matched_sid>60122</if_matched_sid>
    <description>Possible RDP attack: 3 failed logins in a short
period of time</description>
  </rule>
</group>
```

Here, we have the following:

- `<if_matched_sid>`: This option is similar to `<if_sid>` but it will only match if the rule ID has been triggered in a certain period of time. As we want Wazuh to detect the same alert three times within 120 seconds of the timeframe, this is specific to our needs.
- Rule ID `60122` under `<if_matched_sid>`: This rule is used to track multiple Windows event IDs related to login failure. To learn more about this rule and its parent ruleset, visit this page: `https://github.com/wazuh/wazuh-ruleset/blob/master/rules/0580-win-security_rules.xml`.

Next, add the same `netsh` command and active response block to the Wazuh server:

```
C:\\Program Files (x86)\\ossec-agent\\ossec.conf file
<command>
    <name>netsh</name>
    <executable>netsh.exe</executable>
    <timeout_allowed>yes</timeout_allowed>
  </command>

<active-response>
    <disabled>no</disabled>
    <command>netsh</command>
    <location>local</location>
    <rules_id>100100</rules_id>
  </active-response>
```

Save the `ossec.conf` file and restart the Wazuh manager:

```
systemctl restart wazuh-manager
```

Testing

To emulate this attack, we will launch an RDP brute-force attack using the hydra tool. The Hydra tool comes pre-built with Kali Linux; however, if you want to install it manually on some other platform, you can download it using this link: `https://github.com/vanhauser-thc/thc-hydra`. You can run the following command to execute an RDP brute-force attack on your Windows Server:

```
hydra -l roger -P pass.txt 192.168.29.77 rdp
```

Here, we have the following:

- `-l roger`: This parameter specifies the username `roger` that Hydra will use for the brute-force attack. Change `roger` to the username you want to target.
- `-P pass.txt`: Indicates the `pass.txt` password file, which contains a list of passwords. Hydra will repeatedly try each password for the chosen username by looping over this file. Put your password list's actual filename and directory in place of `pass.txt`.
- `192.168.29.77`: Represents the IP address of the target system where the RDP service is running. Replace this with the actual IP address you want to target.
- `rdp`: Indicates which service protocol to target, which is RDP in this instance. Hydra will make an effort to access the RDP service by logging in using the password list and the supplied username.

Visualizing the alerts

You can view the alerts on the Wazuh dashboard. Go to the **Security events** module and check for the latest alert or apply a filter for rule ID: `100100`. As you can see in the following screenshot, rule `100100` has been triggered from our Windows Server with IP address `192.168.29.77`.

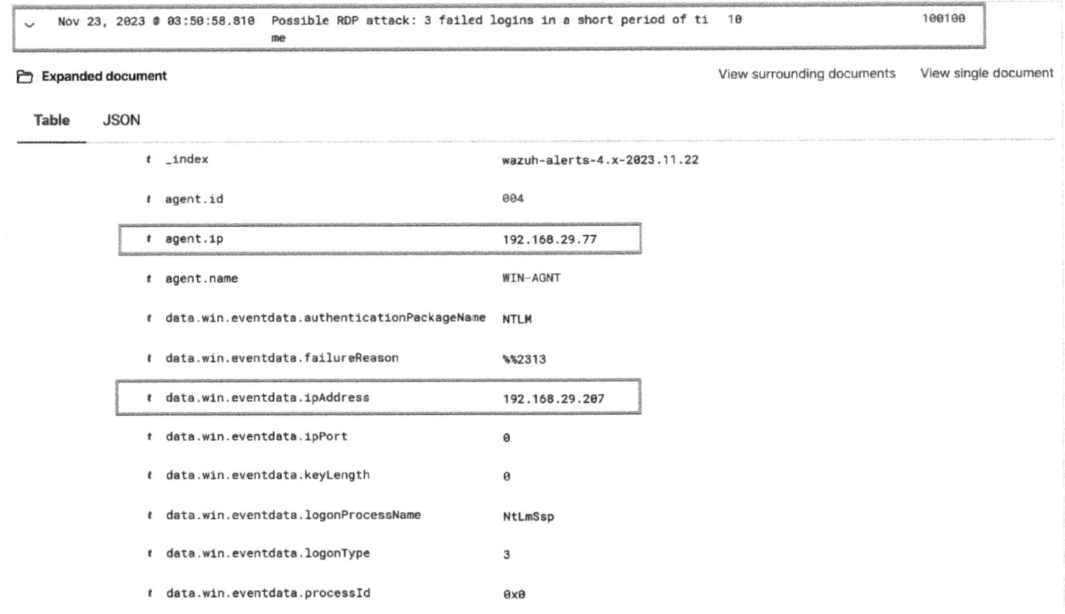

Figure 5.15 – Wazuh alert showing an RDP brute-force attack

Immediately, the Wazuh active response `Netsh` script is activated on the Windows Server.

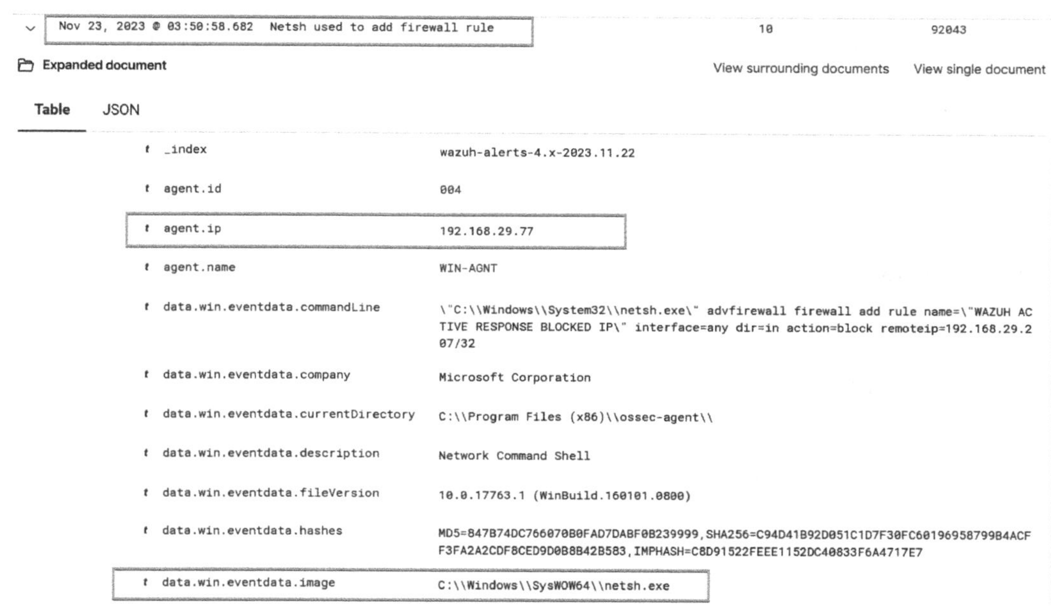

Figure 5.16 – Wazuh alert showing netsh active response

To test whether the attacker machine is blocked or not, you can try launching an RDP session using a Remote Desktop client; it should not work and should give an error, as shown.

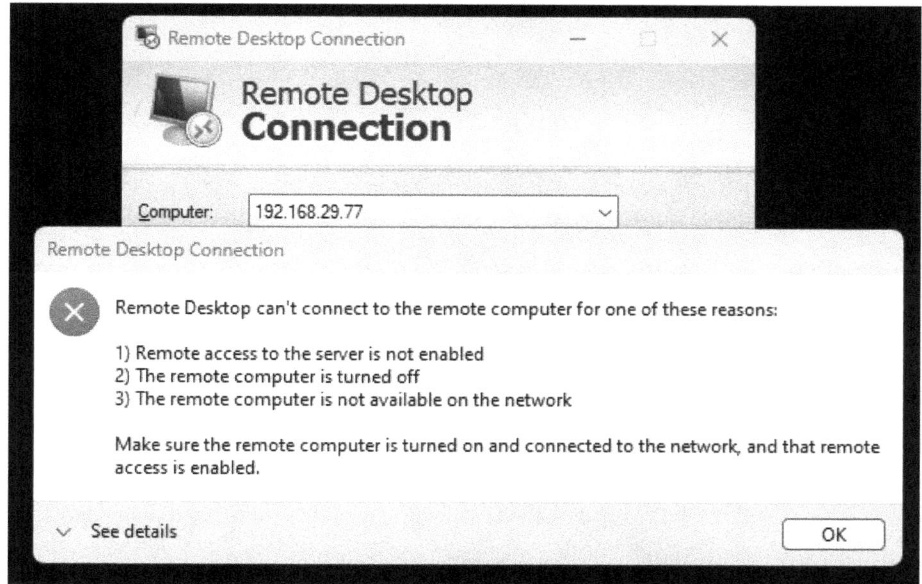

Figure 5.17 – Remote Desktop connection failed

With this, we have learned how to block RDP attack attempts using Wazuh's active response feature.

Summary

In this chapter, we learned about IR phases, Wazuh's active response capability, and some important use cases. We learned how Wazuh's active response module actively blocks unauthorized SSH and RDP access attempts. Additionally, we also learned about Wazuh's capability to isolate infected Windows machines promptly upon detection of malware.

In the next chapter, we will learn how to conduct threat hunting using Wazuh modules. We will learn the importance of log data analysis in Wazuh for better threat investigation and hunting. We will also utilize the MITRE ATT&CK framework to streamline our threat-hunting process.

6

Threat Hunting with Wazuh

Approximately 80% of threats can be mitigated with the assistance of tier 1 and 2 **security operations center** (**SOC**) analysts and automated security tools; the remaining 20% requires your attention. Threat hunting is an important proactive security method for finding threats and holes in security that are hard to spot with regular security measures. Threat hunting uses advanced analytics, threat intelligence, and human expertise to go beyond automated detection and actively seek, find, and fix any security holes or threats that might be hiding in an organization's network. By being proactive, security teams can spot and stop complex threats before they happen. This reduces the time that attackers can stay on the network and stops possible breaches. In this chapter, we will learn how Wazuh can help security teams to proactively detect advanced threats. Wazuh offers an extensive overview of an organization's security features by analyzing large amounts of logs, along with offering real-time monitoring, custom advanced rulesets, threat intelligence, MITRE ATT&CK mapping, and much more.

In this chapter, we will cover the following:

- Proactive threat hunting with Wazuh
- Log data analysis for threat hunting
- MITRE ATT&CK mapping on Wazuh
- Threat hunting using Osquery
- Command monitoring

Proactive threat hunting with Wazuh

Organizations can use Wazuh for proactive threat hunting, a security practice that helps them find and report possible security threats before they become significant threats. This can take the form, for example, of analyzing network traffic patterns to detect anomalous behavior that may indicate a potential cyber threat. By contrast, the main goal of reactive cybersecurity defenses is to react to threats once they are identified or after an incident has taken place. As an example, antivirus software detects and eradicates known malware, and firewalls prevent malicious traffic from entering the network based on predefined rules by the security team.

When you do proactive threat hunting, you look for possible risks or weaknesses in a network before any damage can be caused. Instead of waiting for alerts or known signatures, we can use Wazuh to conduct threat hunting by performing real-time log analysis across multiple platforms, correlating events to detect potential security issues, along with integrating third-party tools to enhance our event visibility and detection capabilities.

In this section, we will cover the following:

- Threat-hunting methodologies
- Threat-hunting steps
- How to use Wazuh for proactive threat hunting

Threat-hunting methodologies

When threat hunters look into a system, they assume that attackers are already there and look for strange behavior that could indicate that bad things are happening. While conducting proactive threat hunting, the first step of looking for a threat usually falls into three main categories:

- **Hypothesis-based investigation**: Threat hunters often start hypothesis-based investigations when they find a new threat within the pool of attack information. This gives them information about the newest **tactics, techniques, and procedures** (**TTPs**) that attackers are using. Once threat hunters have found a new TTP, they check whether the attacker's unique behaviors are common in their own area. For this, our Wazuh platform needs the following configured:
    - File integrity monitoring rules to detect any unauthorized changes
    - Enabling rootkits behavior detection
    - Log collection from different security solutions such as Antivirus, **Endpoint Detection and Response** (**EDR**), and email security
    - Vulnerability detection
    - Command monitoring

- **Intelligence-based hunting**: Intelligence-based hunting is a way to actively look for threats in response to different sources of intelligence. IOCs, IP addresses, hash values, and domain names are some of the threat intelligence sources that you can exploit. In order to accomplish this, Wazuh should be integrated with the following:

    - Third-party threat intelligence tools such as VirusTotal or AbuseIPDB
    - MISP
    - OpenCTI

  Host or network artifacts from **computer emergency response teams** (CERTs) or **information sharing and analysis centers** (ISACs) allow you to export automated warnings or communicate crucial information about fresh threats in other businesses. These are mostly paid services, but they do offer highly curated information.

- Investigation using **indicators of attack** (**IOA**): This is one of the most popular and widely used methods for threat hunting. The idea is simple: "Not every threat group is after you" or even if they are, why you should prioritize them. The first step is to identify the threat group based on its target location, industry, and software by using a free detection playbook called **ATT&CK Navigator**. This online platform is built by MITRE, a not-for-profit organization that operates **Federally Funded Research and Development Centers** (**FFRDCs**) in the United States.

Threat-hunting steps

A proactive threat-hunting method consists of three stages: the *initial trigger phase*, the *investigation phase*, and the *resolution phase* (or, in some situations, an escalation to other teams as part of a communications or action plan). Let's examine these three steps of the threat-hunting process in more detail:

1. **Choosing the right trigger**

    - Threat hunting is usually an in-depth effort. The threat hunter gathers data about the environment and formulates hypotheses on potential threats.
    - Next, the threat hunter selects a trigger for further investigation. This might be a specific system, an area of the network, a hypothesis brought on by a disclosed vulnerability or patch, knowledge of a zero-day exploit, an abnormality seen in the security dataset, or a request coming from another department within the company.

2. **Investigation**

    - After a trigger has been identified, the hunt continues to focus on proactively looking for anomalies that support or contradict the theoretical threat.
    - The threat hunter works with the assumption that "*My network is compromised by a new malware or exploit*" and conducts reverse engineering to prove the assumption.

- Threat hunters employ a variety of tools to help them analyze logs from multiple devices and security controls including server logs, Sysmon, antivirus logs, and spam filter logs.

3. **Resolution and reporting**

   During the investigative phase, threat hunters gather crucial information and provide answers to the following questions:

   - *Who?* – i.e., perhaps an insider threat was involved
   - *What?* – A timeline of incidents in chronological order
   - *Where?* – Details of the affected system including computers and servers
   - *Why?* – A lack of security controls, poor planning, human error, an external attack, and so on

   This information is circulated to other teams and tools during the resolution phase so that they may respond, prioritize, analyze, or retain the data for future use.

Proactive threat hunting with Wazuh

Proactive threat hunting with Wazuh entails an ongoing and methodical search for indicators of potential security threats in the environment of your organization. To conduct threat hunting, Wazuh can be leveraged by security teams for comprehensive log data analysis, seamless integration with MITRE ATT&CK, and the utilization of Osquery (an endpoint analytics tool) and regular monitoring. Let's cover each of these Wazuh capabilities in detail:

- **Log data analysis**: Threat detection is significantly more effective when log data generated by various devices and systems within an organization is analyzed. Wazuh functions as a centralized platform for log management and analysis, receiving and examining data from a wide range of origins, including endpoints, servers, and network devices. In order to conduct a log analysis of each of the devices in your network, you need to have decoders for each of them. Wazuh extracts meaningful information from log data obtained from various sources using decoders.
- **MITRE ATT&CK mapping**: The internationally acclaimed MITRE **Adversarial Tactics, Techniques, and Common Knowledge** (**ATT&CK**) framework offers a thorough, current knowledge base on adversary tactics and techniques. Wazuh uses MITRE ATT&CK to map observed security events to certain ATT&CK approaches, improving threat-hunting capabilities. Security teams can gain a better understanding of prospective adversaries' strategies by using this mapping.
- **Osquery integration**: An open-source, cross-platform endpoint security framework called Osquery enables organizations to communicate with and query their endpoint devices to obtain important data for threat hunting. Wazuh and Osquery combine to give an organization's endpoints a comprehensive picture with endpoint visibility and live querying.

- **Command monitoring**: You can use Wazuh's command tracking feature to track the output of certain commands and treat that output as log content. Command monitoring can be used for threat hunting to monitor many system properties, such as disk space usage, load averages, changes in network listeners, and the state of processes that are already running.

Let's get some deeper and more practical knowledge of Wazuh's log data analysis functionality. This capability of Wazuh helps us to perform manual threat hunting by analyzing tons of log information.

Log data analysis for threat hunting

Log data analysis is a critical component of threat hunting. It involves inspecting and retrieving useful information from log files generated by various systems, applications, and devices. Traditional security methods may miss suspicious patterns or events, but threat hunters can detect them through constant monitoring and analysis of logs. Threat hunters examine log data in search of certain **Indicators of Compromise** (**IOCs**). These IOCs could be domain names, IP addresses, file hashes, or other identifiers linked to known security risks. The problem is that not all logs are the same. Depending on the source of the logs you want to gather, you may need to create a tailored Wazuh decoder. In this section, we will review the following:

- Wazuh decoders
- Building decoders
- Log collection
- Log data analysis

Wazuh decoders

A **Wazuh decoder** is a component that interprets and extracts useful information from raw log data. It collects data from log files or events created by many sources, such as operating systems, applications, and network devices, and converts it into a standardized format that can easily be analyzed and related. We don't have to create decoders every time we onboard a new endpoint as Wazuh has a selection of prebuilt decoders for sources such as Linux, Windows, and macOS.

Wazuh decoders are normally provided as XML files and stored at `/var/ossec/etc/decoders`. Each decoder is tailored to a certain log source such as `0025-apache_decoders.xml` for Apache, `0100-fortigate_decoders.xml` for FortiGate firewalls, and so on. These decoders specify how to parse log data, extract pertinent information (such as timestamps, IP addresses, user IDs, and so on), and transform it into a structured format suitable for security analysis and threat hunting. Wazuh decoders are extremely customizable, allowing users to create custom decoders for specific log sources as needed.

Building decoders

Creating a custom Wazuh decoder begins with the creation of an XML file that explains how to decode and parse log data from a given source. If you want to build a custom decoder, you need to first take a look at an example event from the source. For example, let's take a Check Point Firewall log from the decoder file available on GitHub at `https://github.com/wazuh/wazuh-ruleset/blob/master/decoders/0050-checkpoint_decoders.xml`:

```
Jan 21 15:15:45 myCP Checkpoint: 21Jan2019 15:15:45 monitor 10.0.10.1
<bond0 Protection Name:Header Rejection;Severity:4;Confidence
Level:4;protection_id:HttpHeaderRejection;SmartDefense Profile:SU2_
Protection;Performance Impact:2;Industry Reference:CVE-2002-0032,
CAN-2003-0237, CAN-2002-0254, CVE-2002-0155, CAN-2003-0397,
CAN-2002-0314;Protection Type:protection;Signature Info:^User-
Agent[^I ]*:[^I ]*.*esb|ESB;Update Version:634182243;rule:26;rule_
uid:{405CB782-3274-4D7F-8AAA-4FB24CE726A0};resource:<http://
dnl-02.geo.kaspersky.com/bases/av/kdb/i386/kdb-i386-1211g.xml.
klz;reject_id:5accf7c4-10053-c00080a-c0000003;web_client_type:Other:>
*BcfBAAAAgCCAAEFBAAwQfKXVzrzGvyfPESboPxow0mHhxRLAXAQAAIAAKAA=;Attack
Info:WSE0100001 header rejection
pattern found in request;attack:Header
Rejection;src:10.20.10.1;dst:1.1.1.1;proto:6;proxy_
src_ip:10.10.10.1;product:SmartDefense;service:80;s_
port:51642;FollowUp:Not Followed;product_family:Network
```

Once you have the log, pay close attention to its format. Divide your log into two parts: *prematch* and *custom match*. **Prematch** consists of the date, time, and device name. In our example, it will be `Jan 21 15:15:45 myCP Checkpoint: 21Jan2019 15:15:45`. Second, the **custom match** section varies every time. We can also call these the *parent decoder* and *child decoder* respectively. Let's begin by writing the prematch decoder first.

Parent decoder

When creating a Wazuh decoder, it is a good practice to create a parent decoder and then a child decoder to simplify and organize the decoder rules in a file. The parent decoder usually consists of the date, time, and device name, and the child decoder consists of a specific pattern match. To extract the relevant information from the logs, we need to use a regular expression. A regular expression is a sequence of characters defining a search. The parent decoder is defined using the following `<prematch>` tags:

```
<decoder name="checkpoint-syslog">
  <program_name>^Checkpoint</program_name>
  <prematch>^\\s*\\S+ \\d\\d:\\d\\d:\\d\\d </prematch>
</decoder>
```

In the preceding regular expression, we can see the following:

- The `\d` operator is used to denote numeric characters from 0 to 9 for the time field.
- The `\s` operator is used to represent alphabetical characters from `a` to `z`.

Child decoder

The following decoder rule already exists in the Wazuh decoder ruleset with the filename `0050-checkpoint_decoders.xml`. To extract further information from the Check Point firewall log, multiple decoder rules have to be created. These are used to extract items such as the source IP address, destination IP address, source port, destination port, and service. All the rules must start with the parent decoder "`checkpoint-syslog`":

```
<decoder name="checkpoint-syslog-fw">
  <parent>checkpoint-syslog</parent>
  <type>firewall</type>
  <prematch offset="after_parent">^drop|^accept|^reject</prematch>
  <regex offset="after_parent">^(\\w+)\\s+\\S+ \\p\\S+ rule:\\.+</
regex>
  <regex>src: (\\S+); dst: (\\S+); proto: (\\S+);</regex>
  <order>action,srcip,dstip,protocol</order>
</decoder>

<decoder name="checkpoint-syslog-fw">
  <parent>checkpoint-syslog</parent>
  <type>firewall</type>
  <regex offset="after_regex">service: (\\d+); s_port: (\\d+);</regex>
  <order>dstport,srcport</order>
</decoder>

<decoder name="checkpoint-syslog-ids">
  <parent>checkpoint-syslog</parent>
  <type>ids</type>
  <prematch offset="after_parent">^monitor|^drop</prematch>
  <regex offset="after_prematch">attack:\\s*(\\.+);\\s*</regex>
  <regex>src:\\s*(\\S+);\\s*dst:\\s*(\\S+);\\s*</regex>
  <regex>proto:\\s*(\\S+);</regex>
  <order>extra_data, srcip, dstip, protocol</order>
  <fts>name, extra_data, srcip, dstip</fts>
  <ftscomment>First time Checkpoint rule fired.</ftscomment>
</decoder>
```

While you are building your decoder, you can get help from the Wazuh built-in decoder validator module by running `/var/ossec/bin/wazuh-logtest`. You can also perform this test on the Wazuh dashboard by navigating to **Ruleset Test** under the **Tools** section. Once you execute the module, you need to enter your original Check Point log:

```
root@Wazuh-DLHI:~# /var/ossec/bin/wazuh-logtest
Starting wazuh-logtest v4.5.2
Type one log per line

Jan 21 15:15:45 myCP Checkpoint: 21Jan2019 15:15:45 monitor 10.0.10.1  <bond0 Protection Name:Header Rejectio
n;Severity:4;Confidence Level:4;protection_id:HttpHeaderRejection;SmartDefense Profile:SU2_Protection;Perform
ance Impact:2;Industry Reference:CVE-2002-0032, CAN-2003-0237, CAN-2002-0254, CVE-2002-0155, CAN-2003-0397, C
AN-2002-0314;Protection Type:protection;Signature Info:^User-Agent[^I ]*:[^I ]*.*esb|ESB;Update Version:63418
2243;rule:26;rule_uid:{405CB782-3274-4D7F-8AAA-4FB24CE726A0};resource:http://dnl-02.geo.kaspersky.com/bases/a
v/kdb/i386/kdb-i386-1211g.xml.klz;reject_id:5accf7c4-10053-c00080a-c0000003;web_client_type:Other: *BcfBAAAAg
CCAAEFBAAwQfKXVzrzGvyfPESboPxow0mHhxRLAXAQAAIAAKAA=;Attack Info:WSE0100001 header rejection pattern found in
request;attack:Header Rejection;src:10.20.10.1;dst:1.1.1.1;proto:6;proxy_src_ip:10.10.10.1;product:SmartDefen
se;service:80;s_port:51642;FollowUp:Not Followed;product_family:Network

** Wazuh-Logtest: WARNING: (7612): Rule ID '100001' is duplicated. Only the first occurrence will be consider
ed.

**Phase 1: Completed pre-decoding.
        full event: 'Jan 21 15:15:45 myCP Checkpoint: 21Jan2019 15:15:45 monitor 10.0.10.1  <bond0 Protection
 Name:Header Rejection;Severity:4;Confidence Level:4;protection_id:HttpHeaderRejection;SmartDefense Profile:S
U2_Protection;Performance Impact:2;Industry Reference:CVE-2002-0032, CAN-2003-0237, CAN-2002-0254, CVE-2002-0
155, CAN-2003-0397, CAN-2002-0314;Protection Type:protection;Signature Info:^User-Agent[^I ]*:[^I ]*.*esb|ESB
;Update Version:634182243;rule:26;rule_uid:{405CB782-3274-4D7F-8AAA-4FB24CE726A0};resource:http://dnl-02.geo.
kaspersky.com/bases/av/kdb/i386/kdb-i386-1211g.xml.klz;reject_id:5accf7c4-10053-c00080a-c0000003;web_client_t
ype:Other: *BcfBAAAAgCCAAEFBAAwQfKXVzrzGvyfPESboPxow0mHhxRLAXAQAAIAAKAA=;Attack Info:WSE0100001 header reject
ion pattern found in request;attack:Header Rejection;src:10.20.10.1;dst:1.1.1.1;proto:6;proxy_src_ip:10.10.10
.1;product:SmartDefense;service:80;s_port:51642;FollowUp:Not Followed;product_family:Network'
        timestamp: 'Jan 21 15:15:45'
        hostname: 'myCP'
        program_name: 'Checkpoint'

**Phase 2: Completed decoding.
        name: 'checkpoint-syslog'
        parent: 'checkpoint-syslog'
        ftscomment: 'First time Checkpoint rule fired.'
        dstip: '1.1.1.1'
        extra_data: 'Header Rejection'
        protocol: '6'
        srcip: '10.20.10.1'

**Phase 3: Completed filtering (rules).
        id: '20100'
        level: '8'
        description: 'First time this IDS alert is generated.'
        groups: '['ids', 'fts']'
        firedtimes: '1'
        mail: 'False'
**Alert to be generated.
```

Figure 6.1 – Executing Wazuh's decoder validator

In the preceding screenshot, we can see the following:

- The phase 1 output shows the pre-decoding, which simply takes the log and processes it
- The phase 2 and phase 3 output shows that the decoder name `checkpoint-syslog-ids` has been detected properly and we receive information such as `srcip`, `dstip`, protocol, and `extra_data`

After creating both the parent and child decoders, we need to create a Wazuh rule to trigger an alert once there is a match.

Creating Wazuh rules

Wazuh rules examine the extracted decoder fields to determine the type of message received. The final rule that is matched determines whether an alert is created, as well as its level and category groups. For any event that triggers the Check Point FW decoders, the following grouping rule will issue an alert:

```
<group name="checkpoint-syslog,">

  <!--Generic rule -->
  <rule "d="64"00" lev"l""3">
    <decoded_as>checkpoint-syslog</decoded_as>
    <description>Checkpoint $(type) event</description>
  </rule>
```

In the preceding code, `<decoded_as>` represents the name of the decoder.

Alright, we have learned to create a decoder and the corresponding Wazuh rule, taking a Check Point firewall log as an example. Once you have a decoder, you can then create a Wazuh rule. If there is a match against any of the events received by the Wazuh manager, it will generate a security alert on the dashboard. To conduct a comprehensive threat-hunting program, all types of events have to be available on the Wazuh platform and hence, building a custom decoder should also be part of this process. In the next section, we will learn how Wazuh collects and categorizes different types of log data.

Log data collection

Log data collection means getting logs from different network sources and putting them all together. It is critical for threat hunters to access all types of logs from across endpoints, servers, security devices, and so on. The Wazuh indexer is responsible for log analysis as it stores and indexes alerts generated by the Wazuh server. By default, Wazuh will give you alerts that are triggered by Wazuh rules. However, we need access to all the events for better threat-hunting practice. We will learn to pull out all the events and archive them on the Wazuh server. Let's first discuss the different indices used to store our event types.

wazuh-alerts

This is the default index that stores the alerts generated by the Wazuh server. When normal events get triggered by a rule with high priority, we see the alert and it gets stored in the `wazuh-alerts` index.

All the information in the **Security Event** tab comes from the `wazuh-alerts` index. To see the `wazuh-alerts` index, navigate to the **Discover** tab under **OpenSearch Dashboards**. By default, the `wazuh-alerts` index will be selected.

Figure 6.2 – wazuh-alerts index

wazuh-archives

This index keeps track of all events that come in from the Wazuh server, even if they don't set off alerts. The `wazuh-archives` index stores logs and allows queries that give more information about what's happening on monitored endpoints. `wazuh-archives` is disabled by default to save space on the Wazuh server. Remember, to run an effective threat-hunting program, it is crucial to enable this index. Please follow these steps to turn it on, and once it is configured, two new files will be created to store all the events, `/var/ossec/logs/archives/archives.log` and `/var/ossec/logs/archives/archives.log`:

1. **Edit the Wazuh manager config file**: In the `/var/ossec/etc/ossec.conf` file, set the value of `<logall>` and `<logall_json>` to `yes`:

   ```
   <ossec_config>
     <global>
       <jsonout_output>yes</jsonout_output>
       <alerts_log>yes</alerts_log>
       <logall>yes</logall>
       <logall_json>yes</logall_json>
   </ossec_config>
   ```

2. **Restart the Wazuh manager**: In order for the Wazuh manager to put into effect your changes, you are required to restart it with the following command:

   ```
   systemctl restart wazuh-manager
   ```

3. **Enable visualization**

   To enable visualization on the Wazuh dashboard, you need to enable the archiving feature on the `filebeat` service by editing `/etc/filebeat/filebeat.yml` and changing `archives:` value to `true`.

   Next, restart the `filebeat` service as follows:

   ```
   systemctl restart filebeat
   ```

4. **Discover events**: To discover all the events from the `wazuh-archives` index, go to **Stack management** > **index patterns** and click on **Create index pattern**.

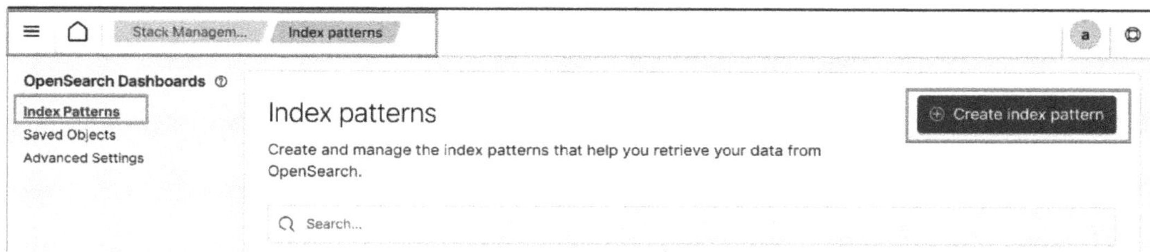

Figure 6.3 – Create index pattern

5. **Define an index pattern**: Next, define the `wazuh-archives-*` index pattern to match all available indices, as shown in the following screenshot, and click on **Next step**.

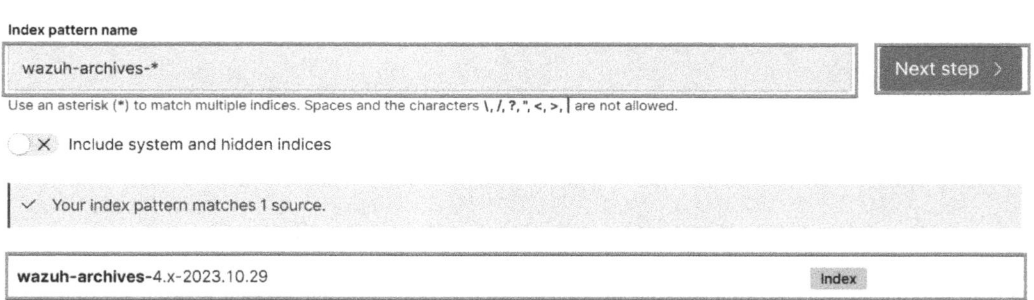

Figure 6.4 – Define index pattern

6. **Set the timestamp**: Next, set the `timestamp` in the **Time field** box.

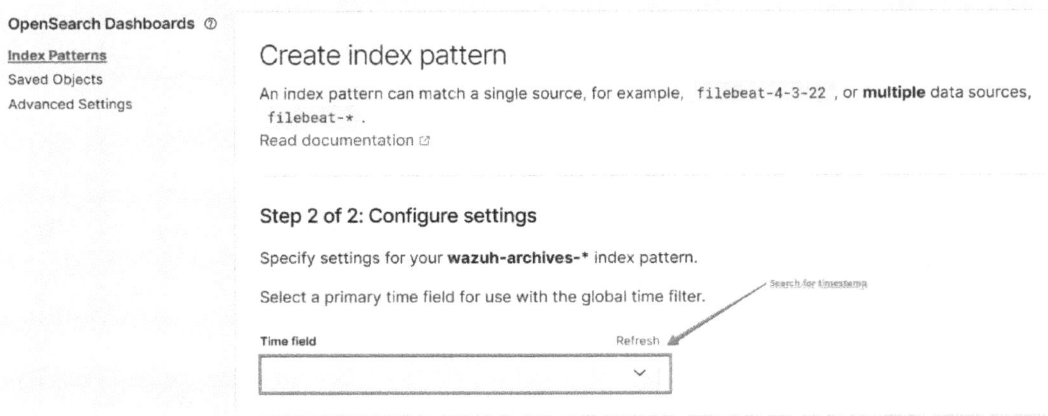

Figure 6.5 – Set primary time field

7. **View the dashboard**: Now, to view the events on the dashboard, navigate to **Discover** under **OpenSearch Dashboards**.

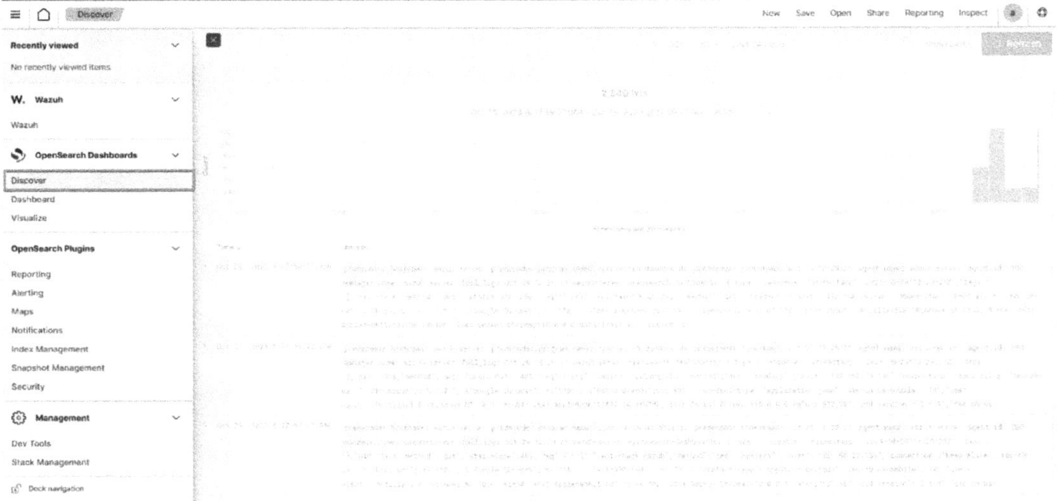

Figure 6.6 – Discover under the OpenSearch Dashboards menu

Make sure you select the **wazuh-archives** index and finally, we get all the events.

Figure 6.7 – Select wazuh-archives

wazuh-monitoring

This index keeps track of information about the state of Wazuh agents over time. The Wazuh agent's state could be *Pending*, *Active*, *Disconnected*, or *Never Connected*. This information is very helpful for finding Wazuh agents that aren't reporting to the dashboard for a number of reasons that need to be looked into. If you want to see all the events from the `wazuh-monitoring` index, navigate to **Discover** and then change the index to **wazuh-monitoring**.

Figure 6.8 – Select wazuh-monitoring

Everything you see under the **Agents** tab comes from the wazuh-monitoring index.

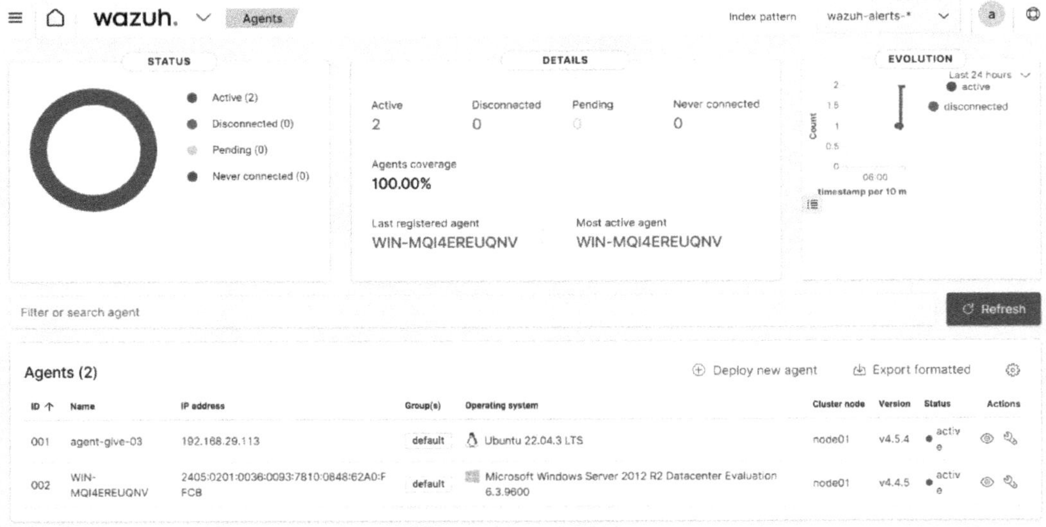

Figure 6.9 – Wazuh Agents tab

wazuh-statistics

This index holds information about the Wazuh server's overall performance. This information is very important for making sure that the Wazuh server uses its computing resources in the best way possible.

Log data analysis

Log data analysis is a critical component of threat hunting because it gives you a lot of information about the activities of systems, and networks. This information helps you find security threats early, spot unusual activity and also helps you find IOCs. Also note that log collection and log analysis are also important in incident response, forensic investigations, security compliance, and many more areas. Let's do some live testing with our `wazuh-archives` log events. We will run some notable MITRE ATT&CK techniques on Windows Server 2012 Server using APT Simulator and then we will conduct some log data analysis. Let's get started:

> **Prerequisites**
>
> You will need Windows Server 2012 or higher.

1. **Sysmon installation**: In this first step, we need to install Sysmon and integrate it with Wazuh. Please refer to *Chapter 2, Malware Detection Using Wazuh*, the *Integrating Sysmon to detect fileless malware* section in particular, as it covers the step-by-step process to install Sysmon on Windows machines.

2. **Installing and executing the APT Simulator**: APT Simulator is an interesting project built by Nextron Systems. To know more about APT Simulator, please refer to *Chapter 2, Malware Detection Using Wazuh*, the *Integrating Sysmon to detect fileless malware* section. Once you download this script to your Windows Server instance, open the Command Prompt, go to the `APTSimulator-0.9.4` folder, and execute the `APTSimulator.bat` file.

   Type `0`. This will run every test including collection, command and control, credential access, defense evasion, discovery, execution, lateral movement, persistence, and privilege escalation.

3. **Testing**: Now, let's log in to Wazuh and navigate to **Discover** under **OpenSearch Dashboards**. Then, filter the results to `agent.id`. In my case, `agent.id` is `002`.

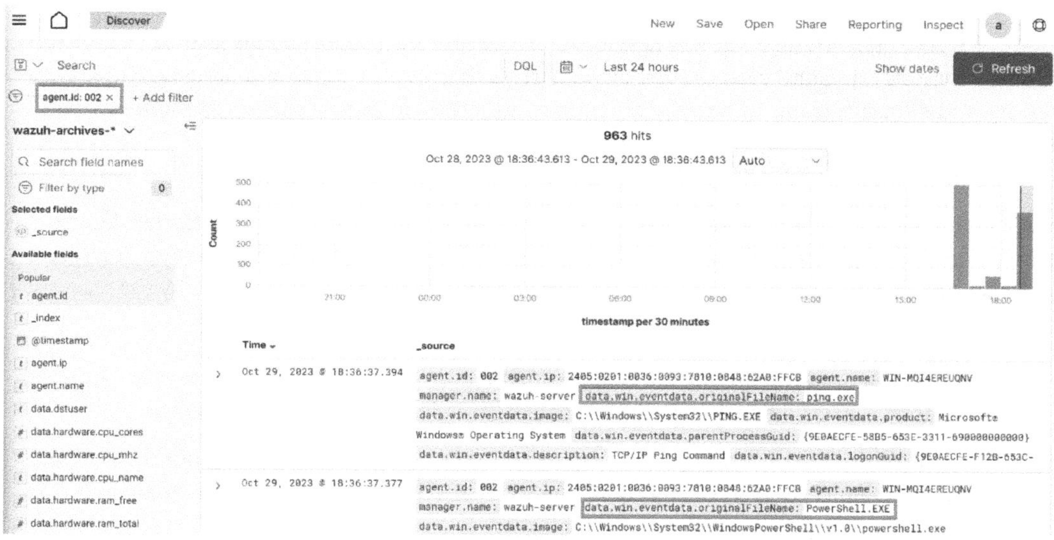

Figure 6.10 – Visualizing APT alerts

We have learned to create custom decoders, covered the different Wazuh log data indices, and analyzed the log data. In the next section, we will explore the MITRE ATT&CK framework and how Wazuh maps the MITRE ATT&CK tactics and techniques.

MITRE ATT&CK mapping

We cannot begin threat hunting by assuming everyone in the world is after us. We need a targeted threat actor or threat campaign-based approach. This is where both Wazuh and MITRE ATT&CK become helpful. Wazuh can collect and trigger any alerts, but for threat hunting, we need to focus on relevant and high-priority threats to our business and need to map this to our Wazuh rules. The MITRE ATT&CK framework helps threat hunters to focus on these kinds of threats and Wazuh allows us to map each of the techniques of those threat actors to Wazuh rules. As a result, threat hunters can hone their focus and save tremendous amounts of time. In this section, we will cover the following topics:

- What is MITRE ATT&CK?
- The ATT&CK framework
- Prioritizing the adversary's techniques
- MITRE ATT&CK mapping

What is MITRE ATT&CK?

The **MITRE ATT&CK** framework was developed by the MITRE Corporation to provide a uniform taxonomy for analyzing and categorizing cyber threats. It provides a common language that both defensive and offensive teams in security operations can utilize to improve their capabilities.

Tactics, techniques, and procedures (TTPs)

The **MITRE ATT&CK framework** is used to categorize and comprehend cyber attackers' **tactics, methods, and procedures** (**TTPs**) during security operations. TTPs are used for organizing threat intelligence, threat detection, building an effective incident response, conducting a security gap analysis, and threat hunting. Let's first understand what the TTP concept involves:

- **Tactics**: These are the main modes of action that attackers use to reach their targets. Consider tactics as the "*what*" of an attack, such as gaining initial access or causing damage.
- **Techniques**: Techniques are precise ways or acts that attackers use to carry out their tactics. They are the "*how*" of an attack, outlining the processes or tools utilized to achieve an objective.
- **Procedures**: Procedures involve greater levels of specificity and detail in comparison to techniques. Procedures are like "*step-by-step instructions*" for carrying out an attack.

ATT&CK framework

MITRE ATT&CK is made up of several critical components that work together to provide a thorough understanding of adversary TTPs:

- Matrices
- Tactics
- Techniques
- Procedures
- Groups
- Software

Matrices

The ATT&CK framework has three matrices: *Enterprise*, *Mobile*, and *Cloud*. The Enterprise Matrix is the most widely used matrix in the ATT&CK framework. Let's understand some of the technologies covered under each of these matrices as follows:

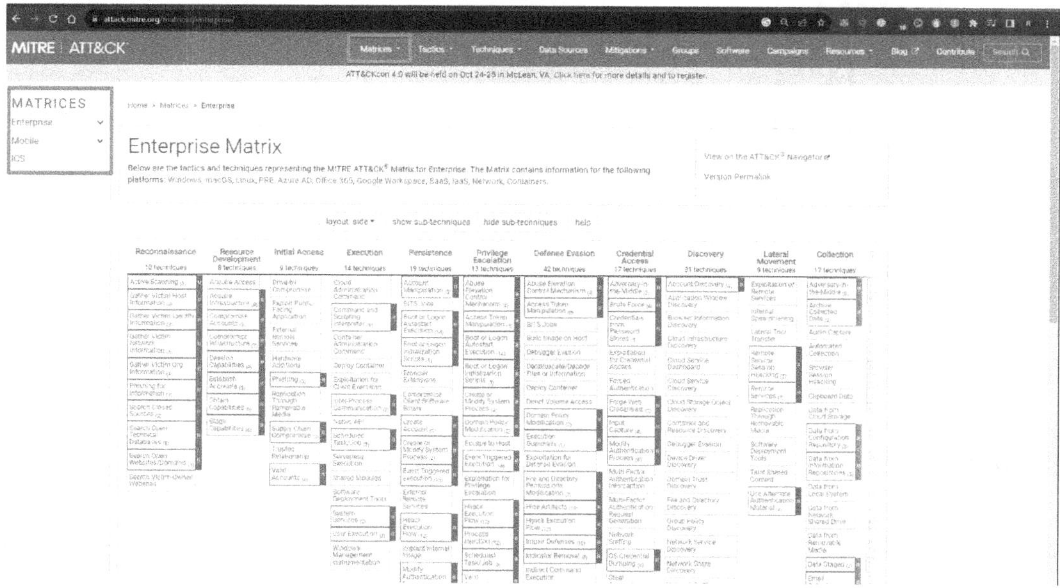

Figure 6.11 – MITRE ATT&CK matrices

- The Enterprise Matrix contains information about platforms such as Windows, macOS, Azure, Office 365, SaaS, IaaS, network, and cloud
- The Mobile Matrix covers techniques used by adversaries related to Android or iOS
- ICS covers industrial control system-related tactics and techniques

Throughout this chapter, our primary focus will be on the Enterprise Matrix.

Tactics

MITRE ATT&CK provides 14 **tactics** that consist of several sets of techniques. In the following screenshot, you can see at the top of each column all of the tactics, and under each tactic column, you can find several techniques.

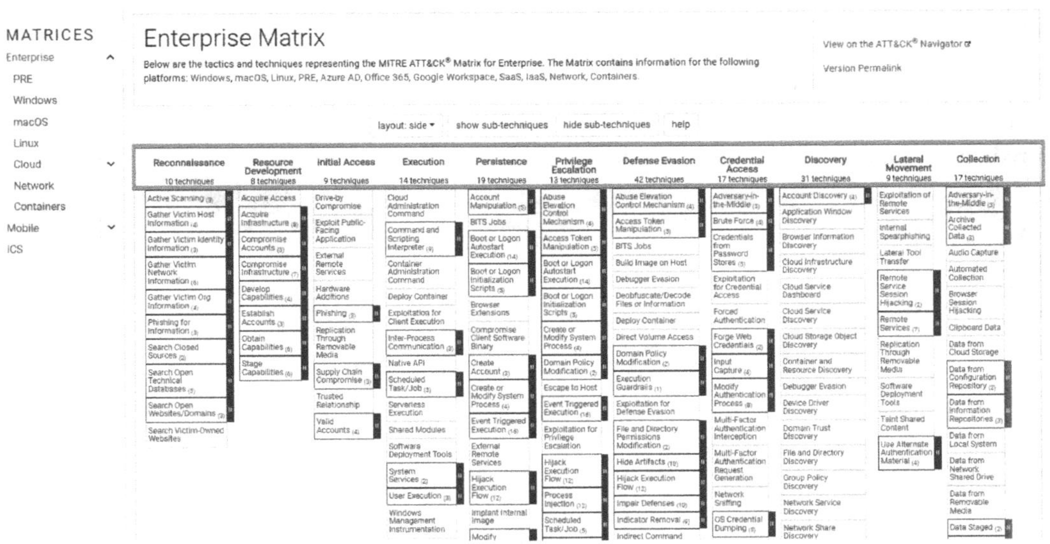

Figure 6.12 – MITRE ATT&CK Tactics

Techniques

Techniques are specific means or procedures used by opponents to carry out tactics. For example, under the *Execution tactic*, you might find techniques such as *Command-Line Interface* or *Scripting*. Visit `attack.mitre.org` and click on any technique to display a list of sub-techniques. As an example, I selected the **Reconnaissance** tactic, then under that I clicked on the **Gather Victim Network Information** technique, and as a result, I got six sub-techniques: **Domain Properties**, **DNS**, **Network Trust Dependencies**, **Network Topology**, **IP Addresses**, and **Network Security Appliances** as shown in the following screenshot.

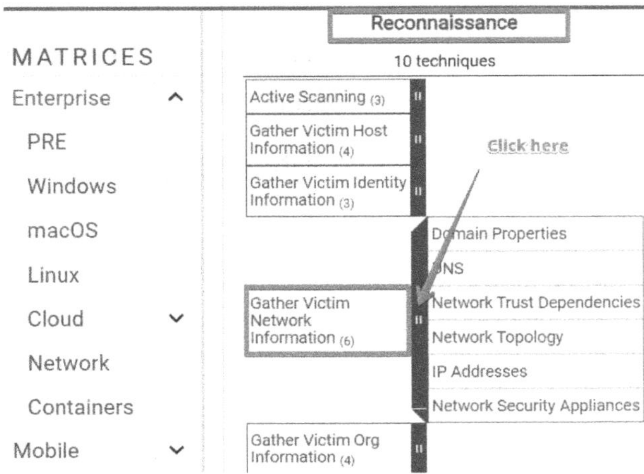

Figure 6.13 – MITRE ATT&CK techniques

Procedures

Procedures describe step by step and in detail how adversaries perform various techniques. In our preceding example, we got six sub-techniques. Click on any of those sub-techniques and you will land on a page with a list of example procedures.

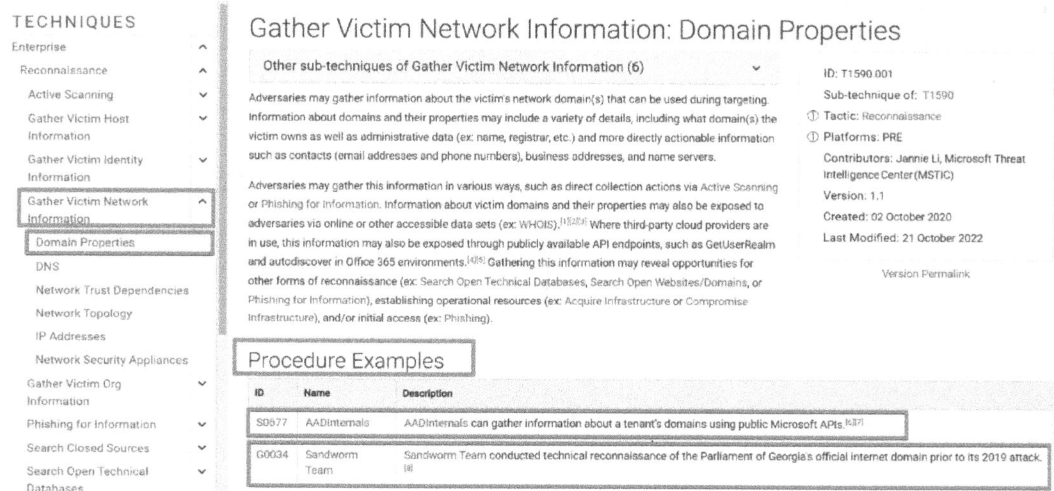

Figure 6.14 – MITRE ATT&CK procedures

Groups

Groups are sets of threat actors or cybercriminal organizations that are known to use specific TTPs. You can refer to a list of all threat actors documented by MITRE ATT&CK at `https://attack.mitre.org/groups/`.

Software

Software lists the exact pieces of malware, tools, and software that attackers use to carry out their objectives. This helps threat hunters to identify the threat group based on the tools they use.

Prioritizing the adversary's techniques

ATT&CK Navigator is a powerful analytical tool developed by MITRE as a part of the MITRE ATT&CK framework. It provides a web-based interactive interface, helping threat hunters and security professionals to explore, visualize, and prioritize techniques used by threat actors. ATT&CK Navigator also helps in aligning security controls against known adversary techniques. You can access the tool at `https://mitre-attack.github.io/attack-navigator/`:

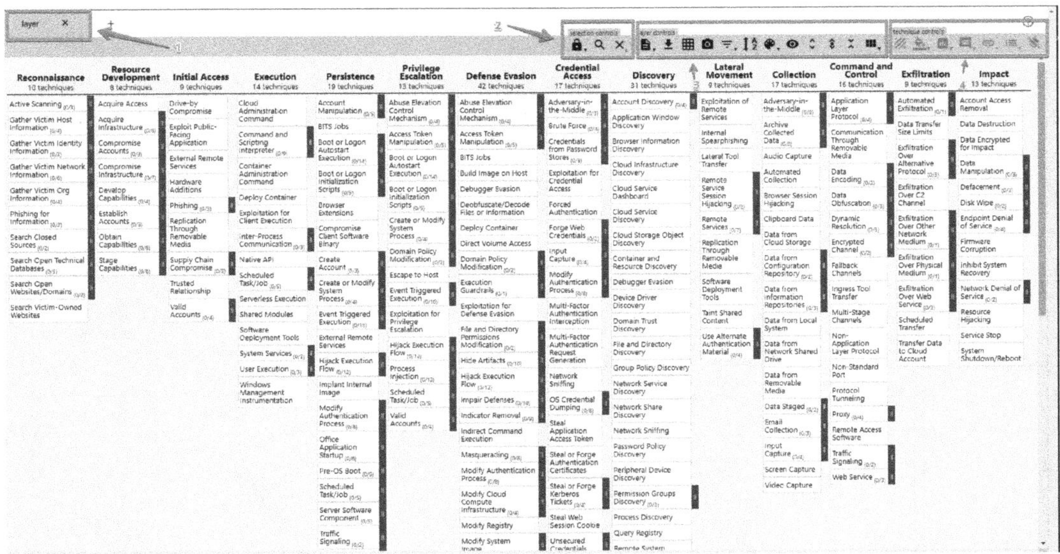

Figure 6.15 – ATT&CK Navigator

The numbers in the preceding screenshot refer to the following:

- **1** is **layer**, used to create multiple ATT&CK framework layers.
- **2** is **section controls**, which gives the following options:
    - Selection behavior
    - A search button for selecting techniques, threat groups, software, campaigns, data sources, and more
    - The option to deselect all techniques
- **3** is **layer controls**, which have the following options:
    - The option to add metadata information to each layer, including a name, description, and other custom metadata
    - Download the layer in JSON format
    - Export the layer in XML format
    - Download the layer in SVG format
    - A filter option to display techniques based on Linux, macOS, Windows, containers, and so on
    - Sorting the techniques based on AI
    - Color setup: You can choose a specific color for certain tactics on the interface

- **4** is **technique controls**, which is useful to mark specific techniques with a color and score. We will use this feature when we combine multiple layers to identify overlapping techniques of multiple threat actors.

Practical use case using MITRE ATT&CK

Let me take you through a practical use case to perform threat hunting using MITRE ATT&CK. Imagine yourself as a threat hunter working for a financial services organization based in the United States. After doing some research on the **Groups** page (`https://attack.mitre.org/groups/`) of the MITRE ATT&CK official website, you settled on two relevant threat actors that target financial services organizations based in the United States. These are APT19 and APT38. (Remember, this is only an example – I suggest you do your research based on your specific industry, software, target countries, and so on.) To discover the priority techniques, we need to find common techniques used by both APT19 and APT38. To do this, we need to customize the ATT&CK Navigator layers as explained in the following steps:

1. Open ATT&CK Navigator, click **Create New Layer**, and then select **Enterprise** as shown in the following screenshot.

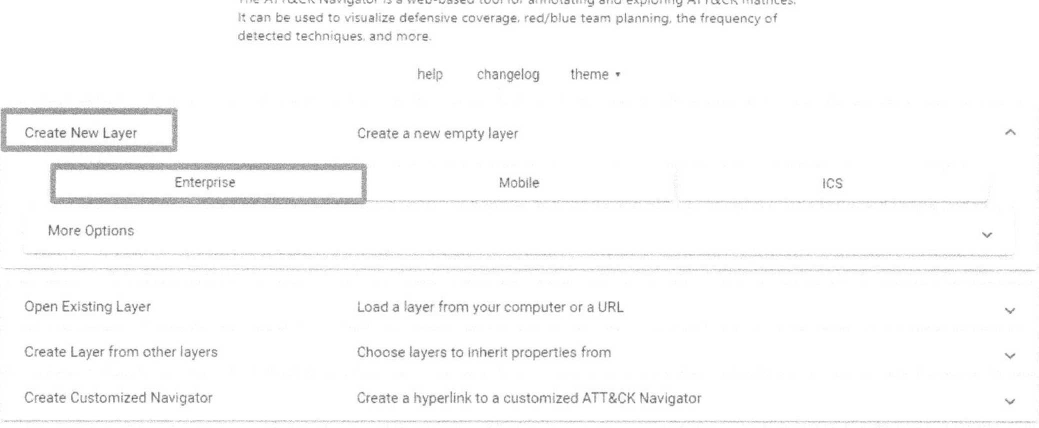
MITRE ATT&CK® Navigator
The ATT&CK Navigator is a web-based tool for annotating and exploring ATT&CK matrices. It can be used to visualize defensive coverage, red/blue team planning, the frequency of detected techniques, and more.
help
changelog
theme
Create New Layer
Create a new empty layer
Enterprise
Mobile
ICS
More Options
Open Existing Layer
Load a layer from your computer or a URL
Create Layer from other layers
Choose layers to inherit properties from
Create Customized Navigator
Create a hyperlink to a customized ATT&CK Navigator

Figure 6.16 – Create a new layer in ATT&CK Navigator

2. Click the search button under **section controls** and search for **APT19** under **Threat Groups**.

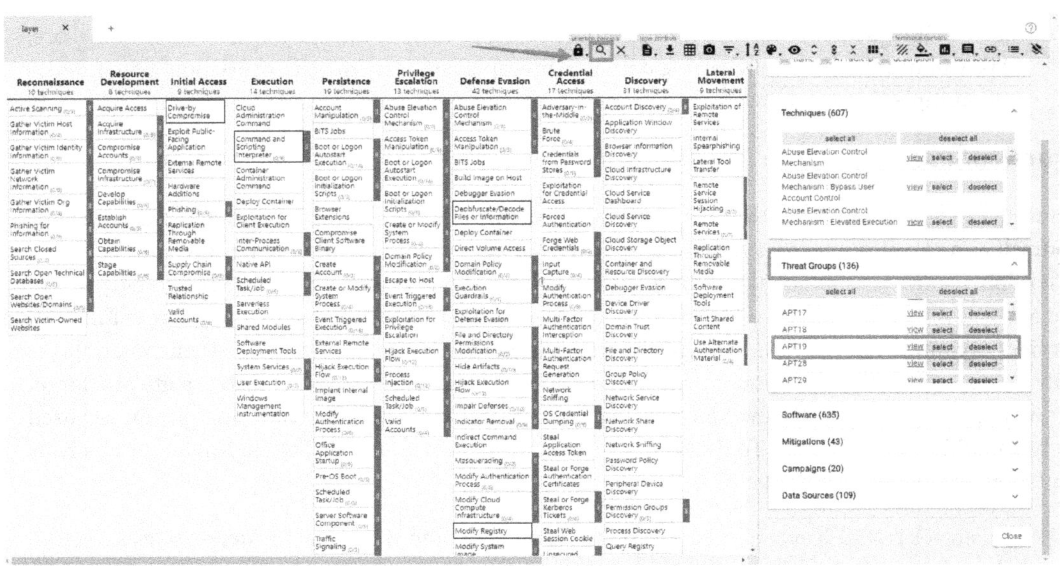

Figure 6.17 – Select APT19 from Threat Groups

3. Next, click the layer information button under **layer controls** and enter the name `APT19` with the description `TTPs of APT19 - Initial threat analysis`.

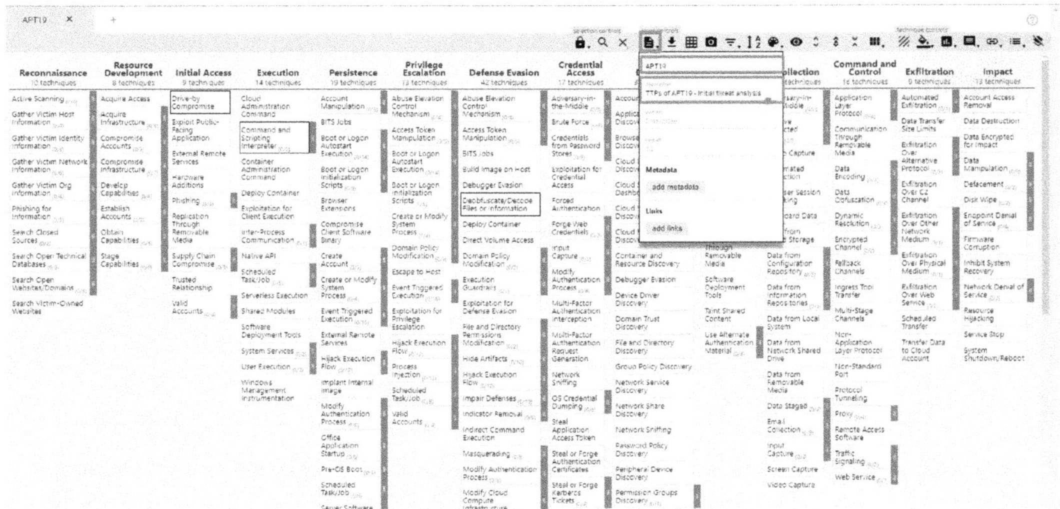

Figure 6.18 – Enter basic information about the layer

4. Next, set the color of the APT19 techniques to red. To do this, click on the background color button under **technique controls**.

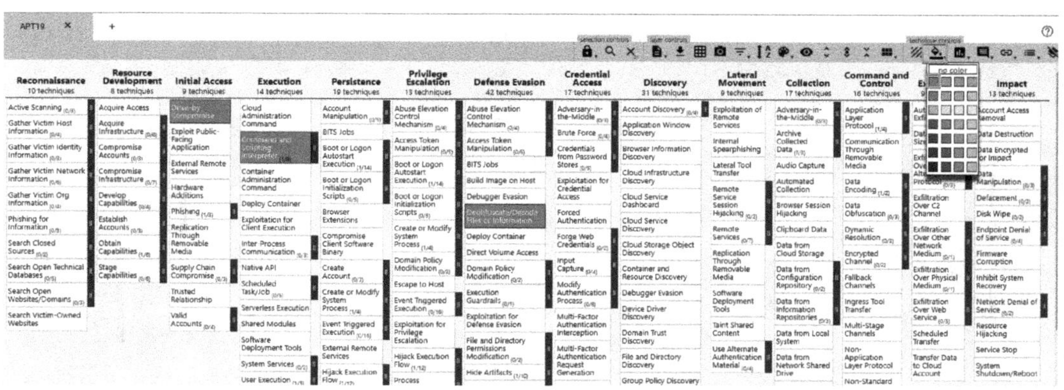

Figure 6.19 – Apply a color to the APT19 techniques

5. Next, click on scoring under **technique controls** and set it to `1`.

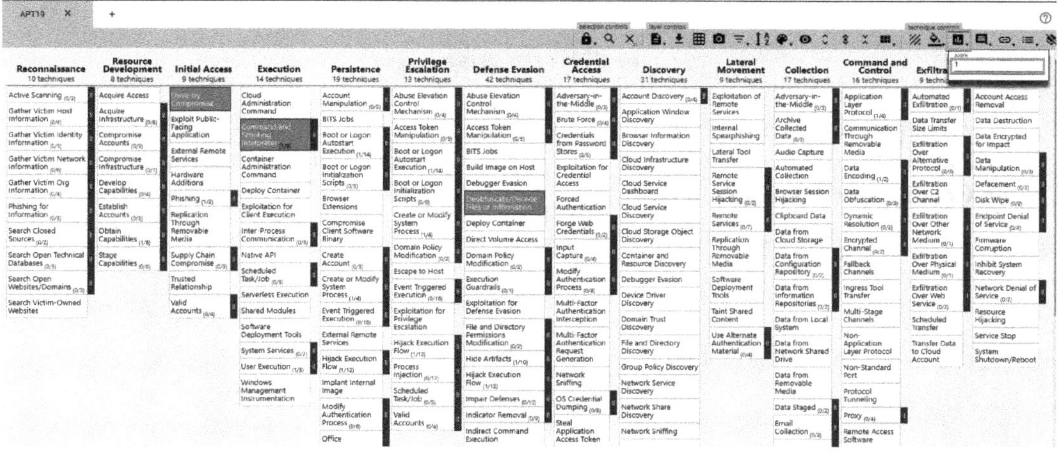

Figure 6.20 – Set a score for the APT19 techniques

6. Repeat the same steps for APT38 with the following details:

   I. Create a new layer.

   II. Click the search button under **section controls** and search for **APT38** under **Threat Groups**.

   III. Click the layer Information button under **layer controls** and enter the name `APT38` with the description `TTPs of APT38 - Initial threat analysis`.

   IV. Set the color of the APT38 techniques to green by clicking on the background color button under **technique controls**.

   V. Click on scoring under **technique controls** and set it to `2`.

The final APT38 layer will look like the following.

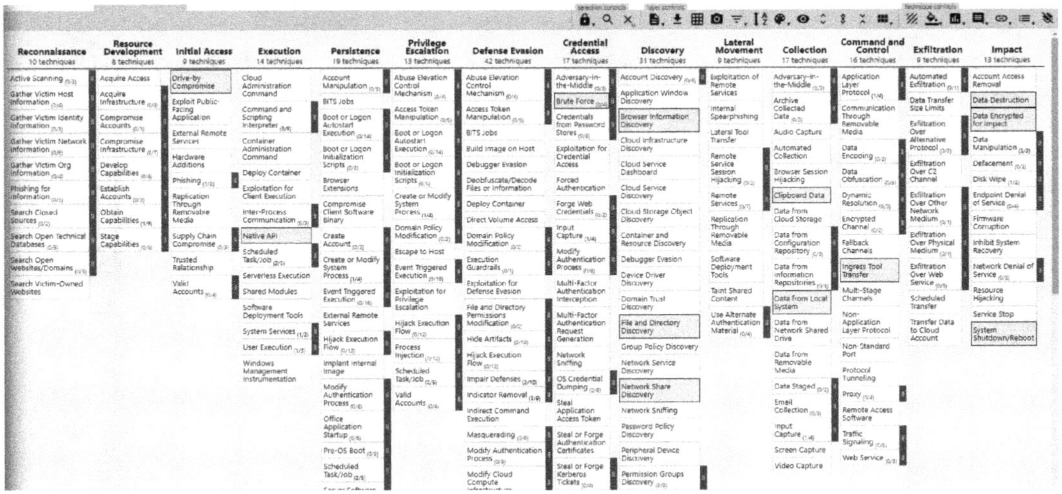

Figure 6.21 – APT38 layer

7. Now, merge both layers to get the common techniques used by both APT19 and APT38. This will help us to prioritize the adversary's techniques. Click on **Create New Layer** and then click on **Create Layer from other layers**.

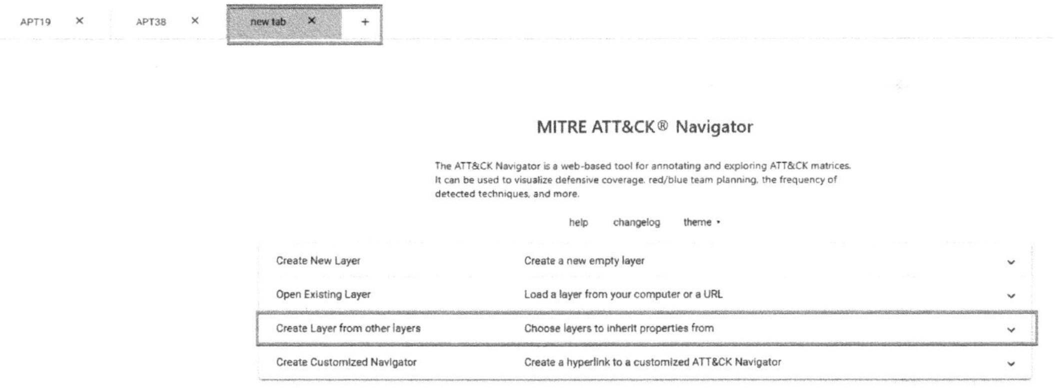
APT19
APT38
new tab
MITRE ATT&CK® Navigator
The ATT&CK Navigator is a web-based tool for annotating and exploring ATT&CK matrices. It can be used to visualize defensive coverage, red/blue team planning, the frequency of detected techniques, and more.
help
changelog
theme
Create New Layer
Create a new empty layer
Open Existing Layer
Load a layer from your computer or a URL
Create Layer from other layers
Choose layers to inherit properties from
Create Customized Navigator
Create a hyperlink to a customized ATT&CK Navigator

Figure 6.22 – Create Layer from other layers

Enter the following information:

- **domain**: `Enterprise ATT&CK v13`
- **score expression**: `a+b`

You can leave everything else blank, then click on the **Create** button at the bottom.

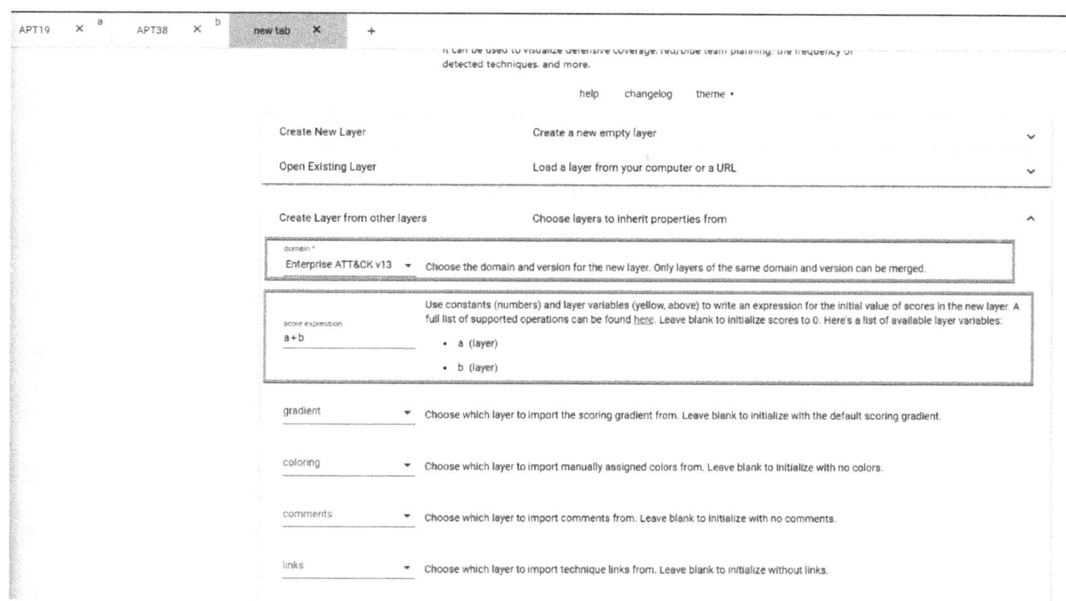

Figure 6.23 – Provide the domain and set expression

1. Once you click on **Create**, you will find a new layer with red techniques from APT19, yellow techniques from APT38, and green techniques that are common to both APT groups, as shown in the following screenshot.

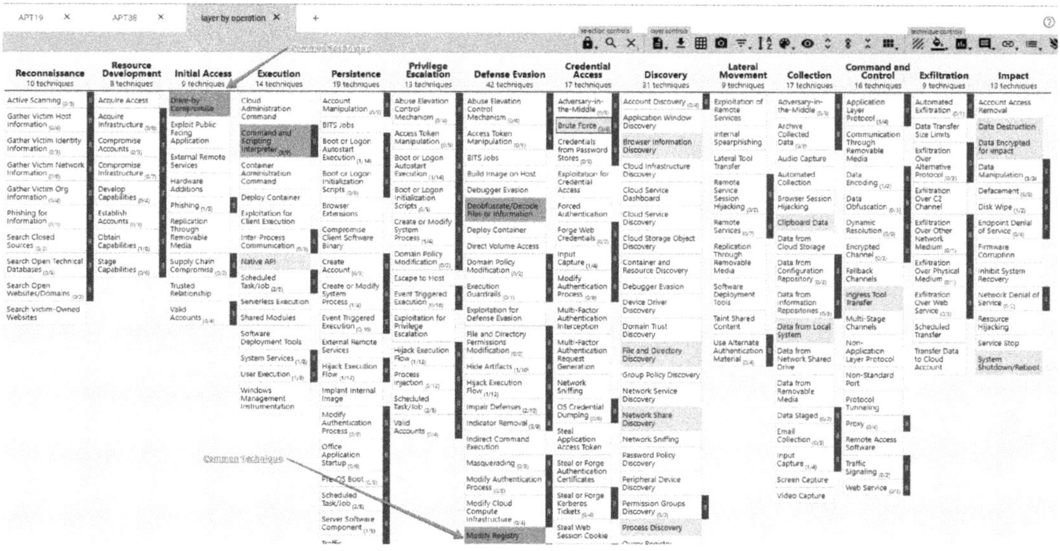

Figure 6.24 – Layers showing techniques from APT19 and APT38

Based on the final layers, there are four common techniques. The threat hunter could now start their hunting process by focusing on these four techniques:

- **Drive-by Compromise** with technique ID T1189 under the **Initial Access** tactic
- **Modify Registry** with technique ID T1112 under the **Defense Evasion** tactic
- **System Information Discovery** with technique ID T1082 under the **Discovery** tactic
- **System Owner/User Discovery** with technique ID T1033 under the **Discovery** tactic

Wazuh MITRE ATT&CK mapping

Wazuh maps the security events in the environment to the MITRE ATT&CK framework's TTPs. Wazuh helps security teams by matching them with known threat groups' TTPs. In order to map a MITRE ATT&CK technique ID to a specific Wazuh event, you need to add the `<mitre>` tag under the given rule. For example, if you want to create a Wazuh rule to associate SSH brute-force attacks with MITRE technique ID T1110, you will use the following rule:

```
<rule id="100009" level="10" frequency="8" timeframe="120"
ignore="60">
    <if_matched_sid>100001</if_matched_sid>
    <description>sshd: brute force attack</description>
    <same_srcip />
    <mitre>
      <id>T1110</id>
    </mitre>
  </rule>
```

You can also verify all the security events related to MITRE ID T1110 by going to the MITRE ATT&CK module in Wazuh and searching for **T1110** under **Techniques**.

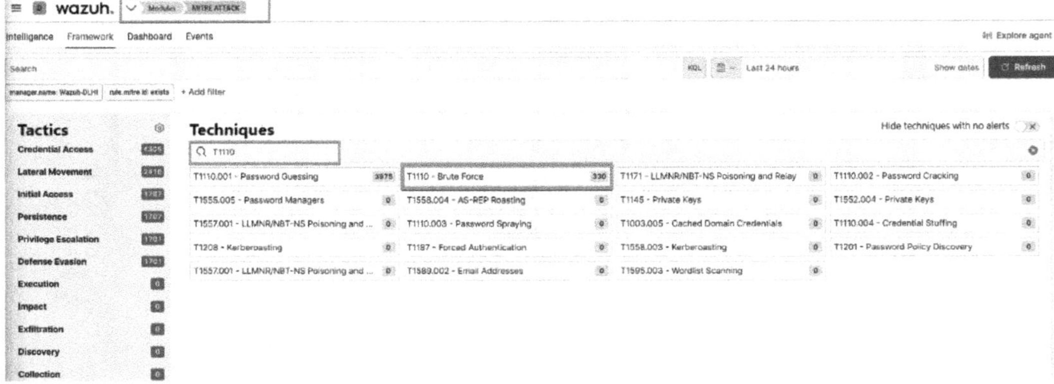

Figure 6.25 – MITRE ATT&CK visualization in Wazuh

Once you click on **T1110**, you will see all the security events associated with this MITRE ID, as shown in the following screenshot.

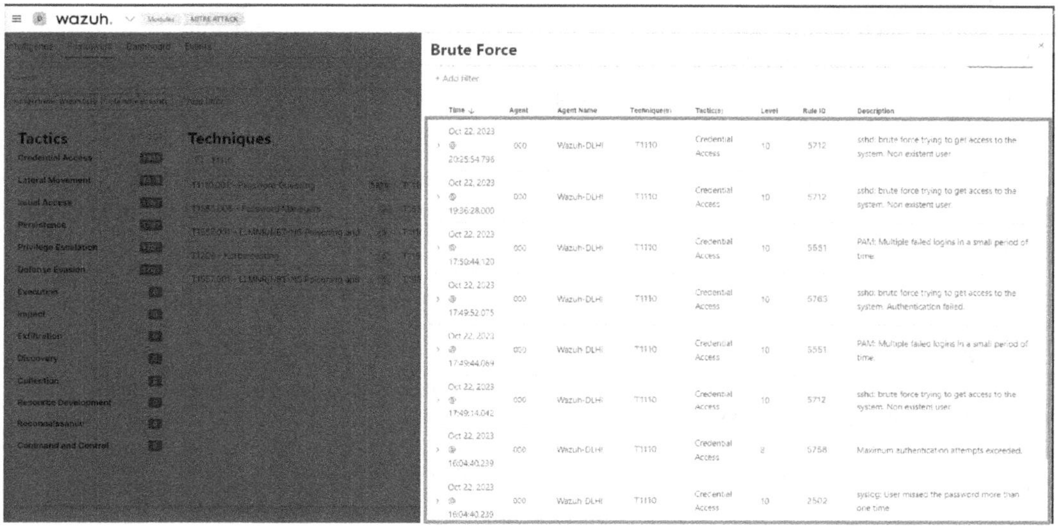

Figure 6.26 – Security events related to MITRE ATT&CK technique ID T1110

We have learned to prioritize techniques using ATT&CK Navigator and created a Wazuh rule mapped to a MITRE ATT&CK technique ID. This helps security teams and threat hunters to discover triggers to start their investigations. In the next section, we will learn to utilize the Osquery tool to conduct comprehensive threat hunting.

Threat hunting using Osquery

When it comes to threat hunting, we need in-depth visibility of endpoint activities and the ability to run queries to allow the threat hunter to retrieve IOCs, suspicious activities, and vulnerabilities in a given endpoint. **Osquery** is the ideal tool for this purpose. It helps threat hunters treat their entire IT infrastructure, including endpoints, as a structured database that can be queried using SQL-like commands. You can get real-time, detailed information about your systems with Osquery and keep an eye on them for signs of compromise. In this section, we will cover the following topics:

- What is Osquery?
- Installing Osquery
- Integrating Osquery with Wazuh
- Threat hunting with Osquery and Wazuh

What is Osquery?

Osquery is an open-source tool built by Facebook in 2014. It converts the target operating system into a relational database and allows us to ask questions from the table using SQL queries containing things such as information about the state of remote machines, running processes, active user accounts, active network connections, and much more. Osquery can be installed on Windows, Linux, macOS, and FreeBSD.

Osquery is heavily used by security analysts, **digital forensic and incident response** (**DFIR**) analysts, and threat hunters. Before we discuss how threat hunters can utilize Osquery with Wazuh, let me first share with you some simple use cases of Osquery:

- **Use case #1 – query for the top 10 largest processes by resident memory size**

  To get the list of the top 10 largest processes by memory size, use this query:

  ```
  select pid, name, uid, resident_size from processes order by
  resident_size desc limit 10;
  ```

```
osquery> select pid, name, uid, resident_size from processes order by resident_size desc limit 10;select pid, name, uid, resident_size from processes
 order by resident_size desc limit 10;
+------+-----------------+-----+---------------+
| pid  | name            | uid | resident_size |
+------+-----------------+-----+---------------+
| 993  | agent           | 115 | 184532992     |
| 1552 | process-agent   | 115 | 97705984      |
| 1189 | trace-agent     | 115 | 66035712      |
| 4813 | osqueryi        | 0   | 43880448      |
| 842  | snapd           | 0   | 28942336      |
| 437  | multipathd      | 0   | 27750400      |
| 960  | unattended-upgr | 0   | 22159360      |
| 3334 | packagekitd     | 0   | 21200896      |
| 838  | networkd-dispat | 0   | 19476480      |
| 734  | systemd-resolve | 102 | 14163968      |
| 993  | agent           | 115 | 184532992     |
| 1552 | process-agent   | 115 | 97705984      |
| 1189 | trace-agent     | 115 | 66035712      |
| 4813 | osqueryi        | 0   | 43880448      |
| 842  | snapd           | 0   | 28942336      |
| 437  | multipathd      | 0   | 27750400      |
| 960  | unattended-upgr | 0   | 22159360      |
| 3334 | packagekitd     | 0   | 21200896      |
| 838  | networkd-dispat | 0   | 19476480      |
| 734  | systemd-resolve | 102 | 14163968      |
+------+-----------------+-----+---------------+
```

Figure 6.27 – Result of top 10 largest processes by memory size

- **Use case #2 – query the list of the top 10 most active processes with process counts**

  In this use case, we will utilize Osquery to retrieve from the system the top 10 active processes based on their frequency and process count. The query is as follows:

  ```
  select count(pid) as total, name from processes group by name
  order by total desc limit 10;
  ```

Once the query is executed, you will get the result in the form of a table with the process names and corresponding frequencies. The output is shown in the following screenshot.

```
osquery> select count(pid) as total, name from processes group by name order by total desc limit 10;
+-------+-----------------+
| total | name            |
+-------+-----------------+
| 2     | systemd         |
| 2     | sshd            |
| 1     | zswap-shrink    |
| 1     | writeback       |
| 1     | wazuh-syscheckd |
| 1     | wazuh-modulesd  |
| 1     | wazuh-logcollec |
| 1     | wazuh-execd     |
| 1     | wazuh-agentd    |
| 1     | watchdogd       |
+-------+-----------------+
osquery>
```

Figure 6.28 – Result of the top 10 most active processes with process counts

Before we integrate Osquery with Wazuh, we need to install Osquery in each of the individual Wazuh agents.

Installing Osquery

The process of installing Osquery is different for each platform. In this section, we will cover the installation of Osquery on an Ubuntu machine and a Windows machine.

Installing Osquery on Ubuntu Server/Desktop

Installation of Osquery on the Ubuntu Server requires the OSQUERY KEY and downloading the official Osquery package, explained as follows:

1. **Set the OSQUERY KEY environment variable**

   This step involves the creation of an environment variable called `OSQUERY_KEY` to store the GPG key used to validate the Osquery package's authenticity. This key is required to confirm that the packages you download are from a reliable source:

   ```
   export OSQUERY_KEY=1484120AC4E9F8A1A577AEEE97A80C63C9D8B80B
   ```

2. **Import the GPG key**

   Import the GPG key into the APT keyring with the `apt-key` command. This key is necessary to validate the Osquery packages you will be installing:

   ```
   apt-key adv --keyserver keyserver.ubuntu.com --recv-keys
   $OSQUERY_KEY
   ```

3. **Add the Osquery repository and update the package**

   Next, you must add the Osquery repository to the list of software sources on your system. The Osquery package will be installed from this repository:

   ```
   add-apt-repository 'deb [arch=amd64] https://pkg.osquery.io/deb>
   deb main'
   apt-get update
   ```

4. **Install Osquery**

   After adding the repository and updating the package list, use the `apt-get install` command to install Osquery. This will get Osquery from the newly added repository and install it:

   ```
   apt-get install osquery
   ```

Installing Osquery on Windows

Installing Osquery on Windows desktops is pretty simple. Please visit the official website of Osquery and download the packages. The website is `https://www.osquery.io/`.

Integrating Osquery with Wazuh

The good news is that Wazuh is already integrated with Osquery. We just need to enable it and make some minor changes to the Osquery configuration file. Follow these steps to complete the installation:

1. **Enable Osquery**: Open the `ossec.conf` file in the Wazuh agent and change the `<disabled>` tag value to no under `<wodle name="osquery"`:

   ```
   <!-- Osquery integration -->
   <wodle name="osquery">
   <disabled>no</disabled>
   <run_daemon>yes</run_daemon> <log_path>/var/log/osquery/
   osqueryd.results.log</log_path> <config_path>/etc/osquery/
   osquery.conf</config_path> <add_labels>yes</add_labels>
    </wodle>
   ```

   In the preceding code, we can see the following:

   - `<log_path>` represents the location of the Osquery logs
   - `<config_path>` shows the location of the Osquery configuration file

2. **Copy the Osquery config file**: By default, the Osquery configuration file is located at `/opt/osquery/share/osquery/osquery.example.conf`.

   Let's copy the file to `/etc/osquery/osquery.conf` using the cp command:

   ```
   cp /opt/osquery/share/osquery/osquery.example.conf /etc/osquery/
   osquery.conf
   ```

Wazuh has already modified the Osquery configuration and added some important packs. You can run `nano /etc/osquery/osquery.conf` to view the default packs:

```
    "packs": {
          "osquery-monitoring": "/opt/osquery/share/osquery/packs/
osquery-monitoring.conf",
          "incident-response": "/opt/osquery/share/osquery/packs/
incident-response.conf",
          "it-compliance": "/opt/osquery/share/osquery/packs/
it-compliance.conf",
          "vuln-management": "/opt/osquery/share/osquery/packs/
vuln-management.conf",
          "hardware-monitoring": "/opt/osquery/share/osquery/
packs/hardware-monitoring.conf",
          "ossec-rootkit": "/opt/osquery/share/osquery/packs/
ossec-rootkit.conf"
      }
```

- In the preceding code, we can see the following:
- `osquery-monitoring.conf` is an Osquery configuration file to collect information about every Osquery pack, including general performance and versions
- `incident-response.conf` retrieves information about crontab, the loginwindow process, a list of open sockets, a list of mounted drives, and so on
- `it-compliance.conf` collects information about active directory, the operating system, shared services, browser plugins, Windows drivers, a list of USB drives, and so on
- `vuln-management.conf` retrieves information about installed applications, browser plugins, and Chrome extensions
- `hardware-monitoring.conf` gathers hardware-related information such as PCI devices, fan speed, an inventory of USB drives, kernel modules, and so on
- `ossec-rootkit.conf` collects information about rootkits

3. **Restart Osquery**: Now, you need to restart Osquery for your changes to take effect:

```
systemctl restart osqueryd
```

Threat hunting with Osquery

Osquery gives you a SQL-like way to query requests and get real-time information about how a system is running. This lets security teams do proactive investigations and find threats. Threat hunting with Osquery involves actively searching for system information such as suspicious processes, unwanted software or modules, abnormal network connections, registry settings, file integrity, and more. For testing purposes, we will write some Osquery queries based on popular MITRE ATT&CK techniques.

It is sufficient to run the queries on a single endpoint for testing purposes and to demonstrate the information retrievable by Osquery. However, keep in mind that the true power of Osquery presents itself when it is widely deployed and administered centrally by the Wazuh manager. Let's focus on discovering persistence tactics in our environment by utilizing a few of its associated techniques.

Local Job Scheduling (MITRE ATT&CK ID T1168)

Adversaries utilize local job scheduling to schedule and execute tasks or jobs on a hacked system. It is covered by MITRE ATT&CK framework under *technique ID 1168*. On Linux-based systems, adversaries can schedule their multi-step attack jobs by abusing the Cron service. They may set up new Cron jobs to run harmful scripts or commands on a regular basis. You can use the following query to retrieve information about local Cron jobs:

```
select command, path from crontab;
```

Once this query is executed, you will see the result in the form of a table with the command and corresponding path, as shown in the following screenshot:

```
osquery> select command, path from crontab;
+------------------------------------------------------------------------------------------------------
---+-------------------------+
| command
   | path                    |
+------------------------------------------------------------------------------------------------------
---+-------------------------+
| root cd / && run-parts --report /etc/cron.hourly
   | /etc/crontab            |
| root test -x /usr/sbin/anacron || ( cd / && run-parts --report /etc/cron.daily )
   | /etc/crontab            |
| root test -x /usr/sbin/anacron || ( cd / && run-parts --report /etc/cron.weekly )
   | /etc/crontab            |
| root test -x /usr/sbin/anacron || ( cd / && run-parts --report /etc/cron.monthly )
   | /etc/crontab            |
| root test -e /run/systemd/system || SERVICE_MODE=1 /usr/lib/x86_64-linux-gnu/e2fsprogs/e2scrub_all_cr
on | /etc/cron.d/e2scrub_all |
| root test -e /run/systemd/system || SERVICE_MODE=1 /sbin/e2scrub_all -A -r
   | /etc/cron.d/e2scrub_all |
+------------------------------------------------------------------------------------------------------
---+-------------------------+
```

Figure 6.29 – Resulting list of local Cron jobs

Kernel Modules and Extensions (MITRE ATT&CK ID T1215)

Adversaries can ensure that their code runs each time the system reboots by installing a malicious kernel module or extension at startup or during system initialization. This makes it difficult to identify and uninstall. This is described under MITRE ATT&CK technique *ID T1215*. Kernel modules are pieces of code that can be dynamically loaded and unloaded from an operating system's kernel. The query to retrieve the kernel modules is as follows:

```
select name from kernel_modules;
```

Once this query is executed, you will get a list of all the kernel modules as shown in the following screenshot.

```
osquery> select name from kernel_modules;

| name                  |
+-----------------------+
| tcp_diag              |
| udp_diag              |
| inet_diag             |
| snd_hda_codec_generic |
| ledtrig_audio         |
| intel_rapl_msr        |
| ip6t_REJECT           |
| nf_reject_ipv6        |
| xt_hl                 |
| ip6_tables            |
| ip6t_rt               |
| snd_hda_intel         |
| snd_intel_dspcfg      |
| snd_intel_sdw_acpi    |
| ipt_REJECT            |
| nf_reject_ipv4        |
| xt_LOG                |
| nf_log_syslog         |
| nft_limit             |
| xt_limit              |
| xt_addrtype           |
| xt_tcpudp             |
| xt_conntrack          |
| nf_conntrack          |
| nf_defrag_ipv6        |
| nf_defrag_ipv4        |
| nft_compat            |
| nft_counter           |
| snd_hda_codec         |
| nf_tables             |
| nfnetlink             |
| binfmt_misc           |
| nls_iso8859_1         |
```

Figure 6.30 – Result of list of kernel modules

Redundant Access (MITRE ATT&CK ID T1108)

Redundant access is a strategy in which adversaries create several paths or techniques for accessing and manipulating a victim machine. This works like a "plan B" for threat actors. To detect redundant access, we need to retrieve information about all the running processes on the endpoint. To get this information, we can run the following query:

```
select pr.pid, pr.name, usr.username, pr.path, pr.cmdline from
processes pr LEFT JOIN users usr ON pr.uid = usr.uid WHERE pr.cmdline
!= '';
```

Once this query is executed, we will get the result in a table containing details on the process ID (`pid`), process name (`name`), `username`, `path`, and command line (`cmdline`) of the running processes, as shown in the following screenshot.

```
osquery> select pr.pid, pr.name, usr.username, pr.path, pr.cmdline from processes pr LEFT JOIN users usr ON pr.uid = usr.uid WHERE pr.cmdline != '';
| pid    | name            | username | path                                | cmdline
| 1      | systemd         | root     | /usr/lib/systemd/systemd            | /sbin/init vultr
| 1013   | wazuh-execd     | root     | /var/ossec/bin/wazuh-execd          | /var/ossec/bin/wazuh-execd
| 101382 | osqueryd        | root     | /opt/osquery/bin/osqueryd           | /opt/osquery/bin/osqueryd --flagfile /etc/osquery/osquery
.flags --config_path /etc/osquery/osquery.conf
| 101384 | osqueryd        | root     | /opt/osquery/bin/osqueryd           | /opt/osquery/bin/osqueryd
| 1108   | wazuh-agentd    | wazuh    | /var/ossec/bin/wazuh-agentd         | /var/ossec/bin/wazuh-agentd
| 1137   | wazuh-syscheckd | root     | /var/ossec/bin/wazuh-syscheckd      | /var/ossec/bin/wazuh-syscheckd
| 1176   | wazuh-logcollec | root     | /var/ossec/bin/wazuh-logcollector   | /var/ossec/bin/wazuh-logcollector
| 1194   | wazuh-modulesd  | root     | /var/ossec/bin/wazuh-modulesd       | /var/ossec/bin/wazuh-modulesd
| 1612   | watchdog        | root     | /usr/sbin/watchdog                  | /usr/sbin/watchdog
| 255689 | fwupd           | root     | /usr/libexec/fwupd/fwupd            | /usr/libexec/fwupd/fwupd
| 259458 | sshd            | root     | /usr/sbin/sshd                      | sshd: root@pts/0
| 259539 | systemd         | root     | /usr/lib/systemd/systemd            | /lib/systemd/systemd --user
| 259541 | (sd-pam)        | root     | /usr/lib/systemd/systemd            | (sd-pam)
| 259626 | bash            | root     | /usr/bin/bash                       | -bash
```

Figure 6.31 – Result of all running processes and their corresponding paths

Writing and organizing queries

There are two ways you can create queries. You can either write a query directly under the `schedule` block of the `/etc/osquery/osquery.conf` file or you can organize them in the form of packs. When you have tons of queries to run, it's always better to create a separate Osquery pack. In our scenario, we will add the following queries to a pack with the name `custom-pack-1.conf`:

```
{
  "queries": {
    "Services": {
        "query": "SELECT * FROM services WHERE start_type='DEMAND_
START' OR start_type='AUTO_START';",
        "interval": 3600,
        "description": "Lists all installed services configured to
start automatically at boot - ATT&CK T1050",
        "removed": false
    },
    "Snapshot_services": {
        "query": "SELECT * FROM services;",
        "interval": 28800,
        "description": "Snapshot Services query",
        "snapshot": true
    },
      "OtherServices": {
        "query": "SELECT name, display_name, status, start_type, path,
```

```
module_path FROM services;",
        "interval": 3600,
        "description": "Services whose executables are placed in
unfamiliar folders- ATT&CK T1543.003",
        "removed": false
    }


   }
}
```

You need to add all the queries under the `queries` field. Each Osquery query can have multiple items of metadata including `query`, `interval`, `description`, and `snapshot`. The following screenshot shows a query pack containing three queries.

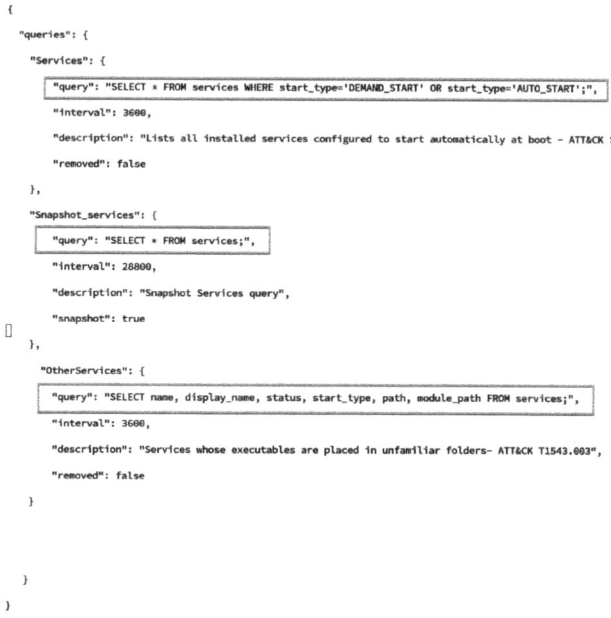

```
{
  "queries": {
    "Services": {
      "query": "SELECT * FROM services WHERE start_type='DEMAND_START' OR start_type='AUTO_START';",
      "interval": 3600,
      "description": "Lists all installed services configured to start automatically at boot - ATT&CK >
      "removed": false
    },
    "Snapshot_services": {
      "query": "SELECT * FROM services;",
      "interval": 28800,
      "description": "Snapshot Services query",
      "snapshot": true
    },
    "OtherServices": {
      "query": "SELECT name, display_name, status, start_type, path, module_path FROM services;",
      "interval": 3600,
      "description": "Services whose executables are placed in unfamiliar folders- ATT&CK T1543.003",
      "removed": false
    }


  }
}
```

Figure 6.32 – Custom Osquery pack

In the preceding screenshot, we can see the following:

- `SELECT * FROM services WHERE start_type='DEMAND_START' OR start_type='AUTO_START`: This query retrieves all rows from the `services` table where `start_type` is either `'DEMAND_START'` or `'AUTO_START'`

- `SELECT * FROM services`: This query retrieves all rows from the `services` table
- `SELECT name, display_name, status, start_type, path, module_path FROM services`: This query retrieves specific columns (`name`, `display_name`, `status`, `start_type`, `path`, `module_path`) from the `services` table

You can save the file and call this under the `/etc/osquery/osquery.conf` Osquery file.

To visualize Osquery events on the Wazuh dashboard, navigate to **Wazuh Modules>Osquery> Events**. You should see all the query results as shown in the following screenshot.

Figure 6.33 – Visualizing Osquery events

We've learned to create custom Osquery queries and visualize the events on the Wazuh dashboard. In the next section, we will learn about command monitoring on Wazuh.

Command monitoring

The most effective way to collect information about an endpoint is to run specific commands on the given endpoint, such as `netstat` (for network connections on Windows), `ps` (to collect process information from Linux machines), and so on. This information plays a vital role in collecting IOCs and running a successful threat-hunting program. The good news is that Wazuh has a built-in feature to monitor the output of specific Windows/Linux commands and show that output as log content. In this section, we will learn the following:

- How does command monitoring work?
- Monitoring Linux commands
- List of Linux commands for threat hunting and security Investigations

How does command monitoring work?

Wazuh runs commands on the endpoints using the *Command* and *Logcollector* modules, and then sends the results to the Wazuh server for examination. The following steps describe the process of command monitoring.

Step 1 – configuration

The process starts when a user chooses to monitor how a particular command is being executed on a system. This can be accomplished locally by adding the necessary command to the local agent configuration file (`/var/ossec/etc/ossec.conf`) or remotely through the `agent.conf` file hosted on the Wazuh server. Wazuh has two modules that let you monitor the results of system commands that are running on an endpoint. The Command and Logcollector modules run and watch commands or executables on Windows, Linux, and macOS targets on a regular basis.

Using the Command module

Wazuh recommends using the Command module as it has checksum verification, allows encrypted communication, and helps in scheduling execution.

The following is an example of the Command module:

```
<wodle name="command">
   <disabled>no</disabled>
   <tag>tasklist</tag>
   <command>PowerShell.exe C:\\activeTasks.bat</command>
   <interval>2m</interval>
   <run_on_start>yes</run_on_start>
   <timeout>10</timeout>
 </wodle>
```

Here, the `PowerShell.exe C:\\tasklist.bat` value in the `<command>` tag is the command to be executed by the Command module. The PowerShell program executes the `C:\activetasks.bat` script.

Using the Logcollector module

Text files, Windows event logs, and straight syslog messages can all send logs to the Logcollector module. It is easy to use and also allows us to format fields such as `timestamp`, `hostname`, and `program_name`.

This is what a simple Logcollector module setup block looks like:

```
<localfile>
<log_format>full_command</log_format> <command><COMMAND></command>
<frequency>120</frequency>
 </localfile>
```

In the preceding code, we can see the following:

- `<command>` reads the output of the command executed by the Wazuh agent.
- `<log_format>` can be set to either `full_command` or `command`. `full_command` reads the output as a single-line entry and `command` reads the output as multiple entries.

Step 2 – execution by the Wazuh agent

Following the configuration of the required command, the endpoint runs the command on a regular basis according to the predetermined frequency or interval.

Under the Command module, we define the `<interval>` tag to execute the command at a specified interval.

Step 3 – monitoring and data forwarding

The Wazuh agent monitors how the configured command is being executed. It records the result of the command along with any associated data, including the timestamp, execution details, and user that started the command. The agent sends this data to the Wazuh server for further analysis.

Step 4 – Wazuh server analysis and alert generation

The data is processed by the Wazuh server after it is received from the Wazuh agent. A number of crucial tasks are carried out by the server, such as pre-decoding, decoding, and matching the received logs against preset rules, explained as follows:

- **Pre-decoding and decoding**: The raw data is converted into a readable format using a Wazuh decoder. So, yes, we need to write a decoder rule too.
- **Matching rules**: The Wazuh server matches the decoded logs to predefined Wazuh rules. These rules identify suspicious or malicious command-related activity using patterns and criteria. If a match is identified, the server alerts security.
- **Alert generation and storage**: Wazuh generates alerts when rules are triggered. Wazuh server log files store alerts for future analysis. These alerts are stored in the `/var/ossec/logs/alerts/alerts.log and /var/ossec/logs/alerts/alerts.json` file on the Wazuh server.

Now that we have understood how command monitoring works, let's take a simple use case of monitoring the output of the `netstat` command on a Linux machine.

Monitoring the output of the netstat command on Linux

`netstat` is a tool for looking at connection information and can be used to find connections that seem suspicious or unusual. As a threat hunter, you may need to focus on a certain endpoint in the context of any unusual network connections. In order to monitor the output of the `netstat` command, follow these next steps:

1. **Installation of net-tools package**: Make sure the `net-tools` package is installed on all the monitored Linux endpoints:

   ```
   sudo apt install net-tools
   ```

   This package gives users and administrators a set of command-line networking tools that can be used to do different network-related jobs such as running `ifconfig`, `netstat`, `route`, `arp`, `rarp`, and so on.

2. **Monitor the netstat command**: Append the Logcollector module to monitor the `netstat` command in the Wazuh agent's `ossec.conf` file:

   ```
   <ossec_config>
   <localfile>
    <log_format>full_command</log_format>
   <command>netstat -tulpn</command>
   <alias>netstat listening ports</alias>
    <frequency>360</frequency>
    </localfile>
   </ossec_config>
   ```

   In the preceding code, we can see the following:

   - `<log_format>full_command</log_format>`: This specifies the log format. In this case, it is set to `full_command`, indicating that the log consists of the full output.
   - `<command>netstat -tulpn</command>`: This indicates the command to be executed. In this case, the `netstat -tulpn` command is used to display active network connections, listening ports, and other related information.
   - `<frequency>360</frequency>`: This represents the frequency at which the preceding command will be executed. It is set to execute every 360 seconds (i.e., every 6 minutes).

3. **Restart and test**: Now, restart the Wazuh agent using the following command and check the Wazuh manager for the alert:

   ```
   systemctl restart wazuh-agent
   ```

4. **Visualizing the alert**: To visualize the alerts, navigate to the **Security alert** module on the Wazuh manager and find the alert related to **Listened port status (netstat)** as shown in the following screenshot:

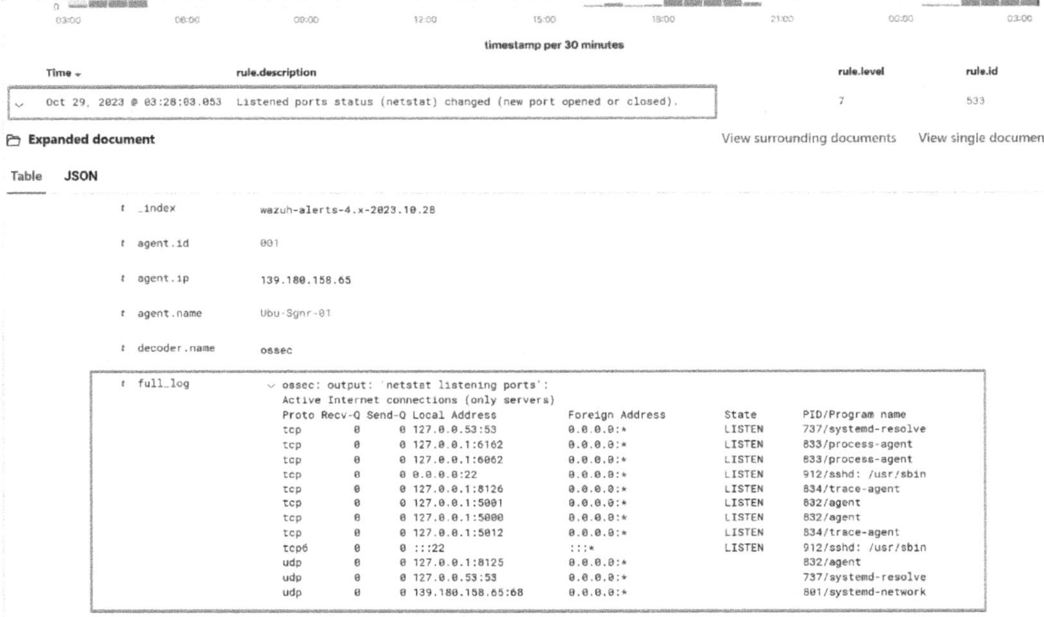

Figure 6.34 – Wazuh alert about netstat listened ports status having changed

You will notice that we didn't even create any Wazuh decoder or rule, but we got the alert. It was possible because Wazuh has a built-in ruleset named `0015-ossec_rule.xml`, containing a rule for netstat listening, as follows:

```
<rule id="533" level="7">
<if_sid>530</if_sid>
<match>ossec: output: 'netstat listening ports</match>
<check_diff />
<description>Listened ports status (netstat) changed (new port opened
or closed).</description>
<group>pci_dss_10.2.7,pci_dss_10.6.1,gpg13_10.1,gdpr_
IV_35.7.d,hipaa_164.312.b,nist_800_53_AU.14,nist_800_53_AU.6,tsc_
CC6.8,tsc_CC7.2,tsc_CC7.3,</group>
</rule>
```

And if you look at the parent rule, you will find the decoder named `ossec` as follows:

```
<group name="ossec,">
<rule id="500" level="0">
<category>ossec</category>
<decoded_as>ossec</decoded_as>
<description>Grouping of ossec rules.</description>
</rule>
</group>
```

List of Linux commands for threat hunting and security investigations

As we bring this chapter to a close, let's quickly review some essential Linux commands for threat hunting and security investigations:

- `ss`: This is a tool used to dump socket statistics and provide information about network connections. The `ss` command is useful to identify open ports, check established connections, and gather network information. It is slightly more advanced than `netstat`.
- `ps`: Using the `ps` command, you can see which processes are active on your system. Examining active processes might assist you in locating unauthorized or suspicious software.
- `top` and `htop`: These commands provide up-to-date details on programs that are currently executing, and the number of system resources being consumed. They can also be used to spot any unexpected or resource-intensive activity.
- `lsof`: You can find open files and network connections with the `lsof` (for *list open files*) command, which can help you keep an eye on behavior that might be suspicious.
- `tcpdump`: This is a very powerful packet capture tool that can be used to detect network-based threats.

Summary

This chapter covered important aspects of modern intelligence and threat-hunting tactics. It started with Wazuh's contribution to proactive threat hunting, then moved on to the importance of analyzing log data, and finally looked at how MITRE ATT&CK mapping improves our understanding of threats. We learned how to use Osquery in Wazuh to effectively perform threat hunting and also learned how to use command monitoring in Wazuh to discover suspicious activities.

In the next chapter, we will learn about the Vulnerability detection and SCA modules of the Wazuh platform. We will learn how to leverage these modules to meet regulatory compliance including PCI DSS, NIST 800-53, and HIPPA.

Part 3: Compliance Management

This part of this book focuses on compliance management using Wazuh and explores vulnerability detection and security configuration assessment modules of the Wazuh platform. You will learn to fulfill some specific requirements of regulatory compliance such as PCI DSS, HIPPA, and NIST 800-53 controls.

This part includes the following chapter:

- *Chapter 7*, Vulnerability and Configuration Assessment

7

Vulnerability Detection and Configuration Assessment

A security vulnerability is a weakness in the program code or a configuration error in the system, such as Log4Shell, code injection and so on, that allows an attacker to directly and uninvitedly access a system or network. The *Hacker-Powered Security Report* from HackerOne in 2022 revealed that over 65,000 vulnerabilities were discovered by ethical hackers in 2022 alone—a 21% increase from 2021. We know that a threat is an adverse or malicious occurrence that exploits a vulnerability. So, why are we so bothered by vulnerabilities? Why can't we work on threats directly? Why can't we prevent threats from happening? The simplest answer is we can't control threats due to their rapidly evolving nature. We can only control and manage vulnerabilities, hence, organizations spend their time and resources on patching security vulnerabilities.

There is a related concept called **security configuration management**. This is the process of identifying misconfigurations of a system's default settings and, as a result, bringing down the number of security vulnerabilities in the network. Vulnerability monitoring and security configuration management are critical for maintaining regulatory compliance such as PCI DSS, NIST, HIPPA, and so on. Wazuh has built-in capabilities to look after both vulnerability detection and security configuration monitoring.

In this chapter, we will get hands-on with vulnerability detection and security configuration assessment modules of the Wazuh platform. We will also learn how to monitor and maintain regulatory compliance.

In this chapter, we will cover the following topics:

- Introduction to vulnerability detection and security configuration monitoring
- PCI DSS
- NIST
- HIPPA

Introduction to vulnerability detection and security configuration management

Vulnerability scanning or detection and security configuration management are critical to keeping the overall security posture of an organization under control. By discovering and fixing vulnerabilities, vulnerability management reduces the likelihood of cyberattacks. By ensuring that systems are configured securely, security configuration assessment helps to prevent data breaches and unauthorized access. Both strategies strengthen the organization's defenses, reducing risks and maintaining trust with stakeholders. Wazuh has modules called Vulnerability Detector to fulfill the requirement of vulnerability scanning and **Security Configuration Assessment** (**SCA**) to maintain the baseline security configuration of endpoints in the network. Let's understand how Wazuh can deliver both services with its built-in features.

Vulnerability Detector

The **Wazuh Vulnerability Detector** module enables the security team to identify operating system and application vulnerabilities on the endpoints being monitored. All valid vulnerabilities are named by **Common Vulnerabilities and Exposures** (**CVE**). You can view the list of all the vulnerabilities on the `cvedetails.com` website and `nvd.nist.gov`. Both sites are managed by the MITRE Corporation. Wazuh is natively integrated with different vulnerability feed providers, such as Canonical, Debian, Red Hat, Arch Linux, **Amazon Linux Advisories Security** (**ALAS**), Microsoft, and the **National Vulnerability Database** (**NVD**). Let's talk about how Wazuh can detect any new vulnerabilities.

How to set up vulnerability detection using Wazuh

Wazuh agents periodically share a list of installed applications from monitored endpoints to the Wazuh server. This inventory of installed applications is stored in local SQLite databases on the Wazuh server.

Let's find out how vulnerability detection works and what needs to be configured to enable vulnerability detection in Wazuh. The workings of Wazuh's vulnerability detection can be explained in three steps:

1. **Step 1: System inventory**

   A system inventory comprises data related to the software and hardware components of the network infrastructure. For the Vulnerability Detector module of Wazuh to work, the system inventory should be up and running. By default, the system inventory module called **Syscollector** is enabled on all Wazuh agents.

   The following block is the default Syscollector configuration present in the Wazuh agent `ossec.conf` file:

   ```
   <!-- System inventory -->
     <wodle name="syscollector">
       <disabled>no</disabled>
   ```

```
    <interval>1h</interval>
    <scan_on_start>yes</scan_on_start>
    <hardware>yes</hardware>
    <os>yes</os>
    <network>yes</network>
    <packages>yes</packages>
    <ports all="no">yes</ports>
    <processes>yes</processes>

    <!-- Database synchronization settings -->
    <synchronization>
      <max_eps>10</max_eps>
    </synchronization>
  </wodle>
```

Let's break this down:

- `<wodle name="syscollector">`: A wodle is a module in Wazuh that allows users to perform syscollector, Command, Osquery, Docker-Listener, and other tasks.
- `<interval>1h</interval>`: This represents the interval at which the syscollector module runs. In this case, it is set to 1 hour.
- `<hardware>yes</hardware>`: This talks about monitoring hardware-related information.
- `<os>yes</os>`: This represents the monitoring of the operating system
- `<network>yes</network>`: This represents the monitoring of network-related information.
- `<packages>yes</packages>`: This talks about the monitoring of packages or the software of endpoints.
- `<processes>yes</processes>`: This talks about the monitoring of all processes of endpoints.
- `<synchronization>`: This contains information related to database synchronization.
- `<max_eps>10</max_eps>`: This specifies the maximum number of events per second (EPS) for database synchronization. In this case, it is set to 10 events per second.

2. **Step 2: Enabling vulnerability detection on the Wazuh server**

   We need to enable the Vulnerability Detector module on the Wazuh server under the `ossec.conf` file.

   Specify `yes` as the value for the `enabled>` tag for each operating system you intend to scan and the Vulnerability Detector module. For example, if you want to enable the Vulnerability Detector for the Ubuntu OS, here is what you should do:

```
<vulnerability-detector>
   <enabled>yes</enabled>
```

```
    <interval>5m</interval>
    <min_full_scan_interval>6h</min_full_scan_interval>
    <run_on_start>yes</run_on_start>

    <!-- Ubuntu OS vulnerabilities -->
    <provider name="canonical">
        <enabled>yes</enabled>
        <os>trusty</os>
        <os>xenial</os>
        <os>bionic</os>
        <os>focal</os>
        <os>jammy</os>
        <update_interval>1h</update_interval>
    </provider>
```

Next, restart the Wazuh manager to apply the changes:

```
systemctl restart wazuh-manager
```

3. **Step 3: Vulnerability alerts generated**

   When the version of packages in the inventory database matches the vulnerability database (list of CVEs), the package will be labeled as *vulnerable* and the Vulnerability Detector module will organize all these vulnerabilities against every agent. You can check the vulnerable packages or applications by navigating to the vulnerabilities module of the Wazuh manager, as shown in the following screenshot.

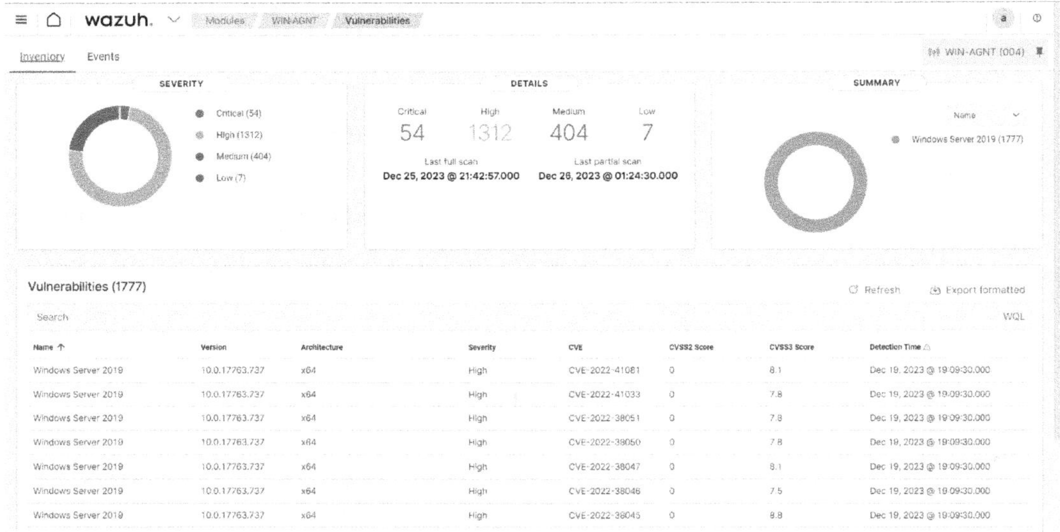

Figure 7.1 – Vulnerable packages or applications in Wazuh manager

> **Note**
>
> When we enable vulnerability detection for the first time, it performs a baseline scan wherein it performs a full scan of the operating system and every package installed. After that, it performs a partial scan where it only scans new packages.

Security configuration assessment

The **Security Configuration Assessment** (**SCA**) procedure validates that every system adheres to a predetermined set of regulations concerning configuration settings and authorized application usage.

Here are a couple of examples:

- Verifying that all the unnecessary open ports (TCP or UDP) are disabled or blocked
- Ensuring that default credentials have been modified

These are some of the most common approaches to bringing down the vulnerability surface of endpoints in the network. Wazuh has a built-in SCA module to scan such misconfigured endpoints and recommend remediation steps. The scanning is conducted based on the SCA policy file, which contains a set of rules. SCA policies can check for the existence of files, directories, registry keys/values, running processes, and so on, as illustrated in the following diagram.

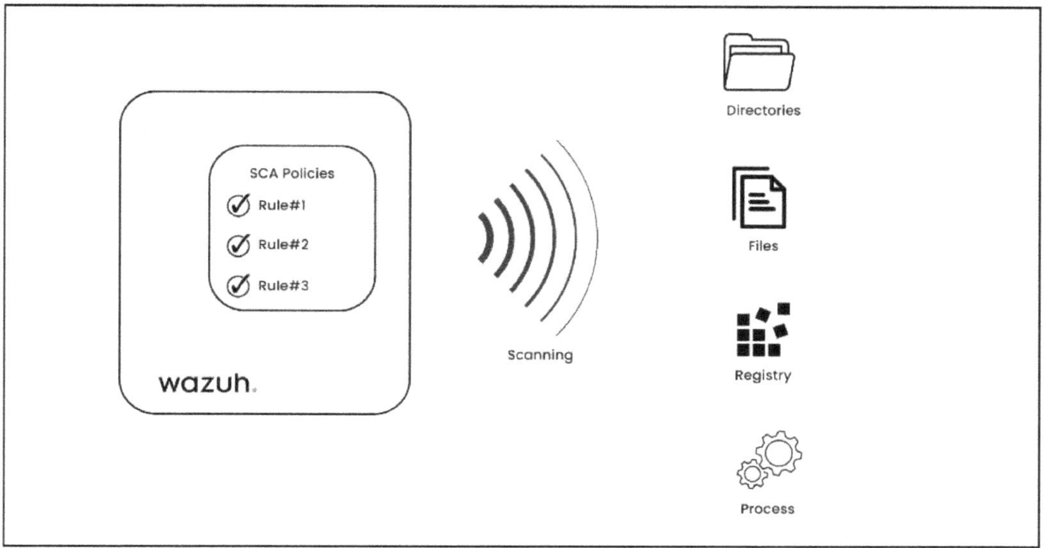

Figure 7.2 – Wazuh SCA check

Wazuh SCA checks that every Wazuh agent maintains a local database in which it keeps the present status of every SCA check. SCA scan results are shown as alerts whenever a particular check changes its status from its last scan.

The Wazuh team and community have built the SCA rules based on the CIS Benchmark. **Center for Internet Security** (**CIS**) is a non-profit, community-driven organization, responsible for building security controls and benchmarks for numerous operating systems and platforms. CIS Controls and CIS Benchmarks are globally recognized best practices for security network infrastructure.

How to set up Wazuh SCA

Wazuh SCA policies are derived from the CIS Benchmark. To configure Wazuh for SCA, start by turning on SCA policies on Wazuh agents. If you have a custom SCA policy, you can push it from the Wazuh manager to all the Wazuh agents. The process is explained as follows:

1. **Step 1: Enabling SCA policies on Wazuh agents**

   By default, Wazuh SCA checks are enabled on the Wazuh agent. However, it uses the default rule present in the `/var/ossec/ruleset/sca` directory for Linux and the `C:\\Program Files (x86)\\ossec-agent\\ruleset\\sca` folder for Windows. You can also create a custom SCA script by utilizing a YML file structure with four sections: `policy`, `requirements`, `variables`, and `checks`, as shown here:

```
policy:
  id: "rdp_audit"
  file: "sca_rdp_audit.yml"
  name: "System audit for Windows based system"
  description: "Guidance for establishing a secure configuration
for Unix based systems."
  references: https://www.cisecurity.org/
    -

requirements:
  title: "Check that the RDP service is not using the default
port (3389)"
  description: "Requirements for running the SCA scan against
the RDP service on Windows."
  condition: any
  rules:
    - 'r:HKEY_LOCAL_MACHINE\System\CurrentControlSet'

variables:
```

```
  $rdp_registry_path: HKEY_LOCAL_MACHINE\System\
CurrentControlSet\Control\Terminal Server\WinStations\RDP-Tcp

checks:
  - id: 3000
    title: "RDP Port: Check that RDP is not running on the
default port (3389)"
    description: "The RDP service should not be listening on the
default port 3389 for incoming connections."
    rationale: "Changing the default RDP port can help reduce
the risk of unauthorized access to the system."
    remediation: "Change the RDP port to a non-standard port for
added security."
    compliance:
      - pci_dss: ["2.2.4"]
      - nist_800_53: ["CM.1"]
    condition: all
    rules:
      - 'r:HKEY_LOCAL_MACHINE\System\CurrentControlSet\Control\
Terminal Server\WinStations\RDP-Tcp -> PortNumber -> d3d'
```

Let's break this down:

- `policy` is a required section.
- `id`, `file`, `name`, `description`, and `references` are some basic metadata for the preceding SCA script.
- `requirements` is an optional section.
- `variables` is again an optional section. It's important for simplifying the rule creation by creating variables for the path or file name and so on.
- `checks` is a required section. This is where we define rules and conditions.
- `'r:HKEY_LOCAL_MACHINE\System\CurrentControlSet\Control\Terminal Server\WinStations\RDP-Tcp -> PortNumber`: This represents the registry value of the RDP port. In this case, the rule checks whether it is `d3d`, which means `3389`.

2. **Step 2: Pushing an SCA policy from the Wazuh manager**

   If you have any custom SCA policy, you can push SCA files directly from the Wazuh manager to all the agents, but it requires enabling remote command execution on Wazuh agents. Once it is done, we can update our custom SCA policy under the `agent.conf` file to push the configurations to all Wazuh agents.

To complete the setup, we need to follow these steps:

I. Enable remote command execution. Set `sca.remote_commands` to `1`:

```
# echo "sca.remote_commands=1" >> /var/ossec/etc/local_
internal_options.conf
```

II. Place the custom SCA policy under the `/var/ossec/etc/shared/default` folder of the Wazuh manager and set the ownership to `wazuh:wazuh`:

```
chown wazuh:wazuh /var/ossec/etc/shared/default/sca_rdp_
audit.yml
```

III. Add the following configuration block to the `agent.conf` file:

```
<agent_config>
  <!-- Shared agent configuration here -->
  <sca>
    <policies>
        <policy>etc/shared/sca_rdp_audit.yml</policy>
    </policies>
  </sca>
</agent_config>
```

We have learned how SCA policies are created and how they are pushed to Wazuh agents. In the next section, we will learn about PCI DSS compliance and how can you use the Wazuh Vulnerability Detector and Security Configuration Assessment modules to meet its requirements.

PCI DSS

Credit card fraud is one of the most common types of bank fraud. A record $34.36 billion was lost to fraud on credit and debit cards in 2022, up almost 5% from the previous year (`http://tinyurl.com/4dymuc8d`). **Payment Card Industry Data Security Standard** (**PCI DSS**) compliance plays an important role because it forces organizations to safely and securely store and process payment card information. This protects both companies and their customers from data breaches and financial losses. For any organization to become PCI DSS compliant, it needs to fulfill 12 requirements drafted by PCI DSS. The Wazuh platform plays a crucial role in fulfilling some of the most critical PCI DSS requirements. In this chapter, we will address some of the important PCI DSS requirements:

- What is PCI DSS compliance?
- Requirements of PCI DSS compliance
- Wazuh use cases for PCI DSS compliance

What is PCI DSS compliance?

PCI DSS compliance was developed by Visa, MasterCard, Discover Financial Services, JCB International, and American Express in 2004 as a set of security standards. This compliance scheme is overseen by the **Payment Card Industry Security Standards Council (PCI SSC)**, with the objective of safeguarding credit and debit card transactions from fraudulent activities and data theft. PCI SSC is an international body that regulates the payment card industry.

PCI DSS is a set of twelve requirements and checklists to ensure that cardholder data is protected and prevent data breaches in organizations. Organizations complying with PCI DSS must meet all 12 requirements, covering the installation and use of firewalls, encryption, endpoint security, network security monitoring, log management, file integrity, access controls, and so on. Let's learn about each PCI DSS requirement in detail and the corresponding security controls.

Requirements of PCI DSS compliance

There are a total of 12 requirements to achieve PCI DSS certification. Each requirement has a few sub-requirements. I will explain each of the PCI DSS requirements with its main points, security controls, and the tools used to fulfill the corresponding requirements, and what Wazuh capabilities or modules can be used to address the same requirements.

- **Requirement #1: Install and maintain a firewall configuration to protect cardholder data**

Main Points	Security Controls and Tools	Wazuh Capabilities
• Install and maintain a firewall configuration to protect cardholder data. • Do not use vendor-supplied defaults for system passwords and other security parameters. • Protect stored cardholder data.	• Firewall • Next-gen Firewall • IPS/IDS: Suricata, Snort, Cisco Firepower	• Security Configuration Assessment (SCA) module

Table 7.1 – Security controls and Wazuh modules for PCI DSS Requirement 1

- **Requirement #2: Do not use vendor-supplied defaults when it comes to system passwords and other security elements**

Main Points	Security Controls and Tools	Wazuh Capabilities
• Encrypt transmission of cardholder data across open, public networks. • Do not store sensitive authentication data after authorization. • Encrypt stored cardholder data.	• Two-factor authentication: Google Authenticator, Cisco DUO	• Security Configuration Assessment (SCA) • Vulnerability detection • Log analysis

Table 7.2 – Security controls and Wazuh modules for PCI DSS Requirement 2

- **Requirement #3: Protect cardholder data**

Main Points	Security Controls and Tools	Wazuh Capabilities
• Keep anti-virus software updated and actively running. • Develop and maintain secure systems and applications. • Protect against malware.	SSL/TLS Encryption solutions: BitLocker	• Security Configuration Assessment (SCA) • File integrity monitoring

Table 7.3 – Security controls and Wazuh modules for PCI DSS Requirement 3

- **Requirement #4: Encrypt Transmission of Cardholder Data Across Open, Public Networks**

Main Points	Security Controls and Tools	Wazuh Capabilities
• Use strong encryption over public networks. • Avoid sending unprotected PANs.	• SSL/TLS Certificates • Remote Access VPN: Cisco AnyConnect, Palo Alto Global Protect etc	• Security Configuration Assessment (SCA)

Table 7.4 – Security controls and Wazuh modules for PCI DSS Requirement 4

- **Requirement #5: Protect all systems against malware and regularly update anti-virus software or programs**

Main Points	Security Controls and Tools	Wazuh Capabilities
• Use updated anti-virus software. • Ensure regular updates and scans.	• Endpoint protection or anti-virus software: Carbon Black, Kaspersky, CrowdStrike, and so on.	• Security Configuration Assessment (SCA) • Malware detection • Rootkit detection • Threat intelligence • Log analysis

Table 7.5 – Security controls and Wazuh modules for PCI DSS Requirement 5

- **Requirement #6: Develop and maintain secure systems and applications**

Main Points	Security Controls and Tools	Wazuh Capabilities
• Identify security vulnerabilities. • Protect systems from known vulnerabilities. • Follow secure software development practices.	• Security testing tools: Checkmarx, Veracode SonarQube, OWASP ZAP, Burp-Suite, Sonatype Nexus, Mend SCA	• Security Configuration Assessment (SCA) • Vulnerability detection • Log analysis • Active response, • File integrity monitoring

Table 7.6 – Security controls and Wazuh modules for PCI DSS Requirement 6

- **Requirement #7: Restrict access to cardholder data by business need to know**

Main Points	Security Controls and Tools	Wazuh Capabilities
• Limit access based on job necessity. • Implement access control. • Restrict physical access.	• Identity and access management: Okta, SailPoint, CyberArk	• Security Configuration Assessment (SCA)

Table 7.7 – Security controls and Wazuh modules for PCI DSS Requirement 7

- **Requirement #8: Identify and authenticate access to system components**

Main Points	Security Controls and Tools	Wazuh Capabilities
• Use unique IDs for system access. • Assign access by job role.	• Network access controls: Cisco ISE, Aruba ClearPass • Remote access VPN: Cisco AnyConnect, Palo Alto Global Protect, and so on	• Security Configuration Assessment (SCA) • Log analysis • File integrity monitoring

Table 7.8 – Security controls and Wazuh modules for PCI DSS Requirement 8

- **Requirement #9: Restrict physical access to cardholder data**

Main Points	Security Controls and Tools	Wazuh Capabilities
• Employ entry controls for physical access. • Differentiate between personnel and visitors.	• Physical access control system • Surveillance cameras • Biometric access system	• Security Configuration Assessment (SCA) • Log analysis

Table 7.9 – Security controls and Wazuh modules for PCI DSS Requirement 9

- **Requirement #10: Track and monitor all access to network resources and cardholder data**

Main Points	Security Controls and Tools	Wazuh Capabilities
• Monitor all network and data access. • Implement automated audit trails.	• Security Information and Event Management (SIEM) tools: Splunk SIEM, IBM QRadar, LogRhythm, and so on • IDS solutions: Snort, Suricata • Log management: Graylog	• Security Configuration Assessment (SCA) • Log data analysis • Active response

Table 7.10 – Security controls and Wazuh modules for PCI DSS Requirement 10

- **Requirement #11: Regularly test security systems and processes**

Main Points	Security Controls and Tools	Wazuh Capabilities
• Conduct regular security tests. • Perform internal and external vulnerability scans.	• Vulnerability scanning: Tenable, Qualys, Rapid7, and so on • Penetration testing: Metasploit framework, Burp-Suite	• Security Configuration Assessment (SCA) • Vulnerability detection • Log data analysis • Active response

Table 7.11 – Security controls and Wazuh modules for PCI DSS Requirement 11

- **Requirement #12: Regularly test security systems and processes**

Main Points	Security Controls and Tools	Wazuh Capabilities
• Establish and disseminate a security policy. • Ensure personnel awareness of security policy.	• Governance risk and compliance software: RSA Archer • Security awareness platform: KnowBe4, Cofence PhishMe, and so on.	• Security Configuration Assessment (SCA)

Table 7.12 – Security controls and Wazuh modules for PCI DSS Requirement 12

When it comes to Wazuh modules to address most of the PCI DSS requirements, **SCA** and Vulnerability Detector are the most common Wazuh modules listed in the preceding tables. Let's understand the use cases of both Wazuh modules to fulfill some of the important PCI DSS requirements as explained in the next section onward.

Vulnerability detection use cases for PCI DSS

As we learned in the *Introduction to vulnerability detection and security configuration management* section, Wazuh detects vulnerabilities in the applications or packages installed on agents using the Vulnerability Detector module. The vulnerability scanning or checks are performed by integrating vulnerability feeds from Debian, Red Hat, Arch Linux, **Amazon Linux Advisories Security** (**ALAS**), Microsoft, the National Vulnerability Database, and many more. Wazuh Vulnerability Detector can be confidently used for Requirement 6 and Requirement 11 of PCI DSS compliance. Use cases for PCI DSS requirements that the vulnerability detection module can fulfill are as follows:

Use case #1: Ensure the detection of and address security vulnerabilities on Windows machines

As per PCI DSS requirement 6, we need to ensure that we detect and address security vulnerabilities. In this use case, we will focus on a Windows machine to detect and address vulnerabilities using a Wazuh module. We can schedule a Vulnerability Detector scan to discover security vulnerabilities. This will require the following steps:

1. Requirements
2. Set up the syscollector wodle on the endpoint
3. Enable Vulnerability Detector on the Wazuh server and restart
4. Visualize the alerts

Requirements

To set up the lab environment to run vulnerability detection on a Windows machine, you require the following systems:

- Windows machine (with the Wazuh agent installed)
- Wazuh server

Set up the syscollector wodle on the Windows endpoint

The Wazuh syscollector wodle manages the information related to hardware, applications, the operating system, and so on. To customize our Windows endpoint, add the syscollector wodle in the `ossec.config` file located at `/var/ossec/etc` in the Wazuh agent, as shown here:

```
<wodle name="syscollector">
    <disabled>no</disabled>
    <interval>1h</interval>
    <packages>yes</packages>
</wodle>
```

Enable Vulnerability Detector on the Wazuh server and restart

To enable vulnerability detection for the Windows platform, you need to edit the `ossec.conf` file in the Wazuh server located at `/var/ossec/etc`. You are required to set `<enabled>` tab to `yes` under the `Windows OS vulnerabilities` section, as shown here:

```
<vulnerability-detector>
    <enabled>yes</enabled>
    <interval>5m</interval>
    <run_on_start>yes</run_on_start>

    <!-- Windows OS vulnerabilities -->
    <provider name="msu">
        <enabled>yes</enabled>
        <update_interval>1h</update_interval>
    </provider>
```

Restart and test the Wazuh manager:

```
systemctl restart wazuh-manager
```

Once the Wazuh manager is finished with the restart, you can see the vulnerability alerts on the **Modules** > **Vulnerabilities** > **Events** tab. The top two vulnerabilities are about the Google Chrome application on the Windows machine.

> **Note**
>
> Once you select Google Chrome Vulnerability CVE-2023-5472, the Wazuh dashboard gives an overview of the alert and the current status of the agent. To know more about all the active CVEs, including information on the affected software, severity rating, links to adversaries, and patches released by the vendor, you can visit `cvedetails.com`. This website is managed by the SecurityScorecard organization.

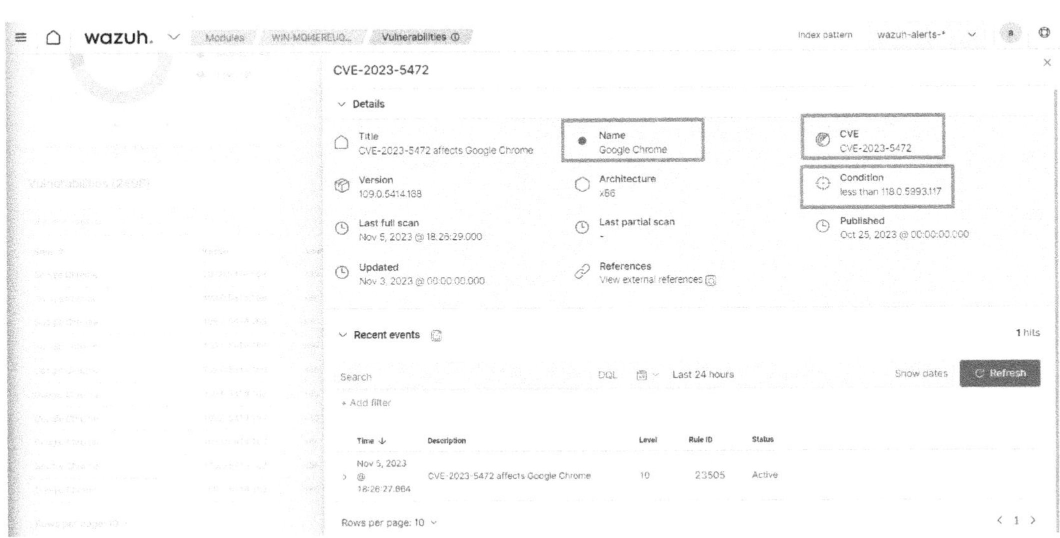

Figure 7.3 – Vulnerability detection for Google Chrome CVE-2023-5472

Use case #2: Identify, prioritize, and address security vulnerabilities regularly

As per *PCI DSS Requirement 11*, we need to identify, prioritize, and address security vulnerabilities. You can apply a filter with `severity=Critical` and you can see all Windows vulnerabilities with critical severity.

Figure 7.4 – Finding critical vulnerabilities with Vulnerability Detector

Security configuration assessment use cases for PCI DSS

Security configuration assessment is an essential Wazuh module, helping you to address multiple PCI DSS requirements. In fact, many of the PCI DSS requirements can be fulfilled by using the Wazuh SCA module. We will address two important PCI DSS requirements using some sample SCA scripts. Please note, both the mentioned use cases are already present in the `cis_win2012r2.yml` file located at `C:\\Program Files (x86)\\ossec-agent\\ruleset\\sca`.

Use case #1: Do not display the last user name on interactive login

PCI DSS Requirement 2 requires enabling only necessary services, protocols, and daemons, and removing or disabling all unnecessary functionality. Let's audit a specific service on Windows Server 2012 R2. We will run an SCA check on whether the account name of the last user to log on to the computer will be displayed on each computer's respective Windows logon screen. It's recommended the feature is disabled.

In the *Security configuration assessment* section, we already covered how to create a custom SCA and the components of each SCA script (policy, requirements, checks). Following is a PCI DSS requirement use case wherein we check if **'Interactive logon: Do not display last user name'** is set to **'Enabled'**. The SCA script is already built by the Wazuh team and compiled by them in the `cis_win2012r2.yml` file located at `C:\\Program Files (x86)\\ossec-agent\\ruleset\\sca`.

One of the sub-requirements under *PCI DSS Requirement 2* requires disabling all unwanted services, protocols, daemons, and functionalities. In this use case, we will run an SCA check to ensure *'Do not display last user name in the interactive Windows logon'* is enabled on the Windows machine. The SCA script has already been built by the Wazuh team and compiled by them in the `cis_win2012r2.yml` file located at `C:\\Program Files (x86)\\ossec-agent\\ruleset\\sca`. This will require the following steps:

1. Requirements
2. Reviewing the SCA policy
3. Visualizing alerts

Requirements

In order to complete the use case of performing an SCA check for *Do not display last user name on Interactive login*, the requirements are as follows:

- Windows machine (with the Wazuh agent installed)
- Wazuh server

Reviewing the SCA policy

We don't need to make any changes in this step. Wazuh has a built-in SCA policy for *'Interactive logon: Do not display last user name'*, set to **'Enabled'** under the `C:\\Program Files (x86)\\ossec-agent\\ruleset\\sca` file as shown here:

```
- id: 15015
    title: "Ensure 'Interactive logon: Do not display last user name'
is set to 'Enabled'"
    description: "This policy setting determines whether the account
name of the last user to log on to the client computers in your
organization will be displayed in each computer's respective Windows
logon screen. Enable this policy setting to prevent intruders from
collecting account names visually from the screens of desktop or
laptop computers in your organization. The recommended state for this
setting is: Enabled."
    rationale: "An attacker with access to the console (for example,
someone with physical access or someone who is able to connect to the
server through Remote Desktop Services) could view the name of the
last user who logged on to the server. The attacker could then try to
guess the password, use a dictionary, or use a brute-force attack to
try and log on."
    remediation: "To establish the recommended configuration via
GP, set the following UI path to Enabled: Computer Configuration\\
Policies\\Windows Settings\\Security Settings\\Local Policies\\
Security Options\\Interactive logon: Do not display last user name."
    compliance:
      - cis: [«2.3.7.1»]
      - cis_csc: [«13»]
      - pci_dss: [«2.2.3»]
      - nist_800_53: ["CM.1"]
      - gpg_13: ["4.3"]
      - gdpr_IV: ["35.7.d"]
      - hipaa: ["164.312.b"]
      - tsc: ["CC5.2"]
    references:
      - 'CCE-36056-0'
    condition: all
    rules:
      - 'r:HKEY_LOCAL_MACHINE\Software\Microsoft\Windows\
CurrentVersion\Policies\System -> DontDisplayLastUserName -> 1'
```

Here, we see the following:

- `condition` is set to `all`.
- `r:HKEY_LOCAL_MACHINE\Software\Microsoft\Windows\CurrentVersion\Policies\System` represents the registry value by using the `r` parameter at the beginning. In our case, we have set the registry value to `1`.

Visualizing the alerts

To verify whether our Windows Server 2012 R2 passed or failed the SCA check, you can go to **Modules** > **Security configuration assessment** and then select the agent. As per the SCA alert shown here, the check has failed.

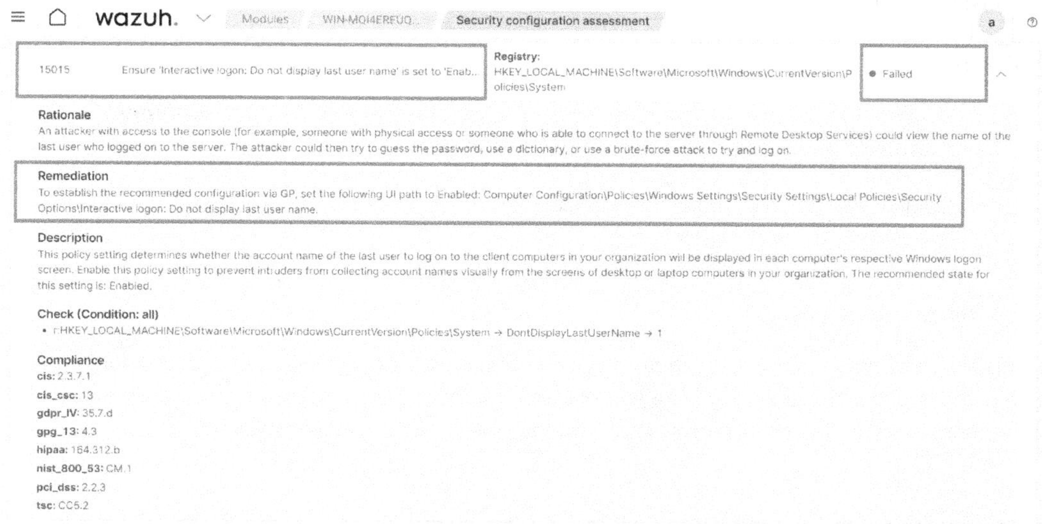

Figure 7.5 –SCA check – Do not display last user name on Interactive login

In order to ensure our Windows machine passes the SCA check for **Ensure 'Interactive logon. Do not display last user name' is set to 'Enabled**, we simply navigate to the registry editor of the Windows machine, navigate to the `HKEY_LOCAL_MACHINE\Software\Microsoft\Windows\CurrentVersion\Policies\System -> DontDisplayLastUserName` registry location and set it to `1`.

Use case #2: Disable anonymous enumeration of SAM accounts and shares

According to *PCI DSS Requirement 7*, businesses should restrict access to the cardholder data environment based on a business need-to-know basis. This simply means that only authorized personnel (engineer/technician/manager) should be able to access cardholder-related data, and that access should be limited based on the job responsibilities and business requirements. One such use case for a Windows machine is to disable the anonymous enumeration of SAM accounts and shares. **SAM** (short for **Security Account Manager**) refers to a database file in Microsoft Windows that stores user accounts and passwords. If we disable the anonymous enumeration of SAM accounts, it will ensure that only authorized users get access to the network. Wazuh has already created an SCA script to fulfill this requirement under the `cis_win2012r2.yml` file located at `C:\\Program Files (x86)\\ossec-agent\\ruleset\\sca` in the Windows agent.

The following topics will be covered in this use case:

- Requirements
- Reviewing the SCA policy
- Visualizing the alerts

Requirements

In order to complete the use case to perform an SCA check for **Disable Anonymous enumeration of SAM accounts and shares**, the requirements are as follows:

- Kali Linux (with the Wazuh agent installed)
- Wazuh server

Reviewing the SCA policy

The following example is a use case where we ensure that anonymous users can't scan SAM accounts and shares. Enabling this policy setting will prevent anonymous users from enumerating network share names and domain account user names on the systems in your environment:

```
- id: 15031
    title: "Ensure 'Network access: Do not allow anonymous enumeration of SAM accounts and shares' is set to 'Enabled'"
    description: "This policy setting controls the ability of anonymous users to enumerate SAM accounts as well as shares. If you enable this policy setting, anonymous users will not be able to enumerate domain account user names and network share names on the systems in your environment. The recommended state for this setting is: Enabled. Note: This policy has no effect on Domain Controllers."
    rationale: "An unauthorized user could anonymously list account names and shared resources and use the information to attempt to guess passwords or perform social engineering attacks. (Social engineering attacks try to deceive users in some way to obtain passwords or some form of security information)"
    remediation: "To establish the recommended configuration via GP, set the following U path to Enabled: Computer Configuration\\Policies\\Windows Settings\\Security Settings\\Local Policies\\Security Options\\Network access: Do not allow anonymous enumeration of SAM accounts and shares."
    compliance:
      - cis: [«2.3.10.3»]
      - cis_csc: [«16»]
      - pci_dss: [«7.1»]
      - tsc: ["CC6.4"]
    references:
      - 'CCE-36316-8'
    condition: all
```

```
    rules:
      - 'r:HKEY_LOCAL_MACHINE\SYSTEM\CurrentControlSet\Control\Lsa ->
RestrictAnonymous -> 1'
```

Here, we see the following:

- `condition` is set to `all`.
- `r:HKEY_LOCAL_MACHINE\SYSTEM\CurrentControlSet\Control\Lsa` represents the registry value of `HKEY_LOCAL_MACHINE\SYSTEM\CurrentControlSet\Control\Lsa`. In our case, it is set to `1`.

Visualizing the alerts

To verify whether our Windows Server 2012 R2 passed or failed the SCA check, you can go to **Modules** > **Security Configuration Assessment** and then select the agent. You can verify whether the SCA check is passed or failed as shown in the following screenshot:

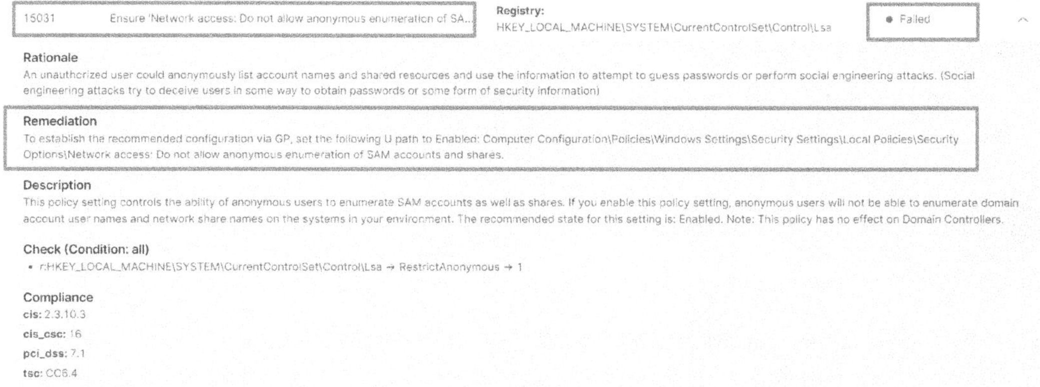

Figure 7.6 – SCA check – Disable Anonymous enumeration of SAM accounts and shares

As per the SCA output, the check failed because the registry value of `HKEY_LOCAL_MACHINE\SYSTEM\CurrentControlSet\Control\Lsa` is not set to `1` on our Windows machine. This means an attacker could list account names and shared resources and use that information to perform a social engineering attack.

The remediation is shown in the above diagram and requires you to set the registry value to 1, then our SCA check will be marked as passed.

In this section, we have learned about PCI DSS compliance and its requirements and utilized Wazuh's Vulnerability Detector and SCA modules to fulfill some of the popular PCI Compliance requirements. In the next section, we will learn about NIST 800-53 controls and how Wazuh modules can be used for some of the NIST 800-53 controls.

NIST 800-53

Over 30,000 cyber security incidents were reported to federal agencies in the United States in the fiscal year 2022-23 – a five percent reduction from the year before (`http://tinyurl.com/2s3msja8`). All federal agencies need to be compliant with the **Federal Information Security Management Act** (**FISMA**). FISMA is a federal law that requires US government agencies to create, document, and implement an information security and protection program. **NIST 800-53** is a cybersecurity standard and guidelines that help federal agencies meet the requirements set by FISMA. The NIST 800-53 framework is developed by the National Institute of Standards in Technology. To summarize, the NIST 800-53 framework helps federal agencies to become FISMA compliant. In this section, we will cover the following topics:

- What is the NIST 800-53 framework?
- List of control families in the NIST 800-53 framework
- Vulnerability detection use case

What is the NIST 800-53 framework?

The NIST 800-53 framework is a cybersecurity standard and compliance framework developed by the **National Institute of Standards and Technology** (**NIST**). It provides a set of guidelines on the security controls needed to build secure and resilient information systems.

What is the goal of NIST 800-53?

The goals of NIST Special Publication 800-53 are the following:

- **Offer a thorough framework**: The goal of NIST 800-53 is to provide an extensive and organized framework for choosing and putting security policies in place to safeguard information systems
- **Enhance information security**: By implementing a set of security controls and best practices, its main objective is to improve the security and privacy of federal information systems and organizations
- **Encourage risk management**: NIST 800-53 advises businesses to recognize, evaluate, and control cybersecurity risks in accordance with their particular requirements and threat environments
- **Facilitate compliance and regulation**: It acts as a guide for companies doing business with the United States government and assists firms in conforming to federal rules and compliance obligations, such as FISMA
- **Encourage continuous improvement**: Organizations can adjust and improve their cybersecurity procedures over time as a result of NIST 800-53's evolution to address new threats and technology

The NIST 800-53 framework provides a number of different controls across multiple security and system access control families. The controls are then organized into 20 security and control families.

List of control families in the NIST 800-53 framework

NIST 800-53 controls are categorized into 20 different security and control families. Each control family has a unique ID and multiple sub-controls. In the following table, we will focus on a wider control family only. Additionally, I'm adding two additional columns to showcase enterprise tools and Wazuh capabilities (modules) available for each NIST 800-53 control.

ID	Family Name	Examples of Controls	Wazuh Capabilities
AC	Access Control	Account management and monitoring; least privilege; separation of duties	• Wazuh log data analysis
AT	Awareness and Training	User training on security threats; technical training for privileged users	• Log data analysis
AU	Audit and Accountability	Content of audit records; analysis and reporting; record retention	• None
CA	Assessment, Authorization, and Monitoring	Connections to public networks and external systems; penetration testing	• Vulnerability detector • File integrity monitoring
CM	Configuration Management	Authorized software policies; configuration change control	• SCA
CP	Contingency Planning	Alternate processing and storage sites; business continuity strategies; testing	• None
IA	Identification and Authentication	Authentication policies for users, devices, and services; credential management	• SCA
IP	Individual Participation	Consent and privacy authorization	• None
IR	Incident Response	Incident response training, monitoring, and reporting	• Active response • Threat intelligence
MA	Maintenance	System, personnel, and tool maintenance	• Log data analysis
MP	Media Protection	Access, storage, transport, sanitization, and use of media	• Log data analysis

ID	Family Name	Examples of Controls	Wazuh Capabilities
PA	Privacy Authorization	Collection, use, and sharing of personally identifiable information (PII)	• None
PE	Physical and Environment Protection	Physical access; emergency power; fire protection; temperature control	• None
PL	Planning	Social media and networking restrictions; defense-in-depth security architecture	• None
PM	Program Management	Risk management strategy; enterprise architecture	• None
PS	Personnel Security	Personnel screening, termination, and transfer; external personnel; sanctions	• None
RA	Risk Assessment	Risk assessment; vulnerability scanning; privacy impact assessment	• None
SA	System and Services Acquisition	System development lifecycle; acquisition process; supply chain risk management	• None
SC	System and Communications Protection	Application partitioning; boundary protection; cryptographic key management	• Threat intelligence • Active response
SI	System and Information Integrity	Flaw remediation; system monitoring and alerting	• File integrity monitoring • Active response

Table 7.13 – List of NIST 800-53 framework controls and Wazuh capabilities

Vulnerability detection use cases for NIST 800-53

The Vulnerability Detector module of Wazuh helps to discover the vulnerabilities of different operating systems. As per the *List of NIST 800-53 framework controls and Wazuh capabilities* table, the *Assessment, Authorization, and Monitoring* control family, with control ID *CA*, uses the Vulnerability Detector module of the Wazuh platform.

Use case: Detect vulnerabilities on Debian-based endpoints

In this use case of vulnerability detection for the NIST 800-53 *Assessment, Authorization, and Monitoring*, control family, we will set up the Wazuh platform to discover vulnerabilities on a Kali Linux machine. Kali Linux is a Debian-based Linux operating system. We will cover the following points in this section:

1. Requirements
2. Setting up the syscollector wodle on endpoint
3. Enabling Vulnerability Detector on the Wazuh server and restarting
4. Visualizing the alerts

Requirements

In order to complete the use case to perform vulnerability detection on a Kali Linux machine, the requirements are as follows:

- Kali Linux machine (with the Wazuh agent installed)
- Wazuh server

Setting up the syscollector wodle on endpoint

Wazuh's syscollector module is responsible for collecting information about the Wazuh agent such as hardware, the operating system, installed applications, packages, and so on. To customize our Debian endpoint, add the syscollector wodle in the `ossec.config` file located at `/var/ossec/etc` in the Wazuh agent:

```
<wodle name="syscollector">
   <disabled>no</disabled>
   <interval>1h</interval>
   <packages>yes</packages>
</wodle>
```

Enabling Vulnerability Detector on the Wazuh server and restarting

To enable vulnerability detection for a Debian-based platform, you need to edit the `ossec.conf` file in the Wazuh server located at `/var/ossec/etc`. You are required to set `<enable>` tab to `yes` under the `Debian OS vulnerabilities` section, as shown here:

```
-- Debian OS vulnerabilities -->
     <provider name="debian">
        <enabled>yes</enabled>
        <os allow="Kali GNU/Linux-2023">buster</os>
        <os>bullseye</os>
      <os>bookworm</os>
```

```
    <update_interval>1h</update_interval>
  </provider>
```

Note the following:

- `<os allow="Kali GNU/Linux-2023">buster</os>` indicates what operating system should be allowed to be monitored for vulnerability scanning. In this case, it is Kali GNU/Linux-2023

Next, restart the Wazuh manager:

```
systemctl restart wazuh-manager
```

Visualizing the alerts

To visualize the vulnerability events, navigate to the **Vulnerabilities** module in the Wazuh manager and check for alerts.

Figure 7.7 – Visualizing vulnerability events of Kali Linux

SCA use cases for NIST 800-53

The Wazuh SCA module scans monitored endpoints to see whether they fulfill secure configuration and hardening standards. Let's cover a use case of Wazuh SCA to support NIST 800-53 controls. We can use Wazuh's SCA module to address multiple NIST 800-53 control requirements. One such use case will be covered in this section.

Use case

We need to change the default SSH port. The **Configuration Management** (**CM**) control family talks about creating and enforcing baseline system configurations. There is a sub-control under the CM control family called CM.1 that focuses on changing the default setting for the port or service on the system. In this use case, we will do SSH hardening checks on a Debian machine. By changing the default port, you may be able to decrease the amount of zombie bot attacks that succeed. The SCA script is already built by the Wazuh team and compiled by them in the `sca_unix_audit.yml` file located at `C:\\Program Files (x86)\\ossec-agent\\ruleset\\sca`. The following topics will be covered in this use case:

- Requirements
- Reviewing the SCA policy
- Visualizing the alerts

Requirements

In order to complete the use case to perform an SCA check for *Change the default SSH port*, the requirements are as follows:

- Kali Linux (with the Wazuh agent installed)
- Wazuh server

Reviewing the SCA policy

We are not required to make any changes to this set. Wazuh has already built tons of SCA policies based on CIS Benchmarks for multiple operating systems. The SCA policy named `sca_unix_audit.yml` will be automatically installed while downloading the Wazuh agent packages. To view the SCA policy for *SSH Hardening: Port Should not be 22*, you can open the `sca_unix_audit.yml` file located at `/var/ossec/ruleser/sca` in the Kali Linux Wazuh agent. You can find the required SCA policy under `rule id: 3000`, as shown here:

```
- id: 3000
    title: "SSH Hardening: Port should not be 22"
    description: "The ssh daemon should not be listening on port 22
(the default value) for incoming connections."
    rationale: "Changing the default port you may reduce the number of
successful attacks from zombie bots, an attacker or bot doing port-
scanning can quickly identify your SSH port."
    remediation: "Change the Port option value in the sshd_config
file."
    compliance:
      - pci_dss: [«2.2.4»]
      - nist_800_53: [«CM.1»]
```

```
  condition: all
  rules:
    - 'f:$sshd_file -> !r:^# && r:Port && !r:\s*\t*22$'
```

Note the following:

- `Condition` is `all`
- `Rules: 'f:$sshd_file -> !r:^# && r:Port && !r:\s*\t*22$` checks for non-command lines indicating the SSH port, excluding lines representing default port 22

Visualizing the alerts

To visualize the SCA check for *SSH Hardening: Port should not be 22*, you can navigate to the SCA module on the Wazuh manager and search for *SSH Hardening: Port should not be 22*. You should see the result as shown in the following screenshot:

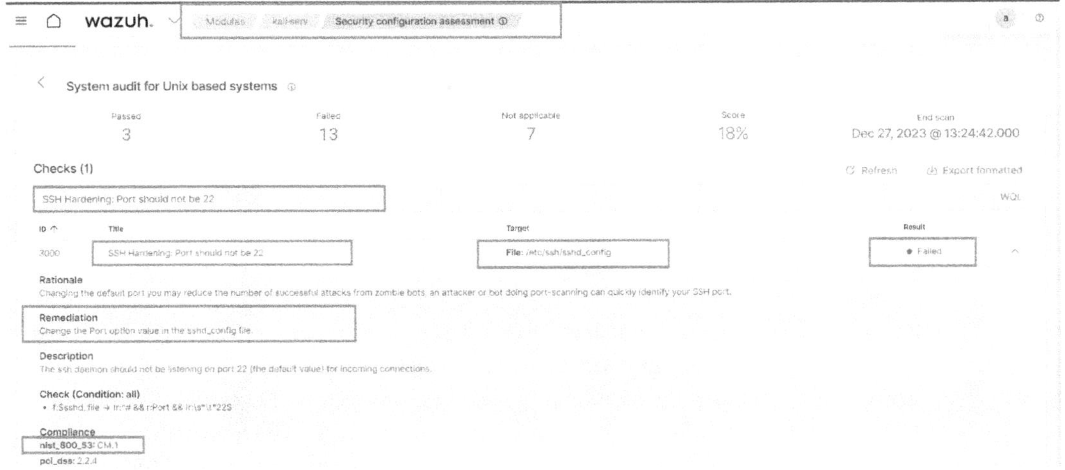

Figure 7.8 – Visualizing SCA check for SSH hardening

Note the following:

- **Title**: **SSH Hardening: Port should not be 22** represents the name of the SCA check.
- **Target**: **/etc/ssh/sshd_config** is the target file location that SCA will validate for the SSH configuration.
- **Result**: **Failed** represents the status of the SCA check. In this case, it is failed.

- **Remediation**: **Change the Port option value in the sshd_config file** explains how to modify the target configuration file if the SCA check fails.
- **Compliance**: **nist_800_53** represents the list of regulatory compliance meeting this requirement.

In this section, we have learned about NIST 800-53 controls and use cases of the Vulnerability Detector and SCA modules to fulfill the requirements of NIST 800-53 controls. In the next section, we will learn about HIPAA compliance in detail.

HIPAA

The HHS **Office for Civil Rights** (**OCR**) data leak portal says that there were about 295 breaches in the healthcare sector in just the first half of 2023. In the first half of the year, healthcare data leaks were linked to more than 39 million people. The **Health Insurance Portability and Accountability Act** (**HIPAA**) is important for many reasons, but the main one is to keep healthcare data private and secure. Wazuh can help health organizations to maintain HIPPA compliance using its in-built capabilities. In this chapter, we will cover the following topics:

- HIPAA compliance rules
- HIPAA security rules
- Vulnerability Detector use cases
- SCA use cases

What is HIPAA compliance?

HIPAA establishes protection standards for sensitive patient health information. HIPAA violations are mainly related to unauthorized access, use, or disclosure of **Protected Health Information** (**PHI**).

Any personally identifiable health information that is communicated or maintained electronically, on paper, or orally is considered PHI. Any information pertaining to a person's past, present, or future health, as well as specifics about medical treatments and payment information that could be used to identify the individual is included in **Health Information** (**HI**). PHI examples are as follows:

- Social Security number
- Name
- Dates of birth, death or treatment, and other dates relating to patient care
- Photographs
- Contact information
- Medical record numbers

HIPAA security rules

The HIPAA Security Rule checklist includes criteria for ensuring the confidentiality, integrity, and availability of PHI created, received, maintained, or transmitted electronically (ePHI). The HIPAA security rules consist of five sections:

- **General rules**: These lay the groundwork for HIPAA compliance, highlighting the importance of privacy and security policies, processes, and worker training
- **Administrative safeguards**: These concentrate on organizational safeguards for ePHI, such as risk assessments, security management, and employee training
- **Physical safeguards**: These cover workstation security, facility security measures, and access controls as they relate to the physical security of data centers and equipment
- **Technical safeguards**: These encompass technical security protocols, including audit controls, encryption, and access controls, which are implemented to safeguard electronic health
- **Organizational requirements**: These focus on the necessity of contracts, agreements, and oversight of business partners' HIPAA compliance and are related to requirements while working with them

As per the scope of this book, we will focus on two categories of HIPAA security rules: administrative safeguards and technical safeguards.

Administrative safeguards

The administrative safeguards, which mandate the designation of a security officer in charge of workforce training, risk analysis, risk and vulnerability implementation, IT continuity supervision, and business associate agreements, form the foundation of security rule compliance.

Standards	**Description**	**Wazuh Capabilities**
Security Management Process	• Risk analysis to detect vulnerabilities regularly • Implementing risk minimization	• Vulnerability detection • Configuration assessment
Assign Security Responsibility	• Designation of a HIPAA security officer • They can also serve as privacy officer	
Workforce Security	• Implement access control for employees • Ensure monitoring for role change and termination access	• Log data analysis • File integrity monitoring

Standards	Description	Wazuh Capabilities
Information Access Management	• Restrict ePHI access to "covered" organizations' workforces • Block parent and connected entities from accessing ePHI	• File integrity monitoring • Configuration assessment • Malware detection
Security Awareness and Training	• Conduct employee security awareness training • Include security reminders and password guidance	• Log data analysis • Action response
Security Incident Procedures	• Implement policies and procedures for incident reporting • Not limited to cybersecurity incidents	• Log data analysis • Active response
Contingency Plan	• Emergency response policies, including data backup and recovery • Routine drill exercise	None
Periodic Evaluations	• Periodic review of policies, procedures, and measures	• Configuration assessment

Table 7.14 – Security controls and Wazuh modules for administrative safeguards of HIPAA compliance

Technical safeguards

The HIPAA technical safeguards ensure that people accessing ePHI are who they say they are, do what they should, and correct issues caused by accidental or malicious actions as soon as possible.

Standards	Description	Wazuh Capabilities
Access Control	• Restrict ePHI access • Ensure authorized users have access rights	• Log data analysis • Configuration assessment
Audit Controls	• Implement system activity recording and analysis • Store ePHI access and modification audit logs	• Log data analysis

Standards	Description	Wazuh Capabilities
Integrity Controls	• Prevent ePHI modification • Implement data integrity checks	• File integrity monitoring
Transmission Security	• Transmit ePHI encrypted • Protect electronic communication	• File integrity monitoring • Configuration assessment
Person or Entity Authentication	• Verify ePHI users' identities • Secure system access with rigorous authentication	• Log data analysis

Table 7.15 – Security controls and Wazuh modules for technical safeguards of HIPAA compliance

Vulnerability Detector use cases

Vulnerability detection plays a critical role in the security management process standard under administrative safeguards. It is about risk analysis and thorough assessment of the potential risks and vulnerabilities. Wazuh's Vulnerability Detector module can be used to address multiple HIPAA requirements under administrative and technical safeguards.

Use case: Detect vulnerabilities on Ubuntu endpoints

In this use case of vulnerability detection for HIPAA compliance, we are addressing the *Security Management Process* standard under administrative safeguards. We will set up the Wazuh platform to discover vulnerabilities on an Ubuntu machine. We will cover the following points in this section:

- Requirements
- Setting up the syscollector wodle on endpoint
- Enabling Vulnerability Detector on the Wazuh server and restarting
- Visualizing the alerts

Requirements

In order to complete the use case to perform vulnerability detection on an Ubuntu machine, the requirements are as follows:

- Ubuntu machine (with the Wazuh agent installed)
- Wazuh server

Setting up the syscollector wodle on endpoint

To customize our Ubuntu endpoint, add the `syscollector` wodle in the `ossec.config` file located at `/var/ossec/etc` in the Wazuh agent, as shown here:

```
<wodle name="syscollector">
   <disabled>no</disabled>
   <interval>1h</interval>
   <packages>yes</packages>
</wodle>
```

Enabling Vulnerability Detector on the Wazuh server and restarting

To enable vulnerability detection for the Ubuntu operating system, you need to edit the `ossec.conf` file on the Wazuh server located at `/var/ossec/etc`. You are required to set the `<enable>` tab to `yes` under the *Ubuntu OS vulnerabilities* section, as shown:

```
<vulnerability-detector>
    <enabled>yes</enabled>
    <interval>5m</interval>
    <run_on_start>yes</run_on_start>
    <provider name="canonical">
       <enabled>yes</enabled>
       <os>bionic</os>
       <update_interval>1h</update_interval>
    </provider>
 </vulnerability-detector>
```

Next, restart the Wazuh manager:

```
systemctl restart wazuh-manager
```

Visualizing the alerts

To visualize the vulnerability events, navigate to the **Vulnerabilities** module in the Wazuh manager and check the alerts, as shown here:

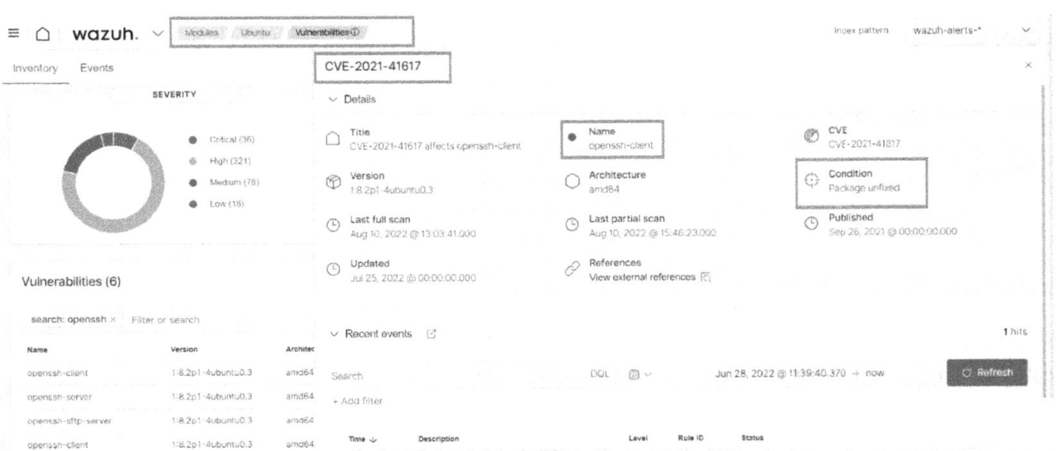

Figure 7.9 – Visualizing the CVE-2021-41617 Ubuntu vulnerability on the Wazuh manager

SCA use case

In this use case, we will go through SCA scripts on Ubuntu machines. As we have already learned, the SCA feature conducts scans on the monitored endpoints to ascertain whether they are properly configured and hardened. These scans evaluate the endpoint's setup by comparing the endpoint's actual configuration to the settings in a policy file.

Use case: Ensure audit tools are 755 or more restrictive

The *HIPAA 164.308(a)(3)(i)* and *164.308(a)(3)(ii)(A)* sections talk about administrative safeguards. All members of a workforce should have appropriate access to electronic PHI to prevent unauthorized access. It is primarily concerned with controlling and managing access to PHI by employees. Let's run SCA checks on an Ubuntu 22.04 machine. In this use case, we will check whether auditd and audit logs are protected with sufficient permissions:

- Requirements
- Reviewing the SCA policy
- Visualizing the alerts

Requirements

In order to complete the use case to perform an SCA check to *Ensure Audit tools are 755 or more restrictive*, the requirements are as follows:

- Ubuntu machine (with the Wazuh agent installed)
- Wazuh server

Reviewing the SCA policy

The SCA policy file called `cis_ubuntu22-04.yml` gets installed while installing the Wazuh agent package on an Ubuntu machine. This file consists of all the SCA policies related to Ubuntu version 22.04. To view the SCA policy for `Ensure audit tools are 755 or more restrictive`, you can open the `cis_ubuntu22-04.yml` file located at `/var/ossec/ruleser/sca` in the Ubuntu Wazuh agent. You can find the required SCA policy under `rule id: 28610`, as shown here:

```
  - id: 28610
    title: "Ensure audit tools are 755 or more restrictive."
    description: "Audit tools include, but are not limited to, vendor-
provided and open source audit tools n>     rationale: "Protecting
audit information includes identifying and protecting the tools used
to view and >    remediation: "Run the following command to remove
more permissive mode from the audit tools: # chmod go->    compliance:
      - cis: [«4.1.4.8»]
      - cis_csc_v7: [«14.6»]
      - cis_csc_v8: [«3.3»]
      - mitre_techniques: [«T1070», «T1070.002», «T1083»]
      - mitre_tactics: [«TA0007»]
      - cmmc_v2.0: [«AC.L1-3.1.1», «AC.L1-3.1.2», «AC.L2-3.1.5», «AC.
L2-3.1.3», «MP.L2-3.8.2»]
      - hipaa: ["164.308(a)(3)(i)", "164.308(a)(3)(ii)(A)",
"164.312(a)(1)"]
      - pci_dss_3.2.1: ["7.1", "7.1.1", "7.1.2", "7.1.3"]
      - pci_dss_4.0: ["1.3.1", "7.1"]
      - nist_sp_800-53: ["AC-5", "AC-6"]
      - soc_2: ["CC5.2", "CC6.1"]
    condition: none
    rules:
      - 'c:stat -c "%n %a" /sbin/auditctl /sbin/aureport /sbin/
ausearch /sbin/autrace /sbin/auditd /sbin/aug>
```

Note the following:

- `condition` is set to `none`
- The `'c:stat -c "%n %a" /sbin/auditctl /sbin/aureport /sbin/ausearch /sbin/autrace /sbin/auditd /sbin/aug>` rule checks for the permissions of auditd and related permissions

Visualizing the alerts

To visualize the SCA check for `Ensure audit tools are 755 or more restrictive`, you can navigate to the SCA module on the Wazuh manager and search for `Ensure audit tools are 755 or more restrictive`. You should see the result shown in the following screenshot:

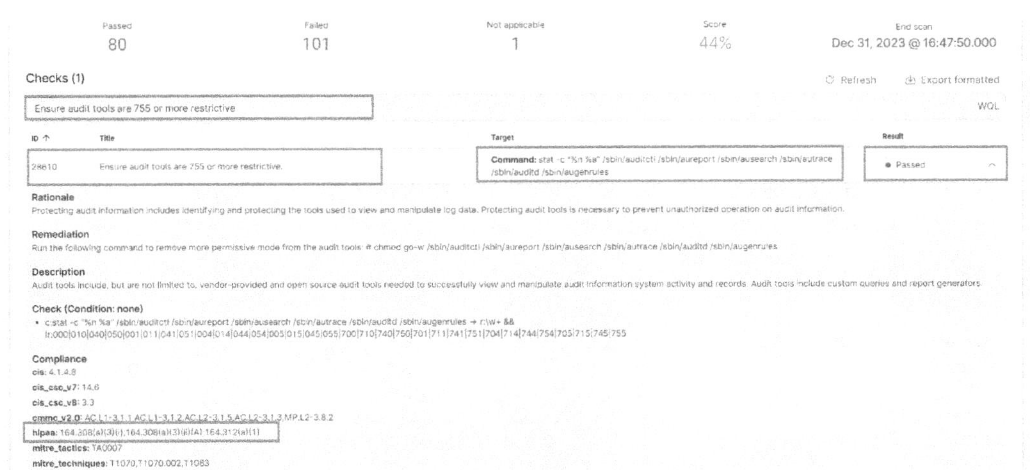

Figure 7.10 – SCA check – Ensure audit tools are 755 or more restrictive

Note the following:

- **Title**: **Ensure audit tools are 755 or more restrictive** represents the name of the SCA check.
- **Target**: **/etc/ssh/sshd_config** is the target file location that SCA will validate for the SSH configuration.
- **Command: stat -c "%n %a " /sbin/auditctl /sbin/aureport /sbin/ausearch /sbin/autrace /sbin/auditd /sbin/augenrules**: This command displays the file names and their access permissions (in octal format) for specified files in the `/sbin` directory.
- **hipaa: 164.308(a) (3)(1), 164.308(a)(3 (MA).164.312(a)(1)**: HIPAA requirements under *164.308(a)(3)(i)* emphasize conducting risk analysis, while *164.312(a)(1)* focuses on implementing access controls to safeguard **electronic protected health information** (**ePHI**).
- **Result**: **Passed** represents the status of the SCA check.

With this, we have come to the end of the chapter.

Summary

This chapter has shed light on the critical role of the Vulnerability Detector and SCA modules of the Wazuh platform. We have learned how to configure vulnerability detection with different customizations of packages, operating systems, applications, and so on. We also went through the workings of the Wazuh SCA module and how to create a custom SCA script from scratch. We learned how to fulfill requirements of the regulatory compliance framework such as PCI DSS, NIST 800-53 Controls, and HIPAA using the Vulnerability Detector and SCA modules.

In the next chapter, we will cover some important rules and custom Wazuh rules for different security use cases.

8
Appendix

We have now reached the *Appendix* chapter. Here, we will cover several custom Wazuh rules. Wazuh has already built thousands of rules to enhance its detection capabilities. However, we will write some important custom Wazuh rules to detect PowerShell, Linux Auditd, Kaspersky, and Symon-related alerts. This chapter covers the following topics:

- Custom PowerShell rules
- Custom Auditd rules
- Custom Kaspersky Endpoint Security rules
- Custom Sysmon rules

Custom PowerShell rules

To enhance the Wazuh detection capabilities for Windows machines, we need to integrate some custom PowerShell Wazuh rules. Each rule can be created with specific conditions, severity levels, and other optional configurations. We will cover the following types of rules in this section:

- PowerShell event information
- PowerShell error logs
- PowerShell warning logs
- PowerShell critical logs

PowerShell event information

We can create a custom PowerShell rule to get event information, as shown in the following:

```
<rule id="200101" level="1">
    <if_sid>60009</if_sid>
    <field name="win.system.providerName">^PowerShell$</field>
    <options>no_full_log</options>
    <group>windows_powershell,</group>
    <description>PowerShell Log Information</description>
  </rule>
```

Here, we have the following:

- `<if_sid>60009</if_sid>`: This represents the list of rule IDs. It will match when a rule ID on the list has previously matched. Rule ID `60009` is a pre-built Wazuh rule for Windows informational events.
- `<field name="win.system.providerName">^PowerShell$</field>`: The `<field>` tag is used as a requisite to trigger the rule. It will check for a match in the content of a field extracted by the decoder. In this case, it will check whether the `win.system.providerName` log field has the `PowerShell` keyword.
- `<group>windows_powershell,</group>`: This enforces that the alert will be categorized under a specific group. In this case, it is `windows_powershell`.

PowerShell error logs

PowerShell error logs typically contain information related to errors, warnings, and other events. To detect such PowerShell error logs, we can create custom Wazuh rules, as shown here:

```
<rule id="200102" level="7">
    <if_sid>60011</if_sid>
    <field name="win.system.providerName">^Microsoft-Windows-
PowerShell$</field>
    <mitre>
      <id>T1086</id>
    </mitre>
    <options>no_full_log</options>
    <group>windows_powershell,</group>
    <description>Powershell Error logs</description>
  </rule>
```

Here, we have the following:

- `<if_sid>60011</if_sid>`: This represents the list of rule IDs. It will match when a rule ID on the list has previously matched. Rule ID `60011` is a pre-built Wazuh rule for Windows error events.
- `<field name="win.system.providerName">^Microsoft-Windows-PowerShell$</field>`: The `<field>` tag is used as a requisite to trigger the rule. It will check for a match in the content of a field extracted by the decoder. In this case, it will check whether the `win.system.providerName` log field has the `Microsoft-Windows-PowerShell` keyword.
- `<group>windows_powershell,</group>`: This enforces that the alert will be categorized under a specific group. In this case, it is `windows_powershell`.

PowerShell warning logs

PowerShell also generates non-critical alerts during script execution. This is helpful for security investigation. To detect such alerts on the Wazuh manager, we can create custom Wazuh rules, as shown here:

```
<rule id="200103" level="5">
    <if_sid>200101</if_sid>
    <field name="win.system.providerName">^Microsoft-Windows-
PowerShell$</field>
    <field name="win.system.severityValue">^WARNING$</field>
    <options>no_full_log</options>
    <group>windows_powershell,</group>
    <description>Powershell Warning Event</description>
  </rule>
```

Here, we have the following:

- `<field name="win.system.providerName">^Microsoft-Windows-PowerShell$</field>`: The `<field>` tag is used as a requisite to trigger the rule. It will check for a match in the content of a field extracted by the decoder. In this case, it will check whether the `win.system.providerName` log field has the `Microsoft-Windows-PowerShell` keyword.
- `<field name="win.system.severityValue">^WARNING$</field>`: It will check whether the `win.system.severityValue` log field has the `WARNING` keyword.
- `<group>windows_powershell,</group>`: This enforces that the alert will be categorized under a specific group. In this case, it is `windows_powershell`.

PowerShell critical logs

PowerShell generates critical alerts where there are some severe errors during execution. To detect such alerts, we can create custom Wazuh rules, as shown here:

```
<rule id="200103" level="12">
    <if_sid>60012</if_sid>
    <field name="win.system.providerName">^Microsoft-Windows-
PowerShell$</field>
    <mitre>
      <id>T1086</id>
    </mitre>
    <options>no_full_log</options>
    <group>windows_powershell,</group>
    <description>Powershell Critical EventLog</description>
  </rule>
```

Here, we have the following:

- `<field name="win.system.severityValue">^WARNING$</field>`: It will check whether the `win.system.severityValue` log field has the `WARNING` keyword.
- `<group>windows_powershell,</group>`: This enforces that the alert will be categorized under a specific group. In this case, it is `windows_powershell`.

This completes some of the important custom PowerShell rules. In the next section, we will cover Wazuh rules for Linux Auditd modules.

Custom Wazuh rules for Auditd

Custom Wazuh rules for Auditd provide a tailored method to enhance Wazuh's capabilities to detect Linux command executions. This will also help the security team to detect critical security events, track user activities, and ensure regulatory compliance.

Auditd syscall rule

We can create a Wazuh rule to detect any system call (syscall) events, as written here:

```
<rule id="200200" level="3">
  <decoded_as>auditd-syscall</decoded_as>
  <description>Auditd: System Calls Event </description>
  <group>syscall,</group>
</rule>
```

Here, we have the following:

- `<decoded_as>auditd-syscall</decoded_as>`: This represents a requisite to trigger the rule. It will be triggered only if the event has been decoded by a specific `decoder`. In this case, it is `auditd-syscall`.

Auditd path

Linux Auditd generates an event for every path record. We will create a Wazuh rule to capture the event for Auditd path messages, as shown:

```
<rule id="200201" level="3">
  <decoded_as>auditd-path</decoded_as>
  <description>Auditd: Path Message event.</description>
  <group>path,</group>
</rule>
```

Here, we have the following:

- `<decoded_as>auditd-syscall</decoded_as>`: This represents a requisite to trigger the rule. It will be triggered only if the event has been decoded by a specific `decoder`. In this case, it is `auditd-path`.

Detecting a change in the user environment

To detect any changes in the user environment, we can create a custom Wazuh rule to detect changes in `bash_profile`, as written here:

```
<rule id="200202" level="12">
  <if_sid>200201</if_sid>
  <list field="audit.directory.name" lookup="address_match_key">etc/
lists/bash_profile</list>
  <description> Auditd: Detects change of user environment</
description>
  <group>path,</group>
  </rule>
```

Here, we have the following:

- `<list field="audit.directory.name" lookup="address_match_key">etc/lists/bash_profile</list>`: The `<list>` tag performs a CDB lookup, and the `field` attribute is used as a key in the CBD list. In this case, the CDB list `audit.directory.name` is used and `address_match_key` is used to search for the IP address and key.

We've learned how to build custom Wazuh rules for Linux Auditd modules. In the next section, we will build Wazuh rules for Kaspersky Endpoint Security solutions.

Custom Wazuh rules for Kaspersky Endpoint Security

Kaspersky Endpoint Security is a leading security provider, delivering cloud security, embedded security, threat management, and industrial security. To enhance Wazuh's capability to detect Kaspersky endpoint alerts, we need to create custom Wazuh rules. In this section, we will cover the following topics:

- Kaspersky's general rules
- Rules to detect events when a Kaspersky agent restarts
- Rules for quarantine alerts

Kaspersky's general rules

Kaspersky Endpoint Security generates some general alerts. To detect those alerts, the following Wazuh rule needs to be created:

```
<rule id="200300" level="0">
  <if_sid>60009</if_sid>
  <field name="win.system.channel">^Kaspersky Event Log$</field>
  <options>no_full_log</options>
  <description>Kapersky rule for the System channel</description>
</rule>
```

Here, we have the following:

- `<field name="win.system.channel">^Kaspersky Event Log$</field>`: It will check whether the `win.system.channel` log field has the `Kaspersky Event Log` keyword

Rules to detect events when the Kaspersky agent restarts

To detect events when the Kaspersky agent restarts, a custom Wazuh rule needs to be created, as shown here:

```
<rule id="200301" level="10">
  <if_sid>200300</if_sid>
  <field name="win.system.providerName">klnagent</field>
    <field name="win.system.eventID">1</field>
    <description>Kaspersky Agent Restarted</description>
 </rule>
```

Here, we have the following:

- `<field name="win.system.providerName">klnagent</field>`: It will check whether the `win.system.providerName` log field has the `klnagent<field name="win.system.eventID">1</field>` keyword. This represents another field within the Windows event log. This rule triggers if the value of `eventID` is `1`. In Windows event logging, `eventID` 1 often represents system startup or the start of a logging session or a restart of the Windows Time service.

Rules for quarantine alert

To detect whether a suspicious file has been quarantined, we can a custom Wazuh rule to trigger the alert, as shown here:

```
<rule id="200302" level="10">
   <if_sid>200300</if_sid>
   <field name="win.system.providerName">klnagent</field>
   <field name="win.system.message" type="pcre2">(?i)^"Quarantine</
field>
     <description>Kaspersky Agent - Quarantine Event</description>
  </rule>
```

Here, we have the following:

- `<field name="win.system.message" type="pcre2">(?i)^"Quarantine</field>`: It will check whether the `win.system.message` log field has the `Quarantine.<field name="win.system.message" type="pcre2">(?i)^"Quarantine</field>` keyword. This specifies another field within the Windows event log; this time it is the `message` field. This rule triggers if the message contains the `Quarantine` keyword. This is done by using a regular expression library called **Perl Compatible Regular Expressions** (**PCRE2**).

We have learned how to build custom Wazuh rules to detect Kaspersky Endpoint Security events. In the next section, we will build custom rules to detect Sysmon events.

Custom Wazuh rules for Sysmon

Sysmon – a Windows Sysinternals tool – provides an in-depth view into system-related activities. Sysmon helps us detect a wide range of activities, such as process creation, file creation and modification, registry changes, driver loading, DLL loading, named pipe creation, process access, and DNS query logging. In order to expand Wazuh's detection capability, we need to build a custom Wazuh rule to generate alerts. There is a total of 30 Sysmon events, as explained on the official Microsoft website (`https://learn.microsoft.com/en-us/sysinternals/downloads/sysmon`). However, we will cover the most important Sysmon events that are mapped with some specific MITRE

ATT&CK techniques. These rules are developed by taking reference from the official GitHub account of SOCFortress – a SaaS-based cybersecurity platform. You can also refer to the list of all the Wazuh rules mapped with MITRE techniques against Sysmon events here: `https://github.com/socfortress/Wazuh-Rules/tree/main/Windows_Sysmon`. In this section, we will cover some of the important Sysmon events, as mentioned here:

- Sysmon Event 1: Process Creation
- Sysmon Event 2: Process changed a File Creation Time
- Sysmon Event 3: Network Connection
- Sysmon Event 7: Image loaded
- Sysmon Event 10: Process Access
- Sysmon Event 11: File Creation
- Sysmon Event 12: Registry Event (Object create and delete)
- Sysmon Event 13: Registry Event (Value Set)
- Sysmon Event 14: Registry Event (Key and Value Rename)
- Sysmon Event 15: File Creation StreamHash
- Sysmon Event 17: Pipe Creation
- Sysmon Event 18: Pipe Event
- Sysmon Event 22: DNS Request

Sysmon Event 1: Process Creation

A Wazuh rule for the detection of a *Process Creation* event allows the security team to monitor suspicious unauthorized processes being executed and is written as follows:

```
<rule id="200401" level="3">
    <if_sid>61603</if_sid>
    <description>Sysmon - Event 1: Process creation $(win.eventdata.
description)</description>
    <mitre>
<id>T1546</id>
</mitre>
    <options>no_full_log</options>
    <group>sysmon_event1,windows_sysmon_event1,</group>
  </rule>
```

Here, we have the following:

- <if_sid>61603</if_sid>: The <if_sid> tag is used as a requisite to trigger the rule. In this case, rule 200401 will be triggered only when the parent rule 61603 matches. Rule ID 61603 is already created in the Wazuh manager under the filename 0595-win-sysmon_rules.xml.

Sysmon Event 2: Process changed a File Creation Time

The File Creation event of the Sysmon module detects the creation of potentially infected files or unexpected file changes, providing insights into file-based malware threats. The custom Wazuh rule for Sysmon Event 2 can be created as follows:

```
<rule id="200402" level="3">
  <if_sid>61604</if_sid>
  <field name="win.eventdata.RuleName">^technique_id=T1099,technique_
name=Timestomp$</field>
  <description>Sysmon - Event 2: A process changed a file creation
time by $(win.eventdata.image)</description>
  <mitre>

  <id>T1099</id>
  </mitre>
  <options>no_full_log</options>
  <group>sysmon_event2,</group>
  </rule>
</group>
```

Here, we have the following:

- <if_sid>61604</if_sid>: The <if_sid> tag is used as a requisite to trigger the rule. In this case, rule 200402 will be triggered only when the parent rule 61604 matches. Rule ID 61604 is already created in the Wazuh manager under the filename 0595-win-sysmon_rules.xml.

Sysmon Event 3: Network Connection

Sysmon Event 3 is generated when it detects any unusual or unauthorized network connections. To detect such a network connection, we can create a custom Wazuh rule, as shown here:

```
<rule id="200403" level="3">
<if_sid>61605</if_sid>
<field name="win.eventdata.RuleName">^technique_id=T1021,technique_
name=Remote Services$</field>
<description>Sysmon - Event 3: Network connection by $(win.eventdata.
```

```
image)</description>
<mitre>
<id>T1021</id>
</mitre>
<options>no_full_log</options>
<group>sysmon_event3,</group>
</rule>
```

Here, we have the following:

- <if_sid>61605</if_sid>: The <if_sid> tag is used as a requisite to trigger the rule. In this case, rule 200403 will be triggered only when the parent rule 61605 matches. Rule ID 61605 is already created in the Wazuh manager under the filename 0595-win-sysmon_rules.xml.

Sysmon Event 7: Image loaded

The Image Loaded event is generated when malicious code is injected into a normal process. The Wazuh rule to detect such events is shown here:

```
<rule id="200404" level="3">
<if_sid>61609</if_sid>
<field name="win.eventdata.RuleName">^technique_
id=T1059.001,technique_name=PowerShell$</field>
<description>Sysmon - Event 7: Image loaded by $(win.eventdata.
image)</description>
<mitre>
<id>T1059</id>
</mitre>
<options>no_full_log</options>
<group>sysmon_event7,</group>
</rule>
```

Here, we have the following:

- <if_sid>61609</if_sid>: The <if_sid> tag is used as a requisite to trigger the rule. In this case, rule 200404 will be triggered only when the parent rule 61609 matches. Rule ID 61609 is already created in the Wazuh manager under the filename 0595-win-sysmon_rules.xml.

Sysmon Event 10: Process Access

The Process Access event helps the security team to detect suspicious activities such as process memory modification or injection, often linked to an advanced attack chain. To visualize such events, the following Wazuh rule needs to be created:

```
<rule id="200405" level="3">
<if_sid>61612</if_sid>
<field name="win.eventdata.RuleName">^technique_id=T1003,technique_
name=Credential Dumping$</field>
<description>Sysmon - Event 10: ProcessAccess by $(win.eventdata.
sourceimage)</description>
<mitre>
<id>T1003</id>
</mitre>
<options>no_full_log</options>
<group>sysmon_event_10,</group>
</rule>
```

Here, we have the following:

- `<if_sid>61612</if_sid>`: The `<if_sid>` tag is used as a requisite to trigger the rule. In this case, rule `200405` will be triggered only when the parent rule `61612` matches. Rule ID `61612` is already created in the Wazuh manager under the filename `0595-win-sysmon_rules.xml`.

Sysmon Event 11: File Creation

The File Creation event provides redundancy for file creation monitoring and helps provide maximum coverage for file-based malware threats. A Wazuh rule to detect such events can be created, as shown here:

```
<rule id="200406" level="3">
<if_sid>61613</if_sid>
<field name="win.eventdata.RuleName">^technique_
id=T1546.011,technique_name=Application Shimming$</field>
<description>Sysmon - Event 11: FileCreate by $(win.eventdata.image)</
description>
<mitre>
<id>T1546</id>
</mitre>
<options>no_full_log</options>
<group>sysmon_event_11,</group>
</rule>
```

Here, we have the following:

- `<if_sid>61613</if_sid>`: The `<if_sid>` tag is used as a requisite to trigger the rule. In this case, rule `200406` will be triggered only when the parent rule `61613` matches. Rule ID `61609` is already created in the Wazuh manager under the filename `0595-win-sysmon_rules.xml`.

Sysmon Event 12: Registry Event (Object create and delete)

Sysmon Event 12 captures logs when a new registry key or subkey is created or an existing one is deleted. This is useful for detecting unauthorized changes to the registry, which may indicate the presence of file-less malware. A Wazuh rule can be created to detect such events, as shown here:

```
<rule id="200407" level="3">
<if_sid>61614</if_sid>
<field name="win.eventdata.RuleName">^technique_
id=T1546.011,technique_name=Application Shimming$</field>
<description>Sysmon - Event 12: RegistryEvent (Object create and
delete) by $(win.eventdata.image)</description>
<mitre>
<id>T1546</id>
</mitre>
<options>no_full_log</options>
<group>sysmon_event_12,</group>
</rule>
```

Here, we have the following

- `<if_sid>61614</if_sid>`: The `<if_sid>` tag is used as a requisite to trigger the rule. In this case, rule `200407` will be triggered only when the parent rule `61614` matches. Rule ID `61614` is already created in the Wazuh manager under the filename `0595-win-sysmon_rules.xml`.

Sysmon Event 13: Registry Event(Value Set)

Sysmon Event 13 is triggered when a new value is set, or an existing value is modified within a registry key. This event is important to detect changes related to malware persistence or privilege escalation techniques. A Wazuh rule can be created to detect such an event, as shown here:

```
<rule id="200408" level="3">
<if_sid>61615</if_sid>
<field name="win.eventdata.RuleName">^technique_
id=T1546.011,technique_name=Application Shimming$</field>
<description>Sysmon - Event 13: RegistryEvent (Value Set) by $(win.
eventdata.image)</description>
```

```
<mitre>
<id>T1546</id>
</mitre>
<options>no_full_log</options>
<group>sysmon_event_13,</group>
</rule>
```

Here, we have the following:

- `<if_sid>61615</if_sid>`: The `<if_sid>` tag is used as a requisite to trigger the rule. In this case, rule `200408` will be triggered only when the parent rule `61615` matches. Rule ID `61615` is already created in the Wazuh manager under the filename `0595-win-sysmon_rules.xml`.
- `<field name="win.eventdata.RuleName">^technique_id=T1546.011,technique_name=Application Shimming$</field>`: The `<field>` tag is used as a requisite to trigger the rule. It will check for a match in the content of a field extracted by the decoder. In this case, it will check whether the `win.eventdata.RuleName` log field has the `technique_id=T1546.011,technique_name=Application Shimming l` keywords.

Sysmon Event 14: Registry Event(Key and Value Rename)

Sysmon Event 14 is triggered when a registry key or value is renamed. These techniques can be used by advanced attackers to evade anti-malware detection or disrupt the system. A Wazuh rule can be created to detect such events, as written here:

```
<rule id="200409" level="3">
  <if_sid>61616</if_sid>
  <field name="win.eventdata.RuleName">^technique_
id=T1546.011,technique_name=Application Shimming$</field>
  <description>Sysmon - Event 14: RegistryEvent (Key and Value Rename)
by $(win.eventdata.image)</description>
  <mitre>
  <id>T1546</id>
  </mitre>
  <options>no_full_log</options>
  <group>sysmon_event_14,</group>
  </rule>
```

Here, we have the following:

- <if_sid>61616</if_sid>: The <if_sid> tag is used as a requisite to trigger the rule. In this case, rule 200409 will be triggered only when the parent rule 61615 matches. Rule ID 61615 is already created in the Wazuh manager under the filename 0595-win-sysmon_rules.xml.
- <field name="win.eventdata.RuleName">^technique_id=T1546.011,technique_name=Application Shimming$</field>: The <field> tag is used as a requisite to trigger the rule. It will check for a match in the content of a field extracted by the decoder. In this case, it will check whether the win.eventdata.RuleName log field has the technique_id=T1546.011,technique_name=Application Shimming 1 keyword.

Sysmon Event 15: File Creation StreamHash

Sysmon Event 15 captures the file creation activities with the hash of the file. To create a Wazuh rule to detect such events, we can create a custom rule, as shown here:

```
<rule id="200410" level="3">
<if_sid>61617</if_sid>
<field name="win.eventdata.RuleName">^technique_id=T1089,technique_
name=Drive-by Compromise$</field>
<description>Sysmon - Event 15: FileCreateStreamHash by $(win.
eventdata.image)</description>
<mitre>
<id>T1089</id>
</mitre>
<options>no_full_log</options>
<group>sysmon_event_15,</group>
</rule>
```

Here, we have the following:

- <if_sid>61617</if_sid>: The <if_sid> tag is used as a requisite to trigger the rule. In this case, rule 200410 will be triggered only when the parent rule 61617 matches. Rule ID 61617 is already created in the Wazuh manager under the filename 0595-win-sysmon_rules.xml.
- <field name="win.eventdata.RuleName">^technique_id=T1089,technique_name=Drive-by Compromise$</field>: The <field> tag is used as a requisite to trigger the rule. It will check for a match in the content of a field extracted by the decoder. In this case, it will check whether the win.eventdata.RuleName log field has the technique_id=T1089,technique_name=Drive-by Compromise 1 keyword.

Sysmon Event 17: Pipe Creation

Sysmon Event 17 records the creation of named pipes, which allows for inter-process communication on a system. This helps to identify any suspicious activities related to the setting up of named pipes. A custom Wazuh rule can be built to detect such events, as shown here:

```
<rule id="200411" level="3">
<if_sid>61646</if_sid>
<field name="win.eventdata.RuleName">^technique_
id=T1021.002,technique_name=SMB/Windows Admin Shares$</field>
<description>Sysmon - Event 17: PipeEvent (Pipe Created) by $(win.
eventdata.image)</description>
<mitre>
<id>T1021</id>
</mitre>
<options>no_full_log</options>
<group>sysmon_event_17,</group>
</rule>
```

Here, we have the following:

- `<if_sid>61646</if_sid>`: The `<if_sid>` tag is used as a requisite to trigger the rule. In this case, rule `200411` will be triggered only when the parent rule `61646` matches. Rule ID `61646` is already created in the Wazuh manager under the filename `0595-win-sysmon_rules.xml`.
- `<field name="win.eventdata.RuleName">^technique_id=T1021.002,technique_name=SMB/Windows Admin Shares$</field>`: The `<field>` tag is used as a requisite to trigger the rule. It will check for a match in the content of a field extracted by the decoder. In this case, it will check whether the `win.eventdata.RuleName` log field has the `"technique_id=T1021.002,technique_name=SMB/Windows Admin Shares` keyword.

Sysmon Event 18: Pipe Event

Sysmon Event 18 captures additional information about pipes, such as opening, closing, or reading to named pipes, and helps in detecting anomalous behavior in the system. A Wazuh rule can be created to detect such events, as written here:

```
<rule id="200412" level="3">
<if_sid>61647</if_sid>
<field name="win.eventdata.RuleName">^technique_
id=T1021.002,technique_name=SMB/Windows Admin Shares$</field>
<description>Sysmon - Event 18: PipeEvent (Pipe Connected) by $(win.
eventdata.image)</description>
<mitre>
```

```
<id>T1021</id>
</mitre>
<options>no_full_log</options>
<group>sysmon_event_18,</group>
</rule>
```

Here, we have the following

- `<if_sid>61647</if_sid>`: The `<if_sid>` tag is used as a requisite to trigger the rule. In this case, rule `200412` will be triggered only when the parent rule `61647` matches. Rule ID `61646` is already created in the Wazuh manager under the filename `0595-win-sysmon_rules.xml`.
- `<field name="win.eventdata.RuleName">^technique_id=T1021.002,technique_name=SMB/Windows Admin Shares$</field>`: The `<field>` tag is used as a requisite to trigger the rule. It will check for a match in the content of a field extracted by the decoder. In this case, it will check whether the `win.eventdata.RuleName` log field has the `technique_id=T1021.002,technique_name=SMB/Windows Admin Shares` keyword.

Sysmon Event 22: DNS Request

Sysmon Event 22 records DNS requests initiated by processes on the machine. This helps us to monitor requests to potentially malicious servers or commands and control centers. A Wazuh rule to detect such DNS requests can created, as shown:

```
<rule id="200413" level="3">
<if_sid>61644</if_sid>
<description>Sysmon - Event 22: DNS Request by $(win.eventdata.
image)</description>
<mitre>
<id>T1071</id>
</mitre>
<options>no_full_log</options>
<group>sysmon_event_22,</group>
</rule>
```

Here, we have the following:

- `<if_sid>61644</if_sid>`: The `<if_sid>` tag is used as a requisite to trigger the rule. In this case, rule `200412` will be triggered only when the parent rule `61644` matches. Rule ID `61644` is already created in the Wazuh manager under the filename `0595-win-sysmon_rules.xml`.

We've learned how to create custom Sysmon rules for Wazuh. We can create multiple granular rules under each category of Sysmon events. To explore a list of all the custom Sysmon rules for Wazuh, you can visit the official SOCFotress GitHub repository here: `https://github.com/socfortress/Wazuh-Rules/tree/main/Windows_Sysmon`.

Summary

In this chapter, we have covered some of the important custom Wazuh rules for different types of events, such as PowerShell events, Linux Auditd events, Kaspersky endpoint protection events, and Sysmon events. In the next chapter, we will cover a list of important terms related to the Wazuh platform.

9
Glossary

This chapter features a glossary of some of the important topics related to the Wazuh platform and its peripheral technologies. This chapter serves as a comprehensive guide to learning fundamentals of Wazuh's technical landscape. Whether you are an experienced security professional or a newcomer to the security landscape, this chapter will provide you with a useful summary of Wazuh's capabilities and its related concepts.

The glossary is covered in alphabetical order.

A

- **Active response**: Active response is a Wazuh module that automates response actions based on specific triggers. This helps security professionals to manage security incidents in a prompt and effective manner. Some actions that can be executed include a firewall drop or block, account block, deleting malicious files, blocking a suspicious network connection, and isolating an infected endpoint. To learn more, check out the following links:
    - **Wazuh official documentation on active response**: `https://documentation.wazuh.com/current/user-manual/capabilities/active-response/index.html`
    - **Configuring active response for malicious files**: `https://wazuh.com/blog/detecting-and-responding-to-malicious-files/`
    - **Integrating Suricata with Wazuh for a network attack response**: `https://wazuh.com/blog/responding-to-network-attacks-with-suricata-and-wazuh-xdr/`

- **AWS instances**: An AWS instance is a virtual machine that runs cloud-based applications on the AWS platform. The cloud-based infrastructure lets you do things without having to buy a computer or server. AWS instances come in various types, such as general-purpose, compute-optimized, memory-optimized, and storage-optimized. To learn more, visit the following websites:
    - **Amazon EC2 instances – AWS documentation**: `https://docs.aws.amazon.com/AWSEC2/latest/UserGuide/Instances.html`
    - **AWS EC2 instance types – AWS**: `https://aws.amazon.com/ec2/instance-types/`

B

- **Brute-force attack**: Brute-force attacks are a type of hacking technique where passwords, login credentials, and encryption keys are cracked through a process of trial and error. It is a straightforward yet effective strategy for getting unauthorized access to user accounts, company networks, and systems. Until they discover the right login details, the hacker attempts a variety of usernames and passwords, frequently testing a large range of combinations on a machine. To learn more, check out the following links:
    - **Brute-force attack**: `https://www.crowdstrike.com/cybersecurity-101/brute-force-attacks/`
    - **Brute-force attack by OWASP**: `https://owasp.org/www-community/attacks/Brute_force_attack`

C

- **CDB lists**: **CDB** (**Contant Database**) lists in Wazuh are text files that can hold user lists, file hashes, IP addresses, and domain names. You can also store other things in them, such as network ports. You can use CDB lists to make "white" or "black" lists of users, files, IP addresses, or domain names. By searching to see whether their signatures are in a CDB list, they can also be used to find malicious files. To learn more, visit the following websites:
    - **CDB lists and threat intelligence**: `https://documentation.wazuh.com/current/user-manual/capabilities/malware-detection/cdb-lists-threat-intelligence.html`
    - **Using CDB lists**: `https://documentation.wazuh.com/current/user-manual/ruleset/cdb-list.html`

- **ClamAV**: ClamAV is an open source antivirus software that can find and get rid of malware, viruses, and other online activities that are harmful to your system and database. It's compatible with Windows, Linux, and Mac devices. To learn more, visit the following websites:
  - **ClamAV – official documentation**: `https://docs.clamav.net/`
  - **ClamAV log collection on Wazuh**: `https://documentation.wazuh.com/current/user-manual/capabilities/malware-detection/clam-av-logs-collection.html`
- **Command monitoring**: Command monitoring allows you to monitor several things, such as how much disk space is used, the average load, changes in network listeners, and running processes. Command monitoring works on all endpoints where the Wazuh agent is installed. To learn more, visit the following websites:
  - **Wazuh – command monitoring**: `https://documentation.wazuh.com/current/user-manual/capabilities/command-monitoring/index.html`
  - **Monitoring root actions on Linux using Auditd and Wazuh**: `https://wazuh.com/blog/monitoring-root-actions-on-linux-using-auditd-and-wazuh/`
- **Compliance (regulatory)**: Compliance (i.e., security compliance) is the process that businesses use to make sure they follow rules, standards, and frameworks for security. The purpose of security compliance is to follow the law, government rules, best practices in business, and agreements made in writing. Some of the popular security compliances are as follows:
  - **Payment Card Industry Data Security Standard** (**PCI DSS**)
  - **Health Insurance Portability and Accountability Act** (**HIPAA**)
  - **Federal Information Security Management Act** (**FISMA**)
  - **Sarbanes-Oxley Act** (**SOX**)
  - EU's **General Data Protection Regulation** (**GDPR**)

  To learn more, check out the following links:
  - **What is PCI DSS compliance?**: `https://www.imperva.com/learn/data-security/pci-dss-certification/`
  - **Using Wazuh for GDPR compliance**: `https://documentation.wazuh.com/current/compliance/gdpr/index.html`

- **Container**: Containers keep software separate from its different environments, such as the development and staging environments. They also help teams that use different software on the same infrastructure work together more smoothly. A container image is a lightweight, standalone piece of software that can be run on an application. It has all the code, runtime, system tools, system libraries, and settings that a program needs to run. To learn more, check out the following links:
    - **What are containers?**: `https://www.ibm.com/topics/containers`
    - **Container security by Wazuh**: `https://documentation.wazuh.com/current/getting-started/use-cases/container-security.html`

D

- **Docker**: Docker is a free tool for making apps, sending them out, and running them. Docker helps you to keep your applications separate from your infrastructure, which speeds up the delivery of software. You can manage your infrastructure with Docker in the same way you run your apps. To learn more, check out the following links:
    - **Docker official documentation**: `https://docs.docker.com/`
    - **Monitoring Docker events on Wazuh**: `https://documentation.wazuh.com/current/proof-of-concept-guide/monitoring-docker.html`

E

- **Endpoint**: An endpoint is a device or node in a network, such as a computer or server, which is monitored by Wazuh agents for security purposes. You can learn more about endpoint from the following link:
    - **What is an endpoint?**: `https://www.paloaltonetworks.com/cyberpedia/what-is-an-endpoint`

F

- **File Integrity Monitoring (FIM)**: FIM is an IT security procedure and practice that examines and verifies application software, databases, and **operating system** (**OS**) files to see whether they have been altered or corrupted. If FIM finds that files have been changed, updated, or corrupted, it can send out alerts to ensure further investigation, and if necessary, remediation takes place. To learn more, check out the following links:
    - **What is FIM?**: `https://www.crowdstrike.com/cybersecurity-101/file-integrity-monitoring/`

- **Setting up FIM on Wazuh**: `https://documentation.wazuh.com/current/getting-started/use-cases/file-integrity.html`

G

- **GDPR compliance**: The **General Data Protection Regulation** (**GDPR**) is a digital privacy legislation about digital privacy that tells businesses how to gather, use, and keep personal data about people who live in the **European Union** (**EU**). This law also controls the sending of personal data outside of the EU. By granting users (often referred to as data subjects) authority over the collection, sharing, and use of their personal data, GDPR compliance enhances privacy rights. To learn more, check out the following links:
  - **What is the GDPR?**: `https://www.cloudflare.com/learning/privacy/what-is-the-gdpr/`
  - **Using Wazuh for GDPR compliance**: `https://documentation.wazuh.com/current/compliance/gdpr/index.html`
- **GitHub**: GitHub uses Git, an open source version control software, to allow multiple people to make changes to web pages at the same time. This makes it possible for teams to collaborate in real time while creating and editing the content for their websites. To learn more, check out the following links:
  - **What is GitHub and how to use it?**: `https://www.geeksforgeeks.org/what-is-github-and-how-to-use-it/`
  - **Using Wazuh to monitor GitHub**: `https://documentation.wazuh.com/current/cloud-security/github/index.html`

H

- **HIPAA compliance**: HIPAA compliance is a set of standards and protocols that healthcare organizations must follow to protect the privacy and security of sensitive patient data. If an organization deals with **protected health information** (**PHI**), it need to make sure that it follow HIPAA rules about physical, network, and process security. To learn more, check out the following links:
  - **What is HIPPA compliance?**: `https://www.proofpoint.com/us/threat-reference/hipaa-compliance`
  - **Using Wazuh for HIPPA compliance**: `https://documentation.wazuh.com/current/compliance/hipaa/index.html`

I

- **IDS (Intrusion Detection System)**: An IDS is a network security solution that checks network data and devices for known malicious activity, unusual activity, or security policy violations. When there are known or potential threats, an IDS detects and alerts a central security tool, such as a **security information and event management** (**SIEM**) system. To learn more, check out the following links:
    - **What is IDS?**: `https://www.geeksforgeeks.org/intrusion-detection-system-ids/`
    - **Network IDS integration with Wazuh**: `https://documentation.wazuh.com/current/proof-of-concept-guide/integrate-network-ids-suricata.html`

J

- **JSON (JavaScript Object Notation)**: JSON is a simple text-based format for sending and storing info. When data is sent from a computer to a web page, JSON is often used. It is a data serialization format that enables consistent data transmission between many platforms, applications, and systems. To learn more, check out the following link:
    - **What is JSON?**: `https://www.w3schools.com/whatis/whatis_json.asp`

K

- **Kubernetes**: Kubernetes is a portable, expandable, open source platform that makes automation and declarative configuration easier for managing containerized workloads and services. In a production setting, you need to keep an eye on the containers that run the apps and make sure they don't go down. Containers are a good way to bundle and run your applications. To learn more, check out the following links:
    - **What is Kubernetes?**: `https://cloud.google.com/learn/what-is-kubernetes`
    - **How to deploy Wazuh on Kubernetes?**: `https://documentation.wazuh.com/current/deployment-options/deploying-with-kubernetes/index.html`

L

- **Log data collection**: Log data collection is the process of getting logs from different network sources and putting them all in one place. Collecting log data helps security teams maintain compliance, identify and remediate threats, and find failures in applications and other security problems.

- To learn more, check out the following link:
  - **How log data collection works**: `https://documentation.wazuh.com/current/user-manual/capabilities/log-data-collection/how-it-works.html`

M

- **Malware IOC (Indicators of Compromise)**: This is forensic data that shows that an attack has been executed in an organization's network or endpoint. IOCs can be IP addresses, domains, hashes of malware files, and so on. An IOC can also include metadata about a file, such as author, the date of creation, and the file version. To learn more, check out the following links:
  - **What are IOCs?**: `https://www.crowdstrike.com/cybersecurity-101/indicators-of-compromise/`
  - **Malware detection using Wazuh**: `https://documentation.wazuh.com/current/user-manual/capabilities/malware-detection/index.html`
- **MITRE ATT&CK**: A **MITRE ATT&CK** (**MITRE Adversarial Tactics, Techniques, and Common Knowledge**) is a framework that assists organizations in determining their security readiness and locating vulnerabilities in their defenses. The MITRE ATT&CK framework offers an exhaustive taxonomy of adversary techniques and tactics and is characterized by its level of specificity. It is built on observations of cybersecurity threats in the real world. To learn more, check out the following links:
  - **What is the MITRE ATT&CK framework?**: `https://www.ibm.com/topics/mitre-attack`
  - **Enhancing Wazuh's detection with the MITRE ATT&CK framework**: `https://documentation.wazuh.com/current/user-manual/ruleset/mitre.html`

N

- **NIST 800-53 framework**: The **National Institute of Standards and Technology** (**NIST**) **800-53** is a cybersecurity standard and compliance framework. It is a set of guidelines that specify the bare minimum-security controls for all federal information systems in the United States, excluding those that are critical to national security. To learn more, check out the following links:
  - **What is the NIST SP 800-53 framework?**: `https://www.forcepoint.com/cyber-edu/nist-sp-800-53`
  - **Wazuh for compliance with NIST 800-53**: `https://documentation.wazuh.com/current/compliance/nist/index.html`

O

- **OpenSearch**: OpenSearch is an open source search engine and analytics suite, used for log analytics, website information search, and real-time application monitoring. OpenSearch is a fork of Elasticsearch and Kibana, launched in 2021. It is licensed under the Apache 2.0 license and is Lucene-based. OpenSearch provides functionality for searching using keywords, multiple languages, natural language, and synonyms. To learn more, check out the following links:
  - **OpenSearch official documentation**: `https://opensearch.org/docs/latest/`
  - **Wazuh and OpenSearch integration**: `https://documentation.wazuh.com/current/integrations-guide/opensearch/index.html`
- **OSSEC**: OSSEC is an open-source **host-based intrusion detection system** (**HIDS**) that's compatible with multiple operating systems. It is a scalable program that checks logs, makes sure files are correct, keeps an eye on the Windows system, enforces policies centrally, finds rootkits, sends real-time alerts, and many more. To learn more, check out the following links:
  - **What is OSSEC?**: `https://www.ossec.net/ossec-downloads/`
  - **How to migrate from OSSEC to Wazuh**: `https://wazuh.com/blog/migrating-from-ossec-to-wazuh/`
- **Osquery**: Osquery is a tool used to query and monitor systems using SQL-like syntax. It works with Windows, Linux, and macOS. With Osquery, you can query thousands of system data points and receive structured data back. Because it can return data in machine-readable formats such as JSON, it is useful for integrating with your existing security or monitoring tools and scripts. To learn more, check out the following links:
  - **What is Osquery?**: `https://www.uptycs.com/blog/osquery-what-it-is-how-it-works-and-how-to-use-it`
  - **Threat hunting using Osquery and Wazuh**: `https://documentation.wazuh.com/current/getting-started/use-cases/threat-hunting.html`

P

- **PCI DSS compliance**: **PCI DSS** (**Payment Card Industry Data Security Standard**) compliance is a set of requirements that talks about how an organization should store, process, or transmit credit card information to achieve a secure environment. It's an international security standard that helps prevent fraud and data breaches while providing consumers with a baseline degree of protection. PCI DSS compliance is not a one-time activity; it's a continuous process that involves assessing infrastructure that handles cardholder data, analyzing the system vulnerabilities, and remediating the exploitable vulnerabilities to secure the network.

- To learn more, check out the following links:
  - **What is PCI DSS compliance?**: https://www.techtarget.com/searchsecurity/definition/PCI-DSS-Payment-Card-Industry-Data-Security-Standard
  - **Using Wazuh for PCI DSS compliance**: https://documentation.wazuh.com/current/compliance/pci-dss/index.html
- **PowerShell**: Built on.NET, PowerShell is a task-based command-line shell and scripting language that saves you a lot of time and effort, and it can also help you to improve the efficiency of your IT infrastructure. To learn more, check out the following links:
  - **What is PowerShell?**: https://learn.microsoft.com/en-us/powershell/scripting/overview?view=powershell-7.4
  - **How to use Wazuh to monitor Sysmon events**: https://wazuh.com/blog/using-wazuh-to-monitor-sysmon-events/

R

- **Rootkit**: A rootkit is a type of software that allows hackers to gain unauthorized access to a network or machine while hiding its presence. Rootkits can be difficult to discover and hide for a very long period. To learn more, check out the following links:
  - **What is Rootkit?**: https://www.fortinet.com/resources/cyberglossary/rootkit
  - **Rootkit detection using Wazuh**: https://documentation.wazuh.com/current/user-manual/capabilities/malware-detection/rootkits-behavior-detection.html

S

- **SCA Policy**: In the Wazuh platform version 3.9.0, the SCA module was added. It offers unique tests that are applied to hardened systems. All platforms supported by Wazuh (Linux, macOS, Windows, Solaris, AIX, and HP-UX) can run the module. The SCA tool gives you a way to read and run configuration checks that are written in the YAML format. Also, having policies set up front makes it easier to follow rules such as HIPAA or PCI DSS, as well as guidelines such as those provided by the **CIS** (**Center for Internet Security**). To learn more, check out the following link:
  - **SCA by Wazuh**: https://documentation.wazuh.com/current/user-manual/capabilities/sec-config-assessment/index.html

- **SSH (Secure Shell)**: The SSH protocol is a protocol for securely sending remote commands to a computer over an unsecured network. SSH encrypts and verifies device connections using cryptography. To learn more, check out the following link:
  - **What is SSH?**: `https://www.geeksforgeeks.org/introduction-to-sshsecure-shell-keys/`
- **Syslog**: Syslog is used to send informational, analytical, and debugging messages, as well as general informational, analysis, and debugging messages. You can use it to keep track of different kinds of events, such as when a system is turned off, an unstable internet connection, system restarts, or the change of port status. To learn more, check out the following links:
  - **How does syslog work?**: `https://www.solarwinds.com/resources/it-glossary/syslog`
  - **Configuring syslog on the Wazuh server**: `https://documentation.wazuh.com/current/user-manual/capabilities/log-data-collection/syslog.html`
- **System call**: A system call is a programmatic method by which an operating system software runs on a computer and asks the kernel for a service. Programs can communicate with the operating system via system calls. When computer software asks the kernel of the operating system for anything, it initiates a system call. Through the **Application Program Interface (API)**, system calls give user programs access to the operating system's services. To learn more, check out the following links:
  - **What are system calls?**: `https://www.geeksforgeeks.org/introduction-of-system-call/`
  - **Monitoring system calls using Wazuh**: `https://documentation.wazuh.com/current/user-manual/capabilities/system-calls-monitoring/index.html`
- **System inventory**: The system inventory module of Wazuh collects data regarding a monitored endpoint. Details about the hardware, operating system, network, and running processes are all included in this data. To learn more, check out the following link:
  - **Wazuh's system inventory**: `https://documentation.wazuh.com/current/user-manual/capabilities/system-inventory/index.html`

T

- **Threat intelligence**: Threat intelligence is data that is gathered, processed, and studied to figure out why a threat actor does what they do, who they attack, and how they do it. Threat intelligence lets us make faster, smarter data-based security decisions. It also changes the way threat actors act, from being reactive to being proactive, in the fight against them. To learn more, check out the following links:
  - **What is cyber threat intelligence?**: `https://www.crowdstrike.com/cybersecurity-101/threat-intelligence/`
  - **Building IOC files for threat intelligence with Wazuh**: `https://wazuh.com/blog/building-ioc-files-for-threat-intelligence-with-wazuh-xdr/`
- **Trust Services Criteria (TSC) compliance**: The **Assurance Services Executive Committee** (**ASEC**) of the AICPA developed the **Trust Services Criteria** (**TSC**), which are standards for evaluating control objectives. These standards include measures for the safety, availability, processing integrity, privacy, and confidentiality of all of an organization's information and systems. These measures also relate to more specific parts of the entity, such as a division, a process, or the type of information that the entity uses. To learn more, check out the following links:
  - **What is the TSC?**: `https://drata.com/glossary/trust-services-criteria`
  - **Using Wazuh for TSC compliance**: `https://documentation.wazuh.com/current/compliance/tsc/index.html`

V

- **Vulnerability**: An information system vulnerability is a weakness or an opportunity that hackers can take advantage of to get into a computer system without consent. Vulnerabilities make systems less strong and allow hackers to attack them. To learn more, check out the link below:
  - **What is vulnerability?**: `https://www.upguard.com/blog/vulnerability`
- **Vulnerability Detector module**: The Wazuh Vulnerability Detector module helps users find weaknesses in an operating system and apps that are installed on the endpoints that are monitored. The module works by integrating Wazuh natively with external vulnerability feeds from Microsoft, **Amazon Linux Advisories Security** (**ALAS**), Canonical, Debian, Red Hat, Arch Linux, and the **National Vulnerability Database** (**NVD**). To learn more, check out the following link:
  - **How vulnerability detection works**: `https://documentation.wazuh.com/current/user-manual/capabilities/vulnerability-detection/`

- **Windows Defender**: Windows Defender is a built-in antivirus and antimalware solution in Microsoft Windows. It scans for malware on a computer and looks for any unusual behavior in the system. To learn more, check out the following link:
  - **Windows Defender logs collection**: `https://documentation.wazuh.com/current/user-manual/capabilities/malware-detection/win-defender-logs-collection.html`

Y

- **YARA**: YARA is a tool that helps malware analysts to detect and classify malware samples. YARA rules are instructions that describe what a certain kind of malware or threat looks like. YARA rules check files and networks for patterns, scripts, and signatures that show the presence of malicious software. To learn more, check out the following links:
  - **What is YARA?**: `https://virustotal.github.io/yara/`
  - **Detecting malware using YARA integration**: `https://documentation.wazuh.com/current/proof-of-concept-guide/detect-malware-yara-integration.html`

Index

A

B

C

D

M

N

R

S

T

U

X

Y

packtpub.com

Subscribe to our online digital library for full access to over 7,000 books and videos, as well as industry leading tools to help you plan your personal development and advance your career. For more information, please visit our website.

Why subscribe?

- Spend less time learning and more time coding with practical eBooks and Videos from over 4,000 industry professionals
- Improve your learning with Skill Plans built especially for you
- Get a free eBook or video every month
- Fully searchable for easy access to vital information
- Copy and paste, print, and bookmark content

Did you know that Packt offers eBook versions of every book published, with PDF and ePub files available? You can upgrade to the eBook version at packtpub.com and as a print book customer, you are entitled to a discount on the eBook copy. Get in touch with us at customercare@packtpub.com for more details.

At www.packtpub.com, you can also read a collection of free technical articles, sign up for a range of free newsletters, and receive exclusive discounts and offers on Packt books and eBooks.

Other Books You May Enjoy

If you enjoyed this book, you may be interested in these other books by Packt:

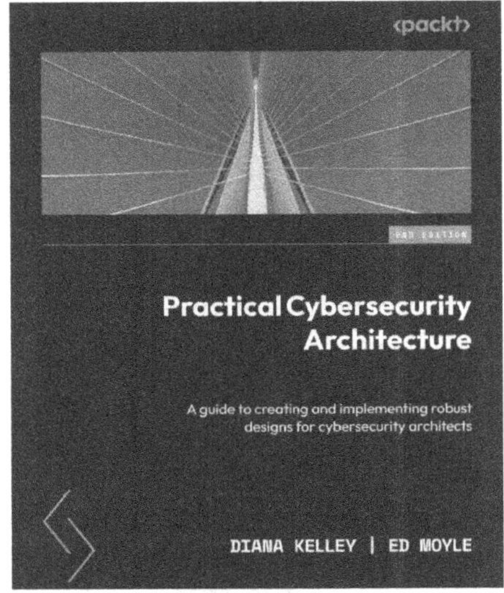

Practical Cybersecurity Architecture

Diana Kelley, Ed Moyle

ISBN: 978-1-83763-716-4

- Create your own architectures and analyze different models
- Understand strategies for creating architectures for environments and applications
- Discover approaches to documentation using repeatable approaches and tools
- Discover different communication techniques for designs, goals, and requirements
- Focus on implementation strategies for designs that help reduce risk
- Apply architectural discipline to your organization using best practices

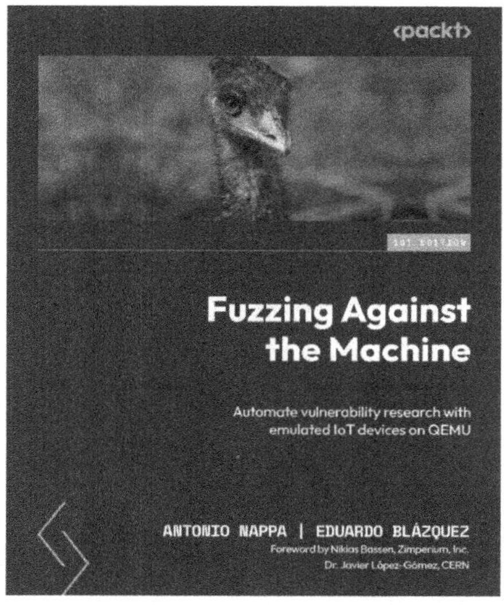

Fuzzing Against the Machine

Antonio Nappa, Eduardo Blázquez

ISBN: 978-1-80461-497-6

- Understand the difference between emulation and virtualization
- Discover the importance of emulation and fuzzing in cybersecurity
- Get to grips with fuzzing an entire operating system
- Discover how to inject a fuzzer into proprietary firmware
- Know the difference between static and dynamic fuzzing
- Look into combining QEMU with AFL and AFL++
- Explore Fuzz peripherals such as modems
- Find out how to identify vulnerabilities in OpenWrt
-

Packt is searching for authors like you

If you're interested in becoming an author for Packt, please visit `authors.packtpub.com` and apply today. We have worked with thousands of developers and tech professionals, just like you, to help them share their insight with the global tech community. You can make a general application, apply for a specific hot topic that we are recruiting an author for, or submit your own idea.

Share Your Thoughts

Now you've finished *Security Monitoring with Wazuh*, we'd love to hear your thoughts! Scan the QR code below to go straight to the Amazon review page for this book and share your feedback or leave a review on the site that you purchased it from.

`https://packt.link/r/1-837-63215-4`

Your review is important to us and the tech community and will help us make sure we're delivering excellent quality content.

Download a free PDF copy of this book

Thanks for purchasing this book!

Do you like to read on the go but are unable to carry your print books everywhere?

Is your eBook purchase not compatible with the device of your choice?

Don't worry, now with every Packt book you get a DRM-free PDF version of that book at no cost.

Read anywhere, any place, on any device. Search, copy, and paste code from your favorite technical books directly into your application.

The perks don't stop there, you can get exclusive access to discounts, newsletters, and great free content in your inbox daily

Follow these simple steps to get the benefits:

1. Scan the QR code or visit the link below

`https://packt.link/free-ebook/9781837632152`

2. Submit your proof of purchase
3. That's it! We'll send your free PDF and other benefits to your email directly

www.ingramcontent.com/pod-product-compliance
Lightning Source LLC
Chambersburg PA
CBHW080624060326
40690CB00021B/4808

* 9 7 8 1 8 3 7 6 3 2 1 5 2 *